MENNONITE
TOURGUIDE
To Western Europe

less Recalled Earlier

MENNONITE TOURGUIDE
To Western Europe

Jan Gleysteen

1984

 HERALD PRESS

Scottdale, Pennsylvania
Kitchener, Ontario

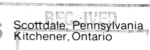

Library of Congress Cataloging in Publication Data

Gleysteen, Jan.
  Mennonite tourguide to western Europe.

  1. Europe—Description and travel—1971- —Guide-
books. 2. Mennonites—Europe—History. I. Title.
D909.G556 1984   914'.04558   84-683
ISBN 0-8361-3360-9 (pbk.)

MENNONITE TOURGUIDE To Western Europe

Library of Congress Catalog Card Number: 84-683
International Standard Book Number: 0-8361-3360-9
Printed in the United States of America

  Illustrated and designed by the author

90 89 88 87 86 85 84 10 9 8 7 6 5 4 3 2 1

To my wife, Barbara;
to Arnold and Rhoda,
Wilmer and Janet,

partners in the
TourMagination ministry
of sharing the story
of our people and our faith

CONTENTS

Foreword by Paul N. Kraybill 9
Pilgrims and Strangers 13
Getting Ready 17

Overall planning/19, travel agents/19, group tours/20, individual travel/21, efficient itineraries/22, travel literature/23, tour information (national)/25, tour information (local, regional)/26, maps/28, tourist assistance/29, open air museums/29, learning a language/30, crossing the Atlantic/30, jet lag/31, passports/34, cash and travelers cheques/35, sending money/37, travel insurance/37, luggage/38, missing bags/39, customs and immigration/40, public transportation, Eurailpass/43, the 24-hour clock/44, timetables/44, rail travel/45, car rental and driving/45, internationall road signs/47, parking regulations/49, domestic air service/49, bicycling/49, hiking, 50, books on Mennonite history/50, Mennonite churches in Europe/52, relief and service in Europe/52, Mennonite World Conference/53, tracing family history/54, lodging/55, restrooms/57, how to say thanks/57, food/58, drink/59, souvenirs/59, traveling with children/62, traveling with the handicapped/63, photography/63, films and airport security/65, scissors/65, voltage converters/66, the metric system/66, writing home/67.

Switzerland 69
Germany 113
Austria 161
Liechtenstein 189
Holland 193
Belgium 233
Luxembourg 255
France 261
Italy 305

Who Goes There? 330
In Appreciation 331
Personal Notes, Additions, etc. 332
The Author 340

Note: Throughout this Tourguide passages pertaining to Anabaptist-Mennonite history are indicated by a color bar in the margin.

FOREWORD

After World War II North Americans became aware of the tragedy that had fallen on their fellow humans in Europe. Mennonites, for the most part, had tried to avoid involvement in the military for conscience reasons. But the postwar period provided an opportunity to express constructively their willingness to be involved and make sacrifices, even though during the war many had been accused of cowardice. Many North American Mennonites went to Europe after the war when others were returning as war veterans.

They found themselves among the hungry and homeless of Europe. This was a new world for them, coming as they did from the comfortable rural farms of traditional Mennonite communities, often quite isolated from the realities of the larger world and its political tensions.

Few of these families had been touched by the grim daily casualty lists in the newspapers of almost every major North American city.

But these young volunteers did work hard to assist in the massive task of restoring and reconstructing a devastated continent.

This postwar encounter with a new culture was a dramatic experience. Men and women from quiet provincial Mennonite communities were thrust into a "new" world. Differences in customs and practice put a new perspective on their own background. They were reaching across a figurative ocean of differences that separated them from their distant cousins in Europe.

For many this opened up new vistas of understanding. Their forebears, years before, had left the shores of Europe for the great new world that lay to the west, promising a new life of comfort and prosperity. Now the old and the new met and tried to bridge the gap that had grown between them in the intervening years.

Walking through the ruins of cathedrals, apartment blocks, massive old government buildings, heavy with history and sturdily built, the North American volunteers became aware of the contrast with the superficiality of their own sleek modern culture. The sense of tradition, stability, and history they found on the continent contrasted with the shallow efficiency of American life. They both were caught up in tradition, but the North Americans began to realize that they lacked the roots and maturity of Europe.

So from the ashes of Europe arose not only a new reconstructed continent, but a group of North American Mennonites were sensitized in a small way to the issues they confronted in a continent where the relevance of tradition, heritage, and history took on new meaning.

Some took time to explore these questions more deeply and to search for new meanings for their "Mennonite" life. This led them to libraries and universities, to the Mennonite congregations, to students, professors, teachers, and pastors. And also to the historical places. Meanwhile in America historical research was beginning to reconstruct a new understanding of the Anabaptist vision, and heritage which had been twisted and distorted by unsympathetic scholars. And so what was being written in America was being experienced on the continent by these young men and women as they struggled with these issues.

The journey and pilgrimage of these young workers took them to Zurich, Witmarsum, to Strasbourg and Schleitheim, to Dordrecht and to Rottenburg. One of them, Paul Peachey, in 1967 published a pamphlet *Mennonite Guide Through Switzerland,"* which is still carried by American tourists tracing the story of the beginnings of the Anabaptist movement in Zurich.

Today a new generation of visitors are going to Europe. The post-World War II Pax boys and relief workers are now grandparents, successful business entrepreneurs, professors, and professionals. They are returning to the Europe of their memories to call to mind once more those days and to tell their children and grandchildren the stories of their past. And then there is the second generation of wandering youth with a railpass, an extra pair of jeans, and a bedroll in their backpack. There are tour groups, choirs, college-sponsored courses in the arts and music, junior year abroad, exchange programs, and a host of other reasons that are bringing a steady stream of North Americans to the continent.

Too often there is the temptation to go fast, see everything, get a sketchy impression, and go back home to join the ranks of those who can say, "I was there." Unfortunately, many never learned that their superficial journey robbed them of what could have been an enriching experience. They were not aware of the distress of their European friends, who watched this parade of naive tourists who never really saw the real Europe.

This is not the place to defend or promote tourism. The fact is that people travel—Mennonites travel. Some do it well, some not so well. Some of us who have lived in Europe as expatriate North Americans, and have been confronted with the reactions of our brothers and sisters, have been aware of at least some of the less-than-complimentary remarks that often follow another fleeting glimpse of American tourists.

On the other hand, tourists are warmly welcomed and hosted with grace and patience that gently overlooks the Americans' style. And there are many North Americans who do care and are eager to travel responsibly.

Travel books abound and probably Mennonites cannot compete with the flow of highly sophisticated materials that are available in every American bookstore. But even though we have been traveling ever since Michael Sattler arrived in Strasbourg in 1526 and in spite of a commendable publishing industry, we have a sparse library of helpful travel material.

This book was conceived out of the need to update the original *Mennonite Guide Through Switzerland* prepared by Paul Peachey, which has remained unchanged to this date and is still being carried by many tourists, although a German revision was prepared and printed in 1975.

Jan Gleysteen is noted for his ability to popularize, and his unequaled slide collection of Anabaptist historical sites taken by his own hand, assuring us that he indeed was there. Added to that is the careful eye and skilled pen of a mapmaker. This is a heady combination and Jan Gleysteen is at his best in this book.

So if you are going to Europe you need at least three things—a ticket, a passport, and the *Tourguide.* You may want a few more things, but don't go until you have at least these three.

Jan Gleysteen and Herald Press have done us all a notable service. This is more than a guide to Europe—it is more than an atlas of maps. It is in fact a resource for your trip to enable you to travel intelligently, to learn as you go, to speak knowledgeably, and to gain new insights and understandings. It is a testament to the fact that while our years of pilgrimage and flight are no longer marked by suffering and distress, we should not allow ourselves to heed the temptation simply to wander aimlessly over the face of the earth. Gleysteen calls us to travel with a purpose, and leave behind us the touch and memory of a sensitive tourist.

This book will help you break the culture barrier and open up new doors for an exciting experience of learning and insight. This is a form of peacemaking to join hands in friendship and understanding with your brothers and sisters in other lands. Perhaps we can plant some seeds, and some will be planted in us as well, that will prevent us from aligning with the political pressures of our time which divide people into friends and enemies for political purposes. That is not the way of God's people. This book is a small step toward achieving a new level of meaningful tourism.

Don't leave home without it! Bon voyage!

 Paul N. Kraybill
Executive Secretary
Mennonite World Conference

PILGRIMS AND STRANGERS

In the late 1920s my grandmother and my mother's younger sister and brother traveled to Canada on the Holland America Line's proud ship *Volendam*. (Twenty-five years later that same steamer was to transport two shiploads of Russian Mennonite refugees to Paraguay, where they established a colony that now bears the ship's name). Although the fares then paid (around a hundred dollars) seem low compared to today's wages and prices, they represented quite a sum of hard-earned money when my widowed grandmother undertook her long journey to settle on the virgin prairies of southwestern Manitoba.

Having said her good-byes at the docks in Rotterdam, Grandmother did not expect ever to see Holland or her older daughters again. And she didn't. I knew her only as a somewhat stern-looking lady on a fading brown photograph.

In those days travel for travel's sake was for the privileged rich and famous. On a more modest scale it was undertaken by journeymen craftsmen in search of experience in their trades and by young scholars bound for the great European universities. Heidelberg was a favorite with the Americans, and Sigmund Romberg immortalized the era in his operetta *The Student Prince*. A whole generation of ambitious Mennonite scholars sharpened their ancestral German to explore the source materials which led to the recovery of the Anabaptist Vision.

Some journeys off the beaten track were undertaken by a bold and adventurous few, who reported on the hazards and the triumphs of their undertakings in the illustrated weeklies. Common folks, who seldom had occasion to travel, followed with interest the progress of the Citroen-Haardt expeditions across the trackless Sahara or the steppes of Outer Mongolia.

Since World War II tremendous sociological and technological changes have occurred. The Americans emerged from the war with all of their land and resources still intact and with unprecedented economic power. For a decade and a half the "almighty dollar" was pegged at a rate of better than 1 to 4 against the stronger of the European currencies. Due to this favorable and fixed rate, agreed upon by the Allies at Bretton Woods, New Hampshire, in 1944, the Americans were just about the only ones who could afford to travel. By the thousands they boarded the great ocean liners to "do Europe."

The Europeans, on the other hand, were still fully occupied with the task of restoring their war-ravaged economies and were not yet permitted to spend any of their governments' sparse financial resources for personal pleasure.

For the most part the American tourists traveled in deluxe air-conditioned coaches which quickly became mobile ghettos that stopped at all the "must-see" points on the itinerary, but which isolated their occupants from the real essence of Europe. Where encounters took place the Americans, inspired by the confidence of the Eisenhower era and empowered by Norman Vincent Peale's positive ways of thinking, talked about bigger and better things back home—like the New York skyscrapers, contour farming, the Santa Fe *Super Chief*, and the Tennessee Valley Authority. When faced with prices marked in Franks or lire, these visitors asked, "How much is that in real money?" And slowly the image of the ugly American was born, the image of a basically good-natured but surprisingly uninformed and not always tactful person, who was convinced that anything and everything could be purchased for a few dollars.

As the European economic recovery progressed, and one government after another was able to lift currency restrictions, the Europeans themselves began to cross their borders in numbers. At first they came on bikes, mopeds, and scooters, and on the rebuilt parts of the rail systems, but sooner or later in VW Beetles and Citroen 2 CV's. Soon all these Americans and Europeans on the move were joined by other nations, including doctors and other professionals from all corners of the former British Empire, oil-rich Arabs, and Japanese with a yen to travel.

The biggest change came during the mid-sixties when the first generation of large jets, the 707s and the stretch-DC8s began to replace their propellor-driven predecessors, such as the Super G Constellation. In less than a decade the proud ships of the transatlantic fleet were driven out of business by these jets and the jumbos that soon followed. Suddenly it was possible for just about anyone to journey, within a matter of hours, to places around the globe our grandparents could only read about.

Another significant factor was the appearance of discretionary time and money. By conservative estimates more than 500 million workers around the world are now receiving annual paid vacations. And though the myth of the rich traveler dies slowly, due to this combination of discretionary time and income, and faster less expensive transportation, the majority of today's tourists are middle-class people. They are men and women who perform quite common and sometimes menial tasks in their home communities. They are store clerks, nurses, meat cutters, truckers, teachers, farmers, secretaries, and children, students, and grandparents.

It no longer serves a useful purpose to debate, as some do, whether one should travel in times like these. People do travel in ever increasing numbers. Reliable statistics, gathered from airline and customs records worldwide, show that more than 32,000 persons leave their home countries every hour of every day and night. The number of intra-country tourists, those traveling within their own borders, is estimated to be at least four times that many.

On a typical summer night the customs officers at New York's Kennedy Airport process 3,000 incoming passengers per hour. That equals twice the number of people that only twenty years ago disembarked from an ocean liner after a weeklong journey. In 1983 American tourists booked 810,000 rooms in Paris hotels! Based on double occupancy, that translates into more than a million and a half U.S. citizens mingling with other visitors out to see the sights of Paris.

This huge flow of people is perhaps one of the most important human factors of all times, a socioeconomic phenomenon capable of exerting a decisive impact on world affairs. The resulting global awareness may just make it a bit more difficult for the superpower governments to tell lies and half-truths to more and more people who have "been there." The potential for peacemaking and bridge-building exists. And experts predict that within fifteen years tourism will be the single most important source of foreign currency income for almost every nation.

Christians come to this new era in travel with a long history of being a pilgrim people. The patriarchs of the Old Testament were nomads. At times they followed some rather unusual road signs: a pillar of cloud by day, and a pillar of fire by night. Later, there was a bright star in the east.

The nomadic experience of the Hebrews gave impetus to specific laws on how they should conduct themselves as sojourners in an alien land, and also on how they should treat the stranger in their midst. In Genesis 18 we read that Abraham was sitting in the heat of the day at the door of his tent by the oaks of Mamre. When three strangers passed by, he invited them in for rest and refreshment. Later, we learn that Abraham and Sarah had entertained angels unawares.

Many other examples of Hebrew hospitality could be cited. David and Nehemiah were known for hospitality shown to travelers, and the queen of Sheba undertook an educational tour to the land of King Solomon that was of great benefit to visitor and host alike.

Jesus was born into this rich tradition, and he depended on the hospitality of many during the years of his Galilean ministry. We remember the Zebedee family on the north shore of the Sea of Galilee. In his teachings Jesus enlarged upon the story of Abraham and Sarah entertaining the three strangers. He taught us that when we welcome strangers, we may actually be inviting in Christ himself.

Over the centuries that thought inspired many of the great saints and entire Christian communities to devote their lives to servanthood hospitality. Examples of these are the Benedictine order, the development of many medieval cities around a monastic hostelry, and the followers of Saint Bernard, who built their hospices at the summit of rugged mountains and trained huge dogs to rescue the lost. Could it be that fresh insights shared by the visitors helped these communities become centers of renewal? What did Blaurock hear from his guests while he was a vicar at Trins? What conversations may Michael Sattler have overheard in the halls of St. Peter's monastery?...

If the hosts had obligations to God, so did the travelers. When Christ sent out his disciples two by two, he gave them good instructions, including the oft-ignored advice to travel lightly. Can you imagine the apostles moving out with matching sets of Louis Vuitton designer luggage?

The Scriptures are replete with interesting stories of exciting occurrences along the way. Jacob met God in a vision on the road between Beersheba and Haran, and the disciples met their risen Lord on the way to Emmaus. Saul set out from Jerusalem—certainly not with the best of intentions—and as he approached Damascus a bright flash blinded him for three days. This roadside experience marked a dramatic turnaround in his life and the beginning of even greater travels in the right spirit. Can our chauvinistic blindnesses be challenged by meeting people of other nations, our airs of religious superiority tempered when we come face to face with genuine holiness in persons of a different tradition?

Not all our travel experiences turn out pleasant. The man who traveled down the winding road from Jerusalem to Jericho fell victim to some local exploiters of tourism. He was beaten up and lost all his luggage. But even that sorry situation carried a blessing in disguise. He learned to respect the despicable Samaritan (read: Cuban, Iranian, Soviet, North Korean, if you will), the only one to come to his rescue. Thoughtful travel experience can help us reexamine or discard some of our shortsighted preconceived notions. The poet Rabindranath Tagore said it well:

> Thou hast made me known to friends whom I knew not,
>   given me seats in homes not my own.
> Thou hast brought the distant near
> and made me a brother to the stranger.

It is in this spirit that the *Tourguide* was written. Informed and purposeful travel has the potential to provide such encounters to more and more people. Across the arbitrary lines drawn by our governments it is possible for Christian travelers to experience that they are first and foremost citizens of a greater and more durable kingdom, one which transcends borders, diverse languages and customs, and even the concept of time. When that happens we may be one step closer to peace.

And, in keeping with another Mennonite tradition of *Living More with Less,* more attention is paid in this book to understanding and relationships than to world entertainment. More space is devoted to roadside picnics than to four-star restaurants.

GETTING READY

Helpful Suggestions
for Overseas Travelers

LAYING A FIRM FOUNDATION

To get the most out of any trip work out the details well ahead of time so that you will not have to worry about them when you should be savoring the sight of seven windmills working. You will not run short of time if you decide on priorities beforehand. Careful plans and day-by-day itineraries are liberating, and make it possible to accomplish a good many of your goals.

On the other hand, don't stick to itineraries too religiously. If you happen upon a costumed folk dance in a fishermen's village, enjoy the occasion. Just alter your plans for the afternoon a bit.

Well-traveled friends can probably suggest places they particularly enjoyed. The best ideas will come from friends whose tastes and styles of travel are similar to yours. Remember that each person has his special interests and that you can't do everything. When your time is limited you must be selective and do what you really want to do.

THE ROLE OF THE TRAVEL AGENT

If you have ever tried to call a major airline or hotel system and were forced to listen to half an hour of their canned music while your reserve of time, patience, and phone budget clocked away, you have already discovered one good reason to work with a travel agent.

A travel agent is supposed to know the way through that confusing maze called the travel industry and provide you with the best possible arrangements for flights, land transportation, car rental, and hotel reservations in keeping with your needs and tastes, requirements and budget, and for that particular season of the year.

Like other professionals travel agents come in various levels of competence and experience. And like editors, secretaries, and mechanics, even the best of them occasionally make mistakes. Unfortunately, mistakes in the travel industry become magnified in the customer's view because one single mistake can drastically alter the course of a long-awaited "vacation of a lifetime."

The travel agent's task has not become easier as deregulation has produced a jungle of ever-changing fares coupled with asterisks and small print that defies all logic. To make matters worse the agent's handiest tools in finding answers—the computer terminals provided to them by two major airlines—are under investigation by the Justice Department on charges of bias in loading.

The question remains, where do you find a competent agent who can serve your travel needs best. The surest way is through the personal recommendation of a frequent traveler among your relatives, friends, and fellow church members whose judgment you respect. In fact, personal reference is considered the backbone of the travel industry.

Some busy agencies will take this even one step further. They accept new clients only on recommendation of their standing customers. When people ask me, "Who do you deal with," I not only give them the address and phone number of our agency, but I will often tell them to ask for a specific person. An expert travel counselor will work hard to get you the best possible airfare and certainly has more clout than you have to secure a room in a tightly booked hotel or two more tickets to an opera at La Scala. There is no reason why your agency needs to be in or near your hometown. Ours is 200 miles away.

There are several agencies staffed mostly by Mennonites which traditionally have serviced Mennonite communities. These agencies include Menno Travel Service (MTS), Prudent Travel, and Assiniboine Travel Service. For addresses and phone numbers consult the most recent edition of the *Mennonite Yearbook*, or check their advertisements in the various Mennonite papers. In addition there are tour organizations which specialize in travel with an Anabaptist-Mennonite emphasis (TourMagination, 1210 Loucks Avenue, Scottdale, Pa. 15683 and Mennonite Your Way, Box 1525, Salunga, Pa. 17538).

THE PROS AND CONS OF GROUP TOURS

To large numbers of people the ultimate tour to anyplace—including Europe—is one on which you do not have to be concerned about any details. Someone else has already worked out the itinerary, provided a comfortable bus, arranged for all or most of the meals, will steer you to the most fascinating places, and will get you to your hotel in decent time.

Package tours haven't always been the greatest and we have all heard about the "Today is Tuesday so this must be Belgium" syndrome. In fact TourMagination was born to provide an alternative to the shepherded disasters we observed in Europe during the late 1960s.

But times have changed and a much better class of escorted tours has become available alongside the still-continuing "Seventeen countries in two weeks" variety. More and more people who can afford and insist on the best are now choosing good escorted tours as the framework for their individual pursuits. They appreciate the idea that the details have already been taken care of and realize that independent travel is considerably more expensive. So they travel with the group, participate in the program for the most part, and stay at the same hotels. But they may occasionally pursue their own interests for a day or two. Even if they don't get a refund on those

parts of the program they skip, they still come out ahead and with a lot less detail to worry about. Still others take in the total group tour, participate in all of the activities of the group, and add an extension of a week or two for personal goals. People who say that they can travel cheaper on their own are probably either poor in math or depend a lot on their overseas relatives and friends.

The number of special-interest tours, apart from the study tours that have always been offered by colleges and universities, has also grown dramatically. Some special-interest tours focus on music and theaters; others on folk festivals, the Reformation, or the Renaissance. There are tours for bird watchers, for dairy farmers, and railroad buffs. Those special-interest tours are often accompanied by guest lecturers, some of them prominent in their field, or otherwise led by professional and knowledgeable leaders.

Whichever you choose, a general or a special-interest tour, returning travelers are nearly unanimous in identifying the quality of the leadership as the single most important ingredient of a successful tour. Good tour directors are professionals known for expertise in their fields who may have lived and studied abroad and who have a basic grasp of the languages. Above all, the best of them have energy, a sense of humor, and a real interest in the people they serve. Qualified tour guides are vital to repeat business and many a traveler will inquire where their favorite guide will go the next season so they can travel with him or her again.

Unfortunately for every tour leader with the required skills, there seem to be ten amateurs who don't know any more where they are or what's going on than the forty people they are supposed to be leading. You can safely double that statistic for the so-called Holy Land tours.

Repeating what we said earlier about finding a good travel agent, a friend's personal recommendation of a certain tour guide or tour organization may be more important than a fistful of four-color brochures that promise you everything.

And speaking about brochures, be sure to read them carefully and do not hesitate to question the tour operator as to what is and what is not included. Too many lovely brochures, when it's all said and done, deliver little more than a glorified airfare-hotel package, in spite of the flowery sentences describing Alpine excursions, boat trips, gourmet dinners, and the like, none of which are actually included in the prices quoted. All too often the seemingly more expensive, but all-inclusive tour, is really the better deal, while the highly advertised cut-rate special is the one you can't afford.

Tours undertaken with Tourmagination by students at Mennonite colleges can be arranged to be taken for college credit, provided certain pre-tour, on-tour, and post-tour requirements are met.

OUTLINING YOUR OWN TOUR

Most people approach tour planning in a dreamlike state, which is perfectly natural. Part of the pleasure of anticipation consists of dreaming about what you will see when you get there.

But along with the dreams you must consider the more practical questions: How much time do you have? Which countries would you really like to see? How much money can you afford to spend? How much distance can you cover in one day? There is no fixed formula for all this other than to be realistic. If you have only two weeks, don't attempt the Grand Tour of Europe. Seeing three or four countries within that time should be enough (or at the most six or seven countries for a three week tour).

You must allow for time to overcome jet-lag, to see the sights in the cities, and on the last day to repack and prepare for the return trip. In flying through from seven to ten time zones, most people find the long-drawn-out flights home more exhausting than the condensed night on the way over.

Once you have settled on the countries you'd like to visit and the towns you wish to explore, you may begin the process of outlining your tour. For this you'll need some of the tour guides and maps described on pages 23 and 28, and a stack of blank calendar sheets. I usually draw a five-week block on an eight-and-a-half-by-11 sheet of paper and take it to the copier to make as many copies as I need for personal and family use.

Then fill in the days and the times of departure and arrival. Be sure to allow for the difference in time. (One of my friends working on his itinerary got himself to Luxembourg by a stroke of magic!) Next mark the dates of any meetings and conferences you wish to attend, and the times of Sunday services in specific churches. Do not forget to take into account the European customs, such as having dinner much later than you are used to in your home country and the stores and offices being closed for about two hours in the middle of the day.

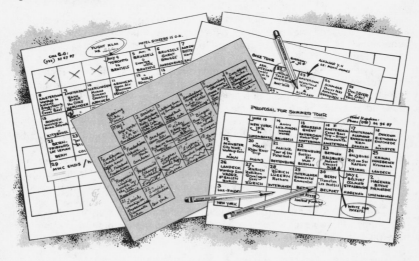

Now with the map at hand begin to fill in the remaining days with achievable distances and sufficient time to explore the various points of interest. It is best to add a free day or a contingency day to keep your itinerary elastic rather than too tight. Should everything work out just perfect, you still have that one day available for an interesting side trip.

Remember that you cannot see "everything" on the first or second or third trip and if you try you won't enjoy anything. The planning process is one of trial and error and much revision and you will soon discover why you need a whole stack of blank calendar sheets.

When at last you have a calendar sheet that is to your liking, check it against a map. Ideally, your routing should look like a loop or perhaps like a figure eight. If you see that there is backtracking and duplication, you will spend too much time and effort on the mechanics of getting around which could be put to better use seeing additional sights.

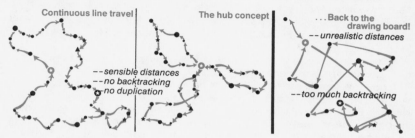

Continuous line travel

The hub concept

...Back to the drawing board!
-- unrealistic distances

--sensible distances
--no backtracking
--no duplication

--too much backtracking

Another model is the hub concept—selecting one, two, or three centers from which to undertake daily excursions, preferably along looped routes. Many municipal tourist offices overseas can advise on local circuits such as a loop of the Münsterland castles, a Friesian lakes circle, or a picturesque harbors road. The advantages of the hub concept are staying in one area long enough to gain a good understanding of the place and lodging at one hotel for several days, eliminating the need to pack and unpack every day.

A common mistake made by inexperienced travelers is to obtain a general road map and then to make a beeline along the red lines connecting major cities. But throughout Europe there are thousands upon thousands of miles of excellently maintained and well-marked secondary roads which lead you through lands enhanced by centuries of living and away from the hassle of modern-day expressway driving.

You may laugh at people who take the two-hour or half-day tours of a city, but in fact most of these tours are pretty good. If you have the time, consider boarding the bus or the boat unless you are one of those rare people who can look at a map and instantly know where you are and how to head to the next point of interest without fail.

BOOKED FOR TRAVEL

The first thing you should do is to find some good books and travel guides. They come in great number and variety and most of them are constantly being updated. Here are some of my favorites in order of preference.

The *Michelin Green Guides* are still by far the best. Michelin, a tire company of worldwide reknown, also has an extensive publishing division which produces some of the finest maps available. A good many of the *Green Guides* covering one country in each volume—Germany, Italy, Switzerland, etc.—are now available in English, as are a number of city and regional guides, such as for the Chataux of the Loire, Paris, the Provence, etc. If you are proficient in either French or German, a much larger selection of *Green Guides* is available to you. Michelin *Green Guides* have more and better detailed maps and street plans than any other guide on the market.

Then there are the trusty *Baedeckers,* perhaps the oldest tour guides in existence. In North America the *Baedecker's* are published/distributed by Prentice Hall. Each *Baedecker* comes with a beautiful fold-out map which, in most cases, appears to be a customized version of the Mair/Shell maps available in Europe. The combination price of the *Baedecker* and map makes it a good deal.

Next come the bulky, paperback tour bibles put out by the four F's: *Fisher, Fodor, Frommer,* and *Fielding;* and *Let's Go,* a Harvard publication. Of these I personally like the 780-page *Fisher's Annotated Travel Guide* the best. In addition there is John Whitman's *Best European Travel Tips,* which contains 2,001 pieces of travel information.

Depending on your interests, each of those guides has its good points, but I must also add my disclaimers.

Now that Temple and Nancy Fielding have retired after forty years of globetrotting and the editorial work has been taken over by others, there may be some changes. But so far the Fieldings have been accused of being snobbish and promoting Ugly Americanism by giving more space to shopping and the exact location of the night spots than to the treasures of the Louvre or the Uffizi. In addition the Fieldings have been unable to locate and recommend any but the most expensive hotels and restaurants. Indeed some travel authorities claim that Fieldings exclusivity increased the budget-minded traveler's fierce loyalty to Art Frommer's *Europe on Twenty Dollars a Day.*

John Whitman's *2,001 Tips* is undoubtedly the most comprehensive compendium of questions and answers on any subject imaginable related to travel—and Whitman's advice appears to be accurate, to the point, and complete. Christian readers, however, may be offended by the explicit information regarding the cost and quality of sex services available in Europe, whether hetero- or homosexual.

An altogether different and delightful book is *Discovery Trips in Europe,* edited and published by the Lane Publishing Company, Menlo Park, California. It is also inexpensive. The latest edition (1983) sells for $5.95 (U.S.). *Discovery Trips* is not a tour guide in the usual sense. Instead, it describes and illustrates in considerable detail anywhere from a couple to a dozen side trips to unusual and fascinating places in each country. Inserted through its pages are good summaries on mountain hiking, staying at quaint inns and guest houses, advice on where to find authentic handicrafts, the best times to visit famous gardens, or where to rent a horse-drawn wagon for a holiday in slow motion. *Discovery Trips* is best described as an idea book and a beautiful book at that.

For more information on a given country it pays to consult the back issues of the *National Geographic* magazine or the entries on that country in one or several encyclopedias. The hefty (42-48 page) travel section of the Sunday edition of the *New York Times* is nearly always worthwhile for reading, clipping, and filing. It usually features a full page or more entitled "What's Doing in Hamburg," [Paris, Leipzig, as the case may be] and a weekly column entitled "Practical Traveler" with the latest information on passports, airfares, the best in travel insurance, traveling for college credit, travel for senior citizens, and car rentals abroad. Compared to the *New York Times* travel section all other travel supplements are weak imitations.

Upon arrival in Europe you'll find the bookstores and the kiosks at the railroad stations loaded with a wide choice of irresistible pictorial volumes on the surrounding country, region, and cities, often with parallel text in three or more languages. My suitcase always gets heavier as the journey progresses.

YOURS FOR THE ASKING

With the exception of the principality of Liechtenstein, each of the European countries maintains a national tourist office in one or more American and Canadian cities. Usually Norway, Sweden, and Denmark pool their services under one Scandinavian Tourist Office. When you write to any of these bureaus requesting specific information on a certain town or province, you will find them very helpful. Here are some of their addresses:

AUSTRIA
Austrian National Tourist Office
545 Fifth Avenue
New York, N.Y. 10017

Austrian National Tourist Office
2 Bloor Street East, Suite 3330
Toronto, Ontario M4W 1A8

BELGIUM
Belgian National Tourist Office
745 Fifth Avenue
New York, N.Y. 10022

DENMARK
(See Scandinavia)

FINLAND
(See Scandinavia)

FRANCE
French Government Tourist Office
610 Fifth Avenue
New York, N.Y. 10020

French Government Tourist Office
372 Bay Street, Suite 610
Toronto, Ontario M5H 2W9

GERMANY
German National Tourist Office
630 Fifth Avenue
New York, N.Y. 10020

German National Tourist Office
2 Fundy, B.P. 417
Place Bonaventure
Montreal, Quebec

GREAT BRITAIN
British Tourist Authority
680 Fifth Avenue
New York, N.Y. 10019

British Tourist Authority
151 Bloor Street West
Toronto, Ontario

ICELAND
(See Scandinavia)

IRELAND
Irish Tourist Board
590 Fifth Avenue
New York, N.Y. 10036

ITALY
Italian Government Tourist Office
630 Fifth Avenue
New York, N.Y. 10020

Italian Government Travel Office
3 Place Ville Marie
Montreal, Quebec

LUXEMBOURG
Luxembourg National Tourist Office
1 Dag Hammarskjold Plaza
New York, N.Y. 10017

THE NETHERLANDS

Netherlands National Tourist Office
576 Fifth Avenue
New York, N.Y. 10036

Netherlands National Tourist Office
1 Dundas Street West
Toronto, Ontario M5G 1Z3

NORWAY

(See Scandinavia)

PORTUGAL

Portugese National Tourist Office
548 Fifth Avenue
New York, N.Y. 10036

SCANDINAVIA

For information on Denmark, Finland,
Iceland, Norway, and Sweden, separately
or combined, write to:

(name of country or countries)
75 Rockefeller Plaza
New York, N.Y. 10019

SPAIN

Spanish National Tourist Office
665 Fifth Avenue
New York, N.Y. 10022

SWEDEN

(See Scandinavia)

SWITZERLAND

Swiss National Tourist Office
608 Fifth Avenue
New York, N.Y. 10020

Swiss National Tourist Office
Commerce Court Postal Station
Toronto, Ontario M5L 1E8

In Europe practically every town has its own tourist information service and many of these in turn work together in regional associations. You can address a request for information to the Municipal Tourist Office of Baden-Baden, Germany, or to the regional bureau representing the entire Black Forest area. In Holland such agencies are called VVV; in France, Syndicat d'Initiative; in Italy, ENIT, and so on. To receive a given town's brochures, address your letter as follows:

Fremdenverkehrsverband	Syndicat d'Initiative
name of town AUSTRIA	name of town FRANCE
Dienst voor Toerisme	Offizielles Verkehrsamt
name of town BELGIUM	name of town GERMANY
Turistbyra	Dept. of Development and Tourism
name of town DENMARK	name of town GREAT BRITAIN
Turistkontor	Bord Fáilte/Tourist Board
name of town FINLAND	name of town IRELAND

Azienda Autonoma di Turismo (ENIT)
_____
name of town
ITALY

Syndicat d'Initiative/Verkehrsamt
_____
name of town
LUXEMBOURG

VVV
_____
name of town
THE NETHERLANDS

Turisttrafikkomiteen for
_____
name of town
NORWAY

Direccion General del Turismo
_____
name of town
SPAIN

Turism och Fritedsbyra
_____
name of town
SWEDEN

Verkehrsbüro/Office du Tourisme
_____
name of town
SWITZERLAND

In general I have found the folders and maps received from these places very helpful. In smaller towns the offices are often staffed by volunteers and the speed of their response varies accordingly. If a small town has exhausted this year's budget for printing and postage, your request may go unanswered. In general you can expect prompt response and relevant material from Northern Europe. I once received a batch of excellent materials from a Danish city within nine days. I wonder whether it arrived on the *Concorde*.

The French and the Italians, on the other hand, are apt to answer you eventually. A time span of two to three months is not uncommon. But your material will come accompanied by a flowery letter embellished with a great assortment of rubber stamps, embossed designs, seals, and stickers, and the gorgeously illegible signature of the Most Honorable Officer in Charge of Public Relations for the city.

MAPS ARE A MUST

In the preparation of your itinerary and for use on the trip itself, good maps are essential. To begin with, don't waste your money on a map of Europe. The scale is too small and the map will not show you what you are looking for any more than you can expect to find Goessel, Kansas, or Lindale, Virginia, on a map of North America.

For an overall map of nearly all the areas covered in this *Tourguide,* the *Michelin Map of Germany,* Red Series No. 987, will do. For excursions further south, the adjoining map of Italy, Red Series No. 988, will cover those parts. The *Red Maps* of France, No. 989; Spain, 990; and Great Britain No. 996, extend the picture to the south and northwest. Add to this No. 991, Yugoslavia, and you will find that together these six maps could make an excellent mural for your office or den. Each of the maps by itself measures about 120 centimeters by 90 centimeters (about four by three feet).

For more detail and for use on your actual trip you will need the maps from *Michelin's Yellow Series.* These include all of the Netherlands on No. 410, all of Switzerland on No. 427, all of Austria on No. 426, and all of Belgium on No. 409. It is also possible to buy the Netherlands in three sheets (Nos. 5, 6, and 1), or Belgium in two (Nos. 1 and 2), and France itself on 43 sheets (Nos. 51 through 93). Map number 87 covers the Alsace. Five more sheets (numbers 202 through 206) cover the nearest adjacent parts of Western Germany, including the Palatinate and the Black Forest.

Once you are in Holland, the best maps to buy are the large-scale *ANWB* maps which cover Holland on thirteen sheets. The legend to the side of these maps is truly exhaustive and carries more than forty marks and symbols identifying tulip fields, wind- and watermills, castles, castle ruins, lighthouses, coal mines, historical markers, prehistoric graves, and even duck nesting places. Yes, the map even tells you on which side of the road to expect the most scenic views. The main office of the ANWB, a Dutch tourist organization, is at Wassenaarseweg 220, Den Haag, Holland.

For all of Germany, all of Austria, and formerly Austrian parts of Italy, the best maps are published by Mair, usually in cooperation with Shell Oil. Mair maps cover Germany in 26 sheets, Austria in eight, and South Tirol in one. Other good maps are published by the firms of Kummerly & Frey, Hallwag, Ravenstein, Freitag & Berndt, Orell Fussli, and by the Italian Automobile Club. Expect to pay between $3 and $8 for a map. Then treat your investment with care and use only soft erasable pencil if you absolutely have to mark on them. Most Provident Bookstores carry a basic selection of maps including the *Michelin Red Series* and a choice of the *Yellow Series* of greatest interest to Mennonite readers. For very special requests of maps, we recommend the Alfred B. Patton Company, Swamp Road (Rt. 313) and Center Street, Doylestown, Pa. 18901, and John Bartholomew and Son, Duncan Street, Edinburgh EH9 1TA, Scotland.

THAT HELPFUL ⓘ

Throughout Europe official tourist information offices are found in or near the railroad stations, air terminals, boat landings, museums, and near the most popular tourist spots. Look for the lowercase letter ⓘ on a blue shield.

The friendly staffers inside will be glad to inform you about current concerts and art shows, help you book a hotel room (for a small fee), arrange a visit to a factory of school, direct you to restaurants that feature salmon, raclette, fresh asparagus (in season), or other local specialties, or tell you which tram will take you back to your hotel. Their services are free, but you may be asked to pay for phone calls, or if you take more than one copy of the maps and brochures.

MUSEUM VILLAGES: EUROPE IN A NUTSHELL

Open-air museums first sprang up in Scandinavia and Holland more than eighty years ago. Today each of the countries described in this *Tourguide* has one or more of these parks in which the architecture of an era is preserved. The majority of the open-air museums are rural in nature but a few preserve the city scene of the past. In German-speaking areas they are called *Freilichtmuseum;* in Holland and in Belgium, *Openluchtmuseum;* in Scandinavia, where they are the most numerous, *Frilandsmuseet.* Most of these museums welcome visitors between April and September and a few are open the year-round.

In a typical open-air museum you will find working farms complete with live animals, herb gardens, bake ovens, wagon sheds, fishermen's cottages and shipyards, windmills and waterwheels, blacksmith shops, toll houses and sawmills, brickyards, sheep sheds and day-laborer cottages, depending, of course, on the character of the region represented.

Most of the buildings are furnished in period style and come equipped with the right utensils and tools. Volunteers in costume may demonstrate old-time crafts and cooking skills, or perform farm chores with antique equipment. Check with the local tourist information offices about these folk museums and the dates and hours that they are open to the public.

Examples of comparable open-air museums in North America include Sturbridge, Massachusetts; Williamsburg, Virginia; and Upper Canada Village in Ontario.

LEARN ANOTHER LANGUAGE

When a foreign representative steps up to the mikes on the White House lawn, when a TV crew interviews a Palestinian family caught in the crossfire in Lebanon, or when a German student bikes across Western Canada, chances are that these persons can express themselves in English that ranges from passable to excellent.

Conversely, North Americans have not been known for such linguistic versatility. The ability to speak another language with a minimum amount of proficiency is no longer even a requirement for applicants to United States foreign services and government assignments abroad. Most American tourists simply assume that they will be able to get by with English only. And especially in Europe that is entirely possible.

But think of how much more fun it would be if you could read the posters, understand the songs, pick up the newspaper, listen to the people in the marketplace or, if you really get good at it, catch a joke. You could buy a *Paris-Match* or a *Panorama* or *Der Spiegel* and get a worldview different from that found in *Time, Newsweek,* or *Macleans.*

There are a variety of language study aids on the market, ranging from simple to sophisticated. For people who like to keep it very simple, I recommend *The First Thousand Words in German,* published in Great Britain by the Usborne Publishing Ltd. as part of a series covering ten languages including French, Italian, and Russian. They are similar to the Richard Scarry books already familiar to millions of parents. Incidentally, don't be surprised if you find the Richard Scarry books in other languages in bookstores overseas.

Looking at words and phrases does not lead to their proper pronunciation unless you have access to an expatriate Dutchman or Austrian living in your neighborhood willing to help you. Here the record stores can help you out. Nearly always in their most out-of-the-way corner the record stores feature records and tapes such as *Living French* [German, Spanish, Hebrew, etc.], and *Berlitz French,* etc. *for Travelers* and the *Converse-a-Phone* series. A fourth system is the *Lingua-Phone Travel Cassette,* which combines a tape and a phrasebook in a vinyl sleeve.

Many communities have clubs such as the *Association Francaise* for people who want to practice their conversational skills. Basic foreign language courses are also taught in most community colleges.

CROSSING THE BIG POND

In the days before jumbo jets and the containerization of freight, a steady parade of proud ocean liners ferried people back and forth to Europe. Three days from home and halfway to Europe, the *Kungsholm* would pass the *Andrea Doria.* The *Groote Beer* would be overtaken by the *Queen Mary* and the *France* would pass the *Seven Seas.* There was always a tiny wisp of smoke on the horizon to mark yet another group of 1,400 souls making the crossing.

But, alas, such is no longer the case. After a decade of rusting away somewhere in the backwaters of a coal harbor, the few remaining superliners have been revived and refurbished to compete with each other on the Caribbean taxi service out of Miami and your chances of catching any boat to and from Europe on a date that suits your schedule are not good.

Because international law requires ships to carry a physician on board for more than twelve passengers, the few remaining freighters which still take on fares have cut the available cabin space down to that number. The only company that takes passengers on its freighters to and from Europe is Polish Ocean Lines, which can accommodate up to 140 passengers per year from East Coast ports such as Galveston, Texas, or Tampa, Florida. The bad news is that, depending on the nature of their cargo, they may drop you off in places like Bilbao, Spain, or Esbjerg, Denmark, or Gdynia, Poland, after a trip of unknown duration. The good news is that whether it takes them ten days or forty days to get you there, the price remains the same. The Russians still run an occasional passenger ship between Montreal and the Baltic ports.

Currently a one-way trip by ship costs about three times as much as a round-trip on a scheduled airliner. Conversely, the transatlantic airfares are among the world's most competitive. They are also complex. At least three dozen major national carriers offer daily scheduled flights to Europe and there are, in addition, a good many charter flights. Some of the world's major airlines and some countries operate affiliate airlines under other names, such as Condor, LTU, Air London, and Martinair.

In a class by itself is Icelandair, the pioneer in low-cost transatlantic fares, which offers its passengers round-trip bus service between Luxembourg and several major German and French cities and one Austrian ski resort. As to air fares, the picture is constantly changing and it is practically impossible for lay persons to pick their way through the many bargains and some that are not. The best approach is to plan well ahead of time, eight to ten weeks is fine, and turn the whole itinerary over to an experienced travel agent and allow for a bit of flexibility.

MINIMIZING THE JET LAG EFFECT

Almost without exception flights to Europe depart in the evening, to arrive at their European destinations by midmorning, local time. There the planes are serviced to leave again in the early afternoon, local time, to arrive—thanks to the time changes—at their American destinations in the late afternoon or early evening of the same day. An exception to this mid-evening departure is the supersonic *Concorde* which leaves at 1:00 in the afternoon and gets you to Europe more than two hours "before you left," at 10:45 in the morning, local time. Your day of two noons costs a little over $2,000 one-way.

The scheme of mid-evening departures allows business people to complete a day's work and then to depart. Tourists are most likely to be people who have arrived at the East Coast airports on connecting flights from elsewhere and need the full daytime to complete that portion of their travels. The late afternoon return allows most passengers to catch an evening flight home. In either direction this scheme saves on time and hotel expenses.

Can you fly from New York to Frankfurt and arrive there with your body and brain already adjusted to Middle-European time? What about those who started their trip at Wichita, Kansas, or Boise, Idaho, and who have crossed ten time zones in the process?

For the vacationer who doesn't want to miss a minute of sight-seeing abroad, or for the business executive who must be sharp at a meeting soon after landing, seven time zones away from home, jet lag is a real nuisance. I have often wondered about the quality of shuttle diplomacy where aged statesmen yo-yo across the Atlantic, making decisions that affect us all.

Jet lag occurs when the body's circulatory rhythms are out of sync with the environment. Jet lag is far more than simply feeling tired and hungry at the wrong times of the day. It is a temporary mental and physical dysfunction that cannot be quickly alleviated by taking a nap or by forcing yourself to adopt the eating and sleeping pattern of your new environment. The more time zones you cross (six or seven hours between Eastern Standard Time and the times in Western Europe), and the faster you cross them (propeller plane, jumbo jet, or *Concorde*), the longer your body needs to make the adjustment.

Formulas for minimizing jet lag include eating lightly en route, checking into the hotel shortly after arrival, going out for a short unhurried walk in the evening, and starting out slowly on the second day abroad. Beware of tour operators who schedule a Rhine River cruise two hours after arrival. Chances are you won't remember much of that lovely excursion.

Recently an anti-jet lag diet, one which attempts to "fool" the body's biological clock, has been developed. Essentially the diet relies on eating and drinking certain kinds of food and beverages for several days before departure. The number of diet days depends on the length of the flight and the number of time zones crossed. For travel to Europe from the East Coast, the jet lag diet requires four days. In principle it works like this:

a. Calculate when breakfast time will be at your destination—for example, 7:30 a.m. in Zurich is 1:30 a.m. EST, 12:30 a.m. CST and 11:30 p.m. MST, and 10:30 p.m. PST.

b. Starting four days before the day of arrival overseas, drink no coffee, tea, or caffeinated soft drinks—if you drink them at all—except between 3:00 and 5:00 in the afternoon. Eat all meals at the regular time.

The first day is a feast day with a high protein breakfast (ham and eggs) and lunch (beans or peas) and a high carbohydrate dinner (lasagne, potatoes, sweet desserts).

c. The second day is a modified fast day. Eat only light meals (simple salads, thin soups, natural juices).

d. On the third day, repeat the diet of the first day.

e. On the day of departure repeat the fast day. If you are flying east, drink stimulating beverages, coffee, tea, etc., only between 6:00 and 11:00 in the evening. If you're flying west, drink them only in the early morning. Don't accept any alcoholic drinks on the plane. Each drink at 30,000 feet has the effect of two at ground level. Sleep as much as you can on the plane.

f. End your diet with a high-protein breakfast at the pre-determined breakfast time of your destination city. Usually that breakfast will be served to you over the ocean. After breakfast do all that you can to stay awake and remain active.

g. Eat the rest of your meals at the customary mealtimes of your environment. If at all possible, eat with other people, since social interaction stimulates wakefulness. Remember the leisurely evening walk.

The high-protein meals and light exercises are intended to induce the body's active cycle. The high-carbohydrate meals stimulate sleep. The modified fast helps to deplete the liver's storage of glycogen (a main muscle fuel) and prepare the body's clock for resetting. Caffeine and its chemical relatives can cause your biological rhythms to shift forward and backward, depending on the time they are consumed. Between 3:00 and 5:00 p.m. their effect is neutral.

On the plane, wear comfortable clothes, slacks, an open shirt, and an old

jacket. Loosen your belt and take off your shoes. And don't brag to anybody about how much last-minute work you did right before you left. It may have been necessary, but it wasn't very smart.

YOUR PROOF OF EXISTENCE

To travel to most other countries an up-to-date passport is required. Never assume otherwise. Not even children are exempt.

The procedure of getting a passport is relatively simple, but you should allow some time. The demand for U.S. passports stands at an all-time high, since the American booklet-type passport was first issued in 1918. In 1983, New York City's Manhattan office, equipped to process 1,200 applications a day, was getting over 2,000, and similar conditions exist at the twelve other offices around the country. The 25 percent overall increase in passport applications is indicative of the fact that more and more people are broadening their horizons.

Unless time is a factor in the preparations, it is best to stay away from the passport office and to apply for your passport at a post office or county courthouse of a larger city. Normally, you will receive your passport in about three to four weeks. In those cities which have a regular passport office, the courthouse and the post office may not be able to offer this service.

Applicants need proof of citizenship, such as a certified copy of their birth certificate, a naturalization certificate, or a consular report of birth, and a driver's license for identification. If you have an expired passport, issued not more than eight years previously, that would be even better. You will also need two identical, recent full-face photos on a plain light background, two by two inches. Vending machine photos and homemade snapshots are not acceptable. Of the three million passport applications processed at the Manhattan center last year, less than five percent were rejected, practically all of them because the photos were technically incorrect.

The clerk at the post office or courthouse will ship these documents along with your completed application to the nearest passport office. All items will be returned with your new passport.

The United States now requires youngsters of all ages to have their own passports. Children under thirteen need not appear personally and because of the possible long wait at passport counters, officials advise parents not to bring them along.

If a U.S. passport is about to expire, you can still use it to leave the country. Just plan to stop in with photos and identification at an American embassy or consulate in one of the countries you will be visiting to get it renewed.

Canadians can make applications in person at any of eighteen regional passport offices or by mail from practically every post office in the country. For Canadian passports the photo should be two by two and three-quarter inches vertical with a half-inch blank signature strip at the bottom. Photos for a Canadian passport must be stamped on the back with the photographer's name and address and the date on which the picture was taken, which must be within the past twelve months.

Canadian passports must be valid beyond the projected return date of the trip. In Canada children under sixteen can still be entered on the passport of one of the parents, not both.

Both Canadian and American passports should be signed on page three before the first trip is undertaken.

As travel moves further into the electronic age, more and more U.S. airports will be installing optical scanning devices capable of reading the latest U.S. passports. The machines, connected to the Treasury Enforcement Computer System (TECS), are capable of verifying the authenticity of the latest machine-readable passports and of rejecting unauthorized alterations, counterfeit passports, stolen passports, and signaling persons that are wanted for crimes. Within a few years all U.S. passports will be machine-readable and other countries are following suit.

Once you receive your passport you should always know its whereabouts and while traveling it should always be instantly accessible. If your passport is lost or stolen, the loss should be reported at once to the nearest police authorities and to the United States or Canadian consulate in that country. Before the consul can furnish you with a new passport, you will again have to provide them with documentary evidence of your citizenship, a new set of photos, and the full fee. Consulates, located usually in capitals and in major administrative cities such as Bonn and Hamburg and Amsterdam, are closed on weekends. This means that if you discover that you lost your passport on Friday afternoon, you may not be able to continue your travels until Monday evening. Consulates are closed on their own national holidays (U.S. Independence Day, Canada's Dominion Day, etc.), as well as on the national holidays of their host countries (Bastille Day, the second days of Easter and Christmas, etc.). Losing your passport and getting it replaced can be time-consuming and costly.

If your passport is stolen and later used for false identification in a major criminal action, you may be asked by your government to participate in a trial far away from home as a witness on your government's side.

One more thing. If you have just received your new passport and discover that the State Department has misspelled your name or switched your first and middle name, DON'T make your own alterations. Personal alterations render the passport invalid. But offical amendments can usually be made within an hour or so at a consulate overseas.

In most countries you will be asked to leave your passport with the hotel receptionist for safekeeping overnight and/or to fill out a lodging slip. This is in keeping with fire, occupancy, and safety laws and helps the authorities to account for all their guests in case of fires and natural disasters. Just be sure to pick up your passport again in the morning or at the end of your stay.

CASH, TRAVELER'S CHECKS, AND CREDIT CARDS

One of the decisions facing travelers overseas is what to do about money. Unfortunately, American and Canadian banks, especially those in smaller towns, can be less than helpful and their answers are often biased in favor of the service they can actually provide. Foreign-exchange dealers at major U.S. and Canadian airports are no better. As you plan your trip, consider these alternatives.

Carrying large amounts of cash is always risky, no matter where you go. For a two-or-three-week trip I recommend taking only from $50 to $75 in U.S. currency, mostly in one and five-dollar bills. These are handy for such incidentals as porters' tips, shuttle service between terminals, and small snacks purchased at times of departure and return.

Foreign-exchange dealers located at all major airports will often urge travelers to convert about one hundred dollars in foreign currency for tips and to pay for small items upon arrival overseas. That advice is best ignored. The exchange offices at the airports overseas, open upon the arrival of all flights, even on Sundays and holidays regardless of the hour, almost invariably will give you a better rate. In the unlikely case that they are not open, your small stock of one and five dollar bills will tide you over. There may be one exception, mentioned here only for those who travel through Europe to other destinations. Foreign currency dealers in the States will sometimes sell you currency for developing countries at better than their official rates. Before you jump into that bargain, however, you'd better find out whether importing such money is legal. In case it is, chances are that the so-called parallel rate within that country is even better.

Traveler's checks are the obvious choice for most travelers. If lost or stolen they can be replaced (though not nearly as fast and easy as demonstrated in the TV commercials), providing you have kept a separate record of the serial numbers of the checks you have not yet spent.

Several companies now market traveler's checks made out in foreign currency. Should you plan an extensive stay in one country, in France for instance, you might consider buying all your traveler's checks made out in French Francs. You should be aware that if the Franc drops, as it did recently, then the checks in your pocket are worth substantially less than what you paid for them. Of course, it could go the other way as well. The German Mark and the Swiss Franc have been considered safe investments.

When you arrive in a country, we recommend that you convert enough traveler's checks to cover your estimated needs for the next few days. It pays to estimate as closely as possible. Service fees for cashing traveler's checks are now per transaction rather than per amount, so it's more advantageous to convert $100 at once than $50 today and $50 more tomorrow. More than likely you'll be asked to show your passport when cashing traveler's checks.

Canadians should consider carrying traveler's checks made out in U.S. dollars. In some countries traveler's checks in Canadian dollars may not be accepted as easily by hotels and stores. Similarly, some Canadian credit cards may not be honored overseas.

Since the Bretton Woods Agreement was abandoned in 1971, the world currencies have been floating, though some would say sinking is a better description for a few. Since then it has become impossible to include a reliable currency conversion chart in a *Tourguide* such as this.

To find out what a dollar is worth as compared to the German Mark or Swiss Franc, consult the financial pages of the big city newspapers. The figures you find there can serve as a guide, provided you keep certain factors in mind. The rates quoted represent the buy-and-sell prices of large amounts of foreign currency between banks on the world's major money markets. Even apart from the processing fees, what you get for your dollar as an individual will always be less.

And in times of international unrest (invasions, terrorist attacks, heavy rhetoric from Washington) there may be a curious discrepancy between the exchange value of cash and traveler's checks. Usually your traveler's checks are worth a bit more.

Major credit cards (Amex, Visa, and Master Card) are honored in the larger stores of most major cities. They are almost useless in the smaller towns. Generally speaking, public services such as transportation and communication—railroad tickets, postage stamps, telephone calls—must be paid for in cash in local currency.

Charging purchases on your credit card abroad can give you free credit for awhile. Don't be surprised, however, if the amount charged to you at time of billing is not exactly the same as the amount you were charged at the time of purchase. Your credit card account is billed on the dollar conversion rate in effect on the day the merchant's bank processes the payment with the international clearinghouse. With the floating dollar, this could work for or against you, but in general the difference is minimal.

MONEY SENT FROM HOME

This is a headache you should try to avoid. If you see that you are going to need more money, it might be wisest to have an Amex money order mailed to you. Not all American Express offices provide this service. But if you need money in a hurry, contact a major bank in the city where you are and find out which bank they deal with in the United States or Canada. Make a phone call to someone at home to have money transferred to that bank to be wired according to the European bank's instructions. The combination of phone calls, service fees, and charges makes this a very expensive process and it cannot be done on weekends.

When two or more persons travel together it is best not to have all the traveler's checks in one person's name and it's certainly better not to keep all traveler's checks, cash, and identification papers in one place. If you feel insecure, and for all travel in southern Europe and the Near East, consider buying a money belt or an under-clothing hip or chest pouch, available at most camping equipment stores.

TRAVEL AND TRIP CANCELLATION INSURANCE

Suppose ... an ice storm delays your takeoff in Indianapolis and the study tour to Europe takes off without you.... You arrive at the dark counters and dead phones of an airline that has gone bankrupt.... You are enjoying the scenery of Europe, when all at once the news reaches you that your sister died and you should come home instantly....

Suppose that the president of the United States, in retaliation for certain world events, announces a sixty-day embargo on flights to or through a certain country, leaving you and thousands of others scrambling for tickets on foreign carriers flying devious routes.... Suppose the departure day of your long-planned vacation coincides with the first day of an air traffic controllers strike ... or a flash flood hits your destination city and the hotel of your choice is battling twelve feet of water in their dining room. It all adds up to inconvenience and expense.

Travel agents and tour operators, caught in the middle as much as you are, are not in a position to reimburse you. All or part of the air fares and the hotel reservation fees become non-refundable after a certain date, usually 60 or 61 days prior to departure.

For that reason most travelers now take out some form of travel insurance. If you have the time it may be well to compare the various types of short-term accident and trip-cancellation insurance available. Some do and some do not cover "unforeseen circumstances" such as earthquakes, landslides, and floods. Practically all travel insurance excludes acts of declared or undeclared wars, riots, and civil disturbances.

Most policies cover emergencies such as death in the family. Breaking up with your boyfriend may seem like the end of the world to you, but it does not count as an emergency. Pregnancy does not meet the insurance company's definition of emergency, but health complications arising from a pregnancy do. Ski accidents are not covered by the standard policy, but skiers can buy a rider to the policy to provide such coverage. Just imagine, for only five dollars more you can break your leg in Interlaken!

Most travel insurance policies carry a most important exclusion, one of which you should be aware. Coverage pertaining to illness may not apply in case of a preexisting condition. If the records of your family doctor show that there has been no change in your condition and that he suggested no change in medication within ninety days prior to your departure, your travel insurance coverage will be in effect. Any change in medication—even a lessening of the dose because you seem to be improving—will be considered an unstable condition and cause for denial of payment.

You should probably not buy trip-cancellation coverage equal to what you have paid for the entire trip, but only on the nonrefundable parts of the price, plus any additional expenses you might reasonably incur in making the return trip. Before you take out insurance against the loss of bags, theft of cameras, etc., check your homeowner's policy. It may be that you are already covered. Your travel agency can advise you at the time you are buying their services.

A HARD LOOK AT SOFT SIDES

Although there are several hundred manufacturers of luggage around the world, basically only three types are available—hardsides, softsides, and soft bags. Hardsides have a rigid frame and sides and are usually molded from plastic or fiberglass similar to that used in safety helmets and molded sportscar bodies. Softsides have a rigid frame covered with a flexible material, such as leather, vinyl, or canvas. Soft bags have no frame at all and are often made of nylon.

Hardsides are today's versions of the trunks once strapped to the running boards of the Model T Ford or carried on trains that gave the pullman case its name. Hardsides do the best job of protecting contents. American-made hardsides, such as Samsonite and American Tourister, are immensely popular with the Europeans and the Japanese who usually recognize a good value when they see one. To protect their valuable instruments, photographers and musicians favor specialized versions of hard-sided luggage.

While hardsides give you the best protection for your money, they tend to pop open, even when locked. This happens especially when they are overpacked. To overcome this problem, the luggage departments in bigger stores carry sturdy and colorful suitcase straps to keep your belongings together.

Overpacking is not as much of a problem with softsides, for they usually have a lot of give. Softsides were developed in the days when the airlines had weight restrictions and fined their passengers for excess weight. Softsides minimize weight by using frames of aluminum or laminated wood and by replacing the hinges and clasps with a zipper and covering the sides with anything from cheap vinyl to expensive leather. Price is a factor in buying softsides, since the less expensive softsides are especially vulnerable to rips and tears caused by the airport's baggage conveyers.

Soft bags, the latest invention, do not even have a supporting frame and easily adapt to the shape of their contents. While this almost always allows one to jam in one more item, soft bags offer no protection whatsoever to fragile items. Neither do they ride well on airport conveyer belts. Soft bags are most appropriate for carryons and for going to destinations where a few wrinkles don't matter.

Many travelers believe that locked bags will prevent theft. My experience has been that if you have kept the keys to your J. C. Penney, Samsonite, Sears, Eaton, or Haliburton luggage for the past ten years, you can probably unlock half of everybody else's suitcases at the airport, regardless of brand name. (Handy knowledge for a tour leader.) At best, suitcase locks keep the bag from accidentally opening during loading and unloading operations. In selecting a suitcase I would pay more attention to the comfort and the sturdiness of the handle than to the always-flimsy locks.

In the store the luggage, beautifully displayed, is empty and light. But try to imagine what the same piece would feel like fully packed and you will discover that the stylishly wrought plastic handle will saw your hand in two and that the cute rope-cum-vinyl creation may not arrive along with your suitcase. When packing, it is best to keep in mind the words of Christopher Fry in Act I of *The Lady Is Not for Burning.*

> *I travel light; as light,*
> *that is, as a man can travel who will*
> *still carry his body around because*
> *of its sentimental value.*

GETTING THERE WITH YOUR LUGGAGE

You know the saga of the jet age: supper in Toronto, breakfast in Brussels, and your baggage went to Mombasa.

The overall record of baggage arrival is excellent. Airlines claim that only about one percent of all baggage is misrouted or lost. That still adds up to around 400,000 misplaced bags a year for every major airline. Long weekend holidays, overbooked destinations, strikes and slowdowns, adverse weather conditions, and subsequent changes and cancellations of flights aggravate the problem. After one particularly long snowstorm several years ago, Chicago's O'Hare Airport had two warehouses full of baggage in distress.

Here are some precautions you can take. Be sure to have all the pieces you take along labeled or tagged twice with your name and address—on the inside and on the outside. Sturdy identification tags are usually incorporated in the canvas straps I recommended for the hardsides.

If you must change planes along the way, and especially if you must change airlines, be wary of checking your belongings all the way from point of origin to destination. If you are making a domestic interline connection, you should seriously consider checking your baggage only to the next connecting point, claiming it there, and checking it again on the next flight. This may seem like a nuisance to you, but it provides the best protection against loss. Then, if the bag didn't come with you from Toledo to New York, you can start the claims process eight or ten hours sooner and in your own language. But be sure that you have sufficient time to do this at your connecting points.

If you find one or more of your pieces missing, report the loss to the airline immediately. With the help of computers airlines can often find your missing bags and deliver them at no cost to you to a Stateside or Canadian address within 48 hours.

Our experience with missing baggage catching up with its owners traveling overseas has not been very good. Lost suitcases seldom connect with people on the move and traveling in areas not served by the last airline on your ticket.

In the States and Canada, most airlines will provide the traveler with "his" or "hers" emergency kits, containing a straight razor, toothpaste, shampoo, and the like, plus $25 in cash. But such kits are not volunteered without your insistence. This same "gesture of goodwill" does not necessarily exist overseas where the claims desk will [rightly] assume that the mistake was made at the point of departure.

Should the baggage be permanently lost, you must document the claim in writing. The airline will eventually reimburse you at the rate of $9.07 per pound for checked baggage up to a limit of $400 per person on an overseas flight, $750 domestic (in U.S. dollars). The process takes between two and three months. Then, if your suitcase does show up a year later, as once happened to a Hesston College student, you will get your belongings back and you may still keep the money.

You probably realize by now that certain items should *never* be checked in but should always be carried. These include your passport, traveler's checks and cash, all medicines and copies of their recent prescriptions, a second pair of eyeglasses, and enough film for the immediate situations, as well as all valuable and irreplaceable items. I well remember one distressed traveler with diabetes stranded at an out-of-the-way destination, whose insulin was traveling somewhere else in the missing suitcase.

CUSTOMS AND IMMIGRATION—OUTWARD-BOUND

First-time visitors to Europe are always surprised at the relaxed informality and ease of entry at most ports of arrival and border crossings. On country roads between Switzerland and France the man in the little office may wave you on without even getting up from his desk inside. The border crossing stations between Belgium and the Netherlands seem to be deserted for good. Customs officers of two or more nations ride the international trains together, spotchecking a passport here and there, stopping perhaps to question a Turkish or Algerian guest worker. The whole low-key approach is a disappointment to those who had hoped to see their brand-new passport enriched with a-half-dozen impressive rubber stamps.

Most European airports use the green lane/red lane system. If you have nothing to declare, you take the green lane and just walk out. If you do, you take the red lane. There the uniformed young men and women will have you on your way in no time.

Almost every country imposes quantity restrictions on the import of tobacco, liquor, and perfume and firearms. In general the use of CB radios is illegal in Europe, so they may question you bringing one along. Some countries have restrictive laws on the books regarding the number of cameras and the amount of film one may bring in, but except for India and the Soviet Bloc countries, such rules are seldom enforced. When in doubt, split up the equipment and the film among the members of your family or group.

On a few international highways there may be some delay at the border. One of these spots is the Autobahn München-Salzburg, which carries massive amounts of overland freight destined for East Bloc nations and the troubled areas of the Middle East and Persian Gulf. A second slow spot is the Franco-Swiss border at Basel-St. Louis, due to a mix of heavy commuter traffic with vacationing foreigners. Both bottlenecks can easily be avoided by crossing the border on less-traveled roads nearby.

If you pick up a hitchhiker (or if you hitchhike), for your own protection insist that your guest and all of his belongings cross the border individually. Though you may not be carrying anything illegal, it is unwise and dangerous to assume that your companion is innocent also. If anything illegal is discovered, *all* occupants of the vehicle will be considered as suspects.

IMMIGRATION AND CUSTOMS—HOMEWARD-BOUND

Your tour of Europe was great and you've just spent a lovely few hours chatting with your seatmate on the plane and now comes customs. That word conjures up visions of long lines of weary travelers waiting endlessly to have their identity probed and their baggage examined. It is an experience most returning travelers do not relish, at least not at that time on their biological clock.

Fortunately, the once notoriously slow United States and Canadian customs have improved considerably over the past few years. Throughout the land, customs agents have improved their methods to speed up the passengers' reentry into the country, while stopping more contraband at the gate. Airlines, passengers, and the customs service themselves, all agree that the processing time has been cut nearly in half.

Briefly explained, the welcome changes are composed of combinations and variations of the following factors:

1. More room to operate. Many customs areas were just not built for the jumbo jet age.

2. A citizens' bypass which separates persons traveling on U.S. passports from the visitors.

3. A one-stop screening process

4. The introduction of the European green lane/red lane system.

At Kennedy Airport, for instance, citizens' bypass means that 45 percent of the arriving passengers no longer need to be interviewed twice, once by the immigration officials and once by customs. However, in cases where one spouse is Canadian—quite common among Mennonites—it still means that the U.S. citizen may have to wait a long time for his or her other half to come through the doors.

Returning U.S. citizens and residents now may bring with them $400 worth of goods duty-free. Persons whose purchases exceed this exemption will be charged a flat 10 percent on the next $1,000 dollars. Anything above the $1,400 ceiling will be charged at the regular rates of duty, which may range from 2 percent to more than 30 percent, depending on the product or its country of origin. Members of an American family living in the same household and traveling together, may pool their exemptions. A family of four would be entitled to a $1,600 exemption and a $5,600 ceiling.

Canadian citizens and residents are allowed to bring with them—after seven days abroad, not counting the day of departure—goods to the value of $300. Canadians may not pool their exemptions. Parents and guardians may sign the declaration for babies and toddlers who are also entitled to a $300 exemption, but the items purchased must be obviously intended for the baby's use—"But, officer, the reason little Jolene needs this telephoto lens is she is an extremely gifted child."

Both the U.S. and Canada have similar laws governing the importation of plants and seeds, the protection of endangered species and the import of art objects. For more details, U.S. citizens should write for the free booklet *Know Before You Go,* available from the U.S. Customs, Room 201, World Trade Center, New York, N.Y. 10048. For the rules and regulations on the import of food, flora, and fauna, write for

Travel Tips, United States Department of Agriculture, Washington, D.C. 20050.
Canadian citizens should write for the corresponding booklets, *I Declare,* available from Revenue Canada, *Bon Voyage, But. . . . ,* available from External Affairs, Canada, and *Don't Bring It Back,* available from Agriculture Canada, all in Ottawa. The titles suggest that the Canadians do not beat around the bush.

One more word of caution. Most of us are by nature, if not by our religious upbringing, inclined to be kind and helpful and we have not learned to be suspicious. Try to imagine that you are standing in the departure hall of an airport overseas. A nice lady approaches you with a small package or maybe just a thick envelope. She wonders whether you'd be so kind as to mail this to her nephew in Boulder, Colorado, or her aunt in Santa Clara, California, and hands you a couple of dollars to cover the cost of postage. What do you do? By all means say no. Chances are good that you become the innocent party in the movement of drugs or restricted currency, but you may end up having to prove your innocence in court. It is of course perfectly all right to render such services to people you have known personally or for new friends that you have met at a church conference.

GETTING AROUND IN EUROPE

Committed to the principles of *More with Less* and good stewardship, let us begin with the suggestion to consider public transportation.

Except during the disruptions of both world wars, Europe's railroads, urban and regional bus lines, river and lake steamers, and tramways and postal services have been fully integrated into a fine web of routes that serve all citizens well with the most energy-efficient and environment-conscious means of getting there.

To illustrate the point, allow me to make a painful comparison. Between Monday and Friday you can find almost 250 passenger trains traversing the entire United States and not quite that many on weekends. On the other hand Luxembourg, one of the smallest countries in Europe, is served by 330 passenger trains daily. In more densely populated countries such as the Netherlands and Belgium, or larger nations such as Germany and France, the number of daily passenger trains is more like 18,000 or 20,000. Washington, D.C., with its Metroliners to and from New York, enjoys this nation's best service with ten trains daily. By comparison Zurich, Switzerland, is served by 512 trains daily on the national railways alone. Additional services in and out of Zurich are provided by the Sihltal, the Uetliberg, and the Forchberg railways, and an extensive network of tram and bus lines.

The punctual arrival and departure of all these trains in Europe meshes with those of ships, ferries, buses, and trams, in clockwork precision and with an overall on-time arrival record of 97.5 percent.

New on the scene is France's earthbound cousin of the *Concorde,* the TGV, currently the world's fastest train. Put in service in 1981, the TGVs, each powered by two 8,500-horsepower motors, maintain an average speed of 260 kilometers (165 miles) per hour between the downtown centers of several major European cities. At that speed the thoroughbred TGVs are only trotting. They are capable of running at a maximum speed of 370 kilometers (230 miles) per hour.

New routes and improved services are constantly being added everywhere. Norway, for instance, has announced a new express train which maintains a speed of 145 kilometers (90 miles) per hour while climbing rugged mountains to well above the timberline through lands of perpetual snow.

43

It follows that with all these services available, the Eurailpass and the Eurail Youth Pass remain the world's greatest travel bargains. These unlimited mileage passes can be purchased for fifteen or 21 days, or for one, two, or three months. With the Eurailpass for a one-time fee you have access to more than 160,000 kilometers (100,000 miles) of railroads in sixteen countries, from Finland to Spain, or between Ireland and Greece.

In addition the Eurailpass entitles you to hundreds of free bus and ferry rides and greatly reduced fares on nonaffiliated lines. It is hard to believe, for instance, that the seventeen-hour boat trip between Le Havre, France, and Rosselare, Ireland, is free, but to the holder of a Eurailpass it is. The services of all the ships on the Swiss lakes are free as are the cruise ships on the Rhine and the Danube.

Great Britain however, is not a party to the agreement and those who wish to visit England, Scotland, and Wales, or to ride the ferries across the English Channel must buy a Britrailpass and a Ferry Supplement. Unless, of course, you plan to swim the English Channel. Swimming the 21-mile channel would save you $25.

Both the Eurailpass and the Britrailpass must be bought in North America sometime prior to departure and you will need to furnish your passport number with the application. Eurailpass and Britrailpasses may be ordered through Menno Travel Service, TourMagination, and Prudent Travelers, or through your local travel agency.

THE 24-HOUR CLOCK

European timetables and official notices are based on the 24-hour clock, eliminating the need to duplicate time in a.m. and p.m. The time between midnight and 1:00 a.m. begins with 00.00. Seventeen minutes after midnight thus becomes 00.17. All times between 1:00 a.m. and 12:59 coincide with the way we normally tell time in North America. But on the 24-hour clock, 1:00 p.m. becomes 13:00. This continues until midnight, which is 24:00.

If this sounds confusing to you in the beginning, simply subtract twelve from all the afternoon and evening times. For example, 14:38 minus twelve equals 2:38 p.m., 21:20 minus twelve equals 9:20 p.m. Once you become accustomed to it, you will find the 24-hour clock the most sensible method for telling time.

POSTER TIMETABLES

At each station you will find large posters with departure times and posters with arrival times, each running chronologically from 00.00 to 24:00 hours. As a rule the departures are printed on yellow sheets, the arrivals on white. Next to the times listed—13:17, 13:23; 13:24, etc.—you'll find a name and number of the train along with its routing from city of origin to its final destination, with a summary of the most important stops between. The last column on the sheet shows the track and the plat-form numbers of the train. On both sheets fast express trains, such as the TEE (Trans Europe Express) and TEN (Trans Europe by Night) and ICs (InterCity trains) are printed in red. Busy stations like Zurich also have huge overhead revolving timetables listing all trains operating within the next few hours, but the principles of these boards are the same.

It is all quite simple. To begin with, you need to know what time it is right now. Let us say it is 14:29. Next you need to know where you want to go. You will find there is a train going in that direction at 14:43. The last column on the departure poster will tell you that it will stop along platform 9A. When you get to the platform you will again see a revolving sign which reconfirms that particular train's number and routing and arrival time.

THE INDIVIDUAL LIVES OF TRAIN COACHES

Do not assume, however, that it is enough to board the right train to get you where you are going. European trains are more than a long string of coaches that stay together toward a common destination. Instead, each car, a part of that great composite master plan worked out annually by an international committee in Bern, Switzerland, may at some stops along the way be switched over to another train to continue its journey.

A train starting off at Amsterdam, for instance, may consist of coaches destined for Vienna, Athens, Istanbul, Basel, Milan, and Rome. They will travel together through all of Holland, but inside Germany the individual coaches will be recombined with parts of trains coming in from Denmark or Belgium on their way to Athens, Rome, or Vienna.

HOW TO RECOGNIZE THE RIGHT COACH

You have reached the right platform at the right time and there stands your train. As you walk alongside the train you will notice that each coach carries a steel or aluminum routing sign with the name of the city where it started printed at the top, the final destination at the bottom, both in large type. In between are names of the most important cities along the way. If you arrive at the platform at the last moment, just board any coach of the train, but find your way through the train to the right coach before this train reaches the next major station. The destinations listed on the outside of each coach are repeated inside on both end platforms.

The operation of bus, tram, and boat services essentially follow the same principles. If you are in doubt, don't be afraid to ask. You will find European train personnel and fellow travelers extremely accommodating.

To save money, it pays to inquire whether the cities you are visiting offer one-day, three-day, or one-week tourist passes, and group or family rates on their transit systems. Some countries, such as the Netherlands, even have a nationwide strip ticket system in which a bus ticket bought in Amsterdam is equally valid on the bus, tram, and metro systems of any other town or city in the country. Cooperation, rather than competition, is the name of the game over there.

BEHIND THE WHEEL IN EUROPE

Italy's Autostradas used to be notorious for the way speeding motorists would blare their horns as they came roaring past. But no longer. The Italian government, in a massive educational campaign, actually succeeded in bridling this Latin exuberance by replacing it with the custom of rapidly blinking the headlights—by day or by night—to let the driver ahead know that somebody is about to pass them.

Headlight-blinking has since become popular in other countries as well and is one of the many customs that a traveler planning to drive overseas should know about. Some other important differences the North American driver should be aware of are the need, in some countries, for an international driver's license, a much stricter compulsory seat belt requirement, and the higher minimum age and lower maximum age limit for drivers.

An important consideration for some travelers is the upper and lower age limit for renting a car. In France and Great Britain cars will not be rented to persons under 25 or older than 65. In most countries the legal minimum age for operating a rented car is 21. For driving a private car it is eighteen. But in either case an older person who assumes the responsibility must ride along.

In most countries the possession of a valid home state driver's license will suffice, but West Germany, Austria, and Italy may require a notarized translation. The U.S. and Canadian embassies in those countries can provide that service, but the problem can more easily be solved by obtaining an International Driving Permit which comes in nine languages. An IDP, which costs $5.00 (U.S.), is valid for one year from date of issue. You can obtain one at your nearest office of the AAA or CAA.

Generally it is to your advantage to book a car rental through your travel agent rather than to deal directly with the rental firms. But either way it is always cheaper to complete the transaction before leaving home. The best rates for tourists are based on advance booking with unlimited mileage.

When you pick up the car over there be doubly sure that the rental company sends you out with all the necessary insurance papers (the so-called green sheets) and border documents. Check to see that they are the originals, not photocopies, or you may find yourself parked at a faraway border until the proper originals are reunited with the corresponding vehicle.

If you have a choice of places where you can rent a car, compare rates, including taxes. These vary considerably from country to country and on an extended trip you can sometimes save a sizable sum by renting your car right across the border. If you will be spending a major amount of time on the road, consider joining a national automobile club. Membership provides many advantages.

If you are staying in Europe for a long period of time, you may want to look into the option of buying a car. Most dealers of European cars have overseas delivery plans. Depending on the make of the car, the savings can be considerable. In other cases there are no savings at all. In either case cars must conform to U.S. or Canadian specifications in order to be legally imported.

In Europe, as in North America, it is probably best to get off the express highways, such as France's Autoroutes and Germany's Autobahnen, to buy fuel and automotive services. Such are usually cheaper in a nearby town. But whereas the food on American toll roads is usually overpriced and atrocious, in Europe that is

quite another matter. The facilities on the Autobahn come in several classes ranging from simple to quite elaborate. Some are equipped with showers, mothers' rooms, playgrounds, picnic areas, and all of them have special facilities for the handicapped. Tasty meals at reasonable prices are served in clean and pleasant quarters. Special diets—less likely to cause drowsiness—have been created with the long-distance driver in mind. While most American drivers would rather get off the turnpike to find a decent meal, in Europe it actually pays to get on.

With the exception of France's Autoroutes and Italy's Autostradas, Europe's expressways are free, though in the Netherlands you may occasionally have to pay a bridge toll and Switzerland and Austria may collect a small fee for the maintenance of their highest Alpine passes. Worth mentioning are the interdenominational worship facilities available to the traveler along some of the superhighways. Watch for the sign *Autobahnkapelle (highway chapel).*

INTERNATIONAL ROAD SIGNS

Because Europeans have always had to contend with a smorgasbord of languages and dialects, they were among the first to adopt the international road signs now in use in most countries around the world.

Most American drivers have no trouble shifting to the pictographic symbols. Illustrations of the signs are found in many travel guides or you may ask for a folder of signs at the desk of your car rental company. The international road signs are based on three geometric shapes: the triangle, the circle, and the rectangle.

Red-bordered triangles call attention to possible dangers ahead. The specific danger itself is illustrated with a black drawing on a white background.

Red-bordered circles give driving instructions, usually prohibitions. Black numbers within a circle indicate the maximum speeds in km/h.

Solid blue circles with a white illustration also give driving instructions, in this case compulsory. White numbers on a blue circle indicate the minimum speed limits, again in km/h.

Rectangular blue signs are informational. P stands for parking. H stands for hospital. A drawing of a wrench will tell you that a garage is nearby. Pictures of tents, picnic tables, youth hostels, and swimming pools tell the rest.

As a concession to the United States military presence, two American signs have appeared in Europe. One is the red stop sign, introduced after Americans continued to drive past the triangular signs with the words *Alto* or *Arret,* with disastrous results. The other one is the upside-down triangle, or yield sign. Or, as the British put it, the give way sign. Railroad crossings are marked with crossed boards like they are over here, but they are usually preceded by three separate barber-pole-striped boards at 80 meter (250 feet) intervals. Just remember, in Europe with the high frequency of rail service and the high speed of the trains, it is a deadly mistake to think you can still make it across ahead of the train.

The same pictographic signs found in the country are also found in the city, but with a few additions. A red circle with a blue center means no parking when the center is slashed by a red diagonal line; no stopping for any reason if the center is slashed with a red X. Others may indicate parking on alternate days. For instance, on odd-numbered days, like the 25th, parking is on the side of the street with the odd-numbered houses. On the 16th of the month it would be on the even side of the street.

A SELECTION OF INTERNATIONAL ROAD SIGNS

No entry

Speed limit

End of speed limit

No passing

Closed to
motor vehicles

Closed to
all traffic

Closed to horse-drawn
vehicles and animals

20:00 - 8:00
Closed to trucks and motorbikes,
8:00 p.m.-8:00 a.m.(Anti-noise ordinance)

No campers

No parking

No stopping

Border:
passport control

Motor vehicles
only

Prescribed
directions

Bicycle path
(may also be used
by mopeds)

 Bike path
(in Holland)

 Bike crossing
(in Holland)

Pedestrians only

Pedestrian
underpass

Signs seen in narrow streets, on one-lane bridges

Begin
limited-access highway

End
limited-access highway

Priority road

End of
priority road

You have the right-of-way

Oncoming traffic
has the right-of-way

Right-hand
curve

Repeated
curves

Slippery
(when freezing)

 200 m
Uneven
pavement

Railroad crossing
(with gates)

(unprotected)

Drawbridge

 30 m
Water's edge

Falling rock

School zone

Road narrows

Right lane ends

Construction
zone

Pedestrian
crossing

Biker's crossing

Deer crossing

Open range,
or cattle crossing

Yield

 800 m
Parking

  WC
Coffee shop,
restrooms

 2 km
Restaurant

 1500 m rechts
Repair service

First-aid
station

 500 m links
Youth hostel

 8:00 - 20:00
Change office

48

THE PARKING DISC

Most cities require the use of a parking disc. You will find one in the glove compartment of your rental car. You dial it to the time you arrived and the card will indicate when you must be back at the car. The disc, correctly set, should be placed inside the windshield. Remember that Europeans have been oriented toward the use of official public transportation and most cities have already banned the private automobile from the downtown areas altogether. Native and tourist alike enjoy the luxury of walking in the middle of the street away from the noise and fumes.

INTER-CITY AIR SERVICES

For those people who are really in a hurry there are flights between most major cities. But if you came to see the country, not the clouds, surface transportation is better and cheaper.

Commuter flights and helicopter services are available, but since airports are always located out of town, Europe's superfast trains invariably provide quicker downtown-to-downtown connections. If you plan your trip right, you will not see the airport again until the day of your departure.

EUROPE ON TWO WHEELS

Few places in the world are better suited to bicycling than Europe north of the Alps. If you have the time, the energy, and the ambition, you should seriously consider seeing all or part of Europe using your own pedal power. At thousands of railroad stations you can rent a bike for an afternoon or for a week. Along your way you'll meet many European cyclists on their way to school, to the office, or to visit friends. Astride a bike you not only see the country, but you can smell the hay, hear the birds, and feel the breeze. You can move at your own speed and stop whenever you feel like it.

If you plan to spend most of your vacation on a bike, you may consider bringing your own or buying a new one in Europe. Most transatlantic airlines will now transport an accompanied bike free of charge provided that you limit the rest of your baggage to one suitcase. While the bike is on the plane, the pedals must be removed, the seat pushed down as far as possible, the tires deflated, and the handlebars turned and fastened parallel to the frame. Be sure to consult your specific airline for its policies on transporting bikes before you go.

In Europe you can arrange to transport a bike at little cost by train, ship, or postal bus. The railroad stations in the larger stations maintain guarded bike storage facilities where you can keep your iron steed for a small fee.

Until recently TourMagination/Out-Spokin' have conducted European bike tours with an Anabaptist/Mennonite history emphasis. They have always been popular and there is talk about reviving the idea. The American Youth Hostel Movement will arrange bike tours for groups of six or more people in Europe, usually in cooperation with Icelandair.

For more about bicycling in Europe be sure to read *Bicycle Touring in Europe* by Karen and Gary Hawkins, Pantheon Books, New York, 1980.

For those interested in the history and development of the bike, museums devoted entirely to the bicycle are found at Heerenveen in Holland, at Neckarsulm in Germany, and at Lunéville in France. Worthwhile collections of historic bikes can also be found in museums of transportation and technology.

STROLLING DOWN A VILLAGE STREET

Europeans love to walk and they can keep it up for hours on end. Together these pedestrians have also had the clout to chase the car from the cities. Entire midtown areas, in some cases entire towns, have been declared pedestrian zones. For recreation Europeans may participate in group hikes that cover a specified route over four days or four evenings.

There are literally ten thousands of kilometers of trails in the national parks and through other areas of scenic and historic interest. So why not get in shape and join them. Be sure to bring your comfy old loafers and flat heels to Europe. You can always ditch them at the end of the trip to make room in your suitcase for the mementos you have bought.

BOOKS ON EUROPEAN MENNONITE HISTORY

For students of European Mennonite history a generous array of books is available from which I'd like to recommend a small selection in order of preference. C. J. Dyck's popular *Introduction to Mennonite History*, Herald Press, 1981, is still by far the best overview of Mennonite history in the areas covered by this *Mennonite Tourguide*. Be sure that you have the latest edition. Improvements and additions over the 1967 edition are substantial and have resulted in an almost entirely new book. Chapters one through nine of Dyck's *Introduction* take the story of the European Mennonites up to 1815 and chapter twenty picks up the story from there to the present time.

For more detail on the Anabaptist beginnings in Zurich/Zollikon two books are of interest. The one is the biographical novel, *Conrad Grebel, Son of Zurich*, by John L. Ruth, Herald Press, 1975. Read it before and after you visit Zurich and you can truly say, "I was there." The other is Fritz Blanke's booklet, *Brothers in Christ*, Herald Press, 1961, which details those fateful first weeks of Swiss Anabaptism through the summer of 1525.

It does not take long to read H. S. Bender's classic statement, *The Anabaptist Vision*, Herald Press, 1944, and the cost of it won't ruin your budget. Revisionist historians notwithstanding, this is still an excellent summary of Anabaptist Mennonite principles. Walter Klaassen's *Anabaptism, Neither Catholic nor Protestant*, Conrad Press, 1973, is another well-written and much discussed summary.

More specialized books include *The Golden Years of the Hutterites*, by Leonard Gross, Herald Press, 1980. In it you will find the details surrounding the stories chronicled in this *Tourguide* on Italy, Austria, and South Germany. Three volumes of the Classics of the Radical Reformation can add significantly to your understandings: *The Legacy of Michael Sattler* by John Howard Yoder, Herald Press, 1973; *The Writings of Pilgram Marpeck* by Klassen and Klaassen, Herald Press, 1978; and *Anabaptism in Outline* by Walter Klaassen, Herald Press, 1981. Additional volumes are in preparation. Also in preparation is *A People on the Way*, a pictorial volume on Anabaptist Mennonite history by Jan Gleysteen, Herald Press.

In 1975 the Lancaster Mennonite Historical Association issued *The Drama of the Martyrs*, featuring high-quality reproductions of all of Jan Luiken's engraved illustrations from the 1685 *Martyrs Mirror*. For further information on these and other books contact your nearest Provident Bookstore.

Throughout this *Tourguide* passages pertaining to Anabaptist Mennonite history are indicated by a color bar in the margin.

THE MENNONITE CHURCH IN EUROPE

While traveling in Europe you may wish to worship with one of the 250 Mennonite and Mennonite Brethren congregations, fellowships, and mission outposts. While the larger ones among these meet weekly, the smaller neighboring congregations customarily combine and rotate their services in the various meetinghouses. The beginning time of the services ranges from 9:00 a.m. to 10:45. Because of their northern location, the times of service in Friesland are different in the winter than during the summer. In most Dutch congregations the church service is followed by a coffee hour in the adjacent fellowship hall.

Because these variables are many and our space is limited, it is impractical to list the addresses and the hours of worship of all the Mennonite congregations here. For an up-to-date contact address of each European conference, consult the latest edition of the *Mennonite Yearbook,* Mennonite Publishing House, under the heading Mennonite and Brethren in Christ World Directory, subsection Europe.

To find a Mennonite meetinghouse, the term "Mennonite" and its variations, "Mennists, Mennonit, etc.," may not be of much help. In Holland the word used is *Doopsgezind* (loosely translated, baptism-minded). The place you are looking for is the Doopsgezinde Kerk. The Swiss only recently voted to adopt the name Mennonite over the objection of a few who [correctly] made the point that historically speaking the Swiss Anabaptists never really were Mennonites = followers of Menno. In most Swiss communities it may still be best to ask for the Altevangelische Taufgesinnte Gemeinde (Old Evangelical Anabaptist Community). The church services at any of these places will of course be in their own language(s).

Most of Europe's larger cities have English-speaking churches, usually in the Calvinist and Anglican tradition, attended by British and American embassy personnel and English-speaking tourists, sailors, and businessmen and -women.

Many Mennonites, spiritual descendants of Grebel, Manz, and Blaurock, have found it interesting to worship in the Grossmünster or Fraumünster churches of Zurich, still served today by the spiritual successors of Zwingli.

THE STORY OF RELIEF AND SERVICE IN EUROPE

One area which for the most part was consciously left out of the itineraries in this *Mennonite Tourguide to Western Europe* is the vital work of the Mennonite Central Committee in Europe, especially from 1940 to 1967, when MCC was active throughout many European countries.

Below is a list of some of the more important places in various countries where MCC played an integral role in cooperative ventures in relief work, broadly interpreted. This included *Suchdienst* (tracing the whereabouts of missing relatives and friends); food, clothing, medicine, and housing; refugee resettlement; helping to organize new Mennonite congregations for refugees; and social work of many types and forms, serving infant and aged alike.

MCC workers who want to visit the places where they once lived and worked will need to expect something of the Rip van Winkle syndrome upon returning to their habitats of old. Others who know less of the story of MCC involvement in Europe should be aware of the breadth and depth of this work.

As you travel, make it a point to chart those cities and villages where MCC once was active. Someday MCC may want to put flesh on these bones, but for now, the listing below will need to suffice. (For present-day Mennonite mission and MCC work in Europe, consult current Mennonite yearbooks of the various groups.)

SPAIN—Spanish Border (pre-1940s); Madrid
FRANCE—Southern France (pre-1940s); Nancy, Valdoie, Wissembourg/Weiler
ENGLAND—London
HOLLAND—Amsterdam, Heerewegen, Roverestein, Walcheren Island
BELGIUM—Brussels, Bullange
GERMANY—Backnang, Bad Dürkheim, Bechterdissen, Berlin, Bielefeld, Bremen, Enkenbach, Espelkamp, Frankfurt, Gronau, Hamburg, Heilbronn, Kaiserslautern, Kiel, Krefeld, Lübeck, Neustadt, Neuwied, Stuttgart, Wedel, Weierhof
AUSTRIA—Linz, Salzburg, Vienna, Wels
SWITZERLAND—Basel
ITALY—Naples, Torre Pellice
(MCC also was active in the following countries: Denmark, Greece, Hungary, Poland, Yugoslavia).

MENNONITE WORLD CONFERENCE

The existence of Mennonite World Conference is the fulfillment of the dreams and efforts of Christian Neff, pastor of the Weierhof congregation in the German Palatinate, an outstanding leader among the European Mennonites during the first half of this century. It was "Onkel Neff," as he was lovingly called by his friends, who personally issued a call for such a meeting in the middle 1920s.

The first Mennonite World Conference was held at Basel, Switzerland, in 1925 and commemorated the 400th anniversary of the birth of the Anabaptist movement in that country. Attendance at the first World Conference was small and North America sent only one delegate, H. J. Krehbiel. The second conference was held in Danzig in 1930 and concerned itself with the urgent needs of the Russian Mennonite refugees to resettle in Brazil and Paraguay. Christian Neff and W. J. Kuhler spoke on the history of the Mennonite relief efforts and one young American, H. S. Bender, reported on current Mennonite relief efforts. An appeal was made to Mennonites everywhere to come to the aid of the Russian Mennonite emigrants. The third conference was held in Holland in 1936 and focused on the 400th anniversary of Menno Simons joining the Anabaptist movement.

World War II made the convening of the fourth Mennonite World Conference in 1940 impossible and Christian Neff died in 1946. MCC organized the next conference to meet in the States by holding two similar sessions of 2½ days each at Goshen, Indiana, and Newton, Kansas. The sessions are remembered as very full with an average of three speakers assigned to each of ten major topics. The attendance was large, but the number of non-American delegates (which included practically all of the Mennonite foreign students studying in the States), numbered only 27.

The fifth Mennonite World Conference was held at Sankt Chrischona near Basel in 1952. One day of the conference was held in historical celebration in Zurich and Zollikon. IBM simultaneous translation equipment was used for the first time.

The sixth Mennonite World Conference was held in Karlsruhe, Germany, in 1957. A trilingual hymnal was printed for the occasion and an "unofficial" communion service was held after the conference for those who wished to participate. Since then, Mennonite World Conferences have been held at regular five-year inter-

vals through 1972, at which time the interval was changed to six years. The complete
list of Mennonite World Conferences held so far reads as follows:

I	1925	Basel, Switzerland	June 13-16
II	1930	Danzig, Free City of Danzig*	Aug. 31-Sept. 3
III	1930	Amsterdam, Elspeet, and Witmarsum, Holland	June 29-July 3
IV	1948	Goshen, Indiana, and Newton, Kansas, USA	Aug. 3-10
V	1952	Basel (St. Chrischona) and Zurich, Switzerland	Aug. 20-15
VI	1957	Karlsruhe, Germany	Aug. 20-16
VII	1962	Kitchener, Ontario, Canada	Aug. 1-7
VIII	1967	Amsterdam, Holland	July 24-29
IX	1972	Curitiba, Brazil	July 18-23
X	1978	Wichita, Kansas, USA	July 25-30
XI	1984	Strasbourg, France	July 24-29
XII	1990	(to be announced)	

*Since 1945: Gdansk, Poland

TRACING OUR ROOTS TO THE OLD COUNTRY

More and more travelers are combining their European tours with a bit of
amateur genealogy. The Mennonites with their strong concept of church and family
are no exception. On TourMagination tours, which specialize in Anabaptist/Men-
nonite history, the number of family historians is high and many TM participants
have extended their stay for a week or more to go after specifics.

If you want your root digging side trips to be a success, it pays to do a lot of
spadework well in advance. Some countries and some airlines have published
leaflets with suggestions on how to proceed. Most of these point to resources in the
British Isles, Scandinavia, or southeastern Europe, and are not as helpful when it
comes to Germanic origins. However, some of the principles of genealogical research may apply.

After doing the obvious, that is, interviewing the older members of the clan,
consulting existing family records, searching county and state archives, Mennonites
can best turn to the following resources:

ARCHIVES OF THE MENNONITE CHURCH
1700 South Main, Goshen, Ind. 46526

LANCASTER MENNONITE HISTORICAL SOCIETY
2215 Millstream Road, Lancaster, Pa. 17602

MENNONITE HISTORICAL LIBRARY OF EASTERN PENNSYLVANIA
Christopher Dock Mennonite School, Lansdale, Pa. 19446

You may want to subscribe to either, or both, of the following magazines:

PENNSYLVANIA MENNONITE HERITAGE
2215 Millstream Road, Lancaster, Pa. 17602

MENNONITE FAMILY HISTORY
Main Street, P.O. Box 171, Elverson, Pa. 19520

For those Swiss-German Mennonites whose ancestors lingered in the Pfalz (Palatinate) for several generations (and that includes many in the [Old] Mennonite Church), it pays to contact the Heimatstelle Pfalz, a fabulous research center in Germany:

HEIMATSTELLE PFALZ
Benzinoring 6/Postfach 2860
D 6750 Kaiserslautern, West Germany

Mennonites and Mennonite Brethren of Dutch-German-Russian background should contact either of the following archives:

MENNONITE LIBRARY AND ARCHIVES
North Newton, Kan. 67117

MENNONITE HERITAGE CENTRE
600 Shaftesbury Boulevard, Winnipeg, Manitoba R3C 2H6

CENTER FOR MENNONITE BRETHREN STUDIES
4824 East Butler, Fresno, Calif. 93727

For additional addresses of Mennonite archives and libraries in the U.S. and Canada, consult the current edition of *Mennonite Yearbook*.

In addition, two non-Mennonite organizations should be mentioned. The first one is:

HISTORICAL SOCIETY OF GERMANS FROM RUSSIA
1139 South Seventh Street
Lincoln, Nebr. 68502

The other one is the Church of Jesus Christ of the Latter Day Saints which maintains vast repositories of general information at its headquarters in Salt Lake City, available to persons of all faiths.

MORE WITH LESS IN LODGING

Conrad Hilton once said, "Each of our hotels is a little America." That may be the best reason, but not the only one, for not staying at these hotels. What is the purpose of traveling halfway around the world to a new and exciting location only to stay overnight at a hotel that is exactly like the one in the town next to yours?

The same applies to Holiday Inns, Sheratons, Novotels, and the other multinationals, which now unfortunately circle the globe. Apart from their cookie-cutter sameness, the problem with multinational hotels is one of propriety. In their manner of doing business and in the immodesty of their architecture, the large multinationals owe their allegiance, not to the customs and environment of the host country, but to the dictates of their corporate headquarters. If we accept the idea that tourism should benefit the people of the countries visited, the massive return of tourist income to shareholders overseas should be disturbing to us.

To be sure, Europe can handle this, but where the same chain hotels are located in less-developed countries, their presence invariably results in a net outflow of resources. There are better places we can patronize.

Europe, which has a long history of tourism—it would not be incorrect to say that it started with the Romans—offers a kaleidoscopic variety of facilities ranging from the bed-and-breakfast tradition to the Ritz. There are literally hundreds of thousands of pleasant hotels and pensiones, guest houses, old inns, mountain lodges, as well as the old hostelries established by the church centuries ago. The very words "hostel," "hotel," "hospital," "hospitality," all date back to the days when monks and nuns first extended the welcome of an open door to the weary traveler.

Except during the height of tourist season or at times of special events, such as the Passion Play, the Olympics, or a Holy Year, it is not necessary for one or two persons traveling together to book hotels ahead of time, unless you prefer to do so. The municipal tourist offices located in or near the main railroad station will be glad to assist you in finding a room. The same office usually sponsors programs like *Get in Touch with the Dutch, Meet the Danes, Don't Miss the Swiss,* and the like, through which you have a chance to meet foreign nationals of like interests or profession. Usually 24-hour notice is required to arrange for the encounter. And be sure to be explicit in describing your interests or else a housewife who enjoys needlepoint is going to find herself face to face with a practitioner of acupuncture!

Throughout southern Germany, in all of Austria, in parts of northern Italy, and elsewhere, you may notice the sign *Zimmer Frei* (rooms available) on farms and village homes. This means that the family takes in overnight guests. The rates they may charge are set by the provincial or cantonal government and are most reasonable. The family may not speak your language, but they have already entertained Finns and Frenchmen, Hollanders and Hungarians, for years and you too will learn to gesture with eloquence.

For the young and the young at heart there are always the youth hostels which feature simple but adequate accommodations from the north of Norway to the south of Spain. Youth hostels are found in castles, in retired ships, lighthouses, historic farms, ancient warehouses, and former monasteries. Other youth hostels are in new buildings.

To make use of the youth hostels, Americans should take out membership beforehand in the American Youth Hostel organization (and Canadians with the Canadian Youth Hostel organization). The address of the AYH is American Youth Hostels, Inc., National Administrative Offices, 1332 I St., N.W., Suite 800, Washington, D.C. 20005. The address of the CYH is 333 River Road, Vanier City, Ottawa, Ontario K1L 8B9.

Buying a membership outside the country of your own nationality may not be easy and in Switzerland and the Flemish-speaking part of Belgium it is expressly forbidden. When applying for your membership you may want to order a copy of the *International Youth Hostel Handbook and Map,* which covers Western Europe.

The Youth Hostel organization promotes traveling on one's own power: biking, hiking, skiing, canoeing, horseback riding, and living the simple life. Arrival at hostels by bus or by car is not prohibited. But if the hostel is full, those who came in under their own power will be given preference.

Most hostels operate on a self-help basis. Performing the small housekeeping tasks assigned by the hostel parents is considered part of the agreement.

For those who enjoy camping or caravaning, Europe has many campgrounds. To make use of these you must have an International Camping Carnet. The ICC serves in lieu of a passport on many campgrounds where the manager may wish to

Jan Gleysteen/'84

hold on to some security until you leave. At other camps, it may entitle you to a reduction in fees. In several countries having an up-to-date ICC is a legal requirement for all campers. American and Canadian campers may apply for their Carnet from National Campers and Hikers Association, 7172 Transit Road, Buffalo, N.Y. 14221. The membership includes International Camping Carnet. The fee covers the entire family.

A WORD ABOUT WATER CLOSETS

A book could be written about the variety of sanitary facilities around the world. Of course they are not marked "men" and "women" in English, but rather *Messieurs* and *Dames*, or *Mucy* and *Czerny,* or *Karlar and Konnur*. And she who thinks *Herren* means "hers" may be in for an embarrassing moment. In many places graphic designs help you to the right WC (water closet). Flushing them would make another chapter in the study. You may have to pull a chain, lift a knob, push a button, kick a lever, or pull a tube. In public places, such as museums, railroad stations, and on board ships, lady attendants normally "man" the restrooms. After using the facilities, it is customary to leave the attendant a tip.

HOW TO SAY THANKS

In certain places you may have occasion to express in a tangible way appreciation for the hospitality or for services rendered. You may want to bring along some small gifts that are typically American or Canadian to leave with your new friends. Items which do not take up a lot of space include: printed decorative towels and calendar towels, locally made ceramics, glass bud vases, pictorial calendars, a color-picture book of your home state or province, Appalachian wood carvings, and blocks of commemorative stamps for the collectors.

While cookbooks are always popular, do not take them along as gifts unless the amounts are given in the metric system.

Be sure to get the full name and address of your new friends and their postal code. A short letter sent upon your return or a card written at Christmastime serves as a great bridge-builder.

BETWEEN BREAKFAST AND THE MIDNIGHT SNACK

A good appetite and a willingness to try new and different foods can add another dimension to your trip—you may be in for some delicious discoveries. The renowned and hearty Continental Breakfast—freshly baked hard rolls, butter, various cold cuts and cheeses, a soft-boiled egg, and piping hot coffee—is usually included in the price of the lodging of the place where you are staying. Some hotels feature a real breakfast smorgasbord. You will probably be asked to give your room number or to show your room key before being seated.

For lunch there are two things you can do. Prepare your own picnic or do some adventurous sampling around the neighborhood. We will start with the latter. In Amsterdam you could head for a stand-up sandwich shop, such as *Broodje van Kootje*, where men in white coats can quickly fix you a tasty sandwich loaded with the best of cheese, ham, fish, shrimp, cold cuts, etc. Street-corner vendors in Munich and Nurnberg stand ready to serve you a choice of hot sausages. In all Belgian towns french fries (with or without piccalilli), shrimp, mussels, and oysters are available in great abundance.

In Münster, Westfalen, it is pumpernickel. In 1648 the pope's representative at the Münster Peace Talks (see page 143), Count Chigi, complained, "All they have in Münster is pumpernickel bread and rain, rain, rain." Things haven't changed much and you owe it to yourself to try some of that black Gothic bread with cheese and ham, rain or shine.

Belgium features waffles that are a real work of art, and France has its crêpes. For those who love pancakes, Holland, being a small country, comes up with some very small, dollar-sized pancakes called *Poffertjes,* made to order before your very eyes on a gas-fired grill in circus style surroundings. In addition to being fun, snacks like these are the perfect answer for travelers who want to save time and who prefer to avoid a heavy mid-day meal.

If, in addition to saving time, you hope to cut expenses, a picnic lunch is the answer. Roadside picnicking is common in Europe, especially along rural roads. But you can also picnic in any of the numerous city parks. Good manners dictate that you do not trespass and that you carry away all trash. In the Alpine regions, where the growing season is very short, it is best to stay out of farmers' fields altogether.

Shopping for the ingredients is an educational experience in itself. In most towns you'll need to visit several stores to gather your supplies. You will find bread at the bakery, meat at the butcher, cheese, butter, milk, and yogurt at the dairy store, cookies and pastries at the sweetshops, and fresh fruit at the open-air market. In the larger cities, you can find supermarkets and co-ops. In Switzerland the Migros chain has just about everything you might need, while Albert Heyn is the name to look for in Holland. In Germany some Kaufhof department stores may have a food department in their basements.

One thing you'll soon notice is that the Europeans are extremely ecology-conscious. They not only turn off their motors when the railroad crossing gates are down, they also refuse to buy groceries wrapped up in excessive amounts of packaging, plastic bubble packs, and the like. Some stores will, therefore, not be able to provide you with shopping bags because their regular customers insist on bringing their own reusable containers and carriers. Bring your own string net, nylon pouch, or shopping basket to carry out your purchases, unless you come in wearing a coat with many oversized pockets.

For the evening meal find a restaurant which specializes in local or regional dishes. Usually the municipal tourist office can advise you which specialties are in season. Most hotel restaurants have their menus posted outside, so it is easy to compare choices and prices between neighboring restaurants. In Europe it also pays to check out the railroad restaurants. Some of these serve award-winning meals at reasonable prices. These *Bahnhof Buffets*, accustomed as they are to serving train passengers in a hurry, are also good places to consider for a group meal on short notice. An advance phone call is all it takes.

WATER, WATER EVERYWHERE AND NOT A DROP TO DRINK

The drinking water you find in European cities and towns is usually of good quality and perfectly safe to drink. Exceptions to this are ornamental fountains that carry the sign *Kein Trinkwasser* or *Eau non potable*, and the water in the restrooms of railroad coaches, which are likewise labeled.

On the other hand, most Europeans do not share the American custom of drinking water with their meals or at other times. If you want water with your meals, ask for it. Chances are that your waiter will look puzzled and repeat *"Wasser?"* to make sure he heard you correctly. He may still come back with a bottle of mineral water. If he does, you owe him the money for it. Better go native and ask for a bottle of *Apfelsaft* (apple juice) to begin with, or any of the other delicious fruit drinks. Try *Johannisbeersaft* (black currant juice), the juice of white or red grapes, or apricot juice, to mention just a few.

Europeans, including most Mennonites and other Christians, may drink an occasional glass of wine or other alcoholic beverage. Others may be convinced total abstainers. In general the teaching in Europe leans toward moderate and responsible usage. Laws against drunk driving are tough and strictly enforced. In Germany the fine payable on the spot amounts to about $250 (U.S.) coupled with the surrender of your driver's license for a month. Normally, when a group goes out for dinner, one person is designated the driver and that person takes only fruit juice. When that group goes out again at a later date, someone else will do the driving. Cafes and restaurants cooperate fully with the program.

Europeans are sometimes annoyed with North American Christians who maintain a position of strict abstinence and who feel it their duty to lecture to them about the evils of alcohol when they have a glass of wine with their meals. One should be able to differentiate between alcohol use and alcohol abuse and when there is clearly no problem, both sides would probably benefit more from a discussion on the theology of Hans Küng or on French Impressionism.

SOUVENIRS OR LASTING MEMENTOS?

A business that has not kept up with the times and probably is unable to is the souvenir industry. The amount of gaudy and useless trinkets flooding the world is staggering. From the Great Smokies to Jerusalem, from Amsterdam to Nairobi, the towns are full of little shops crowded with objects you may regret having acquired once you are safely back home.

There is no denying the popularity of souvenirs. I have seen lovely and intelligent couples buy an extra suitcase while on tour in order to carry home one knickknack from each country for each of their grandchildren. I observed a minister on a study tour marking up a Hummel catalog while half-listening to a guest lecturer because for him shopping had become an all-consuming compulsion.

The souvenir dilemma is simply one of logistics. There will never be enough good-quality creative artists and craftsmen in the world to keep up with the growing demand any more than there will be enough gifted writers, poets, and musicians to create masterpieces for around-the-clock television on forty channels. Lots of chaff will continue to surround the occasional grain.

However, you can come home with some unique and useful mementos. (Please note that I didn't write souvenirs.) Try to locate the arts and crafts centers in the cities you visit. In Switzerland the larger cities have stores which feature *Heimatwerk*—homemade products. In these stores you will find artistic ceramics, woodcarvings and wood products, beautiful weavings, embroidery and linens of good quality, and other products, at reasonable prices. For the best value, concentrate on buying only those products which are indigenous to the country, or even the province or canton, you are visiting.

When you discover an item you really like, think of buying it in multiples to give to friends and relatives. Once you are back home you may discover that the purchase is even more attractive or practical than you first realized. Now if only you would have purchased a few more to share with those special people!

Avoid buying any merchandise from roving street peddlers. It is almost always inferior in quality and seldom if ever representative of the country you are visiting. This warning does not apply to the sidewalk hobby markets where private stamp collectors, book lovers, and the like, come to socialize and to swap and sell their du-

CLOTHING SIZES
IN AMERICAN, BRITISH, AND EUROPEAN
EQUIVALENTS

All equivalents are approximate.
Sizes may differ slightly from country to country and between manufacturers.
Try things on for size whenever possible.

CHILDREN — Boys and girls, suits and dresses

American and British	2	4	6	8	10	12
European	40-45	50-55	60-65	70-75	80-85	90-95

JUNIOR MISSES

American and British	7	9	11	13	15	17
European	34	36	38	40	42	44

WOMEN — Blouses and sweaters

American	30	32	34	36	38	40	42	44
British	32	34	36	38	40	42	44	46
European	38	40	42	44	46	48	50	52

Dresses, skirts, and coats

American	8	10	12	14	16	18	20
British	30	32	34	36	38	40	42
European	36	38	40	42	44	46	48

Shoes

American	5	5½	6	6½	7	7½	8	8½	9
British	3½	4	4½	5	5½	6	6½	7	7½
European	35		36		37		38		40

Stockings

American	8	8½	9	9½	10	10½	11
British and European	0	1	2	3	4	5	6

MEN — Suits and coats, sweaters

American and British	34	36	38	40	42	44	46	48
European	44	46	48	50	52	54	56	58

Shirts

American and British	14	14½	15	15½	16	16½	17	17½
European	36	37	38	39	40	41	42	43

Shoes

American	7	7½	8	8½	9	9½	10	10½	11	11½	12
British	6½	7	7½	8	8½	9	9½	10	10½	11	11½
European	39		40		41		42	43		44	45

Socks

American and British	9½	10	10½	11	11½	12	12½	13
European	39	40	41	42	43	44	45	46

The numbering system for glove sizes (men's and women's) is universal.

plicates. In Paris, for instance, you will find the stamp collectors on the Avenue Gabriel on Thursdays. In Amsterdam the stamp collectors gather on Saturday afternoons on the Nieuwezijds Voorburgwal.

Here are some suggestions for worthwhile purchases. Both Germany and Switzerland are good places to buy high quality cutlery. Look for the names *Henckel and Son*, or the brand name *Zwillingswerk*. An authentic Swiss army knife makes a nice gift for the camper in your family. Colorful picture books and calendars of a region you particularly like and records or cassettes with folk music don't take up much space in your suitcase. They do add weight. The various ingenious slicers, peelers, and other household gadgets you find in the department store will not ruin your budget.

Some countries are known for their specialties. In Germany it is musical instruments of all kinds as well as sheet music, and in Belgium it is lace and linen. In Holland Delft blue and pewter are good buys. Austria and adjacent parts of Bavaria are known for cut crystal, blouses, plain or embroidered, and children's clothing. Stuffed animals and sturdy wooden toys can be found in many places. Costumed dolls in regional dress make interesting remembrances. For lovers of fine chocolate and tasty cheeses, the choices are endless.

The list goes on with knitwear, fine objects such as binoculars and opera glasses, leather goods, stationery, handsome reproductions from the many fine museum shops, and copperware. Let good sense and good stewardship prevail as you make your selections.

TRAVELING AS A FAMILY AFFAIR

When families travel with children they see the world from an additional perspective, through the eyes of a child. Interesting details overlooked by the adults are quickly noted and long remembered by the youngsters. Call them bridge-builders or ice-breakers, children are often less hesitant to try new things, start a conversation with a stranger, and eat unusual dishes. Family travel generates experiences and memories that will be shared for a lifetime.

It may be good to create advance interest in the trip by allowing school-age children to participate to some extent in planning the tour. Borrow books from school or church library and write for the brochures from the government tourist offices listed on pages 25-26. Some national tourist offices have special folders with recommendations for places of interest to children. Remember to ask for them.

When traveling with children, be careful to include enough activity along with the scenery and plan for variety in methods of transportation, such as tram, boat, train, cable car, bus—double-deckers are exciting!—subways, and horse-drawn carriages.

Some towns have museums and exhibits of special interest to children, such as Madurodam in Holland, the Children's Museum in Belgium, and Legoland in Denmark. And you may want to visit one or more of Europe's outstanding zoos.

Children of all ages will get more out of the trip if they are encouraged to collect items along the way for a scrapbook/diary or album. Such items could include postcards, tram, boat, and museum tickets, snapshots, coins, paper money in the smaller values, maps, stickers and decals, napkins, matchbook covers, and the like. Save the sales slip of their favorite purchase. Keeping a scrapbook of day-to-day happenings is not only fun, but it helps children understand and retain a sense of continuity as they travel from place to place. Come to think of it, it is a good idea for adults too.

When you travel with children, be sure the airline is told that you expect seats together. Such requests are usually honored, but if you do not ask, you may find your clan scattered all over the plane with no one to look after the little ones.

If you expect to travel with small children, you may want to write for the booklets *Tips on Choosing Toys for Plane Travel* and *Tips on Choosing Toys for a Car Trip*, both by Marilyn Sloan. They are excellent and they are free, available from Toys to Grow On, 2695 East Dominguez Street, Box 17, Long Beach, Calif. 90801.

TRAVELING WITH THE HANDICAPPED

As a tour director, I have long been interested in travel possibilities for the handicapped. But I have not been at all successful in combining the needs of the handicapped with a route that follows the footsteps of the Reformation. In corresponding with the authorities overseas, I have found them to be extremely helpful and concerned. All have compiled extensive guides with titles like *Access Holland* or *Austrian Hotel Guide for the Handicapped*. But none of them list the places we like to visit on a tour of a historical nature.

The situation is understandable. Castles were built to keep the enemy out, not to provide easy access to anyone. They have narrow and well-worn winding stairs set in walls fourteen feet thick. The world's most famous art museums, the Louvre, the Rijksmuseum, and the Uffizi, all house their main collections in spacious second and third floors, for the most part in historic buildings that antedate modern conveniences.

Mozart, Rembrandt, Zwingli, Dürer, and other significant personalities of the past lived and worked in cramped quarters on the second or third floor of ancient houses located on steep cobblestoned streets. It is technically, financially, and spacewise impossible to add ramps and elevators to any of these places. Restrooms, where they have been added in modern times are often too small to be accessible to the handicapped.

For tours of a different nature, like birdwatching, fishing, or socializing, Europe has much to offer to the physically disabled, with special fishing piers, park trails, campgrounds, and guest houses designed with the needs of the handicapped in mind. Most countries publish one or more guides with titles like *Where Shall I Go Today*, but none of them are in English nor likely ever will be. As more funds become available, the money will be put into adding more facilities, not into translations that are seldom asked for.

CAPTURING THE SCENE ON FILM

Most everybody wants to take pictures while traveling and you may have just discovered that your antique Argus C-3 is no longer equal to the task. So you need a new camera. This raises a whole new set of questions. Do you prefer color prints, slides, or black-and-white photos, or all of the above? Will you take the pictures as personal mementos or for possible publication? Do your extracurricular activities include recording wildflowers with a close-up lens or shooting birds through the telephoto?

Fortunately, the best tools of the trade today—a Pentax, Canon, Mamiya, Nikon, Minolta, and other 35mm cameras—are both better and less expensive than they ever were. All of the latest models have been designed with the needs and

wishes of amateurs in mind and are much more automated and foolproof than earlier models. Almost every brand of 35mm SLR camera comes with an endless array of interchangeable lenses and 35mm film can be bought at stores around the world.

By comparison the quality of the prints from pocket instamatics, disc cameras, and other gimmicks, is less than satisfactory and films for these are not nearly as readily available overseas.

If at all possible, purchase your new camera well in advance of your trip. Read and reread the instruction booklet, check out the procedures one by one with the still unloaded camera in front of you until you are thoroughly familiar with each step, the possibilities and the exceptions. Finally, shoot a couple of rolls film outdoors and inside and under various conditions of light. Then if you are not satisfied with the result, you can still make the necessary corrections to your technique or to the camera before you take off on your vacation.

The next thing to do is to fill out and mail the guarantee. Then photocopy your part of the guarantee along with the sales slip and keep that with your passport to establish your ownership to the customs inspectors on the way home. Since nearly all cameras are manufactured overseas, customs officers have no way of knowing that you bought it here unless you can prove it to them. To avoid any misunderstanding you may even want to register all of your cameras, tape recorders, and the like with the U.S. Customs Service prior to your departure.

Buy fresh, advanced dated film and store in the vegetable bin of your refrigerator until you pack your suitcase. Then, to save space in packing, throw away the boxes (but not the cans) and put all films together in a bag. While traveling, number and identify each exposed film and mail all films to your photo-finishing lab when you get home. The main reason for this, besides convenience and a small savings, is that with today's terrorism and bomb scares, post offices may have to X-ray all incoming goods, which is guaranteed to ruin your film. Or else you may have to pay duty on your own film even though it originated here.

When it comes to buying film, I must admit to being biased in favor of Kodak. It is a bias based on thirty years of experience. When trying to capture the fine details of old prints and documents and artifacts in archives and museums around the world, or historic buildings in a city setting on various brands of film, the results I have had with Kodak have always been a mite sharper, the colors a bit cleaner, and the fine print a bit more legible. Other good films are Agfa-Gevaert and Fuji in color, Ilford in black and white. All other films are light years behind and are not worth considering. When people tell me that they save 39 cents a roll by buying the department store special, I am not impressed. Why spend hundreds of dollars on a once-in-a-lifetime trip to come home with pictures that look like they were taken through three layers of nylon hose? My advice is to stick with the yellow boxes.

FILM SENSITIVITY AND AIRPORT SECURITY

In spite of the sign on the X-ray machine that says, "Inspection will not harm ordinary film," the fact is that the devices *do indeed damage film*. Our own experience and the findings of the Professional Photographers Association have led to the conclusion that on an extensive trip an average of 17 out 100 films are affected. Articles in aviation magazines have admitted as much.

While it is true that a one-time pass through the machine does not harm the film very much, the effect is cumulative and repeated passes through the machines each time you change planes does affect undeveloped film. And now that Kodak has come out with an extremely supersensitive high speed film (ASA 1000), it has been found that the same film is also correspondingly more sensitive to the effects of airport scanning devices.

Expert travelers carry both their film, whether exposed or unexposed, and their loaded cameras in lead-lined filmshield bags. Each one of these filmshield bags (available in most camera stores) holds about thirty cans of 35mm film or eight reels of 8mm movie film. Filmshield is also available in sheets. The lead bags and sheets are fairly expensive but they are also reusable as long as you have need for them.

In the United States and in Canada, travelers have the right to request hand inspection of their film supplies and cameras. In other countries, including all of the Soviet Bloc nations, Switzerland, Spain, and Luxembourg, travelers do not have these rights. The same is true for some flights and connecting flights to the Middle East or any flights on which an unusual number of Arabs have booked passage. We appreciate that in these troubled times this security is necessary, but photographers must take the necessary precautions to protect their investments.

A WORD ABOUT SCISSORS

This may be the best place for a word about scissors. Some airport security people are touchy about scissors, which they consider dangerous weapons. I always have one or more good scissors along, but to avoid the hassle, I have learned to pack them in my check-in baggage, rather than in my carry-on luggage.

PLUGGING IN ON 220

In the United States and Canada, electricity comes in 110-volt AC. Almost everywhere else in the world, and that includes all of Europe, current is 220 volts. That does not mean that you can shave twice as fast over there. In fact, if you plug in your 110 equipment without the necessary adapters, you will see stars and stripes and other strange sights.

Some small appliances and camera accessories, such as those manufactured by Norelco and Vivitar, are world products designed to operate on either 110, 220, or 230 (Australia and New Zealand) by moving a little slide opposite the correct voltage. For most other equipment you will need a converter as well as a set of adapter plugs to couple the North American flat prongs to the European round-pronged sockets. Persons wearing contact lenses will need the proper converter and adapters to operate their sterilizers.

A traveler's set containing one or more type of converters with an assortment of adapter plugs in a vinyl case can be found at most radio and small appliance stores or ordered through discount and novelty catalogs. You will need a 50 W converter to charge/operate a flashunit or a razor; sterilizers for contact lenses require a 1,000 W converter. A 1,600 W unit is needed for travel irons and hair dryers. Operating larger equipment through converters is both unsafe and illegal.

THE METRIC SYSTEM

Once upon a time the people of this world measured their products and their properties in pints, rods, drams, ells, acres, fathoms, inches, quarts, pecks, gallons, bushels, grains, vats, wersts, yards, feet, and furlongs. The problem with these and more than 600 other units of measurements were that they were interpreted locally, which created great chaos in the marketplace. An *Eimer* (bucket), for instance, could measure anywhere from 29 to 307 liters, depending on local custom.

Seeing a need for some order in this chaos, around 1670 the church first called for a rational, uniform system of measures in length, mass, and capacity. Another century passed before a commission of French scientists proposed the metric system. It was discussed in the French National Assembly for four years and accepted as the only legal system in France in 1799. Other countries followed suit.

The change to the metric system has been slow but continuous. Japan became metric in 1868. In certain scientific industries where accuracy is of vital importance, such as the medical, pharmaceutical, optical, and photographic fields, the switch was made to metric even if the country where they were located did not make the switch. By the 1970s the use of the metric system had become nearly as good as universal. At present there are three countries that have not made the switch. One of them is mostly jungle, one of them is mostly desert, and the third country is the United States.

In the metric system the basic unit of length is the meter, the basic unit of mass is the gram, and the basic unit of capacity is the liter. The scale of multiples and divisions is ten. The names for the multiples were given Greek prefixes. Ten meters is one decameter (dam). Ten decameters is one hectometer (hm). Ten hectometers is one kilometer (km). The names for the divisions were given Latin prefixes. One tenth of a meter is one decimeter (dm). One tenth of a decimeter is called one centimeter (cm). One tenth of a centimeter is called one millimeter (mm). The same prefixes are also used with liters and grams.

Surface areas are measured by the square meter, which is the area of a square whose sides each measure one meter. The multiples go by the square of ten, which is one hundred. One square decameter is equal to 100 square meters, also known as an are. A hectare has a hundred are, or 10,000 square meters. Larger areas, such as countries, are usually measured by square kilometers.

Temperatures are also measured on the decimal system. Water boils at 100 degrees and freezes at 0.

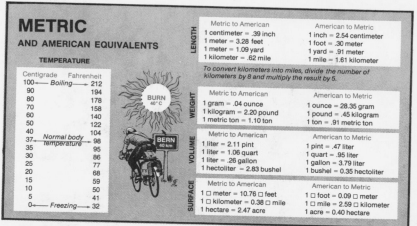

METRIC
AND AMERICAN EQUIVALENTS

TEMPERATURE

Centigrade	Fahrenheit
100 ← Boiling →	212
90	194
80	178
70	158
60	140
50	122
40	104
37 ← Normal body →	98
35	temperature 95
30	86
25	77
20	68
15	59
10	50
5	41
0 ← Freezing →	32

BURN
40° C

BERN
40 km

LENGTH

Metric to American	American to Metric
1 centimeter = .39 inch	1 inch = 2.54 centimeter
1 meter = 3.28 feet	1 foot = .30 meter
1 meter = 1.09 yard	1 yard = .91 meter
1 kilometer = .62 mile	1 mile = 1.61 kilometer

To convert kilometers into miles, divide the number of kilometers by 8 and multiply the result by 5.

WEIGHT

Metric to American	American to Metric
1 gram = .04 ounce	1 ounce = 28.35 gram
1 kilogram = 2.20 pound	1 pound = .45 kilogram
1 metric ton = 1.10 ton	1 ton = .91 metric ton

VOLUME

Metric to American	American to Metric
1 liter = 2.11 pint	1 pint = .47 liter
1 liter = 1.06 quart	1 quart = .95 liter
1 liter = .26 gallon	1 gallon = 3.79 liter
1 hectoliter = 2.83 bushel	1 bushel = 0.35 hectoliter

SURFACE

Metric to American	American to Metric
1 □ meter = 10.76 □ feet	1 □ foot = 0.09 □ meter
1 □ kilometer = 0.38 □ mile	1 □ mile = 2.59 □ kilometer
1 hectare = 2.47 acre	1 acre = 0.40 hectare

Throughout this *Tourguide* all measures are given in the metric system, followed by their American equivalents in parentheses.

HAVING A GOOD TIME, WISH YOU WERE HERE ...

Travel and writing postcards go together like wieners and sauerkraut. Dropping a card to your friends at home and fellow workers at the office is a nice way to let them know you are thinking of them.

Cards mailed from Europe to overseas destinations routinely travel by air at a fixed rate which varies slightly from country to country. In general it has been the least expensive to mail cards from Holland, while Switzerland and Liechtenstein charge the highest rates.

Sending airmail letters from Europe is a bit more complicated. Whereas in the States or in Canada one is charged a fixed rate for the first half ounce, and again a full rate for the next half ounce, in Europe the additional weight is charged by five gram increments rather than a full rate. But it does mean a trip to the post office to have your letter weighed for postage.

It takes about eight or ten days for a card or letter to travel between a small town in Europe and a small town in the Eastern states and provinces—less time between big cities, but longer to points west.

Remember that Dutch stamps are valid only within Holland, and that Germany requires the use of German postage, etc. If you have stamp collectors among your friends, consider buying colorful commemorative stamps available at the philatelic window of major post offices.

Jan Gleysteen/84

SWITZERLAND

CH

Confederatio Helvetica
(Schweiz / Suisse / Svizzera)

Switzerland is a small country covering an area of 41,300 square kilometers (15,941 square miles). At its widest point, it is only 343 kilometers wide (213 miles). Switzerland can easily be divided into three natural regions: the Alps in the south, the Jura Mountains in the northwest, and the Swiss Plateau in the north center.

The blue-green, forest-covered Jura Mountains, which form the boundary between Switzerland and France, extend from Geneva to Basel. The Jura Mountains consist of regular limestone folds, the crests of which form ridges, here and there creating steep-sided, trough-like valleys called *Cluses.* Occasionally a stream will cut across a crest and continue its journey through the next valley.

Stretching from the 4,807-meter-high (12,340 feet) Mont Dolent on the Mont Blanc range in the west to the 3,207-meter-high (10,330 feet) Piz Midon to the east, the Swiss Alps form part of a chain of mountains which begins at the Mediterranean Sea in southern France and extends all the way through eastern Austria. One of the peaks of the Monte Rosa, the Piz Dufour, 4,634 meters (15,220 feet), is the highest summit entirely within Switzerland.

The heart of the Swiss Alps is formed by the magnificent snow-clad peaks gathered around the Saint Gotthardt Massif—peaks which are in every way as spectacular as those of the Mont Blanc which Switzerland shares with France and Italy. Among the best known peaks are the Jungfrau, the Finsteraarhorn, the Matterhorn, and the Weisshorn. The Alps cover 60 percent of the country, but less than 20 percent of the Swiss people live there. Deep snows cover them from three to five months of each year and very little of the land lends itself to cultivation. Still the Alps are a major source of income because their beauty has made Switzerland the classic tourist land for centuries.

During the Middle Ages the great artists traveled the Alps on their way to Italy. Already during the 1700s Switzerland figured prominently on the itinerary of the Grand Tour which young men of good families undertook to complete their education. The stream of visitors continued long after Goethe, Byron, and Shelley extolled the beauty of the region and Brahms had dedicated one of his violin sonatas to the Lake of Thun.

Today Switzerland has more than 8,000 hotels and at least 300,000 persons are employed in the hotel trade. To the Swiss hotel manager and his staff, running a hotel and a restaurant is not just another job, it is a vocation. As a result, complaints about uncomfortable accommodations or poor service are rare. And so it is that people from all over the world come to study the hotel trade at one of the Swiss schools and to do their apprenticeship in Swiss hotels.

The Swiss Plateau is that basin between the Jura and the Alps filled with glacial material deposited during the Ice Ages, long since eroded by time and the many rivers. Its surfaces are rolling with wooded heights and broad cultivated valleys. The steady movement of now-extinct glaciers created many lakes, including Lake Geneva and the Bodensee (Lake of Constance). Though the plateau covers only a third of Switzerland, it is here that more than three fourths of the population live. On the plateau we find all of the larger cities and towns and nearly all of the industry which produces the wide range of specialized high-tech goods for which Switzerland is so well known. The watch industry, however, is concentrated in the Jura.

Switzerland is often referred to as "the water tower of Europe." The mighty Rhine begins its long descent to the North Sea in Switzerland. For 380 kilometers (235 miles) of its long journey it flows through Switzerland or along the Swiss border. Less than 20 kilometers (12 miles) from the sources of the Rhine the gushing waters of the Furka Glacier start the Rhône on its 265-kilometer (165 mile) journey through Switzerland before it reaches the French border, from where it turns south toward the Mediterranean. In the south, the Ticino rushes from the Saint Gotthardt to join the Po in Italy on its way to the Adriatic. In the east the Inn flows through the Engadin to Austria and onward to join the Danube in Germany, thereby linking Switzerland with faraway Russia and Romania at the Black Sea.

During the winter of 1853, one of the coldest ever recorded, far less snow than usual fell in the Swiss mountains. In the spring of 1854 the resulting lack of melting snow lowered the level of all Swiss lakes, exposing wide expanses of mud plains not seen by human eyes for millennia.

The Swiss made the best use of a bad situation by building dams and harbors, by strengthening the shorelines, and even reclaiming some land in the manner of the Dutch. While working in the muck, they discovered the remnants of prehistoric pole villages—fragments of pottery, tools, spears, pieces of bark clothing, leather shoes, bones, bits of basketry, shreds of

The falls of the Rhine at Schaffhausen

Wengen in the Bernese Highlands

netting, and primitive ancient tools. Along the eastern end of Lake Neuchâtel, an amateur archaeologist investigated what appeared to be an artificial mound. He and his crew found a mountain of lances, spears, and short swords, most of the latter still in their scabbards. The site of the discovery was called La Téne—the Shallows—and this name was given to the whole prehistoric culture which once existed from the valleys along the Danube in the east to the plains of Holland and Denmark, and the coasts of Britain and Ireland.

The pole village dwellers of Switzerland were succeeded by a Celtic tribe called the Helvetii, who in turn were joined by the Alemanni. Both groups were later conquered by Julius Caesar in 58 BC. Around AD 443 the Burgundians, who lived at the southern point of Lake Geneva, began to push north, eventually occupying what is now western Switzerland. They mingled with Romanized inhabitants, adopted their customs, and in due time developed a French dialect. At the same time, more Alemanni moved into northern and central Switzerland, replacing most of what remained of the Roman civilization. The people of this region developed several German dialects. Only a few of the Romanized natives withdrew into the remote villages of southeastern Switzerland. Their descendants, one percent of the total population, still speak "Romansch."

While the power of the Roman Empire was declining all over Europe, patrician families everywhere set out to increase their political and economic influence. Among them were the Habsburgs, who were minor landed proprietors in the Aargau, where the ruins of their first castles still stand on the Wulpsberg. From this humble position the Habsburgs consolidated their holdings into a dynasty which soon ruled most of Europe until 700 years later with the fall of Kaiser Wilhelm in 1918.

A clash between the earliest Habsburgs and their closest neighbors gave rise to modern-day Switzerland. In 1239 Rudolf IV, who exercised the Habsburg ability of territorial acquisition with great success, became head of the clan. In 1273, when the bishop of Basel discovered that the prince-electors (so-called Palatines) were about to choose Rudolf as king, he exclaimed, "God in heaven, sit tight on your throne or Rudolf will take your seat!" The same words might well have been spoken by the citizens of three cantons—Uri, Schwyz, and Unterwalden—who already had found it necessary, more than once, to protect themselves against Habsburg ambitions. Meeting in a lakeside meadow at Rütli, they formed the Ewige Bund (the everlasting alliance) and agreed to help each other remain free from foreign rule. The Swiss nation was born.

This alliance was significant for all of Europe because the three Forest Cantons, as these three cantons were called, controlled the Gotthardt Pass, the most important of all the trans-Alpine routes and in fact controlled the trade of central Europe. The ideals of freedom and democracy within the alliance were appealing to other cantons as well. One by one other cantons

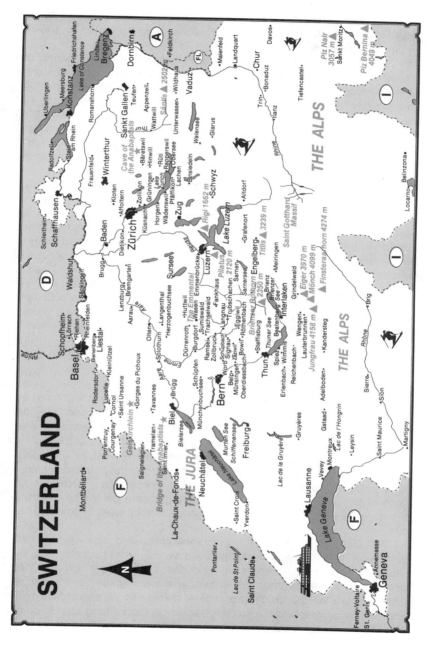

SWITZERLAND

N

THE JURA

THE ALPS

Lake Geneva

Lake Constance

Basel

Zürich

Bern

Geneva

Lausanne

Neuchâtel

Freiburg

Thun

Interlaken

Luzern

Sankt Gallen

Schaffhausen

Bregenz

Vaduz

Chur

Davos

Sankt Moritz

Piz Nair 3057 m

Piz Bernina 4049

Säntis 2502 m

Rigi 1662 m

Pilatus 2120 m

Titlis 3239 m

Eiger 3970 m

Mönch 4099 m

Finsteraarhorn 4274 m

Jungfrau 4158 m

Saint Gotthard Massif

Brünig Pass 2350 m

The Emmental

Cave of the Anabaptists

Bridge of the Anabaptists

Geistkirchlein

73

joined the league, beginning with Luzern, Zurich, Bern, Glarus, and Zug. By 1513 Fribourg, Soloturn, Basel, Schaffhausen, and Appenzell had joined and the Bund now numbered 13 members.

This process continued in spite of religious differences during the time of the Reformation and the interference of Napoleon many centuries later. The Confederatio Helvetica of 22 cantons came into being in 1848. This is essentially the Switzerland we know today, except that Basel, Appenzell, and Unterwalden are now subdivided into half-cantons and in 1978 the (French-speaking) Jura seceded from (German-speaking) Canton Bern to form the new Canton Jura. The process of changing names on public buildings and the lettering on license plates in this new canton is, at the time of this writing, still far from complete.

The Swiss federal policy of neutrality dates back to 1315. The policy was reaffirmed by the Treaty of Westphalia in 1648, and in 1815 the neutrality of Switzerland was guaranteed by the great powers attending the Congress of Vienna. This continued neutrality gives Switzerland a unique position in the world today. Although not a member of the United Nations, Switzerland hosts the European headquarters of that organization at Geneva and at any time will offer facilities for negotiations which might lead to world peace. A current example is the Geneva disarmament talks.

Geneva is the headquarters, also, for WHO (the World Health Organization), the United Nations High Commissioner for Refugees, the Universal Postal Union, and the International Telecommunications Union. Geneva is also home to the International Red Cross, founded there in 1863 by Henri Dunant. The Red Cross flag is the "negative" or reverse image of the Swiss flag.

The Swiss, whether Protestant or Catholic, rural or urban, Swiss-German-, French-, or Italian-speaking, feel that they are first and foremost citizens of one of the 3,095 autonomous communes. Second, they are citizens of the 28 cantons or half-cantons which, though varying in size, have equal rights and representation. Finally, Swiss—that is: citizens of the confederation. Since each canton is a sovereign member of the confederation, a canton cannot be compared with a county in the United States, a municipality in Canada, or a department in France. They resemble the states of the United States, but with one significant difference: their autonomy is greater and their sovereign rights are not limited by the constitution.

The Swiss government is a remarkable institution, one which is truly democratic and one which really does work. In this democracy the referendum is in constant use, and the citizens are called upon continuously to express their opinions on matters of greater and lesser importance, from the construction of a new reservoir to the appointment of a constable. In Switzerland it takes large-scale projects a long time to come into being. But usually they represent solid achievements. The instances of

Lake Luzern and the Urirotstock

"pork barrel projects" and political graft are all but eliminated since such would clearly be against the best interests of the individual communes.

It should not surprise us that Switzerland has had almost 100 years of national zoning laws, and that such laws are quite strict and protective to both the amount and the quality of the environment. Wasteful uses of land, such as the American-style shopping center, are practically unknown and where such shopping centers do exist you'll find them in the industrial zone, built on ground not suitable for farming.

The same quality can be reported for transportation and communication. These services are coordinated by a 62-member commission of professionals which insures that all forms of transportation are complementary and not competitive. The commission also makes sure that the schedules of trains, ships, planes, and the postal services mesh and that all Swiss citizens have access to adequate transportation without consuming more precious energy than necessary—without undue damage to the environment.

With such considerations, the transportation of school-children is provided by the regular trains, trams, and buses, because a nation without natural resources can ill afford a fleet of school buses used only two hours per day.

Switzerland's high standard of living, which so impresses the visitors, should not obscure an important fact. Switzerland, a nation with no mineral resources whatsoever, maintains its position as an exporting country with a trade surplus only by delivering products of consistently high quality. By design, the Swiss import raw and semi-finished materials and turn these into specialty products of high quality destined primarily for the export market. To maintain a high level of employment, the process tends to be labor intensive. Constant research keeps the products up-to-date. The Swiss are leaders in the pharmaceutical, chemical, electrical, and metal-fabricating trades.

Because excessive weight has always been a factor in moving goods up and down a mountain, the Swiss have been way ahead in using aluminum in the construction of trucks, buses, and trains. The technique of welding aluminum was invented in Switzerland. The world's first all-welded aluminum bulk milk tank stands displayed along the highway near Beromünster. The mark "Schweizer Qualitätswahre," (a Swiss quality product), whether seen on cutlery, cheese, watches, chocolate, locomotives, or printed textiles, carries a reputation that the Swiss now intend to live up to. Shoddy merchandise is not seen in the stores.

Most Swiss literature is written in German. Outstanding Swiss works include two children's classics: *Heidi* by Johanna Spyri, and *The Swiss Family Robinson* by the Wyss family. Other prominent Swiss writers include Gotfried Keller and Jeremias Gotthelf.

The great artist Hans Holbein spent many of his years in Basel, the city which was also the home of Erasmus. The Dada art movement originated in Zurich in 1916. Among the best-known Swiss artists are the painter Paul Klee, the graphic artist Hans Erni, and the sculptor Alberto Giacometti. La-Chaux-de-Fonds in the Jura is the birthplace of Le Corbusier, one of the greatest architects of our time.

The Swiss are also proud of their outstanding educator Heinrich Pestalozzi and the Picard brothers, who explored both the stratosphere and the ocean depths in the 1930s.

Richard Wagner lived and worked for some years in a villa outside Luzern, and the composer Arther Honegger, though considered of the French school, was a Zuricher by birth. The major Swiss cities support outstanding symphony orchestras. Almost every town and village has a choir which performs weekly for the local festivals and which may compete in cantonal or national songfests in their colorful regional costumes.

SWITZERLAND, CRADLE OF THE ANABAPTIST VISION

Switzerland is the country where the Anabaptist-Mennonite movement was born within the first decade of the Reformation. It is the original homeland of the immigrant and refugee Anabaptists in the Palatinate (later in Pennsylvania and points west), the Alsace (later in Ohio, New York, Illinois and Ontario), and Polish Galicia (later in Kansas and Nebraska). To understand the Mennonite story, a knowledge of what happened in and around Zurich during the first half of the sixteenth century is essential.

On the one hand, one is inclined to agree with the statement that "Anabaptism was in the air" in various places in northern Switzerland and South Germany during the 1520s. On the other hand, it is now generally accepted that the fellowship in and around Zurich/Zollikon was the first to organize itself as a brotherhood alongside the established Volkskirche, the people's church.

Prominent leaders in this fellowship included the young patrician student Conrad Grebel and his friend Felix Manz, both from Zurich proper, and an ex-priest from Canton Graubünden called Georg Blaurock. Other key figures were the bookseller Andreas Castelberger, also from Graubünden; Wilhelm Reublin, born in the Black Forest, but more recently from Wytikon; and a visitor from the Black Forest named Michael [Sattler]. Several of these men were close followers and supporters of the Zurich Reformer Ulrich Zwingli. But once Zwingli placed his religious reform under the advice and control of the local government—and thereby once again established a state church—the Brethren broke with him.

Though a law was quickly passed to make further meetings and dissent illegal, the Zurich Brethren continued to meet. On the evening of Saturday, January 21, 1525, they confirmed their experience of salvation by baptizing one another as adult believers, though three days earlier the government had reinstated obligatory infant baptism. With great missionary zeal the members of the new movement went out to share their views of a committed discipleship-Christianity with others. In a short time vital fellowships had sprung up not only in Zurich and the surrounding highlands, but also in Sankt Gallen, in Bern, around Schaffhausen, in Appenzell—and beyond the Swiss Confederation, in Austria and in South Germany. A pioneer congregation flourished briefly in Zollikon, just south of Zurich, meeting in farm homes between January and the summer of 1525, but continuous government harassment brought about its early demise.

In the spring of 1525, Bolt Eberli, a farmer-fisherman from Lachen in the Canton Schwyz, was burned at the stake for his beliefs. Eberli is also known as the first Protestant martyr in Switzerland, since the [Catholic] authorities of Schwyz made no distinction between Anabaptist or Protestant heresy. Felix Manz, one of the original Swiss Brethren, was drowned in the

Lachen on the Obersee, home of Bolt Eberli

Limmat River on orders of the authorities in Zurich in January 1527, the first of thousands to die at the hands of the Protestants in Switzerland and throughout Western Europe. Nevertheless, the Anabaptist movement, as one exasperated critic put it, "spread like wildfire."

Over the years there were frequent public hearings both within the cantons and between the cantons regarding the "Anabaptist problem," invariably leading to renewed persecution. These policies enacted by "Christian" governments did not succeed in wiping out the movement as a whole, but by the early 1700s Anabaptism had disappeared from the canton where it had all started.

The earliest and most tolerant place of refuge for the Swiss Anabaptists was Moravia, now part of Czechoslovakia. The first of the Brethren may have arrived there as early as 1526, coming with Balthasar

Hubmaier. From Moravia brave missioners undertook their dangerous return trips to Switzerland to "gather the lambs of the Lord."

A second major place of refuge was the Palatinate, especially throughout the 17th and 18th centuries. In 1671 alone more than seven hundred dreadfully poor and bone-weary Anabaptists, mostly from Canton Bern, arrived there. The mass deportation orders of 1711-1712, Bern's "Final Solution to the Anabaptist Problem," were yet to be issued. At that time a number of Swiss families settled among their Mennonite brothers and sisters in Holland. A glance over the complex chart of Mennonite migrations around the world will show that many Mennonites, particularly those in the States and Canada, have direct family ties to Switzerland.

Though this massive migration of Swiss Mennonites has contributed to the growth of the Mennonite church elsewhere, a remnant of about 2,600 Swiss Mennonites still to exists in Switzerland. The oldest continuous Mennonite congregation, founded around 1530, is located at Langnau in the Emmental. Their first meetinghouse, built in 1888, was recently enlarged. Most of the other Swiss Mennonite churches are in the Jura Mountains. There are two congregations in Basel, one of which relates to the French Mennonite Conference. Near Liestal we find the European Mennonite Bible School, established in Basel in 1951, and moved to its present location on the Bienenberg in 1957.

A Quadrilingual Nation

Switzerland has four official languages: German, French, Italian, and Rhaetisch. You will find all four of them on official documents such as bank notes and at least three of them on public transit and in the telephone booths (plus English for the tourists). More than two thirds of the Swiss people speak German, written as High German in business transactions, but *Schwyzerdütsch* (Swiss-German) is spoken among themselves.

Another 20 percent of the Swiss speak French. Italian is spoken in Canton Ticino (Tessin) and in parts of Canton Graubünden. Raeto-Romansch, or Rhaetisch, is a living remnant of the old Latin and is still spoken in the highlands around Engadin.

The use of multiple languages with equal validity may be confusing to the tourist at first, especially when following road signs. Depending on your route into the city, signs to Geneva read Genf, Genève, or Ginevra. You approach Delemont from the south or Delsberg from the north, but it is the same city. You may also encounter Basel or Bâle, Bern or Berne, Biel or Bienne, Neuenburg or Neuchâtel—alternate names for the cities involved.

But all roads are well marked with numbered road signs (1) in blue for the main routes, (2) in green for the limited-access highways—which in this rugged mountainous territory are not necessarily four lanes wide!—and (3) in white for local roads. All Swiss roads are maintained in excellent condition and beautifully marked, striped, and landscaped. And after traveling these roads for a week, it may suddenly dawn upon you that you have seen neither billboards nor trash and very few power lines to mar the charm of the countryside.

The Climate

The Swiss Alps form a definite dividing line between the moderate climate of northwestern Europe and the subtropical climate of the Mediterranean. On the north side of the Alps there may be considerable rainfall and the summers will be comfortable. An exception to the rule is the city of Geneva, which lies unprotected at the southern end of a long lake. Geneva's temperatures may be high and the local wind, called the Bise, tends to be forceful.

The weather along the Swiss mountain lakes during the summer months is steady and predictable. In general it can be said that it is cloudy in June, that July records the highest temperatures (along with a great number of spectacular thundershowers), and that the skies are bluest in August. The temperature in the mountain lakes ranges between 20 and 25 degrees centigrade (68 to 76 degrees Fahrenheit). A word should be said here about the local wind phenomena such as the Bise and the Föhn. During the summer months the daily rhythm of warming up and cooling off, combined with the depth and the angle of specific valleys creates a wind system as predictable as the ebb and flow of oceans. Many of these winds have names. Toward noon the warm air rises from the fields and forests below carrying the moisture with it. Around the snowy peaks this moisture turns into clouds. The people in Luzern may look up at Mount Pilatus and say, "Pilatus has put his hat on." Around five o'clock the process reverses itself and a cold wind suddenly comes rushing down from the peaks.

While local breezes are predictable the Föhn—which occurs exclusively on the north slope of the Alps—is different. The Föhn is caused by the passage of a deep barometric depression along the north slope of the Alps. Rid of its moisture on the Italian side of the mountains, where there are constant storms and rain, the air drawn in by this depression spills over the crest. It rises in temperature, because of compression, as it loses altitude—one degree centigrade per hundred meters or ten degrees Fahrenheit per hundred feet. It is transformed into a dry and burning wind and the atmosphere becomes strangely clear. When these conditions occur, everyone is on the alert in the mountains. Flash floods are common, avalanches begin to rumble, and the risk of forest fire is great. The citizens live in such a state of nervousness that examinations are suspended in the schools. The Föhn can even be introduced as extenuating circumstance in the defense of criminals.

But the Föhn also has beneficial effects. It melts the snow and enables the cattle to be sent up to the Alpine pastures earlier. Thanks to the Föhn, some valleys, which are suitably situated, can actually grow maize and fruit trees far above the normal elevations.

The Best Times to See Switzerland

Both spring and autumn are favorite times to travel along the mountain lakes. The first signs of spring in Switzerland are seen along the lakes of Canton Ticino. But soon the warm winds of the Fohn bring new life to the shores of Lake Luzern and Lake Thun as well.

Early summer is the best time for the lover of Alpine flora, whether professional botanist or amateur. Most bookstores and the kiosks at the railroad stations feature flower identification guides in many versions and languages. June is also the safest time for glacier excursions because the dangerous crevasses have not yet had time to develop.

In the fall a drive above the vineyards of the southwestern cantons will provide you with the calendar pictures of medieval cities and vistas of luscious grapes set against the background of mirror-like lakes and majestic mountains.

Switzerland has 40,000 kilometers (25,000 miles) of clearly marked mountain trails from which nature lovers can enjoy spectacular vistas. Winter is the time for skiing and sledding and tobogganing throughout Switzerland. However, Canton Graubünden and the Bernese highlands offer the most possibilities.

Holidays and Store Hours

The first of August is a national holiday in Switzerland and the only nationwide legal holiday apart from New Year's Day and Christmas. However, Good Friday is considered a legal holiday in predominantly Protestant cantons. In the predominantly Catholic cantons Three Kings' Day (January 6), St. Joseph's Day (sometime in March), the Festival of God, Ascension Day, St. Peter and St. Paul's Day (in June), Maria Ascension Day (in August), All Soul's Day (November 1), and Maria Immaculate Conception Day and St. Etienne's Day (both in December) are considered legal holidays.

In Switzerland most stores are closed on Monday and/or on a day of their choice. Because the people love fresh baked goods, bakeries open early in the morning, even on Sunday. Post offices close at 11:00 on Saturday morning. Banks are closed on both Saturday and Sunday. However, it helps to know that money can usually be changed at the exchange offices of the major railroad stations.

Special Rules of the Road

In the mountains, uphill traffic has the right-of-way over vehicles coming down, which may be asked to stop or even to back up. Postal buses have the right of way over all other traffic and may choose either side of the road to assure the safe passage of mail and passengers. When passing such buses, follow the instructions of the postal driver.

On narrow country roads, even on the plains, heavier commercial traffic has priority over private cars. Public transportation has the absolute right of way over all over road users (note the THANK YOU sign on the back of the buses).

Speeders lose licenses on the spot, and tourists are not exempt. Sleeping in cars along the highway is tolerated but not encouraged. It is, however, expressly forbidden in Canton Ticino. Children under twelve are not allowed to ride in the front seat.

The Monetary System

The unit of the Swiss national currency is the Frank, or Franc (SFr). The Frank is divided into 100 cents, commonly called Rappen. The money comes in coins of 5, 10 and 20 Rappen, ½, 1, 2, and 5 Franks, all of which are silver metal. The little 5 Rappen and the ½ Frank pieces are easily confused since they are nearly identical in size. Bank notes are issued in values of 10, 20, 50, 100 Franks and higher. All Swiss notes have a fine metallic wire embedded in the paper, as well as a watermark.

The Swiss Frank, along with the German Mark, the Dutch Gulden, and the Japanese Yen, is considered one of the most stable hard currencies on the world money market.

A WALKING TOUR OF ZURICH

Zurich is located along the banks of the Limmat, which flows out of Lake Zurich. Still within the city limits, a second river, the Sihl, joins the Limmat on its way to join the Aare and ultimately the Rhine. The site has been inhabited since the fourth century before Christ. In AD 58 the Romans built a fortress on the heights of the present Lindenhof. According to legend, three early Christians—Felix, Regula, and Exuperanta—were decapitated on the shores of the Limmat on orders of Zurich's Roman governor, Decius.

Note: To serious students of Mennonite history, I strongly recommend the reading of Brothers in Christ *by Fritz Blanke and of* Conrad Grebel, Son of Zurich *by John L. Ruth, before taking the following walking tour. Both are Herald Press publications.*

The best place from which to start a walking tour of Zurich for any reason in any direction is from the centrally located railroad station, one of the busiest in the world. We will do like the Zurichers do and take our first 500 steps toward downtown through the huge underground Shoppingville. We head for the Bahnhofbrücke exit. Before we take the stairs into the daylight, we will stop to watch some people do their shopping from an unmanned, fully automated grocery store.

At the Bahnhof Bridge we stay on our side (west side) of the Limmat. We follow the river to the first bridge, the Rudolf Brun Bridge, and cross the street here. Pedestrians only continue along the Limmat on this side, first via a suspended walkway over the river, then via narrow cobblestone alleys and quays, collectively called Schipfge.

When we are approximately halfway between the Rudolf Brun Bridge and the upcoming Rathaus Bridge, still ahead, we make a sharp right turn and start climbing the narrow street up to the Lindenhof. The old Roman fortress which once stood here is gone, as is the imperial castle that succeeded it. The castle was razed in the 1200s by Zurich citizens who wanted to prove their independence from any distant powers.

The quiet tree-shaded plaza is physically and historically the highest point in Zurich and affords a good panorama of the old town. Throughout the centuries ceremonial meetings and honors banquets, and great festivals have been held on the Lindenhof. Past the fountain which commemorates the role of Zurich's women in the march against the authorities, we descend back down to river level.

The next bridge is the Rathausbrücke (town hall bridge), also known as the Fish Market Bridge. We will skip it for the moment and continue along the river to a point where a boat landing with two lanterns juts into the river's swift, clear waters. From here we have a good view of the massive gray-stone Rathaus. This late Renaissance town hall, built from 1694 to 1698, replaced an earlier partly wooden town hall on the same site.

The 1523 debates between Zwingli and the radical Anabaptists took

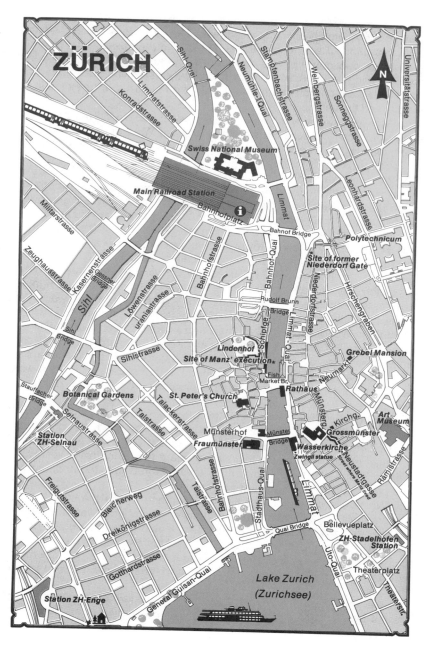

ZÜRICH

Swiss National Museum

Main Railroad Station
Bahnhofplatz

Limmat

Bahnof Bridge

Polytechnicum

Site of former
Niederdorf Gate

Rudolf Brunn
Bridge

Lindenhof
Site of Manz' execution

Grebel Mansion

Neumarkt

Fish
Market Br.

Rathaus

Botanical Gardens

St. Peter's Church

Kirchg.

Art
Museum

Station
ZH-Selnau

Münsterhof
Fraumünster

Münster
Bridge

Grossmünster

Wasserkirche
Zwingli statue

Bellevueplatz

Quai Bridge

ZH-Stadelhofen
Station

Theaterplatz

Station ZH-Enge

General Guisan-Quai

Lake Zurich
(Zurichsee)

place in the earlier town hall. And the ordinance of January 18, 1525, against the Anabaptists was passed here. This ordinance ordered a complete cessation of activity by Grebel, Manz, and their associates, forbade any further public and private discussions on the issues of baptism, communion, and the nature of the church and gave the Anabaptists eight days to join the state church and have their children baptized or be exiled from the city and the canton.

But by the next day the Anabaptists' answer was clear. They could not comply, for their consciences were bound by the Word of God as much (or more) than by the laws of the city—and three days later the first Anabaptist adult baptisms took place.

We continue along the river past the guild house, Zur Meise, one of the most beautiful examples of Rococo architecture in Zurich, until we reach the Münsterhof and the Frauenkirche. The church was a gift to the city by Ludwig the Good in AD 853 in honor of his daughter Hildegard. The church's present appearance dates from the 1200s to the 1400s and ranges from Romanesque to early Gothic architecture. The choir area inside features stained-glass windows by Marc Chagall, installed in 1970.

From the Fraumünster we have a good view of the Grossmünster across the river. But after crossing the Münster Bridge, we first turn right to the Wasserkirche (the water church), where on the south side we find a statue of Ulrich Zwingli, the Swiss reformer. Ulrich (or Huldreych) Zwingli was born in Wildhaus in 1484. After serving as priest for ten years in Glarus, he lived from 1516 to 1590 in the large and magnificent abbey of Einsiedln. While there he became well aware of the scandalous way of life among the monks and saw the need for drastic church reforms. Early in 1519 he was called to Zurich to become the first preacher at the city's "People's Church," the Grossmünster.

Zwingli's statue stands near the place where his ship supposedly landed. That Zwingli is portrayed holding a Bible and a sword is no coincidence. Zwingli perceived the church and state as two parts of a whole—the Christian nation. It had been that way for more than a thousand years and Zwingli wasn't about to change that. It was the radicals, the Anabaptists, who pioneered the separation of church and state.

We now cross the street (Limmatquai) and go up the steps to the Grossmünsterplatz beside the Grossmünster. The church was supposedly founded in the early 800s by Emperor Charlemagne over the grave site of the three martyrs, Felix, Regula, and Exuperantus. High up on the closest of the two spires we see the late-Gothic statue of Charlemagne. It is a more recent copy of the weatherbeaten original, which now can be seen in the crypt below.

We should stop a moment to study the enormous bronze doors created by the sculptor Otto Münch in 1939. The massive doors depict, on four corner panels the coats of arms of the city of Zurich and the church

The coat of arms of the canton of Zurich	Heinrich Bullinger and Leo Jud before the Zurich city council plead for continuation of the Reformation.	Heinrich Bullinger welcomes the Protestant refugees from Locarno (canton of Ticino) May 12, 1555.	The seal of the Zurich church council (Grossmünster)
The execution of the Protestant pastor Jakob Kaiser in Catholic canton of Schwyz May 29, 1529	Johannes Comander at Chur / Berthold Haller at Bern / Ambrosius Blaurer at Constance	Huldreich Zwingli at Zurich / Joachim Vadian at Sankt Gallen / Johannes Oekolampad at Basel	Zwingli's death on the battlefield at Kappel, October 11, 1531

LEADERS OF THE SWISS REFORMATION

The "Mushafen" (soup kitchen) for Zurich's poor, the first social work of the Reformation	Zwingli and Mayor Roist on their way to the Bern Disputation ★ of 1528, accompanied by 200 Reformed soldiers	Milk soup served at Kappel is shared by Reformed and Catholic soldiers during a cease-fire, June 1529	The discussion on the Lord's Supper at Marburg (Hesse) in October 1529: Melanchton, Luther, Prince Phillip of Hesse, Zwingli, and Oekolampad
Zwingli's secret messenger, Thomas Platter, carries out a manuscript in a poultry cage	Zwingli and his family: "Nothing is more precious than love."	Jud, Bibliander, and Zwingli work on the translation of the Scriptures in Swiss-German	Count Ulrich von Hutten on the island of Ufenau, where Zwingli provided him asylum
Zwingli preaches in the Grossmünster shortly after New Year's Day, 1519	The sacking of Ittingen cloister near Frauenfeld by the peasants in 1524	Hans Wirth, lieutenant-governor of Stammheim, beheaded on September 28, 1524, for being a Protestant	The abolition of the mass, and the celebration of the first communion in the Grossmünster, Easter 1525 ★★
Zurich's patron saints: the martyrs Felix, Regula, and Exuperantus	Fourteen-year-old Zwingli makes music in the Dominican monastery at Bern.	Zwingli, as army chaplain, addresses Swiss mercenaries just before the battle of Marignano (Italy) in 1515.	Emperor Charlemagne, founder of the Grossmünster; seal of the congregational superintendent

THE ZWINGLI DOORS

Jan Gleysteen /84

★ The Anabaptists were not welcome at this public meeting (see page 98 for details).

★ ★ The Anabaptists had started the practice three months earlier, in January 1525.

council of Canton Zurich, the three martyrs, and Charlemagne. The remaining twenty panels illustrate the life of Zwingli and moments from the Swiss Reformation.

Continuing around the church, we first go up the Kirchgasse for a short distance. Here a commemorative tablet above the door reads "Zwingli's parsonage. From this house on October 11, 1531, Zwingli left with his army of Zurichers, headed for Kappel, where he died for his faith." Mennonites will find it hard to agree with this statement. How can a follower of Christ press a particular (Protestant) viewpoint upon the citizens of a neighboring (Catholic) canton by means of violence?

We go back down the hill and turn left into the Neustadtgasse. In the Middle Ages, more than 65 percent of the priests and monks, celibacy notwithstanding, did have children. So it was with the canon of the Grossmunster named Manz, who fathered several children, among them Felix, who lived here with his mother on the Neustadtgasse [exact place not known]. Since priests did recognize and assume responsibility for their children, Felix enjoyed all the advantages of his father's high position, including the chances at a quality education.

It was on January 21, 1525, in the home of Felix Manz, three days after the city's ordinances against the Anabaptists were passed that, disregarding the new ordinance, fourteen of the Anabaptist brethren met. Conrad Grebel baptized Georg Blaurock, who in turn baptized all the others. This marks the founding moment of the Anabaptist-Mennonite Church as well as the origin of the first free church in the world—a church which calls for a personal commitment, a Christianity separated from state and citizenship.

We return to the upper side of the Grossmünster, to the Zwingliplatz. We enter the church through another set of massive bronze doors decorated with biblical scenes. In this same church, the Zurichers (among them Grebel and Manz) came to listen to Zwingli's expository sermons in the German language. If the church seems to have a bare look after the cathedrals we have already seen, there is a reason. A group of Zwingli's early followers, including many of the later Anabaptists, removed the statues, altars, tapestries, and paintings from the church in 1523. The only color comes from the stained-glass windows by Alberto Giacometti. Underneath the choir we find the largest hall crypt in Switzerland with graves dating back to the 1200s, as well as the original statue of Charlemagne.

Outside the Grossmünster on the Zwingliplaz we find the more than life-size bas-relief sculpture of Heinrich Bullinger, Zwingli's successor at the Grossmünster. Praised as a fearless leader of the Swiss Reformation and shaper of the Second Helvetian Confession, Bullinger was also one of the most outspoken opponents of the Anabaptists. Even though he had known Grebel, Manz, and the others in person, he did not hesitate to use outright lies (such as the charge of polygamy) to set the people against the Brethren.

We now follow the narrow Münstergasse, which changes its name to Niederdorfstrasse, until we reach the Rindermarkt on the right. We follow this street until it opens up on the triangular Neumarkt. On the left we see the house Zur Eintracht (To Unity), the ancestral home of the Grebel family. Other leading citizens also lived on this square, including several generations of Zurich mayors named Roist. On the Grebel mansion, we find a plaque which reads: "In this house lived, between 1508 and 1514 and 1520 to 1525, Conrad Grebel who, together with Felix Manz, founded the Anabaptist movement." In later years a radical of a different stripe lived here. Nikolai Lenin left this place on the Neumarkt for St. Petersburg to lead the Bolshevik Revolution.

Returning to the river, we note in passing the Froschaugasse, filled with antique stores, restoration workshops, and a few little cafes. Its name reminds us of the pioneer printers Christopher Froschauers (an uncle and a nephew with the same name) who produced the popular Froschauer Bible in 1524, reprinted at least twenty times within the century.

We end our historical walk on a little platform along the Limmat. To our immediate left are the Rathaus and the Fish Market Bridge. Across from us lies the Schipfge and above it we notice the Lindenhof. Let us turn our sights on the Rathaus. In December 1526 the Zurich Council instituted the death penalty for teaching and preaching Anabaptism within the city and the canton of Zurich. A few weeks later, young Felix Manz became the first victim of the new law. On January 5, 1527, the day of execution, the verdicts against Manz and Georg Blaurock were publicly read on the Fish Market Bridge. The executioner led Manz from the Wellenbergturm, which once stood in the middle of the river at the site of the present Quaibrucke, to the place of execution. Manz was accompanied by two pastors of the Grossmünster. One of them was Heinrich Bullinger, who urged Manz to recant in order to save his life. Manz paid little attention to him. Felix's mother and his brothers and sisters were there also and encouraged him to keep the faith. Manz then thanked God for the opportunity to give his life for the truth.

The executioner ran a stick under Felix's knees and over his elbows and tied him up that way, then rowed him out from the Schipfge. It was three o'clock in the afternoon when Manz was held under water until his life had gone. His lifeless body was later buried outside the cemetery walls of the Saint Jacob's Church. This church, but not the cemetery, still exists on the Stauffacherstrasse.

The sad thing is that Manz and thousands after him were not killed on orders of a godless government or heathen invaders, but by Protestant and Catholic Christians to whom the all-inclusive union of church and state— more or less Christian—was to be preferred over the idea of committed Christians "separated unto God."

Still that same afternoon, Georg Blaurock, not a Zurich citizen but an

The Grossmünster dominates Zurich's skyline

outsider, his clothing stripped to the waist, was chased through the Markt-gasse, the Münstergasse, and the Niederdorfstrasse, by a mob of people armed with rods and switches and rocks. At the Niederdorf Gate (no longer in existence but once near the present Banhof Bridge) he was forced to swear an oath never to return. At first he refused to do so, but finally he took the requested vow. Then he symbolically shook the dust off his shoes over the city. Blaurock began a missionary journey which eventually carried him into northern Italy, where he was captured and executed two years later.

While we are still standing at the Limmat, meditating about the events of four and a half centuries ago, we may also notice the St. Peter's Church across the river. Its tower, which once doubled as a defense tower (church and state together), has the largest clock face in Europe, 8.67 meters (28.45 ft.) in diameter). The minute hand alone is four meters (13 feet) long. For every minute its tip moves forward 45 cm. (18 in.).

Please note: About one fourth of the above itinerary coincides with Zurich's red light district, particularly the part between the Grossmünster and the Grebel Mansion. If you start your tour too late in the day, or return to see the buildings illuminated at night, you may find yourself studying anatomy as well as Mennonite history.

The Schipfge, site of Manz' execution by drowning

The imposing buildings of the Landesmuseum—the Swiss National Museum—are located right next to the main railroad station at the confluence of the Limmat and the Sihl. The extensive collections of artifacts within the museum document the history of the Swiss from prehistoric times to our day. Entire 17th-century rooms and halls from castles, cloisters, and patrician homes have been transplanted to this site, complete with tapestries and furnishings. Zwingli's sword and helmet are also on display here.

For a great view of the entire city and most of the lake and the Alps to the south, a trip to the top of the Uetliberg is a must. Trains climbing the Uetliberg leave the Zurich-Selnau station about every half hour. After the 50-minute train ride, it still takes us another 15 minutes to climb the wooded trail to the very top, which provides a fabulous panorama day or night. Zurich offers several boat trips ranging from short excursions on the Limmat and through the downtown area to half-day steamer trips across Lake Zurich to Rapperswil and back.

Between the railroad station and the lake, we find the Bahnhofstrasse, considered the most elegant and expensive shopping street in the world. It is also the home address of many of the famous Swiss banks.

ZOLLIKON, SITE OF THE FIRST ANABAPTIST CONGREGATION

From Zurich it is not far to Zollikon, the first village along the Zurichsee on the road to Rapperswil. The town is served by the Zurich-Meilen-Rapperswil commuter trains and a suburban bus line. On the drive into Zollikon, we follow the Dufourstrasse to the top of the hill. Not more than fifteen feet before we reach a major junction of roads and streets, a small street turns sharp right and steeply downhill. This is the Gstadtstrasse. On Wednesday, January 25, 1525, an important meeting took place on this street in the farmhouse of Rüdi Thomann, presently Gstadtstrasse 23-25.

On that evening several Zurich Anabaptists, sympathizers, and others met here to bid their farewell to Johannis Brötli, soon to be exiled from the city and canton of Zurich. The evening meal turned into an evangelistic meeting and baptism service. A plaque above the door reads: "The concept of the believers' church was first realized in Zollikon by the Anabaptists. In this house on January 25, 1525, one of their earliest meetings was held." Other meetings were held in Zollikon throughout the week and by Friday more than 30 persons had already joined this first Anabaptist congregation in open defiance of Zurich's ordinance of January 18.

Georg Blaurock, a courageous but impulsive man, obviously felt that the entire village could soon be won to the believers' church cause if one made the right moves. But his next move did not prove to be that.

On Sunday morning, January 29, Georg Blaurock arrived at the village church of Zollikon before the village pastor, Niklaus Billeter, was there. When Billeter entered the church, Blaurock asked him, "What are you going to do?" Billeter answered, "I will preach the Word of God." Blaurock countered, "Not you were sent to preach, but I." Billeter reminded Blaurock that he had received his orders from the church and state authorities in Zurich which for ages had appointed the pastors of the parish churches.

Blaurock, however, felt called of God to proclaim the possibility of a believers' church [based on personal commitment] to the villagers in the people's church [based on law and custom]. In this he did not succeed. The local bailiff named Wuest, who was in church that morning, threatened to arrest Blaurock if he did not immediately keep quiet.

Zurich's government now acted quickly. On the next day, Monday, January 30, fifteen members of Zollikon's new Anabaptist congregation found themselves in jail. But three weeks later bailiff Wuest's wife joined the movement.

In spite of the persecution, the Zollikers continued to meet in the homes of Jakob Hottinger, Heini Hottinger, Felix Kienast, and others for more than two years. Jakob Hottinger's statement to the authorities is characteristic of the position of the Zollikon Anabaptists: "The state has no

The Rüdi Thomann house in Zollikon

power over God's Word. God's Word is free." He appealed to the Zurich council not to force attendance at the state churches, but to permit the practice of Christian faith outside the official church. Hottinger called for freedom of worship and the freedom to establish believers' churches. This request was ahead of its time, for it failed in Zollikon.

INTO THE ZURICH HIGHLANDS

Zollikon is situated on a slope between the lake and the Zollikerberg, which in turn is part of the Forchberg. We continue our journey uphill toward Forch, Egg, and Rüti. Just out of Zollikon we reach the village of Zumikon, home of several farmers who joined the Zollikon Anabaptists.

Before Rüti, there are signs for a turnoff to Grüningen. At one time the Grebel family ruled this town and territory and young Conrad Grebel may well have played in the castle yards while his father was Landvogt (governor) here. It was in the Grüningen territory that, after Zollikon, the Anabaptist movement found its strongest expression.

From 1525 to 1528, the Anabaptist movement developed into a real popular movement, against which the magistrates in Zurich seemed powerless. In July 1525 Conrad Grebel returned to his home territory, preaching to the people at Hinwil and Bäretswil. He told his hearers that he had appealed to imperial justice, to divine justice, and to civil justice but had received no justice. He warned them that Zwingli had said that peasants who responded favorably to Anabaptism would be taken to the city and killed.

The Anabaptist movement grew rapidly throughout the fall of 1525. Magistrate Berger reported having a tough time arresting the Anabaptists, for most of the people sided with them. At one time Berger and his assistants, hopelessly outnumbered, watched as a crowd followed the outlaws Blaurock, Manz, and Grebel, and assembled in a field to hear them preach. But eventually arrests were made and Anabaptists did spend their time in the dungeons of the Grebel Castle. And on December 1, 1528, two Anabaptist leaders from Grüningen were drowned in the Limmat, followed by more in March of 1532.

Still the movement managed to stay alive for over one hundred years. On August 29, 1616, three Grüningen Anabaptists were sold as galley slaves. Finally in 1641, the last Anabaptists fled the territory for the Palatinate and Holland.

Our landmark, the Grebel castle, was badly damaged in a fire in 1969, but has been faithfully restored to its 16th-century appearance, even to the wooden dungeons high upon the castle's inner wall.

The castle and town of Grüningen

From Grüningen we continue our pilgrimage to the Cave of the Anabaptists. Going in the direction of Hinwil, we pass the Betzholz, where Manz, Grebel, and Blaurock held their illegal meeting in the presence of Magistrate Berger. Hinwil was long the scene of action for Blaurock, Grebel, and Marx Boshardt, the young son-in-law of Rudi Thomann of Zollikon.

From Hinwil we continue to Bäretswil via Ringwil. In Bäretswil we make a sharp right as soon as we come into town, following the sign for Wappenswil. This is hardly a village at all, with only about two dozen scattered farm buildings beyond the road crossing.

At the first curve of the road, when we reach the last farm buildings on our left, cars and some not-too-large buses can make a sharp right and could possibly continue for another half kilometer (nearly one quarter mile). However, there is no parking area and the farmers do not like vehicles in their fields (the Alpine growing season is short enough). Furthermore, larger vehicles may need to back down this trail, which is not more than one vehicle wide.

From this point of Holenstein it is about a twenty-minute hike up the mountain to the Cave of the Anabaptists (Täuferhöhle). In the process we gain an altitude of about 250 meters (700 feet) and it is advisable that we do not hurry.

The cave once served as the secret meeting place for the Anabaptists of the Grüningen/Hinwil/Bäretswil district, and perhaps as a hideout during times of fierce persecution. The hiking map *Zurich Oberland-Tösstal* (Kummerly and Frey) is the only detailed map available which shows the location of the Täuferhöhle).

LOOKING AROUND IN LUZERN

One hundred years ago, Mark Twain fell in love with Luzern and devoted quite a few complimentary paragraphs to the city in his *Innocents Abroad*. In our time it is still the number one tourist destination in Switzerland, if not in all of Europe, and the *Michelin Guide* simply rates the entire city with three stars. Need I say more?

From the Anabaptist Mennonite perspective the city is not notable, although the second Anabaptist martyr after Eberli Bolt, Hans Krüsi, was executed here already in 1525, after having been abducted from his home in Sankt Gallen in the canton of Sankt Gallen. Apparently Hans Krüsi failed to obey a joint order issued by the governments of four cantons—Zurich, Luzern, Schwyz, and Glarus—to cease his evangelistic services.

Luzern's laws regarding the Anabaptists were exceedingly simple. They were to be killed—no trial was necessary. Apparently Luzern was even willing to go after Anabaptists in other cantons, a tactic which more than once put them into conflict with Canton Bern. (Read details under Emmental, page 107.)

Luzern is blessed with a beautiful setting along both sides of the Reuss River and the shores of Lake Luzern [more correctly called the Lake of the Four Forest Cantons], across from the Rigi, the Burgenstock, and on the west side is Luzern's "own mountain"—the 2,129-meter (6,895 ft.) high Mount Pilatus.

The old inner city is still bordered by the completely intact city wall, crowned by nine medieval watchtowers. Graceful swans float on the Reuss between the city's two famous covered bridges—the Kapellbrücke (built in 1333) and the Spreuerbrücke (built in the early 1400s). The 217-meter (712 ft.)-long Kapellbrücke crosses the Reuss diagonally and meets a small chapel midstream. The joists supporting the long tile roof were decorated in 1614 with 158 oil paintings, of which 112 can still be seen.

Along the Reuss, between the two covered bridges, we find Luzern's Rathaus, built 1602 to 1604. Its colonnaded lower portion serves as a market hall. The entire area between the lake, the Reuss, and the city wall, is one of richly decorated old houses along narrow streets which suddenly widen to form open markets—the Weinmarkt, the Hirschenplatz, the Kornmarkt, and the Mühlenplatz. The entire pedestrian zone is served by a free mini-bus operated by the city.

Mount Pilatus as seen from Fürigen

Worthwhile places to visit in Luzern include the Lion Monument carved out of the red sandstone cliff by Bertel Thorwaldsen between 1819 and 1821, and the adjoining Glacier Garden, a relic of the ice age discovered in 1872. The Bourbaki Panorama is a giant 1,930-square-meter (12,000 square ft.) painting commissioned by the Luzern Society of Pacifists to illustrate the miseries of war.

The Richard Wagner Museum is housed in the villa where between 1866 and 1872 Richard Wagner composed his operas *Die Meistersinger of Nürnberg, Siegfried,* and *Götterdämmerung.* The second floor of the villa also houses a significant collection of Western and non-Western musical instruments.

Luzern's Verkehrshaus is Europe's largest museum of transportation and communication, featuring everything from stagecoaches to space capsules. The oldest steamship in Switzerland, the *S.S. Rigi,* (1847), serves as the museum's restaurant. There are locomotives, trams, trucks, buses and cars, airplanes, snowplows and sleds, and much more. Popular with young and old is a huge model railroad which is an exact replica of the Saint Gothardt Massif, and the three spiral tunnels which carry the trains to and from the Italian frontier.

Luzern's Spreuerbrücke dates back to 1407

FROM LUZERN TO THE MOUNTAINS

Lake Luzern is considered Switzerland's most beautiful mountain lake. From the wharfs near the railroad station, the ships of the Vierwaldstättersee Navigation Company serve most cities along the lake on a regular schedule. A complete circle tour of the lake, an unforgettable experience, takes approximately six hours.

Whether by lake steamer or by land transportation, Luzern is one of the best places from which to reach a number of spectacular mountains. The closest ones—Mount Pilatus, 2,129 meters (6,895 feet) and Mount Rigi, 1,797 (5,896 feet)—can be explored on continuous loop routes which include city bus, cable railway, cogwheel railway, ship and train.

Other options include the 3,239-meter (10,627 ft.) Mount Titlis and the Rothorn. The Brienzer Rothorn Railway, base station at Brienz, is Switzerland's last regularly scheduled steam-powered cog-wheel railway. Both the mountain and the old trains going up it merit a three-star rating.

Continuing in the direction of Bern, we soon arrive at Interlaken, point of departure for even more mountain ascents. Here we are near the Jungfrau, 4,158 meters (13,642 ft.). Below its peak at Jungfraujoch, we find Europe's highest railroad station, 3,454 meters (11,333 ft.) above sea level. For a trip up the Jungfrau and back, we allow a full day.

BERN, CITY OF ARCADES AND FOUNTAINS

Bern, so the story goes, owes its name to an episode in the life of Duke Berchtold V von Zähringen. In 1191, this founder of numerous well-planned cities, went out to hunt and promised to name a new city after the first animal he shot. It happened to be a bear. To this day, Bern's bears are seen everywhere. They are carved in stone and wood, painted on buildings, stenciled on trams and buses, printed on flags, T-shirts, and shopping bags, and cast in chocolate and in marzipan.

Located within a loop of the Aare River, and once protected on the west side by two city walls (former locations are Zytgloggeturm and Käfigturm), the old city has preserved its medieval character. After the death of the duke in 1218, the city grew in power until by the 16th century, the city and the canton of Bern had become the largest canton of the Swiss confederation.

In 1848, Bern was made the capital of Switzerland. Besides the Swiss government, the Swiss National Railways and the postal service have their headquarters in Bern with the result that 20 percent of the people work in government offices. This gives the people in the outlying cantons ample opportunity to make their comments about "den Herren von Bern" (the bureaucrats at Bern).

The Anabaptist movement, which emerged in Zurich in 1525, quickly spread to the neighboring cantons, including Bern. By the summer of 1525, Anabaptists were active in Aarau, in Brügg, and in Zofingen, cities under

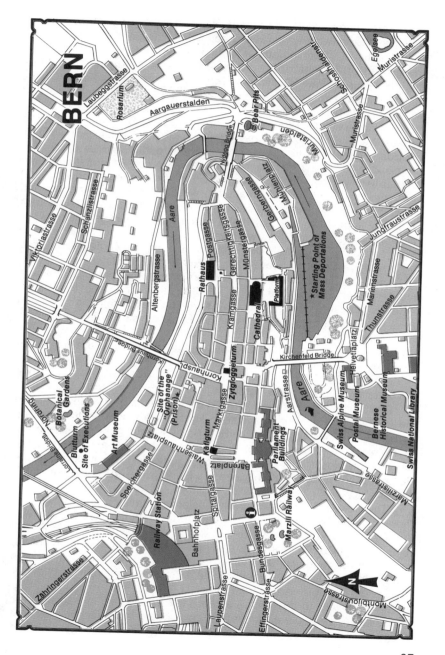

BERN

Laubeggstrasse
Rosarium
Aargauerstalden
Bear Pits

Viktoriastrasse
Schanzlistrasse
Aare
Altenbergstrasse
Nydegg Bridge
Gerberngasse
Postgasse
Rathaus
Gerechtigkeitsgasse
Münstergasse
Kramgasse
Cathedral
Platform
Mühlenplatz
Muristalden
Jungfraustrasse
Marienstrasse
Muristrasse
Muristrasse
Schoschalmistrasse
Egelsee
Muristrasse

* Starting Point of
Mass Deportations

Lorrainebrücke
Nordring
Botanical
Gardens
Blutturm
Site Of Executions
Art Museum
Site of the
"Orphanage"
(Prison)★
Kornhaus Bridge
Kornhaus
Kornhausplatz
Zytglogetturm
Markigasse
Käfigturm
Waisenhausplatz
Bärenplatz
Kirchenfeld Bridge
Aarstrasse
Aare
Parliament
Buildings
Swiss Alpine Museum
Postal Museum
Helvetiaplatz
Thunstrasse
Bernese
Historical Museum
Swiss National Library
Marzilistrasse

Zähringerstrasse
Speichergasse
Railway Station
Bahnhofplatz
Spitalgasse
Bundesgasse
Marzili Railway
Laupenstrasse
Effingerstrasse
Montbijoustrasse

N

97

the control of Bern. In the fall of 1525, Heinrich Bullinger, wrote to Heinrich Simmler in Bern warning him about the Anabaptists. Berchtold Haller, chief pastor at the [still Roman Catholic] church of Bern, informed Zwingli about the growth of the Anabaptist movement in Bern. In August 1527, three cantons—Zurich, Sankt Gallen, and Bern—jointly issued a strict ordinance against the Anabaptists, based on Zwingli's recommendations. Basel had been invited to join them but did not collaborate.

In January 1528 Bern, still in the process of deciding whether to remain Catholic or to switch over to the [Zwinglian] Protestant side, organized a great debate. The meetings were public and everyone was promised a chance to present their views on the Reformation. Eight Anabaptists, among them Georg Blaurock, mistakenly thought that "everyone" included them. Instead, they were imprisoned for the duration of the meetings. On January 22, Zwingli and others held a separate debate with them in the town hall. One of the Anabaptists, a member of Bern's city council, recanted. The others were escorted out of town with the promise that they'd be drowned without mercy should they ever come back. In fact, this is what happened to three Anabaptists in Bern a year later.

The great debate ended with the city's break with Roman Catholicism and the formation of a state church after the pattern in Zurich. In addition, the outcome delivered the death blow to Anabaptism within the city. In the areas under Bern's control, the remaining Anabaptists moved into remote rural regions.

The persecution of Anabaptists in the canton of Bern lasted for centuries. Today most of the descendants of the Bernese Anabaptists, more than 200,000, live in the United States and Canada. Not more than 1,000 remain in the Bernese highlands.

The best way to see Bern is to start from the railroad station. Right on the traffic-filled Bahnhofplatz (station square), you will find the baroque Heilig-Geist-Kirche, Church of the Holy Spirit. Here begins, or rather ends, Bern's main street, which carries five different names. At the other and historically the oldest end, it is called Nydegggasse. Then it becomes the Gerechtigkeitsgasse, the Kramgasse, the Marktgasse, and finally the Spitalgasse.

The view is unmistakenly Bern. Enclosed arcades support three- and four-story facades, leading up to broad gutters and dormers above them. Throughout the summer the street has a festive look with the cantonal and regional flags spaced nearly the full length of the streets, and a flood of red geraniums surrounding the numerous historic town fountains. Goethe once called the Kramgasse section the most beautiful street he had ever seen, and it hasn't changed much since.

We will walk through these arcades toward the next intersection, the Bärenplatz (Bear Square). Dominating this square is the recently restored Käfigturm (tower of cages), once part of Bern's western wall, built and

Bern, as seen from the Aargauerstalden

enlarged between 1232 and 1350. In later years the tower of cages became a prison in which many Anabaptists were locked up and interrogated under torture. Today it houses part of the city's archives. Interestingly, for many years the Bärenplatz was the only spot in Bern where a person could legally smoke in public.

We leave the main street for a moment to continue our walk one block to the left, through the Zeughausgasse. Next to the French Reformed Church once stood the Orphanage, a misleading name for a place which after 1658 served as a concentration camp for a great number of captured Anabaptists. The prisoners were divided into various classes. Some were allowed to die slowly. Others were sold as galley slaves to the Venetian and French fleets. Still others were branded and exiled.

In our time, Bern's small Mennonite fellowship meets on the Zeughausgasse in the same building that houses the Evangelical Bookstore, sharing these facilities with several other denominations.

The Zeughausgasse crosses the Kornmarktplatz and leads into the Metzergasse. About three blocks down, we find Bern's Rathaus (town hall) built from 1406 to 1417. It is considered by many to be the most significant example of secular Gothic architecture. When we compare and contemplate the architecture of this Rathaus and the church next to it, we become aware how much the church and state had become intertwined. Parts of the Rathaus look "churchy," but the church sports defense towers with rifle slots!

The Rathaus is still the seat of Bern's cantonal government. In this same building the Anabaptist problem was discussed again and again, mandates against the Anabaptists were issued for over 200 years, and many death sentences were announced to the public from the impressive balcony of the Rathaus. The Roman Catholic/Anabaptist debate of 1527 and the Reformed/Anabaptist debate of 1527 also took place in this Rathaus. In one corner of this little square, we find an old fountain (1542) showing a Bernese soldier in full armor holding the bear flag.

From the Rathaus we take the Kreuzgasse to the corner of the Gerechtigkeitsgasse and the Kramgasse. From this corner there is a beautiful view in either direction. We are also standing beside the oldest pharmacy in Bern, which began dispensing medicine in 1571.

While we may take in the scenery freely and unhindered, our Anabaptist forefathers were not always so lucky. On the last day of their earthly life, they were chained to a public shame-post, which once stood on this corner. Citizens could come and mock them, shout at them, pelt them with rocks and filthy substance, before they were led to be burned at the stake or beheaded near the middle of this wide street. You wonder about its name—Gerechtigkeitsgasse (street of justice).

We continue through the Kreuzgasse and go around the back of the Münster (cathedral) until we find ourselves standing on the Platform, a massive elevation over the Aare, constructed by monks more then 500 years ago. From the Platform, with its beautiful gardens, a public elevator descends to that part of Bern located at river level and along the Aare harbor. From this harbor, rafts with Anabaptist exiles were shipped down to the Rhine and to Holland. Because the Platform afforded an excellent view to thousands of spectators, Anabaptists were often publicly drowned here. Another spot used for execution by drowning was beside the Blutturm on the opposite side of the old town's peninsula.

You may want to take some time to visit the Münster (cathedral) of St. Vincent. It is the last and also the best example of Swiss late-Gothic architecture. Baumeister Ensinger, who also directed the building of the great cathedrals of Ulm and Strasbourg,put his emphasis in Bern on the harmony of architecture, sculpture, and decoration. The tower carillon includes the largest church bell in Switzerland, ten tons of bronze with a far-reaching voice. We return now to the Kramgasse, taking note of the many ornate fountains along the way. Soon we stand before Bern's trademark, the Zytgloggeturm, built around 1250. From the Kramgasse you can admire the tower clock and the Glockenspiel (carillon), which goes into operation four minutes before each full hour. Long ago, two yardsticks were cemented into the arches of this tower, so that skeptical buyers could remeasure their purchases. From the Zytgloggeturm we continue through the Marktgasse to the Käfigturm. This completes our circle as far as the Anabaptist tour of Bern is concerned.

Further points of general interest include the Bärengraben (bear pits) across the Nydegg Bridge, the Bundeshaus (which houses the parliament), and the Botanical Gardens which specialize in Alpine flora. Excellent panoramic views of the entire old town are visible from the Muristalden on the road to Luzern or from the Rosengarten, on the road to Olten and Zurich.

The Swiss postal museum is of interest to those who want to learn more about the history of one of the world's most efficient postal services.

THE EMMENTAL:
SCENERY, FOLKLORE, AND SWISS CHEESE

Literally translated, Emmental means "valley of the Emme." In reality there are four rivers named Emme. The Wald (forest) Emme and the Weiss (white) Emme join to form the Kleine (little) Emme near Schüpfheim, then all flow east to join the Reuss north of Luzern. Another Emme and its tributaries flows from the heights of the Brienzer Rothorn past Langnau, Lützelflüh, and Burgdorf to join the Aare at Solothurn.

In everyday usage the term Emmental is used to describe the entire region of about 1,300 square kilometers (about 500 square miles) with its distinct geological features and unique forms of architecture. Along the fast-flowing streams and tributaries, we find lush green fields surrounded

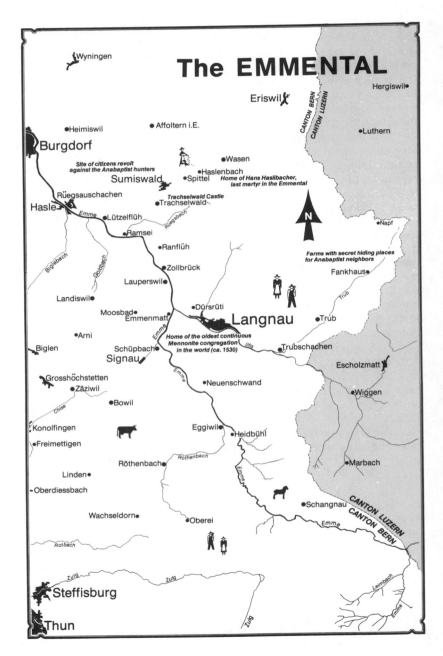

The EMMENTAL

Wyningen

Eriswil

Hergiswil•

•Heimiswil   • Affoltern i.E.   •Luthern

Burgdorf

Site of citizens revolt
against the Anabaptist hunters   •Wasen

Sumiswald   •Haslenbach   *Home of Hans Haslibacher,*
                            •Spittel   *last martyr in the Emmental*

Rüegsauschachen   *Trachselwald Castle*

Hasle•   •Trachselwald•

Emme   •Lützelflüh   •Napf

            •Ramsei

         •Ranflüh   *Farms with secret hiding places*
                                            for Anabaptist neighbors

         •Zollbrück   Fankhaus•

   Lauperswil•

Landiswil•   •Dürsrüti

Moosbad•   **Langnau**
       Emmenmatt•
                                            •Trub
  •Arni
            Schüpbach•   *Home of the oldest continuous*   Trubschachen•
Biglen•   **Signau**   *Mennonite congregation*
                            in the world (ca. 1530)

•Grosshöchstetten   Escholzmatt•
   •Zäziwil
                                                          •Wiggen
      •Bowil

            •Neuenschwand
•Konolfingen
•Freimettigen   Eggiwil•
                                •Heidbühl   •Marbach

    Linden•   Röthenbach•
-Oberdiessbach

   Wachseldorn•   •Oberei   •Schangnau
                                                    Emme

Steffisburg

Thun

CANTON BERN
CANTON LUZERN

N

Biglebach
Goldbach
Ruegsbach
Trub
Ilfis
Emme
Chise
Emme
Röthenbach
Emme
Rotbach
Zulg
Zulg
Zulg
Leimbach
Emme

CANTON LUZERN
CANTON BERN

on all sides by a legion of steep rounded hills leading up to the lower Alps. On their slopes we find fields variably called -eggen, -matten, or -schwanden, fields so steep that they can be worked only with plows pulled along cables by a stationary engine.

Scattered throughout this interesting landscape we find brown wooden Emmentaler farmhouses, clustered in groups of threes and fours, with huge overhanging roofs tiled in red. Some of these buildings are decorated with carvings and paintings akin to the Pennsylvania Dutch decorative arts of Fraktur and tole-painting. Forestry and dairy farming are the main industries and the region is the home of the world-famous Emmentaler and Swiss cheese.

When the early Anabaptists in Zurich and Bern and other Swiss cities faced severe persecution, more and more of them moved into this rural region. The congregation at Langnau is considered the world's oldest continuous Mennonite congregation, dating back to the 1530s. While the mandates were also in effect in the rural areas and persecution took its toll, the remoteness of the region, and a sympathetic attitude of the neighbors toward the Anabaptists, helped to insure the survival of a remnant of Anabaptists in the Emmental throughout the centuries.

In the 1850s, some 325 years after the beginning of Anabaptism in Switzerland, Swiss Mennonites were finally granted civil rights. Until then they had been subjected to deportation, confiscation of property, the forced baptism of their infants by police (last administered in 1812), lifelong imprisonment, or being sold into galley slavery.

The monies taken from the Mennonites were used to train Reformed ministers in their seminaries and to embellish the regional Reformed churches with white towers and imposing clocks. Persons who sympathized with the Anabaptists or gave shelter to them were likewise heavily fined or otherwise punished. Nevertheless, many Emmentalers continued to protect their Anabaptist neighbors from the dreaded Anabaptist hunters.

The heart of the Emmental is Langnau, a charming town halfway between Luzern and Bern. Langnau is the export center for Emmentaler cheese around the world, but it is just as well known for its beautiful wooden houses and for its original linens and ceramics. The "Chuech-lihus," one of the oldest wooden buildings in the region, houses a historical museum. Langnau's Reformed church dates back to 1673.

Right beside Langnau's cemetery we find the Kapelle Kehr, the meetinghouse of the Altevangelische Taufgesinnte Gemeinde (old evangelical Anabaptist congregation) Emmental. The meetinghouse, which looks like a farm home, contains a residence for the pastor as well as a simple but roomy auditorium. A modern addition was completed in 1982.

A stroll through Langnau's well-kept cemetery or a walk through town, reading names on storefronts, clearly establishes the Emmental as the ancestral home of many of our North American Mennonites. All around us we see the names Zurcher, Gerber, Kipfer, Ramseyer, Mosiman, Reist, Zaugg (Zook), Jakob, Aebi (Eby), Ulrich, Moser, Bärtschi, Amstutz, Bigler, Jutzi, Aeschlimann, Wälti (Welty), Thierstein (Derstine), Beyeler, Reber, Liechti, Wüthrich (Widdrick), Neuenschwander, Ruegsegger (Riegsecker), König (King), Bütikofer, Graf (Groff), Lueginbühl, Burckhard, Egli, Steiner, Tschanz, Brächtbühl (Breckbill), Läderach, Hofer, and more.

From the narrow end of the cemetery, a trail leads up to the Dürsrütti, from where we can enjoy a beautiful view over the valleys. The farms along the way were once Mennonite-owned and in the forest reserve, Dürsrütti, we find several of Europe's largest Silbertannen (white firs) under which the Anabaptists once held their secret meetings.

Following the signs to Bern we soon notice an extremely nice cluster of Emmentaler farms on the right side. Just ahead lies the little village of Schüpbach on the Emme. We enter the village through a covered bridge built in 1839. Tradition has it that Schüpbach lent its name to an early Mennonite settlement in eastern Pennsylvania, but the Scotch-Irish neighbors pronounced it Skippack, just as Birkensee became Perkasie.

Just beyond Schüpbach lies Signau, where an overzealous Reformed pastor still continued to harass the Mennonites for a few more years after they had officially been granted freedom to worship.

From Schüpbach south the road leads to Eggiwil-Heidbühl, home of the wood carver, Hans Ramseier, and to Röthenbach, place of origin of many Steiner-Stoner families. The back roads here provide one with delightful ways to get to Thun and Steffisburg, which we will describe later.

But first we go north from Schüpbach and follow the west side of the Emme to Lauperswil and Zollbrück. From Zollbrück we follow the Emme to

Dürrenroth in the Emmental

Ranflüh and Ramsei. Just this side of Ramsei we turn right toward Trachsel-wald and Sumiswald. Immediately after the turn, we pass between the buildings of the Ramseier apple juice factories, whose products delight the palate of the thirsty traveler.

Soon we reach the small town of Trachselwald. The town lies at the foot of the mountain where we find the castle Trachselwald. First mentioned around 1131, the oldest parts of today's castle date back to 1313. In 1408 the castle became the property of Canton Bern and administrative offices of the district government are still housed in it today. The castle was renovated from 1637 to 1641, and from 1749 to 1752, and restored again from 1954 through 1956. An 18th-century access road (not recommended for buses) spirals around the mountain to reach the castle. But most visitors take the steep foot trail from the town of Trachselwald up to the long covered stairs leading into the castle's inner courtyard.

Important to our Mennonite story is the mighty 12th-century keep with its 2.6-meter (8½ ft.) thick walls. Countless Anabaptist prisoners were held in the tower's wooden cells before being transported to Bern. We enter the tower through a door cut into the wall in 1637. To avoid escape, our unfortunate ancestors were placed in the tower through a hole 11 meters (33 ft.) above ground level, since changed into a small window.

We reach the cells reserved for Anabaptists by climbing several wooden stairs followed by a dark and winding staircase in stone. The cells still contain the blocks, the arm and leg irons, and the hole which served as the toilet facility for the prisoners. Sometimes prisoners lost the use of their muscles and their eyesight from the prolonged stay in these places. Ambitious visitors may want to continue climbing to the top floor which served

An Emmentaler barn

as a defense platform in times of war. From this upper level one has a marvelous view of the surrounding countryside.

Before we leave the town of Trachselwald, take a good look at the painted decorations on the town's only restaurant and the beautiful facade of the farm on the corner across from the church.

From Trachselwald we continue north toward Sumiswald-Grunen, not more than one kilometer away. It was particularly in Sumiswald that the population sided with the Anabaptists and always warned them with horns, rattles, and other noisemakers when the Täuferjäger (Anabaptist hunters) were in the neighborhood. As late as 1714, a crowd of about 70 Sumiswalders beat up the Anabaptist hunters and allowed the arrested Anabaptists to escape. For this the town temporarily lost its city privileges and the leaders of the revolt, who were known, were fined and imprisoned. According to the authorities in Bern, Anabaptist sympathizers probably made up the majority of the population in the Emme region.

In Sumiswald-Grünen, immediately after crossing the railroad track, we keep to the right and follow the signs for Wasen. About two kilometers along this road, just before we reach the village of Spitel, we turn right across the tracks. At the first fork of the road we turn left again. And soon we arrive at the small hamlet of Haslenbach, nestled in a curved depression on this plateau.

The large farmhouse on the left, built in the early 1500s, was the home of Hans Haslibacher, the last martyr from the Emmental. He was executed in Bern on October 20, 1571. A detailed description of Hans Haslibacher's imprisonment and execution is found in a 32-stanza poem composed, as the last verse states, by another Anabaptist prisoner. This so-called Haslibacherlied found its way into the *Ausbund,* beginning with the 1622 edition, as well as in the later editions of the *Martyrs Mirror.*

Before his execution Hans Haslibacher had been an Anabaptist leader, active as early as 1532, and a participant in the Great Debate of 1538. He was fined and exiled from the region. More than three decades later, Hans returned home to visit his son. On September 2, 1571, his son, though a member of the state (Reformed) church, was fined for showing hospitality to his aged father, and Hans himself was led away to Trachselwald and from there to Bern. Direct descendants of Haslibacher still live on the farm.

At Haslenbach we can also visit one of Switzerland's approximately 1,600 independent cheesemakers, each of which produce two giant 80-kilo (180-pound) Emmentaler cheeses daily. The Haslibachers and the family of the cheesemaker welcome visits but neither family speaks English.

From Haslenbach we have the option of continuing to Wasen and across the mountains to Eriswil and Hutwil. We can enjoy unforgettable views from either side of the tunnel at Fritzenflüe or from the country road back to Langnau via Lüderenalp.

Another excursion out of Langnau can be made along the Ilfis east to

Trubschachen and then along the Trub River to the villages of Trub, Fankhaus, and Napf. The name Trub is incorporated in the family name Schwartzen*truber* and the original farms of the Schwartzentruber, although no longer in the family, can be seen near Fankhaus.

The Trub valley was also the scene of numerous interesting border disputes in connection with the Anabaptists. Though both the cantons Bern and Luzern hated the Anabaptists with equal passion, Canton Luzern, whose borders run along the east of the Fankhaus Ridge along the Trub, was not too happy about the Bernese Anabaptist hunters violating their border. But sometimes Bern charged Luzern for similar incidents. The Anabaptists, aided by their neighbors, made good use of this invisible line. According to some historians, a number of farms along the Trub used to be equipped with a Taüferversteck (Anabaptist hiding place), usually a double-bottomed grain or potato bin.

ROUND ABOUT THUN

Where the Aare flows from Lake Thun and turns west, there rises on the right bank of the river a high rocky ridge. Already in prehistoric times a Celtic stockade stood on this rock. In fact, the name Thun derives from the Celtic *Dunum*, or stronghold.

During the 12th century the stronghold and surrounding settlement fell into the hands of the city-building dukes of Zahringen. Under Duke Berchtold V von Zähringen, founder of Bern, Freiburg, and other cities, Thun became a city of significance, and the baronial fortress on the castle rock was given its present form.

Between the 1530s and the 1800s many Anabaptists lived in the area in and around Thun at Steffisburg, at Diesbach, and Sigriswil on the north shore, and in the towns of the Simmental on the south. The castle dungeon at Thun held Anabaptist prisoners as early as 1532, among them the Brönnimanns (Brennemans) and Joders (Yoders). In Thun the castle dungeon served not only to store prisoners but the offal of the city's slaughterhouses as well.

Jacob Ammann, founder of the Amish, is said to have come from Erlenbach in the Simmental. Eventually most of the Anabaptists from the Thun area migrated to Holland, to the Swiss Jura, and to America. Today some Brennemans, Stahlis, Amstutzes, Stutzmans, Rissers, Rupps, and Schlappachs (Slabaughs) can trace their ancestry back to these mountains surrounding Lake Thun.

THE JURA, PLACE OF REFUGE

During most of the more than three centuries of persecution in Switzerland, the forest-covered Jura, with its many gorges and sparsely inhabited plateaus, offered the best possible place of refuge for Swiss Anabaptist Mennonites.

For a long time a large part of the Jura belonged to the prince-bishops of Basel, who tolerated the Mennonites for the economic advantages to the region. There were, of course, complaints from the native population against the Anabaptists and orders from on high to enforce the harsh edicts against the Mennonites, but in the Jura such orders were carried out only lightly. So the Mennonites at last found a land where they could live, more or less undisturbed, even though they were long fearful to conduct their worship services openly.

Coming from central Switzerland, we enter the Jura at Biel (or Bienne). Biel is bilingual and in the stores we hear clerks and customers switch back and forth between French and German with ease.

In 1528 Georg Blaurock held meetings in the woods near Biel attended by a sizable group of Swiss Brethren. In 1879 Omega opened its first watch factory in Biel, and today there are more than 300 watch manufacturers in Biel, employing more than 11,000 people.

Just beyond Biel, on the road west toward Sonceboz and Tavannes, persons who have a real interest in Anabaptist history can take a turnoff to the Bridge of the Anabaptists. It is in a gorge high in the Chasseral Ridge of the Jura. For this trip one needs a small car with some power to spare, about an hour and a half of time, and a skilled driver, for the gravel roads leading to the site are steep and narrow. On foot, the trip takes at least four hours. Michelin map number 21 shows the access via Orvin or by Cortébert in reasonable detail.

The Bridge of the Anabaptists is the place where secret meetings were held for many years. The bridge itself was purposely destroyed early in this century because it was no longer safe. But in the gorge below we can still read the initials and dates carved in the rocks by the worshipers. That the name Pont des Anabaptistes shows up on maps and roadsigns suggests that the natives know that the Anabaptists had built the bridge, and that they were aware of the secret meetings. The Anabaptists, and later Mennonites themselves, would hardly have chosen this name.

Descending the Chasseral's north slope, we reach the road to Corgémont, from where we climb the next ridge for four kilometers (2½ miles) to Jeanguisboden. There we find a meetinghouse/school of the Sonnenberg congregation. The main building, which dates back to 1900, also houses the archives of the Swiss Mennonites, a small but interesting collection of books and documents.

Continuing across the mountain we find Tramelan. In this town, several Mennonite families founded the MenSim Watch Factory (MenSim stands for Menno Simons), now owned and operated by Joel Gyger and his wife. MenSim watches in a variety of styles are for sale at their home.

From Tramelan the road goes uphill to Saignelégier. The second road to the right leads to Les Rouges Terres, where we find the chapel of Les Mottes, built in 1928 and enlarged in 1967. The auditorium is large enough to hold 600 persons. The building also houses an apartment for the pastor and caretaker, a dining hall, and part of the sleeping quarters of the adjacent Mennonite retreat center, also named Les Mottes.

Throughout the area one finds magnificent pine forests and impressive farms, some of which are still owned by the Mennonites who settled and improved this land originally. Eighteen kilometers (11 miles) southwest of Les Mottes, past Les Breuleux, we find the Mennonite meetinghouse of La Chaux d'Abel and beside it the oldest Mennonite school in the Jura, built in 1863.

Other fellowships meet alternatively in the farm homes at Chaux d'Abel-Berg, on the Mont Soleil (Sonnenberg), in La Ferrière, and on three farms west of Tramelan. Another congregation meets at Les Bulles, just north of La-Chaux-de-Fonds. It is difficult to find each of the house churches and meetinghouses without a native guide. The Mennonites originally came here to escape, not to be discovered.

From Les Mottes, we turn east again toward Bellelay, where we find an important baroque monastery. Today it belongs to the canton and is used for concerts and mass meetings. The monks at Bellelay are said to have invented the "Tete de Moine" (monk's head) cheese, which is still made here today. (It is made during the summer months only and has ripened by the time the leaves turn.)

A side road leads from just before Bellelay to the small village of Moron, which is almost entirely Mennonite. The Mennonite chapel and school of Moron date back to 1892.

Another five kilometers (3 miles) west and we reach the gorges of Pichoux. Note: The natural tunnel at Le Pichoux may not be tall enough to accommodate buses and other large vehicles. From the Hotel de la Couronne, we climb up a steep rocky trail to a small cave on the right hand side of the path, where secret Anabaptist meetings were once held. It is known as the Geiskirchlein (the Church of the Goat). Since there is not a distinct path from the main trail to the cave, it may be rather difficult to find.

While the first Anabaptists settled in the areas described above, eventually the Mennonites scattered over the entire Jura on both sides of the Franco-Swiss border, all the way toward Basel. A number of Mennonite farms now find some of their fields in France and others in Switzerland, and nearly all Swiss Mennonites have family on both sides of the border.

A visit to all the Mennonite sites in the Jura, therefore, may take several days and a good sense of direction. Furthermore, inns and guesthouses are not plentiful in this part of Switzerland and none are big enough to accommodate tour groups. Tours through the Jura should, therefore, start and end daily in Bern or in Basel.

There are many other points of interest in the Jura. Saint Ursanne is a charming little town founded by Irish missionaries in the 8th century, and a favorite with artists and photographers. The best view of Saint Ursanne is

Climbing to the Geiskirchlein

Basel's 900-year old cathedral overlooks the Rhine

from across the stone arched bridge, the Doubs. Porrentruy is a small city clustered around the fortress of the Basler prince-bishops.

La-Chaux-de-Fonds is the metropolis of the Swiss watch industry. Tower clocks and wall clocks have been made in the city since the 1500s. But not until the early 1700s were the first pocket watches made here. The world's first pocket watch was constructed by Daniel Jean-Richard (1672-1741). He made it in less than 18 months after studying a broken clock left behind by an English horse dealer, and that included the time needed to create the small tools to make the watch. The Jura region produces about half the world's watches and is a major factor in Switzerland's balance of trade. The International Museum of Timekeeping at La-Chaux-de-Fonds is worth visiting.

BASEL, MEETINGPOINT OF THREE NATIONS

Like many other Swiss cities, Basel had its Anabaptist problem. In August 1525 the reformer Oekolampad held a discussion in his home with several Anabaptists concerning baptism and voluntary church membership. The city issued its first mandate against the Anabaptists on June 2, 1526, followed quickly by two more, and then even a fourth one also, listing the fines for Anabaptist sympathizers.

In 1529 Georg Blaurock was confined in Basel's prison, along with a brother in the faith from northern Italy. David Joris, a Dutch Anabaptist, lived in Basel from 1544 to 1556, under the pseudonym Johan van Brugge. Not until three years after his death was his real identity discovered. At that point his corpse was dug up and burned by the authorities. In August 1544, Wilhelm Reublin (no longer Anabaptist) appeared in Basel to conclude his dying days in the city where he had started his theological career. Groups of Anabaptists continued to meet on farms outside the city and in the gravel pits near Lostorf. Some of the Baseler Anabaptists joined the Swiss Brethren and the Hutterites in Moravia. Others migrated into nearby Alsace.

Today we find two Mennonite churches in Basel. The congregation at the Holeestrasse, formerly Amish, belongs to the French Mennonite conference and many of its members live across the border in the Alsace. The congregation at Schänzli-Muttenz dates back to at least 1790 when Christian Röthlisberger assumed the leadership of the congregation. In 1891 a meeting room was built on the Nusbaumer farm at Schänzli. In 1902 a combined farm, residence, and chapel was built on the Basel-Muttenz Road. But this too has since become too small to meet the needs of the growing congregation.

In 1973 some 20 members of the Schänzli congregation decided to form a new congregation at nearby Liestal. On January 21, 1975, exactly 450 years after the founding of the first congregation in Switzerland, the new Liestal congregation became independent from the Schanzli-Muttenz church.

Interesting sights in Basel include the red sandstone cathedral (Münster) with its unique glazed tile roof. The oldest part of this church dates back to 1185 and its style ranges from late Romanesque to Gothic. Among the old gravestones which have been gathered against one wall, we find the gravestone of Erasmus of Rotterdam, who died here in 1536. From the church's terrace there is a beautiful view of the city and the Rhine River. From the foot of the Münster we can cross this river on a current-driven pedestrian ferry "Leu" (lion).

On the market square, which has an active market each weekday morning, we find Basel's massive painted Rathaus built in 1504-1514. East and west of the market square and town hall we find numerous steep and narrow streets with charming houses built between the 13th and 16th centuries. Here and there these streets widen into a small square usually embellished with a pretty fountain.

Basel has many museums and an excellent zoo with 3,200 animals, one of the largest zoos in Europe. During the summer the Basler Passenger Steamship Company offers excursions on the Rhine and the harbors from its dock near the Mittlere Brücke, about two and a half blocks from the Rathaus.

The possibilities for sightseeing in Switzerland are almost unlimited. Rather than providing a listing here, may I suggest consulting the excellent tourist bureaus found in practically every major Swiss railroad station, where they can supply you a wealth of brochures and maps. The friendly multilingual assistants will even work out itineraries.

GERMANY

Deutschland

D

When we talk about "Germany," it is important that we agree on which Germany, for historically that name has carried varied meanings. It once meant hundreds and hundreds of small kingdoms, principalities, duchies, bishoprics, and territories, which together made up the Holy Roman Empire, and whose borders were constantly changing as the result of conquest, princely marriages, or economic alliances.

From 1815 to 1866 Germany meant the German Confederation which then included Austria. In the confederation the great number of German states and territories was reduced from more than 300 to "only" 35 states and four free cities. Prussia proposed a customs union among these cities and states in which the members ended tariffs on goods traded to each other. Prussia was careful, however, to keep Austria, its chief rival for leadership in the confederation, out of the agreement.

From the Franco-Prussian War (1870-1871) until the end of World War I in 1918, Germany became defined as the principal German-speaking area of Europe, apart from Austria and Switzerland. Between the two World Wars Germany was first known as the Weimar Republic and then, under Nazi rule, as the Third Reich.

In 1945 the so-called "Big Four"—the United States, Great Britain, France, and the Soviet Union—assumed authority over a defeated and devastated Germany. The country was divided into four zones of occupation with each power occupying a zone. In the summer of 1945, three of the allied leaders—Truman, Stalin, and Atlee,—met at Potsdam, Germany. They agreed to govern Germany together and to rebuild it as a democracy. They also allowed Russia ten million dollars in wartime reparations and almost at once Russia began to remove entire factories from its zone for shipment to Russia.

Under the Potsdam Agreement, Russia was also allowed to annex each of the three Baltic republics—Estonia, Latvia, and Lithuania,—plus vast areas of eastern Poland, as well as the northern half of East Prussia. The provincial capital of East Prussia, called Königsberg, then became the Russian city of Kaliningrad. Like in a giant chain collision, Poland in turn moved its borders deep into Germany along its Oder and Neisse rivers. As a result, Germany lost more than a fifth of its territory.

Infinitely more disastrous, from a humanitarian point of view, under the Potsdam agreement all Germans living in these areas, and German-speaking minorities living anywhere else in Central Europe, could forcibly be moved from their homes and exiled. In one of the greatest population transfers in history, some thirteen million men, women, and children were chased from their ancestral homes almost overnight. Tens of thousands of these men, women, and children perished in the cruel process carried out on short notice and without provisions, organization, or preparations what-soever. Of these hapless wanderers the majority, some ten million, ended up in displaced persons camps in the three Western zones.

For those who visit Germany today it is hard to imagine the utter de-vastation caused by night after night of saturation bombing. Its industries were gone and its transit system was in shambles, and more than 2½ million of the sixteen million housing units in the areas of present-day Germany had been reduced to rubble. Another 4½ million homes were damaged to the point that they were classified as uninhabitable. With the influx of the ten million displaced persons (DPs) from the east, occupancy rose to more than two persons per available room, even though such a "room" actually might have been an office in a cement factory, a garden shed, or the library of a school.

The situation was aggravated by a shortage of fuel and food, and Germany's money was virtually worthless. In June 1948 the three Western zones carried out a currency reform in which people traded in their old Reichsmark for the new Deutsche Mark (DM) at the ratio of ten to one.

About that same time the United States Secretary of State George Marshall proposed the European Recovery Plan through which the United States contributed thirteen billion dollars in aid and loans to all of Western Europe from 1948 through 1951. Part of this aid also went to the three Western zones, but it was expressly rejected by the Russians for their zone of occupation. The Russians were still bent on revenge and on the disman-tling of the German economy. Their reaction to the Marshall Plan led to the Cold War, the Blockade of Berlin, and the takeover of Czechoslovakia. George Marshall, however, was awarded the Nobel Peace prize for his magnanimous proposal.

The mounting tensions of the Cold War speeded up the need to orga-nize a civil government for western Germany. The trizonal partners ar-ranged for a German assembly to write a federal constitution which was ap-proved in May 1949. On September 21, 1949, the three Western zones were

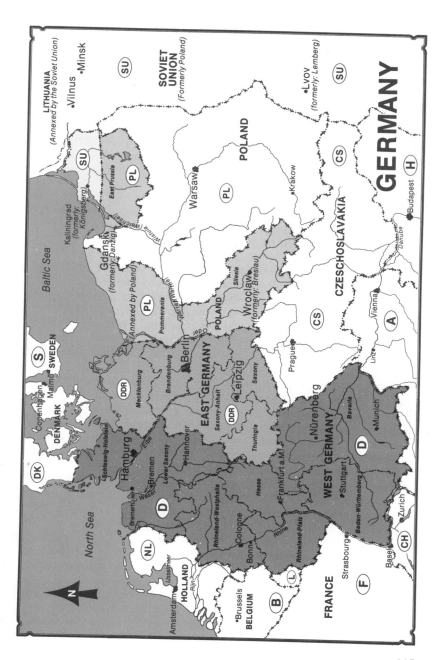

GERMANY

LITHUANIA
(Annexed by the Soviet Union)

•Vilnus   •Minsk

(SU)

SOVIET
UNION
(Formerly: Poland)

(SU)

•Lvov
(formerly: Lemberg)

(SU)

POLAND

•Warsaw   (PL)

•Krakow

(CS)

(H)   •Budapest

Baltic Sea

Kaliningrad
(formerly:
Königsberg)

(SU)

East Prussia

(PL)

Gdansk
(formerly: Danzig)

(Annexed by Poland)

Wisla (Weichsel)

Pommerania

(PL)

Oder

Neisse/Warthe

POLAND

Silesia

Wroclaw
(formerly: Breslau)

(PL)

CZECHOSLOVAKIA

(CS)

•Prague

(A)   Vienna•

Linz•

Danube

Sweden

(S)

Malmö• SWEDEN
Copenhagen•

DENMARK

(DK)

North Sea

Berlin

Brandenburg

Mecklenburg

(DDR)

EAST GERMANY

Saxony-Anhalt

(DDR)

Leipzig•

Saxony

Thuringia

Nürenberg•

WEST GERMANY

Bavaria

(D)   •Munich

Schleswig-Holstein

Hamburg

Elbe

Bremen

Bremerhaven•

Weser

Lower Saxony

Hannover•

(D)

Rhineland-Westphalia

Cologne•

Hesse

Bonn•

Rhine

Frankfurt a.M.•

Stuttgart•

Baden-Württemberg

Rhineland-Pfalz

Zurich•

(CH)

Basel•

Amsterdam•

HOLLAND

Rijn

IJsselmeer

(NL)

•Brussels

BELGIUM

(B)

(L)

Strasbourg•

FRANCE

(F)

N

officially combined into the new Bundesrepublik Deutschland, the Federal Republic of Germany, with Konrad Adenauer as its first chancellor. Two weeks later the Soviet zone became the Deutsche Demokratische Republik, the German Democratic Republic, with Walter Ulbricht as its head.

West Germany, that part of Germany dealt with in this booklet, consists of seven states, each headed by a minister-president, and two city states, each governed by a chief executive and a senate.

The economic pump priming of the Marshall Plan was just what West Germany needed. The Federal Republic astonished the whole world by the speed and the extent of its recovery. This *Wirtschaftswunder* (economic miracle) made West Germany the number one trading nation in Europe by 1959.

Besides the Marshall Plan, credit must go to the Germans themselves. The large labor force of skilled men and women shouldered the obligation of hard work and was willing to forego any wage increases in return for long-term improvements of the total economy. Cooperation rather than confrontation (through strikes) still characterizes the German labor unions. Government encouraged first the rebuilding and later the continuous modernization of industry by well-conceived fiscal policies which encouraged private enterprise. Germany's recovery plan as presented to the Marshall Plan officials favored the production of export goods over consumer goods for the home market. Management, throughout the fifties and early sixties, annually reinvested nearly 25 percent of their profits back into plant modernization. That reinvestment quickly surpassed even the volume of the Marshall Plan aid.

By 1951 Germany, coming out of nowhere, had achieved a favorable balance of trade and began developing a trade surplus. By 1954, no more than six years after its ten-to-one devaluation, the German Mark had become a hard currency commanding a premium on the world money market and investors everywhere began to liquidate their American holdings to reinvest in Germany's growth economy.

Germany has five distinct landscapes which range from the broad North German Plain to the high peaks of the Bavarian Alps. The largest of these five regions, the North German Plain, lies less than 300 feet above sea level. The region is drained by broad rivers flowing north toward the Baltic and North seas. These rivers include the Elbe, the Oder, the Weser, and the Ems, plus that portion of the Rhine from Bonn to the Dutch border, all of which are important commercial waterways with large inland harbors and massive industrial regions lining their shores. In spite of its seeming monotony, the North German Plain actually has a great variety of landscapes, ranging from the wetlands between the river delta to the moors and fields of heather. East Friesland and Schleswig-Holstein resemble parts of neighboring Holland and Denmark. The southern edge of the North German Plain consists of a very fertile, fine, dustlike soil called *Loess*.

Limburg on the Lahn

The Central Uplands consist of a series of plateaus running from the Belgian border in the west to the Czechoslovakian border in the east. Through the Central Uplands the rivers have cut steep and narrow valleys. These rugged gorges, especially those of the Rhine between Bonn and Bingen, have become justly famous. But the sights along the major tributaries, the Mosel, the Lahn, and other rivers, are no less beautiful.

The South German Hills consist of a broad sweep of parallel ranges running from southwest to northeast. Known collectively as the Scarplands, these hills present steep slopes facing west that fall away gently toward the southeast. In Baden-Württemberg these ranges may rise to more than 3,000 feet.

West of these ranges, but separated from them by open undulating country, lies the Black Forest. The South German Hills are drained by the Rhine and two of its tributaries, the Main and the Neckar. But it is also the source of the Danube (Donau), Germany's (and Europe's) only major river flowing east.

The Bavarian Alps are part of the Alps, the largest mountain system in Europe. The highest point in Germany, the 2,963-meter (9,721 feet) Zugspitze near Garmisch-Partenkirchen is found here. In general the political border between Germany and Austria follows the crest of these mountains. One can actually ascend the Zugspitze on the German side and descend into Austria.

A unique area in Germany is the Ruhr territory, perhaps the most densely populated and highly industrialized region in the whole world, long the backbone of German industry. Ever since the industrial revolution of 1850 the proliferation of mills, factories, and manufacturing centers have so completely surrounded the old market towns that today it forms (under many names) one continuous city more than fifty kilometers (30 miles) wide and home to over eight million people.

In 1969 the myriad local coal mines of the Ruhr region were regrouped under a central board. Since that time worker productivity has tripled with the mines producing nearly four tons of coal per man/shift. The Ruhr produces 82 percent of Germany's coal, 64 percent of Germany's steel, 67 percent of the pig iron and all other metals, 80 percent of the coal gas and ammonia and 78 percent of Germany's industrial electric power. While this complex may sound forbidding, the federal government wisely mandated that seven north-south green belts consisting of woods and farmlands would limit the further spread of this industrial buildup.

Germany still lives up to its tradition of having magnificent woods. While the once immense virgin forests are now—after 2,000 years of dense habitation—largely gone, well-managed woodlands are to be found everywhere, especially in the central and southern highlands.

In the Sauerland, homeland of Christopher Dock, Christopher Sauer, and Alexander Mack, the beechwoods are the thickest and the trees the tallest. But large areas of evergreens thrive in Germany as well. The Black Forest, the Swabian Alps, and the Hartz Mountains are all covered with dense mixed forests of beech and spruce. Pines predominate the Alpine scenery below the timberline.

Germans are enthusiastic, one might say, sentimental, lovers of the woods. In 1945 when Berlin lay in ruins, one shocked survivor lamented, "Look what they have done to our trees!" The linden tree especially has many romantic and poetic associations. Many a linden tree has been planted in honor of a great poet or musician and more than a few cities have a square or a boulevard named Unter den Linden.

The same respect for nature shows up in the design and landscaping of highways, in particular the *Autobahnen* (plural for *Autobahn*—espress highway). These roads have been designed not only for speed but also to compliment the regional landscape and the occasional townscape. On the northern plains, where it would have been possible to lay out a straight point-to-point road, the Autobahn sweeps in graceful curves across the land. And in some parts of the country the Autobahn actually offers the tourist a better view of the scenery than before it was constructed. Good examples of this principle can be found on the Stuttgart-Ulm section through the Schwabische Alb.

Germany was one of the first countries to make public education available to all and on all levels. By the 1900s the country had achieved nearly 100 percent literacy. By and large, the present system of German schools dates back to this time before World War I, for despite two wars and Allied attempts to change the system, the tradition prevails.

Two goals are basic to the German system. One is the achievement of a student's highest possible competence consistent with a person's given abilities. The other is the training of individuals for a place in society appropriate to their intellect or ability in which the reality of widely differing talents and interests is taken for granted. In the fourth and fifth grade, students with the highest scores move into accelerated classes that will prepare them to enter a university after spending up to nine years in high school. The most demanding of these classes are in the *Gymnasium,* which emphasizes the classical languages. The remaining students are moved toward vocational and technical education.

Critics within Germany and beyond think that the German system is not democratic and that it perpetuates a class society by denying all people access to identical educational opportunities. The fact remains that in Germany a confectioner, a landscape artist, a shoemaker, or a forester is a person who also has received a quality education.

There are pros and cons to the system. Yes, there is a loss of freedom because one is not allowed to open up a sign shop in Germany without being a *diplomierter* sign artist. But sign shops manned only by qualified professionals avert the visual disasters that greet the visitor approaching any major American city.

The Germans, in turn, would not be impressed with the American system where millions of functional illiterates can show a universal high school diploma just because they "have been there."

When it comes to literature and music Germany's greatest cultural period occurred between the mid-1700s and the mid-1800s. Its outstanding poetic geniuses included Johann Wolfgang von Goethe and Friedrich von Schiller. The great tradition of German music was established by the composers Johann Sebastian Bach and Friedrich Handel, while Haydn and Mozart carried on this tradition in Austria, then considered part of Germany. Later Ludwig von Beethoven, born in Bonn, developed new forms of musical expression. Other German composers included Brahms, Mendelsohn, Schubert, Strauss, and Wagner (see also under Austria).

The Germans' love for art shows up in the architecture of the many Romanesque and Gothic churches and cathedrals and in the lavish decorations of the baroque abbeys in South Germany. In spite of two wars, much of it still stands or has been painstakingly restored for us to enjoy today.

The architecture ranges from 2,000 year-old Roman walls, gates, and mosaic floors to examples of the Bauhaus and Jugendstil. In between these we find literally hundreds of Romanesque, Gothic, Renaissance, baroque sacred and secular buildings, many of them lavishly decorated with sculptures, paintings, and tapestries from the masters of these respective eras. Of these we mention the woodcarver Veit Stoss; the painters Albrecht

Dürer, Matthias Grünewald, Lucas Cranach, and Hans Holbein; the sculptor Tilman Riemenschneider and the more recent sculptor Ernst Barlach. Artists who have been social critics of significance include the illustrator Käte Kollwitz and the playwright Berthold Brecht.

Religion has played a key role in German history and for church historians Germany is a must on the itinerary. The Reformation under Martin Luther and others started in Germany in 1517. By the mid-1600s most of the people in middle and northern Germany had become Protestant (predominantly Lutheran), while those in the south remained Catholic. The post-World War II division of Germany and the arrival of millions of displaced persons resulted in a West Germany with an almost identical number of Catholics and Protestants. Hamburg is considered the largest "Protestant" city in Europe. Cologne and Munich are both considered strong Catholic cities, though neither city is as predominantly Catholic as it once was.

In West Germany the churches have greater influence in public affairs than the official separation of church and state seems to imply. There are two reasons for this. First, more than 90 percent of all Germans claim church membership, and though not nearly as many are active in their congregations, their claim makes them liable to the church tax assessment at income-tax time. And, second, after the collapse of the Third Reich in 1945, the church was the sole surviving institution providing continuity with Germany's past history, and in a position to help bring order out of chaos. In those days of turmoil, the church did indeed provide leadership equal to the task, exemplified by persons such as Hanns Lilje, bishop of Hannover, and Otto Dibelius, bishop of Berlin.

THE MENNONITE STORY IN GERMANY

In April of 1525 Wilhelm Reublin left the fellowship at Zurich and traveled 32 kilometers (about twenty miles) to the town of Waldshut on the Rhine in southern Germany. There he and Conrad Grebel baptized Balthasar Hubmaier, the leader of the local congregation. Together they baptized 360 more people, nearly all of them of Hubmaier's congregation. Still that same year Hubmaier was forced to flee and the young Anabaptist congregation at Waldshut was virtually wiped out. Hubmaier went on to Augsburg and established a congregation there. Augsburg became an influential Anabaptist center and eventually, along with Strasbourg, replaced Zurich in ongoing significance. When Hubmaier moved on to Moravia he left the Augsburg congregation under the leadership of Hans Denck.

Another leader in southern Germany was Michael Sattler. This ex-Benedictine monk, who pastored the Anabaptist fellowships at Rottenburg and Horb on the Neckar River, is credited with editing the Schleitheim Brotherly Agreement, a confession of faith which emerged from of a meeting of Anabaptist leaders in February of 1527. This meeting and the document it produced helped to unify the Anabaptist movement in its early years. Sattler was captured and imprisoned shortly after the meeting in Schleitheim. At his trial he conducted his own defense. The trial is recorded in *Martyrs Mirror*. Sattler was executed on May 21, 1527, outside of Rottenburg on the Neckar. The persecution in South Germany was so intense that by 1616, the beginning of the Thirty Years' War, very few Mennonites were left in the area. According the the *Hutterite Chronicles,* in the town of Alzey alone, 350 Anabaptists are reported to have been executed. Years later, after the Thirty Years' War, Mennonite refugees from Switzerland settled in the Palatinate and worked hard to turn the war-ravaged land into showplace condition. Although the Mennonites were not given complete religious freedom, they were shown tolerance because the rulers of the area needed good workers to rebuild the land. In 1682 a Swiss Mennonite refugee, Peter Krähenbühl, acquired and restored an estate in the Pfalz (Palatinate) called the Weierhof. In time a Mennonite congregation was established there and later a boarding school.

The Anabaptists in North Germany were in closer contact with the Dutch Anabaptists to their west than with the Swiss brethren in the south. In 1534 many Dutch Anabaptists left Holland and went to the city of Munster, where there was a violent uprising. (For more information about this tragedy, turn to page 140.) For a time East Friesland under Countess Anna was a place of refuge for Anabaptists and Mennonites because there they were shown more tolerance.

During the 19th century the German Mennonites gradually lost the privilege of military exemption they had pleaded for during the 17th century. As a result, the Mennonites migrated to Pennsylvania, where they could live according to their faith. Those who stayed behind found it increasingly difficult to practice nonresistance and eventually the practice died out in Germany.

The Mennonites of Germany have been grouped into two conferences, the North German Vereinigung, and the South German Verband. The North German Mennonites, for reasons of geography and history, have been more closely associated with the Dutch Mennonites. The South German Mennonites, for similar reasons and circumstances and through bloodlines, are related more closely to the Swiss and the French Mennonites.

Currently the two groups are in the process of forming one single German Mennonite conference. Since the 1960s thousands of Mennonites and Mennonite Brethren from Soviet Russia (the Umsiedler) have arrived in West Germany. Today these newcomers outnumber the original German Mennonites. While most of the Umsiedler have joined the local Mennonite churches, some have joined the Baptists while another 1,700 have formed seven new and independent Mennonite and Mennonite Brethren congregations in Germany and Austria.

The German Language and Its Variations

The language spoken in Germany from border to border is German. Furthermore, German is also the official language of Austria and one of the official languages of Switzerland and Luxembourg. German is also spoken in eastern France (Alsatian) and in northern Italy (Tirolian). With around 100 million people using German as their national tongue, German is the second most widely used language in Europe after Russian. Spoken as a second language by most other European nationals and by German-speaking immigrants around the world, the total number of people who can communicate in German around the world is estimated at 500 million.

Naturally, in a country as large as Germany, the language comes in a great variety of dialects. Experts divide them into Platdeutsch(Low German) and Hochdeutsch (High German). The best-spoken forms of standard High German are heard around Kassel and Hannover.

The so-called Pennsylvania Dutch (more correctly, Pennsylvania German) can be traced to the Pfälzisch spoken in the Palatinate, although it has picked up a great many English components over the past centuries. The Platdeutsch, spoken by Mennonites of Russian and Prussian descent in various parts of the world, has definite North German origins and has remained purer over the years.

The Climate

Basically, West Germany has two climates, a moderate and coastal climate with considerable moisture in the northwest and a continental climate over most of the rest of the country. The confrontation between air currents coming off the Atlantic Ocean and the North Sea and those of the continent create conditions which can be quite changeable and often turbulent.

The months with the clearest skies are April and May on the coast, June and September further inland. July is almost always the warmest, but at the same time the rainiest, month of the year. April brings bright pleasant days to the Rhine Valley and to South Germany at the time the orchards are decked in flowers.

There are times during October and the first half of November when the people enjoy *Altweibersommer* (old woman's summer), when brilliant sunny days rapidly turn into cool and brisk evenings. During the first cool nights the Bavarian Alps, the Black Forest, and, despite the modest altitude, the Sauerland, begin to accumulate a cover of snow and prepare for the long winter season.

The Best Times to See Germany

Springtime comes early to the plateaus of the Palatinate. In April and May the orchards and vineyards spring into bloom along the Rhine and the Mosel. Icy weather may still surprise travelers until May.

Spring only reaches the shores of Lake Constance (Bodensee) when the warm winds of the Föhn (see page 80) swoop down from the Alps. With all the melting snow everywhere, the Rhine often overflows its banks in early May. When this happens, the Köln Düsseldorfer's great white fleet of Rhine River ships has trouble keeping to a schedule or may even suspend navigation altogether for a few days.

A hot and muggy summer day is a good time to go on a forest walk. Germans are deeply moved by towering trees, babbling brooks, and the animals of field and forest. Germany maintains 37 wildlife observation parks (national parks) totaling more than 10,000 square kilometers (4,000 square miles) and 900 additional nature reserves *(Naturschützgebiete)*. Trails are well marked and rustic benches are placed overlooking the most scenic views.

City parks are meticulously maintained. It is not uncommon for a city to employ 500 or more gardeners. Every two years one of the great city parks is turned into a *Bundesgartenschau*, a federal horticultural exhibition, usually featuring an emphasis such as ecology, organic gardening, landscape architecture, harnessing nature's energy, and the like. The Bundesgartenschaus are held in the odd-numbered years.

Although the first snows often fall in the mountain regions as early as mid-September, autumn can still be a nice season to visit Germany. Many villages in the wine regions celebrate with a *Winzerfest,* when the harvest is in. Winter snows really bring out the beauty of the Hessian and Franconian half-timbered buildings, as well as the painted facades of the Bavarian villages.

Holidays and Store Hours

In addition to the normal holidays (New Year's Day, Easter, Christmas, and the like), all of Germany celebrates Good Friday, Labor Day (May 1), and their national holiday (June 17).

Three Kings (January 6) is a legal holiday in Baden-Wurttemberg and in Bavaria, while Sacraments' Day (the second Thursday after Pentecost) is a legal holiday in predominantly Catholic regions. Maria Ascension Day (midsummer) is a legal holiday in Bavaria and in the Saar Territory. All Saints' Day (November 1) and All Souls' Day (November 2) are legal holidays in predominantly Catholic regions. A Day of Repentance, on the third Wednesday in November, is a holiday in Bavaria. The stores, banks, and post offices are closed on these days.

On some days many restaurants and cafes display a sign: *Heute Ruhetag.* This means that this is the day they spend with their families rather than serving the public.

In general the stores in Germany are open from 9:00 in the morning until 18:30 (6:30) in the evening, with the exception of a two-hour lunch break. Banks are often closed between 13:00 (1:00) and 14:30 (2:30). Money exchanges in all major railroad stations are open continuously between 6:00 in the morning and 21:00 (9:00) in the evening.

Special Rules of the Road

All traffic coming from the right has the right-of-way, even the slower-moving vehicles, unless otherwise indicated. As in other European countries, public transportation (trams, buses, taxis) have the right-of-way over all other traffic. On the Autobahn an advisory speed limit of 130 kilometers an hour (80 miles per hour) is permitted. Traffic moving uphill has the right of way over downhill traffic in the mountain regions.

Passing slower-moving vehicles in heavy traffic is done by taking turns. For a third or fourth car to pull out and pass a whole string of other cars is illegal. When traffic jams or slowdowns cause vehicles to accumulate, those in the right lane are advised to stop or to drive as far to the right as possible and those on the left as far to the left as possible, leaving an unobstructed lane for possible emergency vehicles. Where two heavily traveled roads merge, the principle of blending goes into effect:

one car from the right, one from the left, and so on.

Sleeping in cars along the main highways is forbidden in Germany. Children under twelve are not allowed in the front seat.

The Monetary System

West Germany's monetary unit is the Deutsche Mark (DM). The Mark is divided into 100 Pfennig (Pf.) The money comes in pieces of 1 and 2 Pfennig (in copper, and now seldom seen); 5, 10, and 20 Pfennig (brass), 50 Pfennig (white metal), 1, 2, and 5 Marks (silver alloy). Bank notes are issued in denominations of 5 DM (being withdrawn), 10, 20, 50, 100 DM and higher. All these bills are watermarked and have a fine metallic wire woven into the paper.

THE PALATINATE (PFALZ) AND THE MENNONITES

We start our German itinerary with a tour of the Palatinate not because it is the most important part of West Germany, but because most of the Swiss-German Mennonite families who settled in the Franconia and Lancaster areas of Pennsylvania, in Maryland, in Virginia, and in Ontario, at one time sojourned in the Palatinate for two or more generations. Many of the Swiss-Volhynian families who settled in central Kansas 200 years later also find part of their odyssey here.

If we enter the Palatinate from the west, we probably come through Trier. Arriving from other points within Germany, Mainz or Bingen are our points of entry. Arriving from the south, the first major towns we see are Landau and Zweibrücken.

Named after a Celtic tribe, the Treveri, Trier is the oldest city in Germany. It is, in fact, 1,300 years older than Rome. In AD 117 Trier became the regional capital of the Roman province Belgica Prima and the later the residence of the Roman emperor. With the fall of the Roman Empire, Trier's importance waned but revived when it became the first residence of a Christian bishop north of the Alps.

Even now the Roman presence is still pretty much in evidence in Trier. The Porta Nigra, the mightiest city gate in the entire Roman Empire, still stands, its sandstone portals black and weathered. In 1028 a devout Christian named Simeon had himself bricked into the Porta Nigra's walls in order to spend the last seven years of his life in solitude and prayer.

Trier's Basilica, built around the year 300 by Emperor Constantine, is one of the oldest Christian church buildings in the world. Next to the Pantheon in Rome, Trier's Basilica encloses the largest open interior surviving from the Roman days and stands as proof of the tremendous architectural skills of the Romans. Today the basilica houses a Lutheran congregation.

Adjacent to the basilica stands the bishop's palace. Its present form dates back to the 17th and 18th centuries. Walking through the gardens of the bishop's palace we soon come to the extensive ruins of the Roman imperial baths *(Kaiserthermen)* built during the days of Constantine and

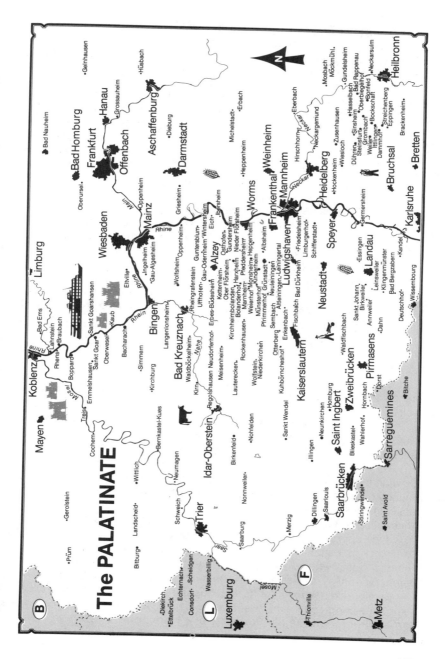

The PALATINATE

N

B
L Luxemburg
F

Mayen
Koblenz
Limburg
Bad Homburg
Hanau
Frankfurt
Offenbach
Aschaffenburg
Darmstadt
Heilbronn
Bruchsal
Bretten
Karlsruhe
Heidelberg
Speyer
Landau
Weinheim
Mannheim
Frankenthal
Ludwigshaven
Worms
Mainz
Wiesbaden
Bingen
Bad Kreuznach
Neustadt
Kaiserslautern
Pirmasens
Zweibrücken
Saint Ingbert
Saarbrücken
Idar-Oberstein
Trier
Sarréguemines
Metz

Rhine
Main
Mosel
Saar
Neckar
Nahe
Rhein

125

expanded under Emperor Gratianus (375-383). A tour of two underground floors shows how the Romans provided for water heating and circulating. Still further along the Olewigstrasse we find a Roman amphitheater dating back to the second century.

Other things to see in Trier are the market square surrounded by beautiful Gothic buildings and the birthplace of Karl Marx. At the Mosel River we find two medieval cranes, once worked by horses on a treadmill.

Mainz, which celebrated its 2,000th birthday in 1962, is one of the oldest settlements along the Rhine. The Romans named it Magontacium and made it the capital of the province of Germania Superior. It was in Mainz that Johann Gutenberg invented the art of printing from individually cast characters.

Among the important things to see in Mainz are the cathedral *(Dom)*, built between the years 975 and 1239, a masterpiece of Romanesque architecture. The Mainzer Dom has a total of six towers of which the mighty central tower (laterna), which crowns the transcept crossing, serves as the city's highly visible trademark.

Across from the Dom we find the Gutenberg Museum of Printing, open daily except Sunday and Monday. The Gutenberg Museum houses a Gutenberg press in the reconstructed workshop of the time and a mass of interesting artifacts related to the history of printing and the technology of papermaking around the world. The museum's prize possession, a 42-line Gutenberg Bible, is kept in a guarded vault, opened to visitors twice daily, 11:00 to 11:30 in the morning and 15:30 (3:30) to 16:00 (4:00) in the afternoon.

Between the Dom and the Gutenberg Museum on the market square stands a town well dating back to 1526, the oldest remaining Renaissance well in Germany.

For lovers of modern architecture, the town hall, designed by the Danish architect Arne Jakobsen, and built between 1971 and 1974, quite strikingly combines Corten steel with sheets of Norway marble.

To the west of Mainz lies Bingen, a small Rhine port serving the wine-growing hinterlands. When we move out of Bingen toward the center of the Palatinate, we soon come to Langenlonsheim, home of Philip of Langenlonsheim, the last martyr in the initial wave of persecution against the Anabaptists. He was executed in 1529 at nearby Bad Kreuznach.

If we approach the Palatinate from France, we enter at Landau, or at Zweibrücken. Landau is the birthplace of the German-American illustrator, Thomas Nast, who designed both the Republican elephant and the Democrat donkey, as well as the North American figure of Santa Claus.

Zweibrücken, known for its fabulous Rosengarten, is also home to the Mennonite congregation of Zweibrücken-Ixheim, the last Amish congregation in Europe to rejoin formally the Mennonite Church in 1937. Zweibrücken was once an important principality, whose territorial holdings stretched almost to the Swiss border. When one of Zweibrücken's ruling princes, Prince Max, became King Max of Bavaria, he transplanted his best farmers, the Mennonites and the Amish, to develop the rough lands along the Danube. In gratitude these Mennonites named one of their Bavarian congregations Maxweiler, now extinct.

For a look at Anabaptist-Mennonite history in the Pfalz, let us start at Alzey. We take the bus or drive our car to the heart of town, the Obermarkt. The bus stops in front of the Nikolaikirche. Inside this church a stone sculpture with seven life-sized figures, depicting the burial of Christ, dates back to 1430.

It is only a few blocks from the church to Rheinhessen Castle, a landmark in Mennonite history. The greater part of the present castle was built between 1250 and the 1500s over the foundations of an earlier Roman stronghold.

The massive round prison tower once held Anabaptist prisoners who lost their lives in the second largest mass execution of Mennonites in history. The *Hutterite Chronicles* placed the number of those executed at 350, based on the testimony of refugees from the Palatinate who reached Moravia. Those who gave up their faith had only their fingers cut off and a cross burned into their forehead with a red-hot iron. After that they were exiled from the Palatinate. Those who remained steadfast, however, were beheaded, drowned, or burned at the stake. The public was so repulsed by this massacre that no further executions took place after 1529.

Thirty years later, around 1560, Anabaptism reappeared in the region in the persons of Hutterite missioners. One of them, Leonard Dax, along with his wife, Anna, and four others were imprisoned in the castle. Not until after peace came to Münster (1648) did the Anabaptists find limited tolerance in the area.

Sixteen kilometers (nine miles) southwest of Alzey, just past the old walled town of Kirchheimbolanden, we find the Weierhof. Once a monastery, secularized during the 1500s, destroyed during the Thirty Years' War, the property was given in hereditary lease to the "Mennist" Peter Krähenbühl (Krehbiel, Kraybill) in 1682.

In his letter to the Pfalzgrave negotiating for the estate, Krähenbühl requested that he and his family be allowed to worship unmolested. The recorded answer given to him by the state council says in part "that what the petitioner wants to read and pray in his house with his children cannot be refused him. But it would have to be done with the express restriction that he will not take on any Anabaptist help or admit any other person of the Anabaptist sect or under any other pretext or appearance form a congregation of such. Otherwise he shall lose even this particular concession and be expelled from the country." Along with Krähenbühl and his nine children, other family names on the Weierhof include Gohl (Galley), Burkhart, Birky (Bergey), Brubacher, Herr, and Ellenberger.

The Rheinhessen castle at Alzey

Today there are two Weierhofs. Closest to the road is the U.S. army base Weierhof, and just beyond it the historic Mennonite settlement. To find the latter, we turn off the main road, make another right, and park on the school grounds.

The old village lies south of the new highway where a sign points to the *Mennonitengemeinde* (Mennonite Church). The road into the village forks twice. We take the first fork left, the second right, and soon we stand in front of the house of Michael Krähenbühl, built in 1712. Notice the initials "M.K." and the date on the half-timbered structure. It was later the home of the well-known Mennonite artist, Daniel Wohlgemuth (1876-1956), whose lithographs and drawings are found in most leading German museums.

Just before we reach the Michael Krähenbühl homestead, through an alley on the right, we can catch a glimpse of a farmhouse. On the second floor of this farmhouse Mennonites were permitted to worship in groups of no more than twenty at a time.

Continuing through the courtyard of the Krähenbühl Hof, we turn left and uphill to the Mennonite cemetery. At the entrance to the cemetery stands an unpretentious and even unattractive little building. This was the first Mennonite meetinghouse, built in 1770. By law it had to resemble a cow shed or a farm storage building so that decent people would not make the mistake of attending the Mennonites' heretical meetings.

In the cemetery graves are cleared away every few years to make room for new ones. Still standing at this time is the grave of the prominent church leader and Mennonite historian, Christian Neff, and his wife, Lydia. "Onkel

Vineyards near Wintersheim

Neff," as he was lovingly called, came up with the idea for Mennonite World Conference and the German *Mennonitisches Lexikon,* which formed the basis for the English *Mennonite Encyclopedia.*

Continuing our tour of the Weierhof on this upward trail we soon come to the back of the current meetinghouse of the Weierhof congregation, built in 1867. The interior was extensively remodeled during the late 1970s. Going down the front steps of the church, we return to the village main street and retrace our steps to the parking lot. That street, by the way, was for centuries *the* highway from France into the German Rhineland and saw the comings and goings of many conquerors, as well as retreating armies and endless lines of miserable prisoners.

The story goes that in the days of Napoleon, citizens were expressly forbidden to show kindness to the prisoners of war, to respond in any way to their pleas for food and water. The Mennonites at the Weierhof kept to the letter of the ordinance, but conveniently dumped a cartload of delicious apples in the gutters along the road past the cemetery. These apples were eagerly picked up by the unfortunate prisoners.

Since the year 1800 the Weierhof has had its own school built up by Michael Löwenberg into an excellent secondary school with boarding facilities. Known as the Gymnasium near the Donnersberg, it became widely known as a quality school among Mennonites and non-Mennonites alike.

Today the school complex occupies nearly all of the space north of the highway which divides the Weierhof. Here we also find the offices of the

German Mennonite Church as well as the rich archives of the German Mennonite Conference.

In addition to the Weierhof, there are many other *Hofs* in the Palatinate of interest to Mennonite historians, genealogists, and others. Nearby we find the Pfrimmerhof and the Münsterhof. Further south are the Kohlhof, the Limburgerhof, and the Branchweilerhof, the Deutschhof, and the Kaplaneihof. Near Zweibrücken we find the Wahlerhof and the Grünbacherhof.

To find the Hofs you will need a good navigator and the map *Rund um Mannheim,* scale 1 to 100,000, published by Haupka and Co., Bad Soden (available in the region's bookstores). The Mennonites, detested heretics for such a long period of their history, were forced to live in semi-seclusion and the ordinary person on the street in Mannheim or Oggersheim still cannot direct you to their former and present hideouts.

From the Weierhof it is not far to Worms on the Rhine, another town with a legendary past history and prestige. On our way to Worms we see several free-standing arches, all that remains of a magnificent railroad viaduct destroyed by General Patton's armies in 1944. Nearby are the villages of Kriegsheim, Monsheim, Pfeddersheim, and Florsheim—places visited by William Penn and his delegation to recruit Quaker and Mennonite settlers for "Penn Sylvania."

In the last village before Worms, Pfifflichheim, we find the remains of an old oak tree under which Martin Luther preached to the peasants before continuing into town to face the Imperial Diet in 1521.

The massive Dom (Cathedral of Worms) soon becomes visible. The Dom of St. Peter is, along with the cathedrals of Mainz and Speyer, one of the most important examples of late-Romanesque style in Germany. The present building, begun under Bishop Burkhard in 1018, was basically completed in its present form by 1171, with the finishing touches and interior details added by 1230. The mighty edifice survived attempts by France's King Louis XIV and the Allied bombs of 1942 to 1945 to destroy it. The cathedral and the *Reichstag* (Imperial Diet) building, which once stood beside it, were the scene of over 100 Imperial Diets or national assemblies.

In 1521 the pope issued a papal bull against Martin Luther and his teachings. Thereupon Emperor Charles V called for an Imperial Diet to be held at Worms and invited Martin Luther to come before it. Luther went there "as though going to his death" but without hesitation and very much encouraged by the enthusiastic crowds along the way. It was at the Diet that he spoke his immortal words, "Here I stand. I cannot do otherwise," and was thereafter banned from the empire.

A reminder of the close cooperation of church and state—the cathedral and the Diet—is the massive *Kaiserportal* (the Emperor's Entrance) cut into the side of the cathedral. It seems that when the emperor and his entourage came to church they did not bother to dismount from their horses. This door is tall enough to accommodate horses and riders, lances, halberds, and banners (the ushers in the Worms Cathedral did more than clean up leftover church bulletins!).

Leaving the Dom we walk around the back of it, stopping to see the recently rejuvenated mosaics which tell us of the changing looks of the Dom and its environment and which lists the bishops and emperors who over the centuries came to hold court in Worms. The mosaics are like a short course in European history. Continuing through the gardens we soon come to the Martin Luther Monument, established in 1868.

One could hardly find a better place to give an illustrated mini-lecture on Reformation history than at the foot of the Luther Monument. Here Luther stands in the center, surrounded by four of the forerunners of the Reformation: Peter Waldo, twelfth century; John Wycliffe, 1330 to 1384; Jan Hus, 1372 to 1415; and Girolamo Savonarolo, 1452 to 1508. At the four corners of the monument we find (in the back) the Protestant theologians Reuchlin and Melanchthon and (up front) Luther's protectors, Phillip of Hesse and Frederick the Wise. Seated women between these corner figures symbolize the cities of Augsburg, Speyer, and Magdeburg, where important events in Lutheran history took place.

The Luther monument in Worms

Among other points of interest in Worms is the Jewish cemetery *(Judenfriedhof)*. In use since the eleventh century, the cemetery has over a thousand ancient gravestones inscribed in Hebrew. It is also one of the better places from which to view the cathedral towers. Not far from the cathedral we find the Church of the Holy Trinity *(Dreifaltigkeitskirche)*. The interior of this church has been adapted to accommodate an exhibit on the Lutheran Reformation. The museum of the city of Worms, located in a former Romanesque monastery, also features special exhibits on Luther among its large historical and artistic collections.

About eleven kilometers (seven miles) north of Worms we find Ibersheim, a village that was destroyed and abandoned after the Thirty Years' War. Mennonite refugees from Bern, Switzerland, reclaimed the land and rebuilt the farms. In 1661—three years before Mennonites elsewhere in Germany received any such concessions—the Mennonites of Ibersheim were recognized as subjects of the Palatinate.

They were even allowed freedom of private (not public) worship, provided that "such not be attended by non-Mennonites living on the estate, much less attract and mislead others of our subjects." The charge was soon made that they abused the privilege. Indeed the inspector discovered in 1671 that the congregation had baptized a formerly Reformed person. The congregation was fined 100 Thaler. It was also noted that 100 persons attended services, far more than the legal limit of twenty. Upon a petition from all the Mennonites in the Palatinate, the law was later amended to read twenty families rather than twenty persons.

After meeting in homes for quite some time, the congregation began to meet in the village school. The present church was built in 1836, the only Mennonite church in south Germany with a tower and a bell. It is also the only church in town. Ibersheim is also the hometown of the Mennonite illustrator and sculptor Fritz Kehr.

South of Worms we find Frankenthal, site of the Frankenthal Debates of 1571. This series was an important discussion between representatives of the Reformed and Lutheran denominations on the one side and the Anabaptists on the other. Since Frankenthal was heavily bombed during World War II little remains there to remind us of that former era and occasion.

A DAY ON THE RHINE

The Rhine is one of the world's most scenic, romantic, and historic rivers and no tour of Germany is complete without a cruise on the Rhine River. I say this without qualification, having made the trip perhaps forty times—first mostly on steam-powered paddlewheelers during the fifties, later on the more recent proud superliners of the inland waters, and once on a hydrofoil.

Although there are six-day cruises from Rotterdam, Holland, to Basel,

The Rhine: treasures of scenery and history

Switzerland, many people travel only the section between Cologne and Mainz, or part of it. The cost of such a trip is not unreasonable, and holders of a Eurail pass may ride the ships free.

There are two classes of ships—the locals, which stop at all towns, and the faster *Schnellfahrt,* (express runs). The *Schnellfahrt,* which leaves Cologne at 7:00 in the morning, is the only trip that runs daily all the way from Cologne to Mainz.

Each of the ships has one or two restaurants and a self-service cafeteria, a shop from which to buy postcards and souvenirs, and a barber shop. Good books found on board explain the castles on the Rhine and a small booklet, entitled *The Finest Legends of the Rhine,* is available. A purser on board provides limited postal and banking services.

For a first-time Rhine River trip an upstream ride is recommended (14 miles per hour against the mighty current) instead of the downriver (24 miles per hour) run.

If time or money is limited, our itinerary may include only that section between Koblenz and and Bacharach. However, by boarding at Koblenz, we will also have to compete for the best deck chairs with hordes of tourists from the international package tours. The sights along the river, the stories and the legends behind them, are explained to passengers over the public-address system in three languages. We will see dozens and dozens of castles, luscious vineyards, ancient towns and cities, the legendary Lorelei, and the never-ending spectacle of life on the river itself. For Mennonite readers, I'd like to point out a few additional sites not explained on the public-address system.

The Thirty Years' War (1618 to 1648) left many towns along the Rhine in ruins, its citizens killed or dispersed. Such was the case with Langendorf, a town once located where the Wied joins the Rhine. In 1652 the landowner Count Friedrich III von Wied wished to establish a new town: Neuwied. To attract people to help him build it, he offered freedom of worship to all, even to the Mennonites. The Mennonite refugees—skilled weavers, farmers, and clockmakers—made a real contribution to the new town's economy.

In 1758, Count Alexander, one of Friedrich's descendants, ordered the Mennonites to build a meetinghouse across from his castle, and on November 6, 1768, the meetinghouse was dedicated in the presence of the count and his family. This old church still stands. Today it is rarely used since the number of Mennonites in Neuwied after World War II has twice grown dramatically—first, through the influx of displaced persons from the east in 1945 and more recently by the arrival of Russian Mennonites *Umsiedler* (resettlers).

Across from Neuwied, beyond Andernach on the way to the Eiffel Mountains, we find a number of former Amish-Mennonite farms: the Kräherhof, the Pönterhof, and Jacobstahl, and a small cemetery in the woods near Eich.

From Bacharach it is only two kilometers (just over a mile) uphill to the little town of Steeg. Members of the Virginia Mennonite Healwole family like to make the pilgrimage to the Hütwohl wineries in Steeg. The name Hütwohl also shows up around Alzey.

THE LOWER RHINE

The Lower Rhine, between Cologne and the Dutch border, had long been the home of independent Christian movements and persons such as Thomas à Kempis, the Brethren of the Common Life, and Meister Eckardt. Thus the soil was well prepared for the later Anabaptists. Very early in our history Anabaptist congregations were formed at Julich, at Millen, Born, Aachen, at Gogh, Kleve, Emmerich, Rees, Krefeld, Rheydt, and in Cologne itself. Of these congregations all but Krefeld have become extinct. Menno Simons himself spent about two years in Cologne.

Cologne, established as a Roman outpost by Emperor Claudius in AD 50, offers its visitors 2,000 years of history packed in a semicircle of not more than two square kilometers (five square miles) of the old inner city. Any brief attempt to summarize Cologne is an exercise in frustration. The *Michelin Guide* does it in six pages of fine print; the usually short-and-to-the-point *Knaurs Kultürfuhrer* gives it sixteen pages. The Kölner Dom (cathedral), one of the most famous in the world, took over 600 years to complete (1248-1880). First-time visitors will be overwhelmed by the sheer size of this edifice. The twin-spired facade in full Gothic style and covered with thousands of sculptures is especially impressive. Each of the Dom's lacy spires rises to a height of 157 meters (515 feet). Ambitious persons may climb one of the towers for a beautiful view of the city.

On the Dom square we find a remnant of the old Roman northeast gate into the city. To the south side of the Dom we find a section of the old Roman harbor road. The Roman-Germanic museum contains three floors of Roman finds, ranging from mosaic floors to a complete temple, a very precious collection of old Roman glass and ceramics, as well as objects from the barbarian and early Christian civilizations.

Older than the Dom itself is the great St. Martin's church, built in Romanesque style between 1185 and 1220. A few blocks up the Rhine from there we find the ultra-modern St. Severin's bridge, a 756-meter (2,480 ft.) long suspension bridge hung from one single central pylon. From this bridge and from the older *Hohenzollernbrücke* there are excellent panoramic views of the old city.

Cologne: from Roman outpost to modern metropolis

The first Mennonite refugees coming from Jülich, Kleve, and Rheydt arrived in Krefeld some time around 1600. Many of them were weavers and contributed to the establishment of Krefeld as an important textile center for several centuries.

In 1683 thirteen families of Krefelder weavers, (all of them until the 1670s members of the Mennonite congregation, but recently having joined the Quakers), left for America. There they founded Germantown, Pennsylvania, now part of Philadelphia. In 1920 a monument to these departing weavers, the so-called *Weberdenkmal* (monument to the weavers), was erected in Krefeld. Other Mennonite and Quaker families from the Rhineland followed the 1683 pioneers in great number.

In 1695 the Mennonites of Krefeld were finally allowed to build a meetinghouse. This church was enlarged in 1843 and partly destroyed by Allied bombs 100 years later in 1943. In 1950 the church was rebuilt.

The history of Krefeld cannot be told without mentioning the van der Leyens, a Mennonite refugee family which came to Krefeld around 1669. For generations these creative linen weavers guided the development of both the congregation and the city. In Krefeld, the van der Leyens pioneered in orderly city planning (six planned additions were made to Krefeld before the van der Leyens lost their prominence).

To improve the quality of congregational life the van der Leyens set aside a sizable endowment to send their ministers to the Dutch Mennonite

Krefeld: the weavers' monument

Krefeld: the town hall

seminary in Amsterdam and specified that from their fund "a well educated and capable preacher should be paid 100 Thaler annually." The van der Leyen endowment to the Mennonite church of Krefeld lasted until the end of World War I, when the defeat of Germany and accompanying inflation wiped it out.

The town hall of Krefeld, van der Leyenplatz number 1, was once the private home of one of the van der Leyens (built 1791-1794). The estate Neu Leyental, in Empire-style, was built in the 18th century as a summer home for the van der Leyens.

When these Quaker-Mennonite pioneers left Krefeld for America in 1683, they were soon followed by thousands of other Germans in a never-ending stream. The German states, alarmed at losing so large a percentage of their population, hastily erected more than fifty customs stations along the Rhine, at which the *Amerika-fahrer* were made to pay exorbitant emigration taxes. Of these customs fortresses Zons-Dormagen stands practically unchanged. Inside the fortress walls the emigrants waited out endless delays in the inns and hostels which were conveniently owned by the customs officers.

BETWEEN THE NORTH SEA AND THE BALTIC

East Friesland was the scene of early Anabaptist activities beginning with the appearance of Melchior Hofmann as traveling evangelist in the 1530s. Hofmann's baptism of 300 persons in Emden not only marks the emergence of the Anabaptist movement in North Germany but in Northwest Europe as well. From Emden, Jan Volkertsz van Trijpmaker took the message to the Low Countries. Later, thousands of Anabaptist refugees from Flanders to Friesland streamed into East Friesland, where they experienced relative freedom. Among those who found a home here during the days of most violent persecution in Holland were Dirck Philips, Leenaert Bouwens, Hans de Ries, and Menno Simons himself. It was in East Friesland in 1549 that the Anabaptists were first called "Mennists."

Schleswig-Holstein, now part of Germany, was Danish during the days of the Reformation. Anabaptist refugees from Holland and Flanders also found refuge here (at first especially in the rural areas) during the 16th century and later. Though most municipalities issued edicts against the Anabaptists and often ordered Mennonites to join the Lutheran congregations, Mennonites did enjoy full rights and privileges in Wüstenfelde, in Glückstadt, and later in Altona. But not until 1863 was a law passed that made it possible for Mennonites to move about freely throughout the entire province.

Today only a few of North Germany's historic Mennonite communities remain. In East Friesland they are Emden, Norden, and Leer. In Schleswig-Holstein they are Hamburg-Altona and Friedrichstadt. More recent congregations and fellowships have been established at Lübeck, Kiel, and Wedel.

HANSESTADT HAMBURG

Hamburg is Germany's second largest city—only Berlin is larger. Along with Lübeck and Bremen, Hamburg retains its old title of a Free and Hanseatic City and with it the status of an independent city state. We notice the HH on the license plates—Hansestadt Hamburg. During the Middle Ages Hamburg profited from the peculiar conditions of the North Sea and Baltic trades. Only lumber and grain ships risked the stormy weather around the north of Denmark, while all other cargoes were unloaded at Lubeck and transported overland to Hamburg and vice versa. Hamburg somehow managed to stay out of the Thirty Years' War and was saved the terrible destruction suffered by most other German cities.

Hamburg grew as a port (today the fifth largest in the world), especially after the independence of the United States and the cultivation of Latin America as a region of important resources. Until World War I the *Hamburg Amerika Linie* was the largest steamship company in the world.

Where other cities have a city center, Hamburg has a lake, the Alster, around which we find grouped the town hall, the city's main road (the Jungfernstieg), five historic churches (the Sankt Jakobi, the Sankt Katherine, the Sankt Peter, the Sankt Nikolai, and the Sankt Michaelis), the Gänsemarkt (goose market), and the opera house. Hamburg, long the most powerful trading metropolis in the world, suffered two great fires, one in 1713 and the other in 1842, and heavy bombing during the Second World War.

In 1601 Mennonites were allowed to settle just outside Hamburg at Altona in an area called the Grosse Freiheit (Great Freedom). The growth of the Mennonite-owned shipping industry benefited the whole city. From 1723 on, with some interruptions, the Mennonites of Hamburg have maintained their own schools until well into the 19th century.

The original Mennonite meetinghouse on the Grosse Freiheit was lost in the fire of 1713. On its site a new meetinghouse was built in 1715. In 1916, during World War I, the congregation erected a new meetinghouse, parish house, and parsonage in Altona on the Mennonitenstrasse 20. The extensive archives and library, which were begun in 1747, are housed in it.

During the American bombings of July 1943 nearly one third of Hamburg's Mennonites lost their homes and property and some lost their lives. The van der Smissen Allee, the Dennerstrasse, the old church in the Grosse Freiheit, and a chapel in the new city were completely leveled. Fortunately, the new church and building, including the irreplaceable archives, though severely damaged, survived when the block-buster bomb which fell within a few feet of the church failed to explode, although the shock of impact caused the roof of the fellowship hall to cave in. In 1946 these buildings were in use again, and in 1948 the restoration was completed.

There are many worthwhile things to do in Hamburg, including a 50-

minute boat trip on the Alster. There are frequent departures between 10:00 and 16:00 (4:00) o'clock. Hour-long boat trips on the harbor are offered between 9:00 in the morning and 18:00 (6:00) o'clock. The Hagenbeck Zoo, established in 1907, one of the most advanced zoos in the world, is popular with zoologists and animal researchers.

Hamburg's Planten un Blomen Park is a proving ground for new and hybrid varieties of flowers, shrubs, and trees. Admission is twenty Pfennig during the daytime and 80 Pfennig at night, when the park features programmed lights, music, and fountains.

HANSESTADT LUBECK

Founded during the 1100s, Lübeck was the capital of the Hanseatic League, an association of Dutch and German ports which, from the 12th to the 16th century, controlled the trade in northern Europe. Lübeck's town center still reflects those days of glory when Lübeck and Cologne, on the Rhine were Germany's largest cities. The completion of the Stecknitz Canal in 1389 was not only a great technical accomplishment for its time, but it assured Lubeck a leading place in the salt trade.

Between 1535 and the 1700s there were often Mennist people in the city, although officially they were not tolerated. Lübeck's common citizens, however, liked the Nederlanders (Menno Simons himself spent some time in the city during the 1540s). With the influx of Danzig and West Prussian Mennonite displaced persons during the 1950s, a new congregation was organized at Lubeck.

The Holstentor, an enormous twin-towered city gate built in 1478, secures the port city from the land side. From the beginning it was as much a symbol of prestige as it was a defense structure. As a tourist in Germany you will probably have a picture of the Holstentor in your pocket (it appears on Germany's fifty-Mark note). Just beyond the Holstentor, along the Trave, we find the Salzspeicher, a group of 16th- and 17th-century red brick warehouses in which the salt coming from Lüneburg was stored. The Dutch influence in Lübeck is seen in the Gothic town hall built from 1230 onward along two sides of the market square. A stone stairway in Dutch Renaissance style was added in 1594.

The composer Dietrich Buxtehude, though not born in Lübeck, spent most of his adult life in the city, serving as organist and cantor of St. Mary's Church from 1668 until his death in 1707. Lübeck was also the birthplace of Willy Brandt, former chancellor of Germany and winner of the Nobel Peace Prize.

Between Hamburg and Lübeck on Route 75 we find Bad Oldesloe, the place where Menno Simons lived and worked in relative security during his final years. Bad Oldesloe and the smaller village of Wüstenfelde belonged to the Danish count, Bartholomeus von Ahlefeldt.

Menno moved here, possibly from Lübeck, in the summer of 1554 and

The Menno-Kate near Bad Oldesloe

died in Wüstenfelde on January 31, 1561. The village of Wustenfelde was leveled during the Thirty Years' War, but the Menno-Kate and printshop remain. In this modest little cottage the printing of Menno Simons works continued until seven years after his death. In front of it stands the large and ancient linden tree supposedly planted by Menno himself. The cottage and the tree are located along the Segebergstrasse.

THE MUNSTER TRAGEDY

The story of Münster and Munsterite Anabaptism is a long and complicated one and almost impossible to summarize. *The Mennonite Encyclopedia* devotes seven pages to it and the historian Cornelius Krahn reports that there are probably more books, articles, poems, and dramas based on Münster than on any other aspect of Mennonite history. And the last words have not yet been written.

The city of Münster is located at the meeting point of several ancient European trade routes. Before the year 300 early Christian missionaries established a monastery to provide the weary travelers with physical and spiritual nourishment—*Monasterilum* (Münster). The city became a bishopric in 804, and a member of the Hanseatic League in 1300.

The city, ruled by powerful craftsmen and trade guilds, was quite receptive to the Reformation, and by 1532 all but one of the city's churches had become Evangelical. These independent Evangelicals accepted Anabaptist innovation, and by 1534 the city was governed by Anabaptists with Bernhard Knipperdolling as the mayor of Münster.

What happened next is hard to describe in a few sentences. The Spanish had begun to persecute the Anabaptists in Holland, Flanders, and Friesland with such ferocity that some Anabaptists actually came to believe that the end time had come. Then the baker Jan Matthijs of Haarlem had an apocalyptic vision in which he saw Münster as the New Jerusalem. Soon thousands of sorely persecuted Anabaptists saw Jan Matthijs' vision as a divine message of deliverance.

From Amsterdam and elsewhere the Anabaptists sailed across the Zuiderzee and started walking toward Münster. In spite of the fact that hundreds were arrested, tortured, and put to death, still greater numbers succeeded in reaching Münster. One eyewitness, Hermann von Gresbeck, reports that Anabaptists from Holland and Friesland continued to arrive in Münster day and night.

The development of an Anabaptist power in his territory greatly annoyed Bishop Franz von Waldeck. He succeeded in bringing together an unlikely coalition of Catholic and Lutheran armies who were willing for the time being to forget their mutual animosity to fight a common enemy, the Anabaptists. Münster came under siege.

On April 4, 1534, Jan Matthijs had the foolhardy inspiration to go outside the city walls with a handful of followers to disperse the enemy as in the days of Gideon. He was killed in the attempt. Later, there was the episode with Hille Feyken, a young woman who sacrificed herself in her attempt to reenact the apocryphal story of Judas and Holofernes. She too was captured and her body was chopped to bits.

Within the walls of Münster, the leadership was passed on to Jan van Leyden, who governed the city with twelve elders. Van Leyden taught that the people within Münster were the children of light fighting against the children of darkness, the bishop's armies. In time he proclaimed himself to be the new King David of an Old-Testament-oriented earthly kingdom of God.

Before we become too critical of this development, we should remember that the ruthless persecution the Anabaptists experienced in the Low Countries could lead only to desperation and fanaticism among people whose true shepherds had already been eliminated by fire and the sword.

The Münster Anabaptists managed to hold out for a long time, but on January 25, 1535, the city fell to the bishop. The victorious Catholic and Lutheran armies conducted a great massacre from which only a few managed to escape. The leaders, Jan van Leyden, Bernhard Knipperdolling, and Bernard Krechting, were cruelly tortured then sent to various parts of the country to be displayed as freaks, and finally they were killed on January 23,

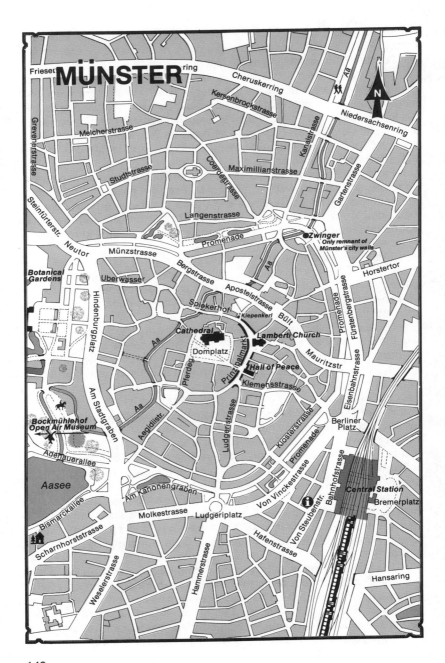

MÜNSTER

Frieset ring / Cheruskerring / Kersenbrockstrasse / Niedersachsenring

Grevenerstrasse / Melcherstrasse / Kanalstrasse

Studtstrasse / Coerdestrasse / Maximillianstrasse / Gartenstrasse

Langenstrasse

Steinfürterstr. / Promenade / Zwinger
Only remnant of Münster's city walls

Neutor / Münzstrasse / Bergstrasse / Aa / Horstertor

Botanical Gardens / Uberwasser / Apostelstrasse / Büt / Fürstenbergstrasse / Promenade

Hindenburgplatz / Spiekerhof / Kiepenkerl

Cathedral / Lamberti Church

Aa / Domplatz / Prinzipalmarkt / Hall of Peace / Mauritzstr. / Eisenbahnstrasse

Pferdeg. / Klemensstrasse

Am Stadtgraben / Aegidiistr. / Aa / Ludgeristrasse / Klosterstrasse / Berliner Platz

Bockmühlenhof Open Air Museum

Adenaueraallee

Aasee / Am Kanonengraben / Promenade / Von Vinckestrasse

Bismarckallee / Molkestrasse / Ludgeriplatz / Von Steubenstr. / Bahnhofstrasse / Central Station / Bremerplatz

Scharnhorststrasse / Weselerstrasse / Hammerstrasse / Hafenstrasse

Hansaring

1536. Their corpses were hung from the tower of the St. Lamberti Church in three iron cages which still can be seen today.

The Münster tragedy was exploited by the Catholics to criticize and combat Protestantism in general and the Reformers conveniently used the Münsterite label for all Anabaptists, including the peaceful Swiss Brethren and the Obbenites of Holland.

Any walking tour of Münster must begin on the Prinzipalmarkt, the most historic, most beautiful, and busiest street in town. The unbroken row of elegant houses with the Renaissance gables were once the residences of rich traders.

Walking along the Prinzipalmarkt, we soon come to the Lamberti Church. If we look up the length of the tower, we will see the three cages in which the bodies of van Leyden, Krechting, and Knipperdolling were once displayed as a gruesome lesson against heresy. The graceful tower itself is 99 meters (323 ft.) tall. The church structure as a whole is considered a significant example of late-Gothic architecture.

Continuing along the curving Prinzipalmarkt we come to a restaurant, the Kiepenkerl, named in honor of the earliest medieval barter traders who came to Münster. A delightful statue of such a *Kiepenkerl* with his wares stands on the little square beside the restaurant.

Just a little farther we turn left to follow a path along the Aa, a small tributary of the Ems River which divides the city. Crossing the first bridge we come to we approach the massive Dom (cathedral) from the rear. The earliest parts of this cathedral date back to the 11th century. We enter the church through the 16th-century south portal. Inside is a large sanctuary surrounded by an ambulatory. There is also an astronomical clock dating back to 1542.

On the Market Square beside the Dom, Jan van Leyden erected a tribune and held court during the last days of the New Jerusalem (1534-1535).

From the Dom Square we return to the Prinzipalmarkt. Straight ahead of us now we see the magnificent Rathaus (town hall) dating back to the 14th century. Inside the Rathaus we find the Hall of Peace. In this richly adorned hall the Treaty of Westphalia (Peace of Münster) was signed in 1648, which ended the Eighty Years' War between Holland and Spain and the Thirty Years' War over the rest of Central Europe. The Peace of Münster resulted in the reorganization of Europe with considerable loss of prestige to the popes and emperors. The treaty recognized the independence of Holland and Switzerland.

The woodwork in the Hall of Peace dates back to 1577. Along the walls we see the painted portraits of the kings and the delegates who signed the peace agreement. Upon request an English tape will be played to tell you the story of the interior of the Hall of Peace.

Among other points of interest in Münster is the residence of the

Münster: the Hall of Peace on the Prinzipalmarkt

prince bishop, built from 1767 to 1787. This late baroque structure today houses several faculty families of the university. We should also visit the Bockmühlehaus, a small open-air museum along the Aasee with a number of original Westphalian rural buildings grouped around a very picturesque windmill.

Near Münster in the Westphalian countryside we find a large number of beautiful moated castles. Once the last refuge of farmers and peasants in times of war, these castles now sleep peacefully on their islands, mirrored in the quiet waters of their moats. There are more than two dozen of them. The city of Münster has a folder, which is available at the Hall of Peace, listing five suggested routes, each of which leads you to five or six of these castles.

GREEN HILLS AND SLATE HOUSES

South of Münster we find the Sauerland, a wooded mountain region which forms the hinterlands to the Ruhr Basin, for which it furnishes water and power by means of dams and reservoirs. Here we find both half-timbered houses in striking black and white, and houses with slate siding and roofs. Sauerland was home to the colonial Pennsylvania schoolmaster, Christopher Dock, and the pioneer Germantown printer, Christopher Sauer.

The Church of the Brethren had its beginning in Schwarzenau on the Eder. Alexander Mack baptized the first members of the fellowship in the Eder River here in 1708. Mack and his followers eventually migrated to Germantown, Pennsylvania. The kinship between Mennonites, Brethren, and Quakers—the three historic peace churches—has always been close. Little evidence remains in Schwarzenau to remind us of the Brethren beginnings except for the naming of a street and a school, the Alexander Mack Schule.

Interesting features of the Sauerland architecture are the lengthy inscriptions on the beams of the half-timbered houses. Some of these provide historical-genealogical information. Others are pious verses and proverbs. Some of these texts also appear on the *Fraktur Vorschriften* (samples of Gothic handwriting) of eastern Pennsylvania and the Niagara peninsula of Ontario.

THE BLACK FOREST

The Black Forest *(Schwarzwald)* is a mountain range which stretches more than 170 kilometers (100 miles) between Karlsruhe and Basel across the Rhine from a similar range, the Vosges in France. Between these mountains lies the Rhine River Plain. The Black Forest and the Vosges are similar in height and both are densely wooded.

The highest point in the Black Forest is the Feldberg, at 1,493 meters (4,899 feet). In the Vosges the highest point is the Grand Ballon at 1,424 meters (4,674 ft.). Because of the density of the trees these high points rarely provide good lookouts, but here and there a steel observation tower fills the need. On clear autumn days it is sometimes possible to see even the Swiss Alps from here.

The northern Black Forest is crossed by several large valleys, such as the Neckar, the Kinzig, and the Murg. The beauty of the woods and streams, the quaint architecture of the Black Forest farm homes, the peace and quiet of the land, the many mineral springs, both warm and cold, have made the Black Forest a popular vacation region for centuries. For Mennonites there is the additional dimension of Anabaptist-Mennonite history.

For tour purposes the region is often divided into the northern Black Forest with the adjacent areas of Baden-Württemberg and the southern Black Forest with the Lake of Constance (Bodensee).

THE WITNESS OF MICHAEL SATTLER

Michael Sattler was born at Stauffen near Freiburg im Breisgau around 1490. The *Hutterite Chronicles* tell us that he was a learned man. Certainly his writings give testimony to that fact. As far as we know he received his education at the University of Freiburg. Michael Sattler entered the Benedictine monastery of Sankt Peter, where he rapidly rose to the position of prior, second only to the abbot.

While in office Sattler began to study the writings of the apostle Paul, only to discover that the ways of life at the monastery were not in harmony with the scriptural teachings on Christian righteousness. In fact the corrupt and immoral lives of the monks and priests and nuns around him so horrified Michael Sattler that he left the order. Soon thereafter Sattler surfaced in Zurich where, under the influence of another native of the Black Forest, Wilhelm Reublin, he joined the Anabaptists. He soon became one of their most zealous missioners.

Although Sattler's major area of activity probably was in the southern Black Forest, Sattler turned up again in Zurich to participate in the Great Debate of November 1525, for which he was arrested and later expelled. He returned to the Breisgau to resume his missionary activities. Because of Austria's absolute intolerance of Anabaptism in that region, he decided to cross the Rhine into Strasbourg, where he spent some time with the reformers Capito and Bucer.

In the fall of 1526 Sattler left Strasbourg to serve the emerging Anabaptist congregations at Horb and Rottenburg. Michael Sattler won a large following, especially around Horb. In the late winter of 1527 Sattler traveled to Schleitheim on the Swiss-German border to help draw up the Brotherly Agreement, also known as the Schleitheim Confession, finalized on February 24, 1527.

As he was on his way home from Schleitheim the congregations at Horb and Rottenburg were betrayed to the authorities. When Sattler

The Benedictine monastery of Sankt Peter in Schwarzwald

reached Horb, he and his wife, plus Reublin's wife, and some others were arrested. The government had made a valuable catch. For on Sattler they found not only the seven articles of the Brotherly Agreement, but important plans for the further evangelization of the Black Forest region.

The government, seeing that most of the population sided with Michael Sattler and his friends, feared a revolt, so Sattler was removed to Binsdorf under heavy guard. A long letter, which he wrote to the congregation at Horb while in prison, has been preserved.

At that time the Black Forest was under the jurisdiction of the Austrian rulers. They decided to make Sattler's trial a show trial with the required presence of all leading personalities in order to teach them once and for all how the Anabaptist heretics should be dealt with.

To their credit the Tübingen, Strasbourg, Freiburg, and other universities were unwilling to send their jurists to take part in this trial with a predetermined outcome—the death penalty. Finally, Ensisheim (in the Alsace) provided several men willing to do this dishonorable job.

Michael Sattler was returned to Rottenburg, where the trial was held May 15-18, 1527. Nine charges were read against Michael Sattler and the brothers and sisters with him. The complete record of this trial can be found in the *Martyrs Mirror*, in *The Mennonite Encyclopedia*, and in John Howard Yoder's biography, *The Legacy of Michael Sattler*, all available from the publisher of this tourguide.

Michael Sattler was taken from the courthouse to the market square and a piece was cut from his tongue. Then he was forged to a cart, tortured

147

with red hot pliers, and taken out of town to be burned on the shores of the Neckar. The execution of the others took place during the next week, and Sattler's wife was drowned in the Neckar eight days after her husband's death.

There are many places of interest to visit to learn firsthand more of the Michael Sattler story. Among them is Stauffen, Sattler's birthplace, which has a lovely little market square and a brightly painted Rathaus. On top of a hill just out of town we find the ruins of Stauffenberg Castle, surrounded by lush vineyards. We may also visit Sankt Peter im Schwarzwald, the Benedictine abbey of which Michael Sattler was prior. This abbey was established by the end of the 11th century. Because the territory was long under Austrian rule, the massive abbey has a distinct Austrian style of architecture. The present baroque facade dates back to 1724-1729.

Freiburg im Breisgau, one of the most attractive cities in Southwest Germany, is located in the Upper Rhine Plains, halfway between the Black Forest and the river. The town was founded by the dukes of Zahringen in the twelfth century, the same family which founded Bern and Thun in Switzerland. The old university city is clustered around a late-Romanesque red sandstone cathedral built between the early 1200s and 1513. There is a good view of the whole city from the top of the Schlossberg, six minutes from downtown by cablecar.

Horb on the Neckar is a pleasant small town. The Rathaus Market (surrounded by its stuccoed or half-timbered houses) and the church are worth a short visit. Horb was the site of one of Sattler's ill-fated congregations.

Rottenburg on the Neckar

Rottenburg on the Neckar is a 700-year-old small city clustered around St. Martin's Dom (1424-1491). On the market square we find the Rathaus, the fourth town hall on the same site. The trial of Michael Sattler was held in one of its early editions. Between the Rathaus and St. Martin's Dom we find the town fountain, a gift to the town from Archduchess Machtild in the 1470s. Rottenburg still has several sections of its old city walls and the remains of five old defense towers. In 1527 Michael Sattler was taken twenty minutes beyond the city walls toward Tübingen, where he was burned along the Neckar. A memorial plaque to Michael Sattler is found in the Evangelical Lutheran Church on the Kirchgasse along the river.

EXPLORING THE BLACK FOREST

In order that tourists may really experience the Black Forest the government has established a number of special highways. The most important among these are the Schwarzwald Hochstrasse (the Black Forest High Level Road), the oldest and still the most spectacular of these roads. It begins at Baden-Baden.

This road, the epitome of peace and quiet, is surrounded by the stillness of immense pine forests. There are about twenty rustic mountain inns along the way, if we care to linger.

Beyond Freudenstadt the road, numbered B500, continues as the Schwarzwald Höhenstrasse (the Black Forest Plateau Road) all the way down to the Swiss border at Waldshut.

Another tourist highway is the Schwarzwald Tälerstrasse, (the Black Forest Valleys Road) (numbered B46 and B294), which winds for 100 scenic and romantic kilometers (60 miles) through the valleys of the Murg and the Kinzig. This road starts at Rastatt and ends at Alpirsbach.

In addition there is the shorter Schwarzwald Panoramastrasse (Black Forest Panoramic Road) from Waldkirch past Breitnau to Hinterzarten in the Southern Black Forest. This road leads past Sankt Peter's Monastery.

In the winter the Black Forest offers 600 kilometers (375 miles) of long-distance cross-country ski trails and 500 kilometers (300 miles) of regional ski trails. The trail system includes meeting points, trail huts, lodges, and even a system-wide backpack transfer service (for a fee). Detailed water- and snow-proof maps of the entire trail system are available.

The beautiful Kinzig Valley is of more than a passing interest to us because the Anabaptist engineer-theologian Pilgram Marpeck once worked here. For the city of Strasbourg he built a series of channel dams, making it possible to float the valuable lumber down to the Rhine. But he was discharged from his job because he continued to hold Anabaptist meetings in those places where he lived and worked.

Gutach, in the heart of the Black Forest is located in a nine kilometer (4 mile) long valley with the most beautiful of the old Black Forest farmhouses. Here we also find the open air museum, Vogtsbauernhof. Grouped

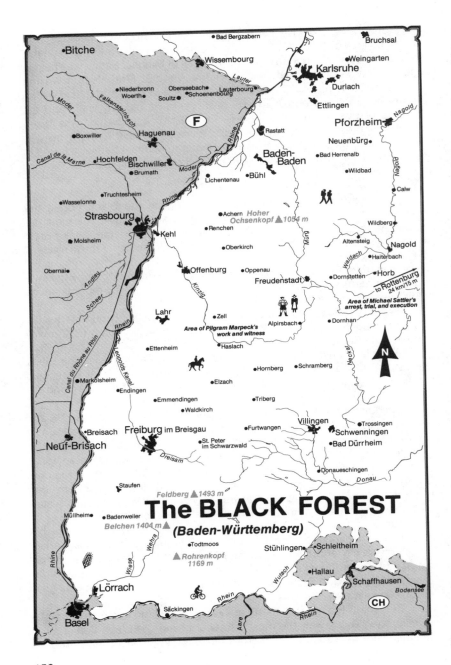

The **BLACK FOREST**
(Baden-Württemberg)

The Black Forest

around an original large farmhouse dating back to 1570, we find a number of other farm buildings dating back to the 16th and 17th centuries. All machinery in the small village is driven by waterpower and can still be put in operation. In Gutach the traditional costume can still be seen, especially on Sundays and holidays.

In the areas around Triberg, Titisee, and Lenzerheide, we may see cuckoo clocks being made. However, cuckoo clocks, ranging from cheap and trashy to handmade works of art, are available throughout the region. When it comes to cuckoo clocks, we usually get what we pay for .

BAVARIA, THE ROOF GARDEN OF GERMANY

Bavaria, the largest state in the German Federation, has long been one of Europe's most popular vacation regions. It is a country of amazing variety from the glamour of its capital, Munich, to the majesty of its Alpine peaks, from the friendliness of its citizens to the incomparable riches of its art and architecture.

In Bavaria the welcome mat was not always out for the Anabaptists. Between 1527 and the 1600s Bavaria's laws regarding them were exceedingly simple. "All Anabaptists will be punished with death. Those who recant will be beheaded. Those who remain stubborn will be burned. Henceforth, none of them will escape execution, even if they recant." *The Martyrs Mirror* records more than 200 martyrs in Bavaria and their memory also lives on in the hymns of the *Ausbund* (see page 158). By the late 1590s the Anabaptists had pretty well disappeared from Bavaria.

Two hundred years later another ruler, King Max I of Bavaria, was more favorably inclined toward the Mennonites and Amish. He remembered them as the best of his farmers on his estate back home in the

Palatinate and invited them to Bavaria. The settlers worked hard for him to turn the tremendous marshes along the Danube into useful farmland. But very few families settled there permanently.

The reason for the early migration of many of these families was a Bavarian law of 1805 which stated that no religious group could be relieved from military obligations. However, for 185 guilders a substitute could be hired. But that was a huge sum of money at that time. Since the Amish and Mennonites had large families and the years of military obligation were many, they simply went broke trying to purchase exemptions. This situation in Bavaria and also in Alsace-Lorraine led to the large-scale migration of Amish and Mennonites to Ontario and to the American Midwest, usually to Illinois.

ART AND ARCHITECTURE IN MUNICH

Munich (München), capital of Bavaria, the third-largest city in Germany, is a cultural center of major importance, rich in architectural treasures of the first order. Great writers and poets, from Goethe to Thomas Mann, and from Heinrich Heine to Gottfried Keller, described their impressions of Munich. We find the most eloquent testimony, however, in the words of Thomas Wolfe who wrote, "How can one speak of Munich but to say that it is a kind of German heaven. Some people sleep and dream that they are in paradise. But all over Germany people dream that they have gone to Munich in Bavaria and really, in an astonishing way, the city is a great Germanic dream translated in life."

The city's rise to power began in the 1150s when Count Heinrich der Löwe von Babenberg und Sachsen destroyed a bridge at Fohring owned by the bishop of Freising. Then he built a new one at Munich, forcing all trade to pass through his city, then only a cluster of houses.

Between the 16th and the 19th century, the kings of Bavaria, knowledgeable patrons of the arts, attracted to Munich scores of architects, sculptors, painters, composers, poets, and dancers, as well as many scientists. In 1802 the Bavarian State University was moved from Landshut on the Isar to Munich.

Generations of architects and artisans have embellished the city with churches, palaces, theaters and art galleries, parks and botanical gardens. Bavaria's secretary of state Benjamin von Rumford introduced the potato to Europe, and George Ohm discovered the laws of electrical resistance. Justus von Liebig invented such items as artificial fertilizer and the bouillon cube, Wilhelm Rontgen pioneered in X-rays and Ferdinand Sauerbruch performed the first lung surgery.

The Norwegian writer Henrik Ibsen wrote a number of his dramas in Munich, and Thomas Mann, who won the Nobel Prize for literature, lived there for forty years. Richard Wagner and Richard Strauss lived and composed in Munich at the invitation of King Ludwig II. Paul Klee, Vassily Kandinsky, and Franz Marc all lived and painted in Munich. To this day Munich is also an important center of quality printing and publishing, particularly of coffee-table-size art books.

The heart of Munich, between the Karlstor and the Marienplatz, is one large pedestrian zone served by underground mass transit and surrounded by busy main traffic arteries. To get into that area, we use the underground passageways, rather than attempt to cross the streets. Munich's drivers are said to hold the world's speed records for commuter traffic.

Along the way we find the late-Gothic Frauenkirche with its twin towers, the old Rathaus, built between 1470 and 1480, and the neo-Gothic new Rathaus of the 1860s. Its carillon and Glockenspiel, Germany's largest, is one of Munich's main attractions.

Around 11:00 in the morning, the crowd collects on the square and every eye is focused on the new Rathaus. Precisely at 11:00 two animated figures (mounted knights) ride out and move past each other. In the next revolution, one of them unseats the other with his lance and a group of red-coated coopers dance to a traditional tune. When that is over, a cock, higher up, flaps his wings and crows three times, a reminder of Peter's denial.

Besides the Frauenkirche, the Sankt Peterskirche, the Sankt Michaelskirche (whose bell-vaulted ceiling is second only to the St. Peter's in Rome), the Theatinerkirche, and the Church of the Trinity (Drei-faltigkeitskirche) are worth visiting. Many of the churches and historic buildings of Munich and Bavaria are finished in the baroque and rococo

Munich, rich in art and culture

153

styles, in which the Bavarians' "love for all things beautiful" is translated in paint and stucco.

The Alte Pinakothek, built in Venetian Renaissance style, houses the imcomparable collection of fine arts gathered by the Bavarian kings since 1528. The works exhibited in thirteen huge galleries and 23 side rooms range from Dürers and Holbeins to Van Goghs and Manets. Truly the Alte Pinakothek ranks with the Louvre in Paris and the Uffizi in Florence as one of the world's greatest art museums.

And then there is the Deutsches Museum located on an island in the Isar, built in 1925 to house the expanding collection of the German Museum of Science and Technology. The museum attempts, according to its directors, "to present the most complex natural phenomena in the simplest possible diagrams and exhibits, to reduce a multitude of technical systems to their basic principles."

The Deutsches Museum is the largest museum of its kind in the world. It is above all known for its many "hands on" exhibits to be tried out and experienced by the visitors. Allow at least a half day to visit some of the departments, from mining to photography, metal foundry to musical instruments, printing to aviation, wind and waterpower, ecology, road construction and chronometry, surveying and minerals, to mention just a few.

On the outskirts of Munich we find the Nymphenburg palace and park and the adjacent Botanical Gardens. The Nymphenburg, built 1664 to 1674 as a separate residence for the Bavarian kings, was enlarged and embellished throughout the 1700s. On summer evenings, concerts are held in its Great Hall, lit up for the occasion by a thousand festive candles.

DACHAU, A LESSON TO BE REMEMBERED

Not far from all this beauty we find a grim reminder of another era—the Dachau Concentration Camp Memorial and Museum. The Dachau Camp, established by Heinrich Himmler in 1933, was the first of many Nazi death camps. This particular camp, soon surrounded by subcamps under the Dachau administration, processed 200,000 captured Jews and Jewish sympathizers from throughout Europe. All in all, some six million people were murdered in camps like Dachau, Buchenwald, Auschwitz, Bergen-Belsen, Maidanek, to mention just a few.

Within the barbed-wire enclosure, the former administration building is now a museum depicting the twelve years of Nazi terror. The exhibits are not suitable for children under twelve nor for the fainthearted. The original death camp has been razed, but two of the barracks have been reconstructed. Excerpts from letters and diaries printed in four languages give us a feel of what went on inside. Just outside the enclosure of the main camps we find the crematoriums. Three chapels—Catholic, Protestant, and Jewish—complete the memorial site. Our emotions will likely be troubled for quite some time after leaving the place.

Nurnberg: the Heilig Geist Spital

WITHIN THE WALLS OF NURNBERG

Nurnberg was one of Europe's intellectual centers during the Middle Ages. The workshops of the sculptors Veit Stoss and Peter Vischer established a reputation for the city, which one of their pupils, Albrecht Dürer, confirmed with his own creative genius. The poet Hans Sachs lived here and the Nürnberger Meistersinger gave a new direction to German literature.

The Reformation occurred in Nurnberg very early and with it came the first messengers of Anabaptism. Hans Denck came to Nurnberg in the fall of 1523 to accept the position of rector at the important Sankt Sebald school. Denck was expelled from Nurnberg in 1525 for his Anabaptist views.

Other early Anabaptists who appeared in Nurnberg were Hans Hut, the printer Hans Hergot, Ludwig Haetzer, and Wolfgang Vogel. In 1527 Nurnberg passed strict laws against "the ungodly and misleading faction." The prisons were soon filled with Anabaptists but this did not stop the movement. Between 1532 and 1537 the Hutterite leader, Peter Riedemann, was imprisoned for four years and ten weeks in the Lug-ins-Land Tower, which can still be seen as part of the city's upper wall.

The old part of Nurnberg was, and still is, divided in two distinct districts. One district is grouped around the Sankt Sebald, the other around the Sankt Lorenz. Because of the swampy conditions of the meadows along the city's Pegnitz River, not until late in history did the two districts, surrounded to this day by one massive city wall, grow together.

Nurnberg, like Munich and so many other European cities, is Fussganger-freundlich. In other words, the pedestrian is king. A prominent tourist site in old Nürnberg is the Dürer Haus. Albrecht Dürer bought this large 15th-century house by the upper city wall in 1509 and lived there until his death in 1528. The house and museum are open to the public.

The 13th-century Gothic Sankt Sebald Church, today a Lutheran Church, houses a number of important works by Vischer and Stoss, as does the similar Sankt Lorenz Church on the south side of the Pegnitz.

On the Hauptmarkt we find the Beautiful Fountain, a 14th-century town fountain covered by dozens of bronze figures of Old and New Testament characters, with some local heroes from the medieval times thrown in for good measure.

The Heilig Geist Spital (Holy Spirit Hospital), built on two arches over the Pegnitz River in 1331, is a favorite target of photographers, as is the Henkersteg, an old covered bridge with a good view of the Sankt Sebald. The Gothic Rathaus (town hall) contains dungeons and a prison museum.

A walk around Nürnberg's city walls totals five kilometers (three miles). From this wall, near the Fürther Tor, there is a lovely panoramic view of the entire old city by day or by night.

From this very site Germany's first railroad, the Nürnberg-Fürth Line started rolling in 1835. It is just a few steps from here to the museum where a replica of the first locomotive and train can be admired, as well as many other exhibits related to Germany's transportation and postal services.

OBERAMMERGAU AND ITS PASSION PLAY

In 1633, when the dreaded plague killed most of the inhabitants of the small village of Oberammergau, a parish priest, driven to desperation, made a vow that he would stage a Passion Play every decade if the plague would vanish. And, as the story goes, no more Oberammergauers died of the plague from that moment on.

A play was written and in 1634 the people of the Ammer Valley were able to fulfill their pastor's promise. The play picks up the story of Christ at the moment of his triumphal entry into Jerusalem and ends with the resurrection. The text of the Oberammergau Passion Play has been revised several times. The current text is basically the one written by a parish priest, Aloys Doysenberger, in the 1850s. Recently it was revised to remove certain anti-Semitic passages. The present musical score dates back to 1815. The Passion Play season comes at each turn of a decade—1970, 1980, 1990— except that the special 350th-anniversary performances were added for 1984. A season consists of approximately nine dress rehearsals and press performances and about 75 public performances. The play lasts from 9:00 in the morning until 17:00 (5:00) in the afternoon, with a three-hour lunch break. The tickets, which include the price of the meal and one overnight accommodation, cost between $80 and $200 (U.S.). The small villages of Ober- and Unter-Ammergau at the foot of the Bavarian Alps are also worth visiting between the plays and definitely less crowded.

THE CASTLES OF KING LUDWIG

King Ludwig II occupies a special place in Bavarian history. Although he is sometimes known as "Crazy Ludwig," we will not use that description in Bavaria, for the 19th-century king is still much admired in that region. Ludwig was of a temperamental and romantic nature and averse to political power. Always in search of peace, Ludwig withdrew into play and fantasies.

During his life Ludwig built three of the world's most extravagant castles: the Herrenchiemsee, an imitation of the Palace of Versailles; the Linderhof, a rococo palace; and the magnificent Neuschwanstein Castle, which has graced the covers of European travel guides in many languages. All three of these castles are within easy reach of Munich.

Ludwig II had the relatively small pastel-colored Linderhof Palace built deep in a wooded hillside surrounded by terraced gardens, reflecting pool, cascades, and playful fountains. The palace itself, built between 1874 and 1879, successfully combines the style of Italian Renaissance and German baroque. Inside, the luxury of the chambers and banquet halls surpasses the luxury of Versailles.

Located in an incomparably beautiful setting, the Neuschwanstein Castle, towering from a sharp peak in the Alpine foothills, was not designed by an architect, but rather by a designer of backdrops and sets of operas, which explains its theatrical appearance. It has been said that the legends and the corresponding operas of *Lohengrin* and *Tannhäuser* provided the inspiration for it. The Sängersaal, or hall of the singers, illuminated by a

Linderhof Palace

multitude of fine chandeliers, occupies practically all of the castle's fourth floor. It was at Neuschwanstein that on June 10, 1886, King Ludwig II learned from a citizens' commission that he had been deposed. Three days later the king and his psychiatrist drowned in the Chiemsee, presumably after a scuffle on a rowboat.

The Chiemsee is the largest mountain lake in Bavaria. Its mirror-like waters are spread over 23 square kilometers (nine square miles) and provide a perfect reflection for the Alps. Two islands in this lake, the Herreninsel and the Fraueninsel, are well worth a visit. The trip to the islands is in itself an adventure.

From the mainline railroad station at Prien, a small steam locomotive, placed on the tracks in 1887, pulls a half dozen equally ancient coaches to the harbor, where the passengers transfer to the ships of the Chiemsee fleet. One of the ships, the S.S. *Ludwig Fessler,* is an equally charming paddlewheeler.

The larger of the two islands, Herreninsel, was bought in 1873 in its entirety by King Ludwig II to save it from the logging interests and to build upon it a palace and formal gardens in the manner of Versailles. Construction was begun in 1878 and continued until 1885. By that time more than twenty million Marks had already been spent and the state treasury was empty. The king had only lived less than a week at this palace—but happened to be at Neuschwanstein—when his death put an end to the dream. The great entrance hall, in which more than forty kinds of marble were used, and the magnificent Hall of Mirrors are only two of the sights awaiting the visitor.

On the way back to Prien, a stop at the Fraueninsel is well worth the time and effort. Although small, this island has a picturesque fishing village and a Benedictine cloister dating back to AD 770. In their *Pensionat* (guesthouse) the nuns will be glad to serve the thirsty traveler with an excellent hot chocolate or any other drink.

PASSAU AND THE AUSBUND

Passau is located on a tongue of land at the confluence of the Inn, the Danube (Donau), and the Ilz. At this point the added waters of the Inn almost double the volume of the Danube, which at Passau becomes a truly major stream. The ancient Celtic town of Passau was Christianized around AD 718 by the great missionary Saint Boniface himself.

Later prince-bishops of Passau became powerful rulers of church and state over vast areas of Germany and Austria. In the 1300s these bishops built the mighty *Oberhaus,* (upper house) fortress-castle on a rocky point between the Ilz and the Danube and below it, at river level. The *Niederhaus* (lower house) formerly exacted tolls from all those who traveled by land or by water. The two strongholds were connected by a defense wall.

In 1537 about sixty Anabaptist travelers were arrested in Passau and

Passau, as seen from the Oberhaus

held in the Oberhaus castle dungeons for about five years. Before nearly all of them died from hunger and torture, the prisoners wrote 51 hymns which formed the nucleus of the *Ausbund,* the first known hymnal of the Anabaptists. Still in use today among the Amish, the *Ausbund* is also the oldest hymnbook in continuous use by any Christian group in the entire world.

GERMANY'S TOURIST HIGHWAYS

Germany has a number of tourist highways, in addition to those already mentioned in this chapter. Each of them is worthy of a few days of driving or an entire vacation. The most important among these are the

Romantic Road, the Great Castle Road, the German Alpine Road, and the German Wine Road.

Linking the Main River with the Bavarian Alps, the Romantic Road (Romantische Strasse) runs from Wurzburg on the Main to Neuschwanstein Castle through peaceful valleys and splendid imperial cities. In part, it follows the ancient Roman Via Claudia. Along the way it touches on the three best-preserved medieval cities in all of Germany—Rothenburg o/d Tauber, Dinkelsbühl, and Nordlingen.

Near the southern end of this road at Steingaden, a short side trip to the Wieskirche is worthwhile. It is the last and the best of the works of the great rococo architect Dominikus Zimmermann. Reluctant to leave his masterpiece, Dominikus spent the last ten years of his life in a little cottage nearby.

Crossing the Romantic Road at right angles is the Great Castle Road (Burgenstrasse), which runs from Mannheim on the Rhine through Heidelberg to Nurnberg.

In between Lindau on the Bodensee and the Austrian border at Salzburg, we find the German Alpine Road (Deutsche Alpenstrasse).

From the French border at Wissembourg to a point west of Worms, meanders the German Wine Road (Deutsche Weinstrasse), with many picturesque towns and villages, some of them of particular interest to Mennonites. (See description of the Palatinate, pages 124-132.)

Other roads include the German Vacation Road, the Green Coastal Road, the Old Salt Road, and the Upper Swabian Baroque Architecture Loop, to mention just a few.

AUSTRIA

Österreich

At times people have asked me, "Which is your favorite country?" I find that question hard to answer. But sometimes I say, without too much hesitation, "Austria." To begin with, Austria is manageable in size. One can cover the country from Vienna to Feldkirch in a one-day train ride that is a railroad buff's dream. With two thirds of the country covered by spectacular mountain massifs, it is the most Alpine country in Europe.

From Vorarlberg, which resembles adjacent eastern Switzerland, to the Burgenland, which has a Balkan flavor, from the Drava Valley to the plains along the Danube, Austria offers an infinite variety of landscapes and experiences. There is Vienna, among the great cities of Europe, second only to Rome in its long and illustrious history, and Salzburg, the city of Mozart.

Throughout the land we find more than 1,500 impressive castles, some strategically placed on mountaintops guarding ancient trade routes. The abbeys and the churches, many in lavish baroque style, are colorful reminders of a great era in art.

To the charm and impressiveness of this scenery is added the charm and the kindness of the Austrians themselves, masters of *Gemütlichkeit,* (the art of making you feel at home). Yes, Austria is definitely at the top of my list of favorite countries.

Once the name Austria stood for an empire which, under the authority of one single monarch, ruled over territories from southern Italy to the Netherlands, but it was reduced to its current size in 1919, when the remains of the Austria-Hungarian Empire were dismantled.

During the 16th century cleverly calculated royal marriages, rather than wars, had brought Austria much of its widespread territory. In 1740 a young empress, Maria Theresa (age 23) ascended the throne. Maria Theresa was a wise ruler. During her forty-year reign, Austria prospered.

Her husband, Francis Stephan, the duke of Lorraine, became Emperor Francis I. But Maria Theresa herself continued to control Austria's national affairs. To better the international connections of Austria, Maria Theresa married off the sixteen of her children who lived to maturity, to kings and princes of other royal houses.

Today nearly every Austrian city has a street, a square, a theater, or a fountain named in her honor. Unfortunately, Maria Theresa must also be counted as one of the most vicious persecuters of non-Catholic minorities, such as the Anabaptists. During her reign, with the help of Jesuit priests, Maria Theresa was able to reduce the large thriving Hutterite brotherhoods to less than a hundred survivors.

The 68-year reign of Franz Josef from 1848 to 1916, one of the longest recorded in European history, ended in failure, with the Habsburg dynasty collapsing two years after his death. Yet Austria also remembers this king for the significant social and economic changes made under his rule. These changes resulted in greater prosperity for the common people and for an artistic revival, especially in urban architecture.

Modern Austria is a federation of one self-governing city (Vienna) and eight provinces, governed by a republican form of government. Austrian politics have been dominated by the People's Party and the Socialists, two parties so well balanced as to require a coalition government. All public appointments, including those of artists and musicians, singers with the opera, and actors in the national theater, are carefully proportioned in keeping with the balance between the two parties. This system, popularly known as *Proporz,* has brought great stability, for it has forced political rivals to work out compromises for the common good of Austria and the Austrians.

Landlocked Austria, bordered by seven other countries (three of them communist and four from the west), faced great difficulties at the end of the war. The wanton looting, rape, and murder committed by Soviet soldiers in their march to conquer "Fortress V" created a continuing deep-seated hatred toward communism in the Austrians. For the first three years after the war, Austrian city dwellers, deprived by the Russians of all supplies, fought a desperate struggle against hunger and cold.

For ten years the eastern part of the country remained occupied by the Russians, who began to remove most of the undamaged property for shipment to the USSR as part of the German war reparations. During these ten years, the entire eastern region, so vital to the country's economy, was completely beyond Austria's control and unable to contribute to the so-necessary reconstruction. The treaty of 1955 provided for the departure of the Russians in return for enormous shipments of goods to the Soviet Union for six years and for most of the country's petroleum for ten years.

Austria came out of the ordeal with an almost universal desire for independence and perpetual neutrality, a status now written into the constitu-

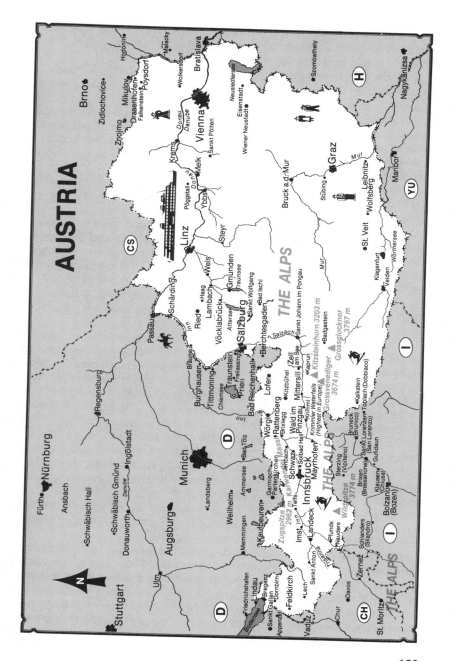

163

tion. This rules out Austria's alignment with either the NATO or the Warsaw Pact forces, or the construction of military bases on Austrian soil. Austria is, in fact, a buffer state between east and west.

When the Soviets squashed the 1956 Hungarian uprising, some 170, 000 Hungarian refugees arrived in Austria, creating a new burden on the country's economy.

To make a comeback possible out of such a desperate situation, labor, industry, and government have cooperated and agreed on hours, wages, and work conditions. In general, Austrian workers have accepted somewhat lower wages in return for quality government-provided social services.

Nearly one quarter of Austria's population lives in Vienna. Except for the four next-largest cities, Graz, Linz, Salzburg, and Innsbruck—the rest of Austria's towns tend to be old and cozy, small and provincial.

Think about Austria and you think of music. Austria has long been the home of great composers. Mozart was born in Salzburg, and Beethoven, Haydn, Schubert, and Brahms all lived and worked in Vienna sometime during their lives. In 1797, Haydn composed the Austrian national hymn, better known to most of us as "Glorious Things of Thee Are Spoken."

Strauss was the name of a Viennese family of composers: a father and three sons. The Strausses really caught the spirit of Vienna and shaped it into a musical form called the waltz.

Johann Strauss, Sr. (1804-1849), began composing waltzes in 1825, organized his first orchestra in 1826 and was soon appointed conductor to the royal court. He wrote about 230 waltzes, polkas, and marches.

Johann Strauss, Jr. (1825-1899), became even more famous. In 1844 he founded an orchestra which he later combined with his father's in 1849. He turned this orchestra over to his brother in 1862, after gaining international fame as a composer/conductor. Johann Strauss, Jr.'s best-known pieces may be *The Blue Danube* and *Tales from the Vienna Woods.* Johann's brothers, Josef and Edward, were not as gifted but still had hundreds of pieces to their name, including *Pizzacato Polka,* which they wrote together. Edward's son, Johann Strauss III, also became an eminent conductor.

The Vienna Philharmonic Orchestra won worldwide acclaim under a succession of great composer-conductors, including Gustav Mahler, Richard Strauss, and currently Herbert von Karajan.

Each year thousands of visitors attend the Salzburg Festival, a great musical event which centers around the music of Salzburg's own musical genius, Mozart. The Landestheater in downtown Innsbruck features the very best in classical opera and drama.

But music also has its local sound. Nearly every mountain village has its own folk music group. You may well hear their joyful sounds in the park by the river at night. And the well-known Christmas hymn "Silent Night,

Holy Night," written hastily as a substitute when the organ broke down, was first sung in Oberndorf, Austria in 1818.

About one fourth of the Austrians make their living directly or indirectly from the forest (which covers nearly 37 percent of the country), one of Austria's great natural resources. The place of timber in Austria's economy is surpassed only by the forest product economies of Finland and Sweden. The forests (80 percent of which are mostly spruce and pine) are carefully managed and harvested and remain a delight to the tourist.

From the early days that waterpower was first harnessed for generating electricity, Austria has exploited this natural resource. Although only 60 percent of the suitable waterpower sites have been developed, Austria is a net exporter of electricity to the European electric grid.

Salt played a major role in Austria's past and—besides Salzburg— many towns include "Salz" or "Hall" (meaning saltworks) in their names. A number of working salt mines are open to the public.

The salt industry also brought about the world's oldest pipelines. To process the salt closer to the market, the authorities during the mid-1700s

The Grossglockner highway

started building wooden pipelines to carry brine from the mines to process-ing plants near the cities. The longest one of these ran from Bad Rei-chenhal (Austria) to Rosenheim (in Germany) and was in use from 1810 to 1958.

The farms tend to be small. Half of Austria's 450,000 farms are less than fourteen acres in size.

One dilemma for Austria is the status of South Tirol, or rather, Austria's minority living in this Italian district. In a secret treaty of 1915, Italy lined itself up with the Allies in return for the right to annex the Austrian province of South Tirol up to the Brenner Pass. Ratified later by the Treaty of Saint Germain, the land and a quarter million Austrians formally became a part of Italy, who renamed it Alto Adige (Upper Etsch Valley).

The Italians under Mussolini began a program of discrimination and 78,000 South Tiroleans actually fled to Austria. Some tried to return to their former homes in 1945. In 1946 South Tirol favored becoming part of Austria, a request vetoed by the Allies. However, Italy promised Austria and the Allies a measure of home rule for the province. South Tiroleans are quick to tell you the promise was nullified when South Tirol was combined with several other provinces into a new administrative department (Alto Adige) in which the Italians outnumber the Austrians two to one.

One of the reasons for including Italy in this tour guide (pp. 305-328) is that South Tirol was the last mission field of Georg Blaurock and the birth-place of the Hutterite branch of the Anabaptist Mennonite family.

ANABAPTISM IN AUSTRIA

In the 1520s Hans Hut brought Anabaptism to Vienna in lower Austria. Here he baptized many believers, including Oswald Glaidt and Leonhard Schiemer who, in turn, spread the faith to other parts of Austria. Schiemer, who previously had been a Barefoot Friar, was one of the most successful Anabaptist missioners. He was martyred in Tirol in 1528. From Vienna the Anabaptist movement spread to Steyr on the Enns in upper Austria, which eventually became the center of the work of Hut, Glaidt, and Schiemer. However, prior to the arrival of these Viennese, Anabaptism had already come to Linz, the provincial capital of upper Austria. During this time the Anabaptist movement was also growing in Tirol and Salzburg. Tirol produced some important leaders. Pilgram Marpeck, from the Inn Valley, and Leopold Scharnslager from Kitzbühel became important leaders in the south German Anabaptist circles, especially in Augsburg and in Stras-bourg. South Tirol was also the home of Jakob Hutter, the founder of the Hutterite Brethren. Peter Walpot, who as a young man witnessed the martyr death of Georg Blaurock at Klaussen in 1529, later became a Hutterite bishop.

So Anabaptism spread throughout Austria. However, the various local authorities dealt with it in diverse ways. Some meted out an immediate

Kitzbühel

death sentence to those apprehended, others decreed "light incarceration" only. In Lower Austria, Emperor Ferdinand issued many mandates against the Anabaptists and hired Dietrich von Hartitsch as the first professional Anabaptist hunter *(Täuferjäger)*. In December 1539, von Hartitsch captured 136 Anabaptists in Steinabrunn alone. They were then taken to Falkenstein Castle. Some managed to escape, but others were sold to Admiral Andrea Doria to become galley slaves in his navy. Balthasar Hubmaier and Peter Riedemann were also among those martyred or imprisoned in Ferdinand's territory. In the 1550s Jesuits brought the Catholic Reformation, better known as the Counter-Reformation, to Lower Austria, the one place where it was very successful. Consequently, Anabaptism died out in Lower Austria after the second half of the 16th century. In Upper Austria, the persecution was much the same as in Lower Austria, but the remaining Anabaptists there went into hiding. The group died out in part because they lacked strong leadership.

Salzburg was ruled by an archbishop who united the forces of church and state to persecute the Anabaptists in his domain. Foreigners who were caught in Salzburg were dealt with particularly harshly because it was thought that they were seducing others into the "unchristian act of rebaptism." Anabaptists trying to escape persecution in Tirol sometimes came to Salzburg, but found no refuge there either. In Salzburg, as in Lower Austria, the Catholic Counter-Reformation ended all Anabaptist activity in the area.

In spite of Ferdinand's Anabaptist hunters and spies, Anabaptism flourished in Tirol for several decades. Apart from the well-known leaders it produced, it is estimated that there were 20,000 Anabaptists in Tirol. Among these there were some nobility, including Christopher Fuchs, Erhard Zimmermann, Anton and Siegmund Wolkenstein (both later recanted), and Countess Helene von Freyberg, one of the followers of Pilgram Marpeck. She offered shelter to Anabaptists in her Münichau Castle, which she left to her sons when she too was forced to flee the country. Most of the Anabaptists in Tirol sooner or later became Hutterites and joined with their brethren in Moravia. After the Hutterites set up their colonies in Moravia, they felt a responsibility for all Anabaptist groups back home in Austria. But after 1600, there were no more native Anabaptists in Tirol. In fact, all martyrs in Austria after 1605 were missioners, usually from Moravia, passing through the country, rather than indigenous Anabaptists.

Recently four Mennonite Brethren churches have been established in Eastern Austria which, together with nine more congregations in Germany, form the European Mennonite Brethren Church, totaling 960 members in these two countries.

The Language

German is the official language of Austria and is spoken by 95 out of every 100 Austrians. For centuries, the area around Vienna has attracted Serbs, Croats, Magyars, Italians, Romanians, and Slovenes, and thus most of the eastern Austrians are of mixed origin.

The Climate

It is practically impossible to talk about the Austrian climate. The country may have a half-dozen climatic conditions at any given time. It all depends on whether we find ourselves on the north or on the south side of the Alps, or whether we are in a valley which runs north to south or one that lays east to west.

Austria's western province of Arlberg enjoys the moderating influence of the Lake of Constance, which accounts for pleasant summers and gentle winters—so much so that the mountains of the Arlberg are dressed in trees and shrubbery all the way to the top, well above what is normally considered to be the timberline.

But as soon as we cross over these mountains into Tirol, the weather and the scenery are entirely different. In the Salzburg area there are sudden changes in temperature and frequent downpours.

Another phenomena to contend with on the north side of the Alps anywhere is the Föhn. (For a description of this wind, see "Switzerland," page 80.)

The Best Times to See Austria

It is only appropriate to start the seasons of Austria with winter. After all, two thirds of the country consists of the highest Alps and there are many winter sports centers of worldwide renown, especially in the provinces of Arlberg, Tirol, and in Salzburgerland. Innsbruck was the site of the 1976 winter Olympics.

Springtime only lengthens the days, making it possible to ski even in the highest altitudes. It is not uncommon to encounter a warmly clad Austrian, skis on shoulders, mixing with the shirt-sleeved tourists sunning in Innsbruck's parks as the skier heads for the 2,344-meter (7,691 ft.) high Hafelekar, towering over the city.

Summer in Austria offers a choice of pleasures: hiking in the valleys or skiing in the heights, swimming in the lakes or enjoing excursions by lake steamer or train.

In the autumn the slanted rays of the sun often light up old castle ruins and villages in spectacular ways. It can be a bit nippy and night comes quickly in the fall after the last rays of the sun disappear behind the mountain masses.

Holidays and Store Hours

In addition to the major holidays of the Christian year, Austria recognizes the following legal holidays: Three Kings' Day (January 6), Day of Labor (May 1), Sacraments Day (the second Tuesday after Pentecost), Maria Ascension Day (mid-August), the Austrian national holiday (October 26), All Souls Day (November 1), and Maria Immaculate Conception Day (December 8). The stores and banks are closed on those days.

In general, stores in Austria are open between 8:00 a.m. and 18:00 (6:00 p.m.) with a two-hour noon break. Most stores close at noon on Saturdays. The post offices in the main railroad stations are open day and night, even on Sundays and holidays.

Special Rules of the Road

Parking on mountain roads is permitted only if the parked car leaves enough paved surface for two more vehicles to pass each other without undue difficulty. In the cities, parking is not allowed in any street with streetcar tracks between the hours of 5:00 in the morning and 20:00 (8:00) in the evening. When we park in Vienna, we must display our parking discs, and we are required to buy coupons from vending machines to cover the amount of time we plan to park.

Sleeping in cars along the main roads is illegal, but it is permitted on country roads, provided the car is safely and legally parked.

Children under 12 are not allowed to ride in the front seat. If certain types of vehicles, like sports cars and vans, only have a front seat, children are not to be transported in them.

When the green of a traffic light starts to flicker, it soon turns orange. Driving through orange is illegal. Hitchhiking in western Austria for boys under sixteen and for girls under eighteen is illegal.

The Monetary System

Austria's monetary unit is the Schilling (Osch). The Schilling is subdivided into 100 Groschen. Coins are minted in the following values: 2, 5, 10 and 50 Groschen (aluminum); 1, 5, 10 and 20 Schilling (white metal); 25, 50, 100 and 500 Schilling (silver) and 1000 (Gold). Paper notes come in denominations of 20, 50, 100, 500, 1000 Osch and higher. A unicum in currency is that the Maria Theresa Thaler, commonly dated 1780, is still considered legal tender, even though its value is pegged to the world silver market rather than at face value.

SALZBURG, CITY OF MOZART AND MUSIC

Salzburg is a city where a dramatic landscape and a rich architectural heritage complement each other. Salzburg is a delight from the first distant sight of the fortress, Hohensalzburg, and does not lose its magic when one wanders through the narrow streets of the Altstadt.

That Salzburg is a city of churches is no wonder. It was founded by the missionary monk, Rüprecht of Worms, in AD 696 as the see of Salzburg. It was elevated to the status of bishopric within a century.

During the 13th century, the archbishops of Salzburg combined the temporal powers of the state with the rule of the church. Their spiritual and temporal control reached from Bavaria deep into Italy. Much of their large revenue came from the mining of salt in the Salzkammergut region. The prince-bishops showed a taste for building and soon converted the little settlement of Salzburg into an architectural showpiece.

In 1587, Wolf Dietrich von Raitenau became archbishop of Salzburg at the age of 28. It was his dream to make Salzburg into a second Rome. Early during his reign, the old city conveniently burned down (arson was suspected), giving von Raitenau the opportunity to rebuild the city in great splendor.

The archbishop's private life was not above criticism. He had twelve children by Salome Alt, his Jewish mistress. Concubinage was not uncommon among the clergy, but after Wolf Dietrich von Raitenau spent a fortune to build his mistress the beautiful chateau and gardens of Mirabel, the pope decided enough was enough. In 1612 the bishop was tried and incarcerated in his own fortress, Hohensalzburg, where he died after five years in the dungeons.

It would be ironic to think that he shared those filthy quarters with the Anabaptists he had so vigorously persecuted, but the dates do not make that altogether impossible.

Archbishop Paris Lodron (1619-1653) took advantage of his long reign to complete the ambitious building projects started by his predecessors. The cathedral, which shows the last expressions of Italian Renaissance, but which is finished in lavish baroque, was completed in 1628. The dedication ceremony lasted eight days. For the occasion, Horatio Benevoli composed a special mass. Written in 53 parts, the mass was performed by eight antiphonal choruses, two string orchestras, two ensembles for brass and woodwinds, and a percussion section, all accompanied by the cathedral's own mighty organ.

To see Salzburg, it is advisable that we leave our car in the newer part

Fortress Hohensalzburg

Salzburg, city of churches

of town, to the right of the Salzach (or our tour bus on the Nonntal bus parking terrains). Old Salzburg is strictly for pedestrians and the occasional horse-drawn *Droschke*. From the Nonntal, little yellow pedestrian signs point the visitors to the Altstadt, but most of the time we might as well just follow the crowds.

Our first stop is the fortress Hohensalzburg, the former stronghold of the archbishops. Hohensalzburg is the largest intact fortress in central Europe, still preserved in its original condition because it was never conquered. It stands on a solid rise of dolomite rock 120 meters (400 ft.) above the Salzach. The castle was frequently enlarged and remodeled to become a comfortable residence of the archbishops. One of the rulers, Leonard von Keutschach (1495-1519), adopted the turnip as his emblem. We see sculptured turnips again and again as we tour the castle.

There are two ways to get to the castle. One is by walking up the steep access road which takes you about twenty minutes. But it is easier to go on the *Festungsbahn,* a funicular railway that takes us straight to the top. The view from the castle's ramparts over the city is unforgettable.

A unique part of the castle is the so-called Salzburger *Steer,* a mechanical organ built in 1502. It received its name from the large opening and final chords of the chorales which are played. The mechanism is a hand-driven drum and plays three times a day at 7:00 a.m., 11:00 a.m., and at 18:00 (6:00 p.m.). A good place to listen to it is from the St. Peter's Cemetery.

Coming down from the fortress, we can turn left into the St. Peter's Cemetery. This charming little resting place abuts the vertical wall of rock on which the Hohensalzburg fortress is located. Elaborate wrought iron gates under baroque arcades enclose the graves of generations of Salzburg's leading families. Tall pines, weeping willows, and well-kept flower beds add to the romance and the beauty of the place.

Next to the cemetery, we find St. Peter's Church, built in 1130, Salzburg's only Romanesque church. Leaving the cemetery and church we come past the St. Peter's mill and cellars in the abbey courtyard. We now find ourselves on the Kapittelplatz, dominated by the cathedral. A feature of this square is the fountain which served as a horse trough. The fountain bears a curious resemblance to Rome's Fontana Trevi, though it was actually built much earlier, in 1732.

Passing through the Dom Arcades, we find ourselves on the Dom Square in front of the cathedral. Salzburg's original cathedral, built in 774, stood on the same site and burned out eight times before Archbishop Wolf Dietrich von Raitenau pulled it down in 1602. The present cathedral was to be of the same size as St. Peter's in Rome, but while the deposed archbishop was spending the last years of his life in the dungeons of his own fortress, the work was completed on a more modest scale.

Even so, Salzburg's cathedral is impressive. The front, flanked by two

Interior of the Salzburger Dom

symmetric towers, is built of light-colored Salzburg marble. We are impressed by the size and by the riches of marble, stucco, and painted decorations of the interior. In 1756, Wolfgang Amadeus Mozart was baptized in the Dom's Romanesque baptismal font. On October 16, 1944, the United States Air Force bombed the cathedral. The dome was destroyed and the interior badly damaged. Repairs took almost twenty years and millions of Schillings.

The original organ was built in 1702-1703 by the organ builder Christopf Egedacher. It has been rebuilt, restored, and enlarged numerous times. It now has 120 registers and 10,000 pipes, the largest of which is 11 meters (34 ft.) high and the smallest measures 3 centimeters (1¼ inches).

From the Dom it is but a few blocks to the Altstadt, the old town. Two circumstances influenced the character of Salzburg's inner city. First, there is precious little space between the steep rock of the Monchberg and the rushing Salzach. Second, the best available space had been taken over by the cathedral, the churches, chapels, and residences of the bishops. Besides St. Peter's and the Dom, we should also mention the Franciscan Church, the Collegiate Church, St. Kajetans, St. Erhardt's, the Nonnberg Abbey, St. Ursuline's, and more.

All this left the city of Salzburg with no other option than to crowd the houses close together and to expand upwards. The results are narrow canyon-like streets, flanked by five- and six-story houses, finished in pastel-colored stucco. The nicest of these streets is the Getreidegasse, with its wrought iron shop signs and richly ornamented storefronts. It is worth our time to take a glance at the courtyards of some of these houses—at numbers 3, 5, and 9, for instance—which remind us of life in the Middle Ages.

The goal of most visitors is Getreidegasse 9. In this house, on the third floor, Wolfgang Amadeus Mozart was born on January 27, 1756 and lived here until age seven. Today it is a Mozart museum covering three floors. The exhibits contain many significant mementoes of Mozart's youth, such as his violins, including the violin he played for Empress Maria Theresa as an eight-year-old child prodigy. His spinet and his musical manuscripts are on display, as well as a selection of portraits and letters.

Across the river we may also visit the house on Markartplatz 8, where the Mozart family lived from 1773 to 1787. A monument to Mozart can be found on the Mozartplatz, not far from the Dom.

The old town hall of 1407 is also located on the Getreidegasse. Where the Getreidegasse changes its name to Judengasse, the street widens into a small market square around the fountain of St. Florian. On the square we find the Salzburg Bank, with its doorway dating back to 1774, and the even older Court Pharmacy, of 1591, which still has its baroque interior fittings. Cafe Tomasselli, also on the square, was founded by an Italian in 1703 and has been in business ever since.

Behind the Getreidegasse near the Neutor stands a monumental horse trough built around 1700 to water the 150 horses of the archbishops. It is embelished with frescoes and statues— all with a horse motif.

Besides the Chateau Mirabel and the second home of Mozart, already mentioned, another point of interest is the Kapuzinerberg. This rock takes its name from a Capuchin monastery which was built on it in the 16th century. Before that it was called the Imberg.

There are two ways up the Kapuzinerberg, both starting from near the Platzl. The shortest is a flight of stairs from the Steingasse to the tiny St. Johann Chapel. Another steep ascent starts from the archway on the

Salzburg: the horse troughs (Pferdeschwemme)

Linzergasse 14, known as the Felix Pforte. A path taking off to the right from these trails leads to the Hettwerbastei, for another fine view of the city and the fortress.

Ever since the 13-year-old Mozart directed his first opera, *La Finta Semplice,* there in 1769, Salzburg has been Austria's city of music. Apart from almost daily Mozart performances in the concert halls and palaces, in and around Salzburg there are the five-week-long Salzburger *Festspiele* in July and August, the Salzburger Marionnetten Theater, the annual performance of the mystery play *Every Man* by Hugo von Hofmansthal, and many impromptu open-air performances by visiting bands and orchestras. Each year in January the Vienna Philharmonic participates in the celebration of a Mozart week.

The city maintains an information and booking office for all its cultural events on the Mozartplatz 5.

In the city and land of Salzburg, where the temporal and spiritual authorities were combined in the office of the archbishop, the struggle against Anabaptist heretics could be carried on with great vigor and almost unlimited manpower.

That the Anabaptists, nevertheless, maintained a vital and courageous fellowship in and around the city can be seen from the numerous sharp mandates issued against them, as well as by the complaints of the archbishops. One of these, Matthias Lang von Wellenburg, wrote that he and his counselors had to work day and night to stamp out the heretics.

In 1528, thirty-two people, present at a secret meeting, were arrested and later executed. Among them was the 16-year-old daughter of the goldsmith Georg Stein. The executioner himself carried the girl to the horse trough and held her under the water until she drowned. She did not recant, did not betray her brothers and sisters at large, and she "laughed" at the sight of the water.

This news traveled as far as the city of Augsburg, where in 1529 one of the city lawyers argued that little could be accomplished by killing Anabaptists. "In Salzburg," said he, "the young girls come running and request to be put to death."

In 1541, one condemned Anabaptist even showed a sense of humor. While he was being burned at the stake, Leonhard Bernkopf told the executioner, "This side is already roasted well enough. Now turn me over to do the other side." Great zeal in persecuting the Anabaptists was shown by Archbishop Wolf Dietrich von Raitenau, who ordered that all the Anabaptists should be killed by fire and the sword and their properties confiscated. It is possible that by 1598 the Anabaptists in Salzburgerland had been indeed wiped out.

MAJESTIC MOUNTAINS, GRACEFUL WATERFALLS

The province of Salzburgerland stretches south and west of the city like a huge reverse of the letter "L," the foot of which reaches the end of the long Pinzgauer Valley, flanked on all sides by towering mountains. Rushing through the entire province are the white tumbling waters of the Salzach. The Pinzgau is the most mountainous part of Salzburgerland, surrounded by the Hohetauern, the Great Venetian Range, the Gross Glockner, the Kitzbüheler Alps, the Leoganger and Lofener Steinberge, and more. It has been generously endowed by nature and carefully cultivated by the inhabitants into one of the world's finest vacation spots. The villages of the Pinzgau lie along the swift Salzach like pearls on a string.

At the valley's western end, near Krimml, we find Europe's highest waterfalls. With a three-stage drop of 380 meters (1,250 ft.), these falls are a favorite with hikers, most of whom make it up to the second stage. For a full ascent to the upper falls, which are even longer than the middle and lower falls, allow 3½ hours. The trail along the falls is always open but the veils of spray and mist make it hazardous in winter.

There are romantic guesthouses in every little town and inexpensive private accommodations in houses which display the sign *Zimmer Frei* (rooms available).

Once upon a time the valleys of the Pinzgau were full of Anabaptists protected by sympathetic neighbors. Of special interest is the story of Veit Grünberger, a Hutterite clockmaker and therefore also called Uhrmacher, a missioner in the area.

176

In the spring of 1570, Veit Uhrmacher and a fellow missioner, Veit Schelch, after completing their mission were heading back to the Hutterite colonies in Moravia. Their presence in the region was known and a price had been set on their heads. When the two stopped in Wald for a meal at the Walderwirt Inn, some local peasants suspected that these were the wanted men. When the two gave thanks before eating their meal, the peasants knew for sure and called the sheriff.

Wald im Pinzgau

While the innkeeper stood guard, the sheriff arrived along with the castle judge, several officers, and the provost of Mittersil. Together they led the prisoners to the dungeons at Mittersil, some 23 kilometers (14 miles) to the east. The sheriff's wife, secretly sympathetic to the Anabaptist cause, saw to it that they received good food, and the sheriff himself apologized for arresting them. He was only doing his job.

Shortly thereafter, they were hauled off to the Hohensalzburg fortress, where the bishop kept them in the dungeons for three years before they were ever questioned. At his trial Uhrmacher contended that true faith shows up in a good lifestyle and pointed out that the Catholic way of life, at that time, was hardly Christian. That viewpoint, Veit said, was illustrated by their cruel ways in dealing with those who tried to be true disciples. Under torture the other Veit recanted and was released, but later rejoined the brotherhood.

Uhrmacher escaped from the Hohensalzburg in 1576 by tying together old rags. In the *Great Chronicle* Uhrmacher attributes his escape to the help and power of God for whom nothing is impossible. Uhrmacher went on many more missionary journeys before his natural death in 1586. Both the inn at Wald, in business since 1423, and the castle at Mittersil, are still in existence.

There is no limit to the number of hikes and excursions we can take from the Pinzgau. This includes mountain hikes in the upper and lower Sulzach valleys, a trip over the spectacular Gross Glockner Alpine road system, a cable car ride to the peaks above Kaprun, a visit to the town of Zell am See, located on the shore of a beautiful mountain lake, or an excursion to the ski resort of Kitzbühel.

INNSBRUCK AND THE INN VALLEY

Ever since the southern border of Austria was brought back to the crest of the Alps, the Inn Valley has become the geographical middle of western Austria. From the steep gorges of the Finstermünz Ravine, where Austria meets both Switzerland and Italy, to the Kufstein Gap, through which the Inn River flows into Germany, the Inn Valley is typical of a landscape in which the powerful forces of the Ice Ages met the immovable Alps. This confrontation in nature resulted in huge light-colored limestone folds on the north side of the valley, the darker, crystaline rocks of the central Alps to the south, and the deposit of spacious plateaus which later became idyllic sites for towns and villages.

The Inn enters Austria rushing north through the steep rocky gap of Finstermünz, which forms a natural border between Tirol, Switzerland's Engadine, and Italy's Upper Adige. For some distance into Austria the influence of the Swiss Rhaetian style of architecture is still noticeable. A couple of humpbacked covered bridges across the river near Pfunds are more than 700 years old.

At Landeck (literally "corner of the country") the Inn turns east taking with it the waters of the Rosanna and the Trisanna, coming from the west. Landeck's massive castle and a series of eagle's nest strongholds nearby bear witness to the city's strategic importance for this part of Austria.

From Landeck to Imst, the valley is narrow and densely forested. But suddenly it broadens into the wide Imst basin with the town of Imst perched on a large plateau. From Imst it is not far to Innsbruck. From time immemorial the shortest and easiest route from the Roman Empire to the Germanic nations led over the Brenner Pass and crossed the Inn at the site of present-day Innsbruck. An improved highway was already in place before the year 1000 and a better bridge across the Inn was built by Count von Andechs in 1187.

At that time the name Innsbruck was chosen for the settlement which rapidly grew into a major city. In 1420 Innsbruck became the capital of Tirol and the seat of the Austrian court of administration. Under Emperor Maximilian I, Innsbruck was made the imperial residence and thus became the

Innsbruck: the Goldenes Dach'l

official center of the expanding Habsburg Empire. In Innsbruck, Maximilian married his first wife, Maria of Burgundy. This marriage increased his territorial holdings as far west as the Netherlands. In 1494 he married his second wife, Bianca Maria Sforza, thereby increasing his influence over additional regions. These marriages inspired a Latin poem: "Let others wage war. Thou, happy Austria, make love. What others owe to Mars, instead, receive from Venus."

Soon after his second wedding the emperor had the famous Goldenes Dach'l set up (description to follow). The emperor also chose Innsbruck as his burial place and directed the building of the lavish Hofkirche (Court Church) as his tomb. However, the Hofkirche never received the emperor's remains, for the citizens in the meantime had become exasperated with the huge unpaid debts run up by Maximilian and all his court members. Therefore, Innsbruck literally closed the doors on him, and Maximilian was buried at Wiener Neustadt instead.

But other royal occasions and the prosperity of the city's merchants left their mark on Innsbruck. The city experienced a new era of splendor under Maria Theresa. In 1765 the city was alive with a new celebration, the marriage of Crown Prince Leopold, grand duke of Tuscany, to the princess of Spain, Maria Ludovica. A giant triumphal arch was built at the head of the present Maria Theresienstrasse. Suddenly consternation spread through the crowds. The husband of Maria Theresa, Emperor Franz I, had died at the Hofburg Palace and the joyous wedding ended in a time of mourning.

In Innsbruck, it may still be possible to find a parking place not far from the heart of town. Tour buses are given a limited amount of time to discharge or to load passengers near the Landestheater, but long-time parking in the area is not permitted. However, in Innsbruck, all points of interest are within easy walking distance.

The heart of old Innsbruck is the Maria Theresienstrasse. This imposing street of irregular width offers visitors the combined view of an historic city with its monuments and churches against the backdrop of the 2,234-meter-high (7,657 ft.) Karwendel Massif, covered with snow for the better part of the year. It is not unusual, therefore, in Innsbruck to see businessmen, nurses, and students devoting their noon break to the ski runs halfway up the Karwendel's Nordkette.

Extending beyond the Maria Theresienstrasse is the narrower Herzog Friedrichstrasse, a busy little shopping street reserved for pedestrians. At the widest spot of the street, we find the *Goldenes Dach'l* (Little Golden Roof), built by Maximilian as a tribune against an otherwise plain building. The emperor used it as a reviewing stand from which to observe the entertainment in the street below. The Goldenes Dach'l, designed by Schwabian artist Niklaus Turing, is covered by more than 3,400 gold-plated tiles and decorated with delicately sculptured scenes relating to the life of Maximilian and his two wives.

On the street corner nearest to the Goldenes Dach'l, we find the ornate Helbling Haus, originally built in Gothic style but completely covered with rich rococo ornamentation in the early 1700s. The Stadtturm, also but a few steps away, affords a wonderful view over the old town, including the Goldenes Dach'l and the Helbling Haus.

The present *Hofburg,* or palace, was built during the reign of Maria Theresa. The long and full facade flanked by two towers was finished in 1777. Its colors are a rich "Maria Theresa yellow" with white trim.

The Hofkirche, (Court Church) was completed under Ferdinand I, who finally realized the unfulfilled plans of his grandfather, Maximilian I. The main building is still Gothic in style though it is finished with Renaissance and baroque additions. In it we find the monumental tomb of the emperor surrounded by 28 more-than-lifesize figures in bronze and copper, standing guard around the still empty tomb. In addition there are the sculptures of 23 patron saints of the Habsburg family. The grace of the saints is more attractive than the sobriety of the giants who guard the tomb, but together these three-dimensional statues provide an invaluable resource for the student of medieval costume. The Hofkirche also contains the tomb of Andreas Hofer, hero of the Tyrolean uprising against Napoleon.

The triumphal arch on the Maria Theresienstrasse recalls the days of joys and sorrow of 1765 when a wedding turned into a funeral.

South of Innsbruck we find the towns of Igls and Patsch along the old Brenner Pass Road. From the meadows beyond Patsch we can admire one of the marvels of modern engineering, the Europa Bridge. As part of the new Brenner Toll Road, connecting Austria with Italy, the Europa Bridge spans the Sill Valley. The bridge is 820 meters (2,690 ft.) long and is supported by pylons 190 meters (620 ft.) high. The immense concrete structure dwarfs the farms below it and makes the cars and trucks on it look like toys. A project of this size could only be undertaken by the hard work of Austrians and Italians and the generous contributions of all other European governments.

Continuing eastward along the Inn from Innsbruck, we soon come to Rattenberg. Until Emperor Maximilian took control of the entire Inn Valley as far as Kufstein in 1505, this small fortified town had been the subject of continued strife between Bavaria and Austria. Once the center of a rich mining area, Rattenberg lost its economic importance when the mines

Rattenberg, home of Pilgram Marpeck

were exhausted by the mid-1600s. Consequently, Rattenberg has maintained the medieval appearance of a small Tirolean city.

Today Rattenberg is best known for its hand-cut and engraved glassware which we can observe in process in the numerous shops on both sides of the main street. Overlooking the town is a small castle. At the western end of the main street we find two unusual houses, the so-called Nagelschmiedehauser, built partly into the steep rocks behind them. As cities go, Rattenberg is small and the duration of our visit depends only on how long we want to watch the glass engravers at work.

The entire Inn Valley was the scene of tremendous Anabaptist activity from as early as 1526 through the 1590s. Most likely the believers' church ideas traveled into Austria from the neighboring Swiss cantons of Graubunden, Sankt Gallen, and Appenzell, where Andreas Castelberger, Conrad Grebel, and a host of others were traveling and preaching, and from where Georg Blaurock undertook his missionary journeys.

At any rate, good-sized Anabaptist fellowships were found at Pfunds, Landeck, Imst, Innsbruck, Schwaz, Rattenberg, Kitzbühel, and Kufstein. The strongest of these fellowships existed in and around Rattenberg. In 1529, Leonard Schiemer was beheaded in Rattenberg and his body burned. There followed seventy more martyrs in that city alone. Twenty more lost their lives in neighboring Schwaz and 68 in Kitzbühel. In Kitzbühel the care of the orphaned children of the Anabaptist martyrs became a great burden to the city treasury. The mining magistrate, Pilgram Marpeck of Rattenberg, left town in the summer of 1528 to continue his Anabaptist activities around Strasbourg, France.

Since many Anabaptists were leaving Tirol to find greater freedom in Moravia and elsewhere, Emperor Ferdinand I issued a special edict on March 26, 1534, to the boatmen on the Inn and the Danube Rivers not to accept any Anabaptist passengers. The government was especially interested in tracing and arresting the evangelist Onofrius Griesinger (according to the warrant of June 8, 1533—"of moderate height, without beard, wearing a rough woolen coat, white trousers, brown socks ... has already baptized quite a number of people here in Tirol"). But Griesinger, helped by a sympathetic population, managed to elude his pursuers and held secret meetings attended by large groups of people. In the summer of 1538, Griesinger held a three-day church and communion service and even had the incredible courage to visit brethren (other Anabaptists) who were in prisons. On August 29 his luck ran out and he himself was taken, bound, to Brixen, to be executed two months later in October 1538. The surviving Inn Valley Anabaptists eventually all migrated to Moravia.

Just outside of Rattenberg, near Kramsach, we find the Open Air Museum of Tirolean Farming. To reach the museum village, drive through Kramsach, past the three mountain lakes *(Badeseeen)* to the museum parking lot. A path leads uphill over a ridge into a lovely valley, a perfect setting for the historic farms. Within the farm homes there may be demonstrations of baking and cooking on smoky wood fires, and costumed elderly volunteers will be glad to tell you all about life on a Tirolean farm—however, not in English.

VIENNA, THE PEARL ON THE DANUBE

Vienna, located on the physical and ideological crossroads of East and West, was for six centuries the residence of the Austro-Hungarian Empire. When that empire was carved up by the victorious Allies following World War I, Vienna was made the capital of the new, and much smaller, Austria. Today Vienna again enjoys considerable prestige as an international center.

Twice during its history, in 1529 and in 1683, Vienna withstood a long siege by the Turks. During the second siege, most of the citizens fled, leaving the town to be defended by 24,000 soldiers facing 300,000 Turks, Tatars and Slavs. For two months the city successfully fought off all attacks and on September 12, 1683, the mighty Turkish army was routed in a surprise attack by the forces from within the city and a relatively small relief force sent by the duke of Lorraine.

It is said that delicious croissant rolls served at European breakfast tables originated from a design patent given to the bakers by the emperor when Vienna's bakers, working at night, heard the noise of the Turkish invaders trying to tunnel their way into town.

As with so many other European cities, parking in Vienna is a problem and it is expressly forbidden on any street with streetcar tracks.

There are two good places from which to enjoy a general panoramic view of Vienna, both of which are located in the northern parts of the Vienna Woods (Wienerwald). The 423 meter (1,388 ft.) high Leopoldsberg overlooks the Danube and the northern and eastern parts of Vienna. On the restaurant terrace near the Leopolds Church, a relief design shows Vienna as it was in 1683 at the time of the Turkish siege. From the Kahlenberg, 483 meters (1,385 ft.), the spire of St. Stephans Dom stands out above the city. Between the panoramic terrace and the city we can view the vineyards of Grinzing.

A third, and more recent, point of view is from the revolving platform of the Donauturm, a 252-meter (827 ft.) television tower built on an island in the Danube. The revolving platform and restaurant are located 150 meters (500 ft.) above the ground and offer a fine aerial view of the entire city across the river below.

Still another possibility is a view from the giant ferris wheel of the Prater, which has a diameter of 64 meters (200 ft.). The Prater itself, a large downtown park, was once the hunting reserve of the aristocracy.

Vienna's landmark, St. Stephans Dom, dating back to the 1450s, suffered during the Turkish siege of 1683 and fared even worse under the

Vienna: St. Stephan's Dom

184

Russian bombings of 1945. After the war all the Austrian provinces pulled together to meet the tremendous cost of the cathedral's careful restoration. Stephans Square, heart of medieval Vienna, is dwarfed by the size of the cathedral, whose single spire rises to a height of 137 meters (450 ft.). The tower is open to the public and can be climbed to the level of 73 meters (240 ft.). The stairway has 344 steps. The smaller north tower can be climbed to the floor where the mighty Pummerin bell hangs, 60 meters (197 ft.) above the square. A wide-angle lens is helpful if we want to take photos of the cathedral's colorful glazed tile roof from either tower. Near the Dom, on Domgasse 5, we find the house where Mozart lived from 1784 to 1787, during the time he composed his *Marriage of Figaro*. The Mozart house in Vienna is open for limited visiting hours daily, except on Mondays.

Vienna has three magnificent palaces: the Upper and the Lower Belvedere and Schönbrunn Palace. Today the two Belvedere palaces, designed by Lukas von Hildebrand for Prince Eugen von Savoie, 1663-1736, house Austria's major art collection, with paintings and sculptures ranging from the medieval to the contemporary.

Schönbrunn is a magnificent residence built to replace an imperial hunting lodge destroyed by the Turks. The exterior of this palace, built between 1695 and 1749, is also finished in "Maria Theresa Yellow." The interior is finished in red, white, and gold baroque ornamentation. Guided tours take you through 45 of Schönbrunn's 1,200 rooms. The palace's formal gardens are open to the public until sundown.

Among the things left behind by the Turks, in their hasty retreat in 1683, were large amounts of coffee. Soon the dark-colored drink became increasingly popular in Austria and even gave its name to those places in which it was served. Eventually the cafés of Vienna, of Budapest, of Innsbruck, and from there on throughout Europe, became the places of rendezvous for the artists, the writers, and the prosperous bourgeoisie. In Vienna, the café is still a time-honored institution.

Horse lovers should not miss the Spanish Riding School, where the training of horses can be seen between 10:00 and noon, Tuesdays through Saturdays, except during July and August. Costumed performances are featured occasionally. The Spanish Riding School is the home of the world-famous Lippizaner horses.

Vienna never had an Anabaptist congregation for any length of time but was the scene of at least 23 executions during the reign of Ferdinand I. Among the prominent martyrs were Balthasar Hubmaier and his wife, executed on March 10, 1528; Jakob Wiedemann, also known as One-Eyed Jakob, an early leader of the Moravian Hutterites; and Oswald Glaidt, the co-worker and later fellow prisoner of Hans Hut.

In 1527, Hut and Glaidt had held a meeting in a house on the Karntertrasse, at which time Hut baptized no less than 50 people. Among these was Leonard Schiemer, who later lost his life at Rattenberg. The well-

Vienna: Schönbrunn Palace

Excursion boats on the Danube, Budapest, Hungary

advertised threat by the emperor to tear down the houses in which such meetings took place, was not always carried out in Vienna. The Inn Freisinger Hof actually lodged Anabaptist missioners later than that.

THE (NOT ALWAYS) BLUE DANUBE

The Danube (Donau) is Western Europe's longest river with a course of 2,826 kilometers (1,757 miles) between its sources in the Black Forest and its Black Sea delta at the Russo-Romanian border. Although the Danube could be navigable at least up to Regensburg in Bavaria, there is very little traffic on the river, at least when compared with the ever-busy Rhine. For centuries the lack of development was due to the uncertainties of Balkan politics. Since the Cold War the strained relations between East and West have hampered the further development of the Danube into the great commercial waterway it could be.

Between May and the end of September, the DDSG Steamship Company, with offices in Vienna, Austria, and Passau, Germany, runs regular passenger services between these two cities, with stops at Krems, Melk, and Linz. Both Austrian and Soviet ships ply up and down the Danube between Vienna and Yalta, on the Black Sea, which is a six-day trip downstream, eight days upstream.

Visas need to be secured for the transit through the Eastern Bloc nations and we camera buffs will discover that there are strict rules on what we may or may not photograph. From personal experience, I know that photographing a charming farm wagon can get you into a lot of trouble if that wagon happens to be located in a restricted area.

For more information on Danube River excursions between Passau and Vienna or from Vienna on east to Russia, write to: DDSG Reisedienst, Mexicoplatz 8, A 1020 Vienna, Austria.

For students of Moravian Anabaptism and Hutterite history, Vienna is a good starting point for trips across the border into Czechoslovakia at Nikolsburg (Mikulov) or at Bratislava, or to Budapest, Hungary, via Hegyeshalom. For details on what to see there, read The Golden Years of the Hutterites, by Leonard Gross, Herald Press, 1980.

IN THE SOUTHEASTERN PROVINCES

Finally we mention the cities of Graz and Bruck an der Mur. Graz was never much of an Anabaptist center but as the only administrative center of any size for three southern provinces, Anabaptists captured throughout the region were usually tried and executed here. In 1529 the painter Kasper allowed his house in Graz to be used for secret meetings and baptisms. When this was discovered, the house was destroyed pursuant to the orders of the emperor and the building site sold to the benefit of the Catholic Church. The site is said to have been a valuable corner lot, not far from the cathedral.

In Bruck an der Mur, nine men and three women were executed in 1528. In a café near the Hauptplatz, we can still see a primitive mural which records the execution of the Anabaptist Hans Oehl for his stubborn heresy. The mural obviously was intended as a warning to other would-be defectors from the true and Catholic faith.

Not far from Graz at Stübing is the Austrian National Open Air Museum. In a secluded valley, three kilometers (two miles) from the main road, more than fifty homesteads and their outbuildings have been reconstructed on a forty-hectare (100 acres) tract. All of the groupings blend beautifully with the landscape and give the visitor a good feel of yesterday's rural Austria, from the thatched-roof Burgenland farms to the square stone farmhouses of Upper Austria. The museum is open from April through October, closed on Mondays.

JanGleysteen/84

LIECHTENSTEIN

FL

Fürstentum Liechtenstein

The tiny principality of Liechtenstein, which covers an area of less than 160 square kilometers (about 60 square miles), is one of the smallest countries in the world. (Washington, D.C., is larger by about eight square miles.) The Fürstentum Liechtenstein, as it is called, is separated from Switzerland by the Rhine, while the first or second range of the steep Bregenzerwald Alps forms Liechtenstein's natural boundary with Austria. The present population numbers about 23,000.

In the days of Charlemagne two dukedoms were set up, Vaduz and Schellenberg. In 1699 Prince Johann Adam von Liechtenstein bought Schellenberg. Fourteen years later he added Vaduz and combined the two dukedoms into one hereditary principality under the Austrian House of Lords. In 1866 Furstentum Liechtenstein became independent but maintained strong economic ties with Austria. With the fall of the Austro-Hungarian Empire in 1918, Liechtenstein severed its economic ties with Austria and began to orient itself toward its western neighbor, Switzerland. In 1924 Liechtenstein signed a customs union agreement with that country. Along with Switzerland, Liechtenstein was able to remain neutral throughout World War II, even though it had no army and only a couple of police officers.

Until 1938 the principality did have an army which consisted of one man who was both general and private and who gave himself marching orders, but one day the entire army died and has never been replaced.

According to one tongue-in-cheek story, Liechtenstein did experience a grave threat to its sovereignty some years ago. A Swiss cavalry unit, out on night exercises, took a wrong turn and ended up in Liechtenstein. The Liechtensteiners made a citizen's arrest and escorted the Swiss invaders to a good restaurant, where they treated them to a sumptuous meal. The Swiss captain apologized, "After all, horses don't have good headlights and

Liechtenstein looks pretty much like Switzerland in the dark." Now if we could only get the White House and the Kremlin to go by this historic precedent.

The country has been ruled by Franz Josef II since 1938. The prince appoints foreign representatives, negotiates trade agreements, calls Parliament into session and must approve all laws. The prince appoints a prime minister who is responsible to a fifteen-member Landtag, elected by Liechtenstein's adult male citizens. The prince owns one of the world's finest private art collections, housed in his castle overlooking Vaduz. It includes originals by Rembrandt, Brueghel, Botticelli, and Rubens.

Perhaps the most fascinating product of this postage stamp-sized country is postage stamps. About a quarter of Liechtenstein's national income comes from the sale of limited edition commemorative issues. Whenever a new bridge needs to be constructed or a government building enlarged or remodeled, another beautiful stamp is designed and printed. Always issued in small editions, Liechtenstein's stamps soon become collectors' items, worth far more than their face value. The new post office building itself was paid for through the one-day sale of a very special issue. Philatelists often line up before dawn to buy their two-set per customer limit of a new series. They say that enterprising students make good money standing in line for those who don't care to get up that early, or by retailing sets to people who didn't get there in time. Many of Liechtenstein's stamp issues are carefully printed full-color reproductions of the prince's famous art collection.

Liechtenstein has no embassies or consulates anywhere, except for their mission in Bern. Wherever they have consular representation, the Swiss also represent Liechtenstein. Because of Liechtenstein's liberal tax policies, more than 10,000 foreign companies have "offices" in the country. In many cases these offices consist of little more than a neatly polished brass plaque on a building that could not possibly house that many working firms with worldwide connections. Other nations that encourage such tax-haven registry are Liberia, Panama, and the Bermudas.

THE ANABAPTIST-MENNONITE STORY

With the early Anabaptist leaders Blaurock, Manz, Grebel, Castelberger, Bolt, and Uolimann extremely active in the neighboring cantons across the Rhine, and with the (for a while) predominantly Anabaptist canton of Appenzell just a few miles away, it is entirely possible that there were Anabaptist conventicles in Liechtenstein as well, though no records of such remain. In the summer of 1526, Conrad Grebel himself died at Maienfeld, just eight kilometers (five miles) south of Liechtenstein. Fifty years later, Hutterite missioners were active in Austria's Vorarlberg and particularly successful at Rankweil, only eight kilometers (five miles) north of Liechtenstein. The last execution of Anabaptists anywhere in Europe, in

The castle of Vaduz, Liechtenstein

Liechtenstein's last soldier

191

1618, took place at Egg, a little town along the same Bregenzerwald which forms the Liechtenstein-Austrian border.

Only recent history provides a direct link between Liechtenstein and Anabaptism. With the rise of Adolf Hitler, members of the Rhon Bruderhof at Sannerz, Germany, found it increasingly difficult to reconcile their consciences with that which was demanded of them. They feared especially the induction of their young people into the *Hitlerjugend* (Hitler Youth) or into Germany's armed forces. In 1934 a number of them fled Germany to establish a new Bruderhof in Liechtenstein. It was located on the Triesenberg above Vaduz and went by the name Alm Bruderhof Silum.

When Hitler annexed Austria in 1938, the occupants of the Alm Bruderhof fled to England. But, because the Brethren were German and anti-German sentiment ran high in England, they were forced to keep moving on. In 1941, when World War II was raging fiercely, Mennonite Central Committee arranged for the group to make the long voyage to Paraguay on a blacked-out freighter, evading the German U-boats. They arrived there safely to establish the Primavera community about 130 kilometers (80 miles) northeast of Asuncion. Today this group of mixed German, English, and now American members, known as the Hutterian Society of Brothers, lives at Farmington, Pennsylvania; Rifton, New York; and Norwalk, Connecticut.

A Summary of General Information

The official language of Furstentum Liechtenstein, wedged between German-speaking Austria and the German-speaking cantons of Switzerland, is German. However, little Liechtenstein is so tourist-oriented that the waiters in cafes and the clerks in the stores can efficiently handle four or five other languages. In some of the bigger stores is at least one of the clerks can give the Japanese or Arabs a good sales talk on cuckoo clocks or jewelry in their own language.

For climate and the seasons, consult this section under *Switzerland,* page 80.

The Swiss authorities take care of the customs formalities on the border between Austria and Liechtenstein and you will not have to go through customs again when you cross the Rhine or head south for Chur.

In Liechtenstein the Swiss Frank is common currency. However, the stores in Vaduz, Schaanwald, and elsewhere accept almost anything within reason from Swedish Kroner and Spanish Pesetas to South African Rands as long as they can make a sale.

Liechtenstein usually shows up on the eastern edge of the maps of Switzerland or on the western edge of maps of Austria. Separate maps of Liechtenstein are hard to find.

HOLLAND

Nederland NL

When we think of Holland we probably have visions of tulips and wooden shoes, canals, windmills, and tall brick houses with fancy gables. Well, we will not be disappointed. They are all still there in great numbers— the tulips, of course, only in season. But there is much more. Few countries can offer you so much scenery and so much history in such a compact area.

Most of the Dutch people use the names Holland and Netherlands interchangeably— *Hol* meaning hollow or low and *Nether* also meaning low—though technically speaking the name Holland applies only to the two western provinces, North Holland and South Holland. People from Friesland and Groningen probably will not agree with the above statement. They always talk about going to Holland when they visit relatives in Haarlem or shop in Amsterdam. They use the word Netherlands only for the country as a whole.

Either way, about three fifths of the country is below sea level. Medieval travelers used to complain that they could not tell where the sea ended and the land began and the early rulers of the land were called the water lords. Since then the water lords and their subjects have gotten things sorted out a bit better but most of the land is still hollow and the process continues. The latest statistics show that the Netherlands has an area of about 2,600 square kilometers, which is almost a thousand square miles more than at the beginning of the century. The Dutch had to fight for this additional territory but they took it from the sea rather than from other nations. Still this battle has its own heroes, for the North Sea has proven itself to be a formidable enemy.

In 1555 this collection of watery lordships came under the rule of Philip II of Spain who thoroughly disliked the country's climate and damp- ness as well as the Dutch people and their Protestant religion. The Dutch, chafing under Philip's rule, found a champion in Willem de Zwijger (William the Silent), a prince of Orange and a man of few words. Willem de Zwijger was far ahead of his contemporaries in his thinking. He greatly influenced the future tolerant and cosmopolitan outlook of the Dutch. "I cannot appreciate," said Willem in 1564, "princes trying to govern the conscience of their subject people and wanting to deprive them of their religious liberties." He said this, mind you, a full century before the Compromise of Augsburg, when later princes and bishops once again agreed to limit the religious freedom of their subjects through the law of *Cuius Regio, Ejus Religio.*

For a while the Spanish were generally successful in land battles but the Dutch controlled the waters. When the Spanish attacked the Dutch rebels in Leiden in 1573 the Dutch broke the dikes surrounding the city and the rebel fleet sailed over the frozen polders to rescue the city. Except for a twelve-year armistice, 1609-21, the Dutch continued to fight the Spanish for eighty years. Willem de Zwijger was assassinated in Delft in 1584, but his son Prince Maurits continued the battle. In 1588 the Dutch joined the British to defeat the Spanish Armada. Sixty years later, in 1648, Spain finally recognized the independence of the Low Countries.

Even as the long war continued, the Dutch grew in power and prosperity and the 1600s became known as Holland's Golden Age. The merchant fleet tripled in size. The East India Trading Company (VOC) was founded in 1602, the West India Trading Company (WIC) in 1621. By 1650 the Dutch provided more than half of the world's shipping with 160,000 sailors serving on 16,289 ships. Jan van Riebeeck established a supply station at the southern point of South Africa and called it Kaapstad, now Capetown. Jan Pietersz Coen established Batavia, now Djakarta, and Jan Abel Tasman explored Australia. His name is remembered in Tasmania.

While the struggle for independence continued, Holland welcomed refugees from elsewhere to its land. The French Huguenots in particular added much to Holland's cultural growth. Others who benefited from Holland's liberal policies were Jews from Eastern Europe and from Spain, the Pilgrims (who later moved on to Massachusetts), the Hernnhutters, Swiss and South German Anabaptists, Quakers, English Baptists, and others. Each of these groups added its own particular skills to the whole which hastened the blossoming of Dutch creativity in the arts and sciences.

Rembrandt van Rijn, Frans Hals, Jan Steen, Jan Vermeer, and Meindert Hobbema were busy painting. The Jewish philosopher Spinoza, a refugee from Spain, found a home with a Mennonite family in Leiden. Hugo de Groot laid down the principles of international law. Jan van Campen and Hendrik de Keyser were the leading architects. Jan van Leeuwenhoek invented the microscope, and Christiaan Huygens, the pendulum clock. The biologist Jan van Swammerdam—using knives so tiny that they had to be sharpened under van Leeuwenhoek's microscope—made important discoveries about the function of nerves and the muscles. Joost van den Vondel wrote magnificent poetry and stage plays. The world's first paved highway was completed in Holland in 1650. Soon the Netherlands played a role in the history of Europe far out of proportion to its physical size and in spite of the continuing struggle against the Spanish until 1648.

Holland thereafter remained a free nation until 1795 when the French invaded it. In 1806 Napoleon renamed it the Batavian Republic and installed his brother Louis Napoleon as king. The Dutch drove out the French in 1813. After the ultimate defeat of Napoleon, in 1815, world leaders meeting at Vienna redrew the map of Europe. They reestablished the Seventeen Provinces of the Low Countries and Willem VI, prince of Orange, became King Willem I of the Netherlands and Luxembourg.

But by this time the language, the temperament, and the religious views of the northern and southern Hollanders differed greatly. Most of the southerners were Catholic and the upper classes now spoke French. In 1830 the five southern provinces seceded from Holland to form a new nation. They invited King Leopold von Saxe-Coburg to become the first king of the new Belgium. Luxembourg seceded from Holland in 1890 when ten-year-old Wilhelmina became queen upon the death of her father, Willem III. Luxembourg's laws did not provide for a female ruler.

Another century of peace and progress followed including a great cultural revival. Josef Israels, the three Maris brothers—Jacob, Matthijs, and Willem—Anton Mauve, Willem Mesdag, and his wife, Sientje Mesdag van Houten, were among those who established the Haagse school of impressionism. Towering above all of them was Vincent van Gogh, a leader among the modern European artists. Within a short time during the first half of this century, seven Dutch scientists won Nobel prizes for their discoveries in physics and medicine.

During World War I, the Dutch managed to remain neutral, even though many Dutch ships were torpedoed by the Germans or confiscated by the Allies, drastically interfering with Holland's worldwide shipping, its chief source of income. After World War I, Holland's prosperity never returned.

On May 10, 1940, Adolf Hitler suddenly and savagely attacked the Netherlands and occupied the country within five days. The royal family and many government people managed to escape to England, just in time, on May 14. Out of frustration the Germans ordered the destruction bombing of Rotterdam that same day. Though the actual number of dead, numbering in the thousands, will probably remain unknown, 25,000 homes and 11,000 other buildings were destroyed and 77,000 persons lost everything they had.

The five-year German occupation left most of the land in ruins and 270,000 people were killed, many of them in Nazi extermination camps, including 104,000 of Holland's Jewish citizens. A liberation attempt by

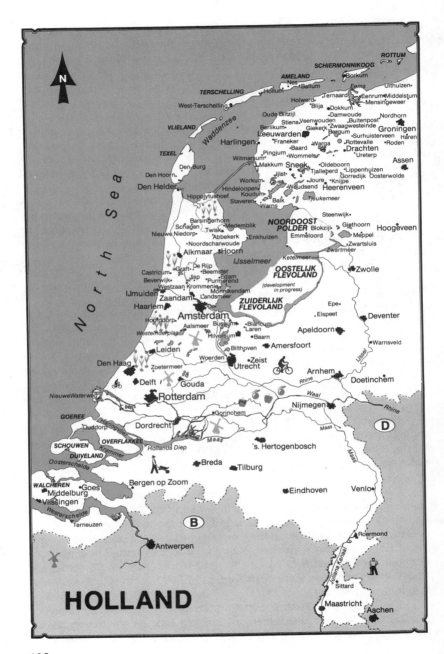

HOLLAND

British paratroopers on September 17, 1944, at Arnhem and Oosterbeek, failed. All of Holland north of the great rivers remained under German occupation until the fall of the Third Reich as a whole in May 1945. By this time the land had suffered starvation, inundation, and massive wanton destruction of property.

When the war ended, industry, labor, and government worked together to put the country back on the road to prosperity. In addition, to alleviate the high population density, the government actively encouraged emigration. Nearly half a million people went to Australia, New Zealand, Canada, South America, and the United States during the first few years after the war. The emigration to Canada is now down to about 9,000 people yearly, while New Zealand and Australia attract between 500 and 600 persons, mostly farmers. Even so, the population density amounts to 895 persons per square kilometer (2,300 persons per square mile) in the western part of the country, one of the highest concentrations of people in the world. The total population of Holland is now around 14 million.

Holland is characterized by three different types of landscapes: (1) along the coast a sand bar is traceable through a chain of islands in the north and the south, and by coastal dunes between these; (2) the eastern uplands with a few hills and ridges of glacial origin, and (3) in the center we find that landscape so characteristic of the Dutch scene—the polders.

In the Roman days the lowlands between the dunes and the uplands consisted of a huge shallow swamp in which the shape of the land was constantly being changed through the effect of wind and the waters. Originally, people tried to settle this land by building mounds called *terpen*. One can still find terpen in Friesland.

By the 1200s the Dutch were busy drying out this land by building dikes and pumping out the water within. The result in each case is a polder. In the beginning such polders were drained and kept dry by windmills and later by steam-powered pumping stations. Today the water level in the polders is maintained by electric pumping stations capable of moving 30,000 gallons of water per minute. Since so much of the country is below sea level, the rivers too must be bordered by dikes. Otherwise they would flood the land.

In 1852 the Dutch succeeded in draining the huge 18,000-hectare (44,500-acre) Haarlemmer Lake between Amsterdam and Haarlem with the aid of steam pumping stations. Today Amsterdam's airport, *Schiphol,* (Ship's Hollow,) is located in one corner of this former lake and jumbo jets regularly put their wheels down on runways laid 16 feet below sea level.

Each polder has an integrated system of drainage ditches and canals to move the ever-present ground water to higher levels and out to the sea. Only in Holland one can see cows grazing below and an ocean-going freighter gliding past between the dikes above. Since the 1950s gigantic steel troughs even carry important waterways over four-lane highways.

"Zeswielen" windmill group near Alkmaar

Land below sea level: ships above and meadows below

Since the 1920s the most ambitious poldering project of all has been taking place and is still in process. From 1927 to 1932 the gigantic 30-kilometer (22-mile) dike connecting north Holland with Friesland was finished under the direction of master engineer Dr. Cornelis Lely. The completion of the dike was a momentous occasion followed with great interest by the whole world. It was the Dutch equivalent of the driving of the Golden Spike. The enclosed arm of the high seas, the Zuiderzee, metamorphosed from a salt-water sea into a fresh-water lake, now called Ijsselmeer. Then the poldering process began.

First the northwest corner was diked in and drained to form the Wieringermeer Polder, completed in 1930, followed by the Noordoost Polder in 1943. The East Flevoland Polder emerged from the waters by 1957 followed by the South Flevoland Polder in 1968. The last and final polder, the Markerwaard, is scheduled to become land sometime during the 1980s. And again Holland will have grown in area by 10 percent since the big dike was completed 50 years ago. Another small sea, the Lauwers Zee, an inland sea between Groningen and Friesland was diked in and reclaimed by 1970.

After each polder becomes land, it takes more years to develop the roads, lay out the farms, and to establish the towns, recreation areas, and industrial zones—all according to plans worked out well in advance. Although a growing population necessitates a policy of continued expansion, the demands made on the environment by industry, housing, transportation, and recreation confront the authorities with complex decisions which can be made only within a framework of national planning and zoning. Ultimately, such decisions can be made only in a European context, and Holland, a pioneer in European integration, will doubtless continue in that direction. Actually Holland, densely populated and highly developed, hopes to become a pioneer in solving those problems that will confront all of Western civilization by the end of the century. To the Dutch, turning garbage into electricity is nothing new. They have had to do it for fifty years, already.

Firm believers in neutrality throughout most of their history, the Dutch have increasingly participated in international organizations during this century. Active in the League of Nations between the wars, Holland became a charter member of the United Nations in 1945. Den Haag (the Hague) was the site of peace conferences in 1899 and 1907, after which it became home to the Permanent Court of Arbitration. To house the court, the Peace Palace was built in Den Haag with finances provided by the American Andrew Carnegie. Holland initiated the Benelux Customs Union and became a founding member of the European Economic Community and the later Euratom. The Dutch as a whole are quite anti-militaristic, and are only halfhearted participants in NATO. They are outspoken in their disgust with big-power leaders who can offer only military solutions to complex social problems.

Of the 10,000 windmills that once dotted the polder landscape, only a few more than 1,000 remain, all duly registered and protected by the Windmill Preservation Society. Many of these are in working order. We have already mentioned that windmills in great number were once used to drain the polders. Mills are also used to make paper, press oil, grind pigments, make mustard and spices, and saw logs. Many still perform many tasks now usually done by more modern machinery. By virtue of its many windmills the land along the Zaan River is considered the world's first truly industrial region.

And Holland still is an industrial nation. The textile industry is one of the oldest industries in the country, with numerous yarn and woolen mills in the cities of Noord Brabant and a cotton industry centered around Almelo and Enschede on the German border. Enschede has a special academy for textile designers. The world's first artificial fiber, Enkalon, was developed by the Enka industry in Arnhem.

Although Holland has no iron ore of its own and depends on imported ores from Sweden and France, the steel mills at Velsen are among the most productive in Europe. Located in a beautiful region of dunes and woodlands, the steel mills are extremely environment conscious. They even developed noiseless locomotives to run ore trains through the residential areas.

In the 1890s Gerard and Anton Philips started a small factory to make light bulbs in the village Eindhoven. With a staff of ten persons, they produced about 500 lamps per day. Today Philips is one of the world's largest electrical manufacturers with 336,000 employees and with plants and sales organizations in 60 different countries.

Though 73,000 workers are employed by the Eindhoven factories, Philips and the Dutch government decided to find an alternative to commuting, considered a waste of precious energy. The result was to take the work to the workers at fifty closer-to-home locations throughout Holland and Belgium. Known around the world as Philips, the company trades in North America under the name Norelco.

Another major Dutch company is Royal Dutch Shell. You have done business with this company if you ever bought a tank of gasoline at a Shell station. The Royal Dutch Airlines (KLM), established in 1912, is the world's oldest airline and runs the world's second largest network of routes.

Being so highly industrialized, Holland has long had a strong labor movement. The four major unions are part of the Netherlands Labor Foundation, an organization of employers and unions designed to work out common goals and to settle industrial disputes. Strikes are practically unheard of.

Although heavily industrialized, the Netherlands depends on agriculture, not only for home consumption, but also for foreign income, exporting fresh vegetables to neighboring countries and dairy products all over

A nationwide network of waterways

Evening rush hour: 14 million people, 10 million bicycles

the world. Holland's famous black-and-white Frisian-Holstein cattle have the highest yield per cow per acre of grassland. Capable of delivering as much as 80,000 pounds of milk per year, the Frisian cattle are much in demand for improving cattle strains in other countries. There is even a monument to the Frisian cow in the city of Leeuwarden captioned "Us Mem" (loosely translated as "the mother of us all"). You can probably find Gouda and Edam cheese (Dutch cheeses) in your neighborhood supermarket.

Tulip bulbs from the fields near Lisse and Hillegom find their way to gardens in the moderate zones of both hemispheres and cut flowers auctioned at Aalsmeer in the morning are flown to florists in Paris, Rome, Chicago, and New York in the afternoon. Horticulture is important both for the number of people employed as well as for overseas earnings. There is an important Higher Institute of Horticulture at Wageningen.

A vast network of canals and waterways totaling over 8,000 kilometers (5,000 miles) reach almost every city of importance. The Dutch National Railways serves all parts of the country with the highest frequency of trains in Europe. Their motto: fast, safe, and inexpensive. The average town in Holland is served by 106 passenger trains daily between the hours of 6:00 in the morning and midnight. Nights are basically reserved for freight trains.

The Dutch are enthusiastic bikers. There are 10.7 million bikes in use among the 14 million inhabitants. Try to cross a busy street in Amsterdam at 5:00 in the afternoon and you'll be convinced that you're dodging half of them. And when you are away from home you can always rent a bike for a modest fee from most of the railroad stations.

Holland has more museums per capita and per square mile than any other country in the world, and the Dutch themselves are avid museumgoers. Through its National Tourist Offices in New York and Toronto (see addresses on p. 26) Americans and Canadians can purchase a Holland Culture Card for approximately $7.50 (U.S.). The HCC, valid for one year, will give you free entry to over two hundred museums and substantial reductions on organ recitals, live theater, ballet and opera performances. The Royal Dutch Airline (KLM) offers a tour which includes a card similar to the HCC.

DUTCH ANABAPTISM, PAST AND PRESENT

Anabaptism came to the Netherlands in 1530 through Jan Volkertsz Trijpmaker, a follower of Melchior Hofmann. A congregation was formed in Amsterdam and the movement spread rapidly. In the formative years, 1530-1534, some Anabaptists were violent revolutionaries. Even though these groups came to a violent end, the peaceful Anabaptists, who united under Obbe Phillips, had to pay dearly, often with their lives, for their association (usually in name only) with the insurrectionist groups. In Holland the most severe persecution of the Anabaptists lasted only about fifty years. The last Anabaptist was executed in 1574. Even though other forms of harassment and special taxation for Anabaptists lasted much longer, congregations were allowed to develop quietly. This was certainly a different situation from that in many other European countries where Anabaptists continued to be openly persecuted for centuries.

One of the most important Anabaptist leaders to come out of the Netherlands was Menno Simons. Menno came from the town of Witmarsum in the northern province of Friesland. For a while he was a priest. He then joined the Anabaptist movement in 1536 after he studied the Scriptures and found no biblical basis for infant baptism or transubstantiation. He soon became a strong, loving leader. He lived his life as an itinerant preacher and although he was in constant flight from the authorities, his influence was widespread. He ministered to congregations in Friesland, Holland, Limburg, western Germany, and in places as far away as Danzig (Gdansk).

In addition to being a leader and a preacher, Menno Simons was an author. He secretly published his books from 1551 until the time of his death in 1561. Menno died a natural death at Oldesloe (then in Danish territory). The name Mennonite had its origins in East Friesland, where Anabaptists were first called "Mennisten" after Menno Simons. However, the Dutch Anabaptists themselves preferred the name *Doopsgezind* (baptism-minded), a term still used today.

There were three main groups of Mennonites in the Netherlands: (1) The Frisians, (2) the Waterlanders, who made their home in the watery lands north of Amsterdam, and (3) the Flemish, who had migrated north to escape the severe persecution in Flanders. Unfortunately, these groups were not at peace with one another. The Frisians were the most conservative. They practiced the use of the ban (excommunication) and retained authoritarian leaders. The Flemish were also conservative but they were culturally different from the Frisians. These cultural and temperamental differences caused many difficulties between the two groups. The Waterlanders also held to the traditional Anabaptist beliefs, yet they were always more tolerant of other Anabaptists and of other Christians. During the first century, many leaders, including Menno Simons and Hans de Ries, labored to settle the differences among the various groups. But it took time. In 1811 the Algemeene Doopsgezinde Societeit, (ADS) a general conference unifying all Mennonite churches in the Netherlands, was organized.

The Dutch Mennonites have a long history of being generous. The Amsterdam Mennonites worked particularly at aiding their persecuted brothers and sisters in other countries. In 1660 and 1662 they collected funds for the distressed Mennonites in Danzig and Poland. In 1672 they helped the Palatine Mennonites financially, and in 1709 they gave aid to the Bernese Mennonites when their government moved with full force to eradicate them. For nearly 300 years there has been a Committee of Foreign Needs. In 1694 the Mennonites of Amsterdam took up two offerings totaling

52,000 Guldens to assist their persecuted Mennonites in the Palatinate. Mennonites also played an important role in the public charitable institutions, including an organization for national welfare and an institute for the deaf in Groningen.

Dutch Mennonites made many cultural contributions to the Netherlands. One of Holland's foremost poets and playwrights, the Shakespeare of Holland, Joost van den Vondel, was a Mennonite for most of his life. Several of the leading artists during Holland's Golden Age were Mennonites. These include Salomon Ruysdael and Jacob Ruysdael and Jan and Casper Luyken. Jan Luyken's etchings illustrate the *Martyrs Mirror,* which was compiled by another Dutch Mennonite, Tieleman Jansz van Braght. And although there is no documentation to suggest that Rembrandt van Rijn was a Mennonite, he was close to, and influenced by, the Waterlander Mennonites. In addition to contributions in the fine arts, Mennonites made other diverse contributions—from Jan van der Heyden's invention of the fire engine to Pieter Pietersz' innovations on the windmill to Jan Adriaansz Leeghwaters' significant work in land reclamation.

The Dutch Mennonites have declined greatly in number over the past century, particularly during the past two decades. Today there are 22,500 baptized members in 140 congregations located, for the greater part, in Friesland and North Holland. They are active in relief and development aid and committed to peace and nonresistance. As small as they are, they manage to support a weekly periodical of high quality, the *Algemeen Doopsgezind Weekblad.* The seminary in Amsterdam was founded in the 1740s and is the oldest Mennonite seminary in existence.

The Dutch Language

The language spoken in Holland is Dutch or Hollands. The people in the northern province of Friesland also speak Frisian, which is divided into Fries and Stads-Fries (City-Fries). In Holland nearly everybody is multilingual and eager to test their skills on visitors.

The Climate

The great Dutch masters of the 17th century, Jacob and Salomon Ruysdael, Meindert Hobbema, Jan van Goyen, have introduced the world to Holland's dramatic skies through their landscape paintings. The same towering masses of rapidly moving clouds are still to be seen today, with occasional rays of sun spotlighting red tile roofs, fresh green willows, and the chugging barges traveling on the nation's rivers. Holland's climate is oceanic, cool and wet. The average annual rainfall amounts to 750 millimeters (30 inches) distributed over 200 days. Dutch summers are probably cooler than one would expect. The winters, however, are more gentle. Only once every four to five years do the canals freeze over hard enough to make skating possible. Because Holland lies so far north, however, during the winter the daylight hours are short and the days are often dark and gloomy.

A forceful western wind blows almost constantly and it doesn't take a compass to find our direction in Holland. Most of the trees are wind-blown and point east. If we plan to bike through Holland, knowing about this prevailing wind direction can save us many hours and a lot of energy.

The Best Times to See Holland

For many the word "Holland" will bring forth images of tulips, windmills, and wooden shoes. If we wish to see the tulips, hyacinths, and daffodils in their full glory, the best time for us to visit Holland is between mid-April and mid-May. The precise time is about as hard to pinpoint as the right weekend for observing maple sugaring in Pennsylvania or for viewing the cherry blossoms in Washington, D.C. Fortunately, the tulip season is fairly long and we are almost certain to see fields in bloom, whether they are the early varieties, the late ones, or all of them at once. Everywhere tree buds are springing open and a fresh green haze forms a fairy-tale background to the annual explosion of colors. Holland is also a paradise for bird watchers at this time, as large wading birds and small song birds are all busy raising the next generation. In the Betuwe region between the great rivers, the orchards are in bloom.

Summer is a good time to explore the dunes along the North Sea or to take boat trips on the rivers, canals, and lakes. On the Hoge Veluwe National Park and in het Gooi the heather will be in bloom. In the autumn the leaves simply turn brown and drop. The scene will not be considered spectacular to those who have seen the autumn colors of Indiana or Ontario. Fall mornings may be foggy and chilly.

Since the 1940s there has been a shift in climate all over the Northern Hemisphere, and winters that bring snow and ice are increasingly rare. There is a good chance, though, that we will see the morning fog frozen to every tree, bridge railing,

Constant winds from the west provide a slanted image

streetlight, and ship's mast, turning each into a fine, white filigree piece of artwork. Since Holland is this far north, the hours of actual daylight are notably short. Any season is a good one to visit Holland's great museums or to listen to its famous orchestras conducted by celebrated maestros.

Holidays in Holland

In addition to the major holidays of the Christian year, the Dutch celebrate the royal birthday, now fixed at April 30, regardless of the current monarch's actual birthday, and Liberation Day, May 5, now celebrated every five years only—1985, 1990, 1995, and so forth. December 6, Sint Nikolaas' Day, is not an official holiday, but it sure seems like one.

Special Rules of the Road

Public transportation—trams, buses, and taxis—have priority over all other traffic, including pedestrians. As noted earlier, Holland is the land of cyclists with 10.7 million bicycles owned by 14 million inhabitants. Accordingly, there are more than 10,000 kilometers (6,000 miles) of bike paths. Beware of striped crossings and of signs that read *Fietsers Oversteken* (Cyclists cross here). Tourists are often surprised by cyclists coming out of the bushes to cross the highway at these places. When facing traffic in a narrow street or on a one-lane bridge, we should go first if the square blue sign with two arrows is on our side. We must wait for the oncoming traffic if the round red-bordered sign with two arrows is on our side.

The Monetary System

Holland's monetary unit is the Gulden (variously abbreviated as *fl, Hfl,* or just plain *f,* all of which stands for the antiquated term *florin).* The Gulden is divided into 100 cents. It comes in the form of 1¢ (now disappearing) and 5¢ pieces (copper); 10 and 25¢ pieces, 1 and 2½ Gulden coins (silver alloy). The 10¢ coin, called *dubbeltje,* is perhaps the smallest coin you have ever seen. Notes come in the denominations of 5, 10, 25, 100 Gulden, and higher.

Holland was the first country to make their paper money identifiable to blind persons. The 100 Gulden note carries one rough dot on the lower left-hand corner, the 25 two, the 10 three, and the 5 has a straight line. Other countries are now developing their particular variations on this principle.

AMSTERDAM BY BOAT AND ON FOOT

Many Dutch towns—Edam, Volendam, Monnickendam, Rotterdam, for example–have a *Dam,* the place where in bygone years the river was dammed up and the few houses around the church formed the beginning of the town. As European cities go, Amsterdam is not very old. The people who built a dam on the Amstel River received their city charter in 1275.

A glance at the map shows that Amsterdam consists of a series of concentric canals around this dam, like growth rings of a tree. With many connecting canals and streets, downtown Old Amsterdam looks pretty much like a spiderweb or a spoked wheel. If we understand this layout, it will help us to reach most destinations with little difficulty.

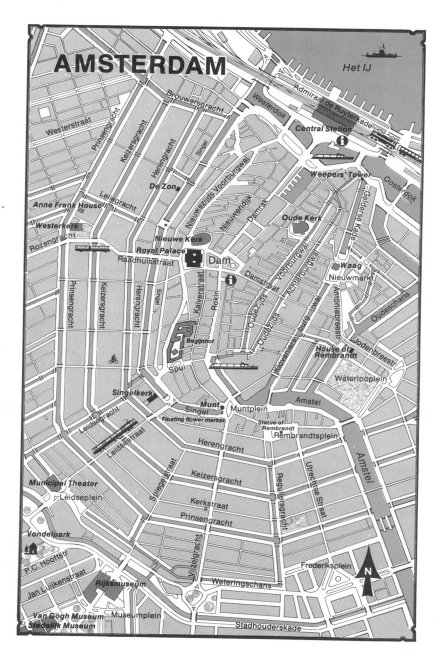

AMSTERDAM

Het IJ

Westerstraat

Brouwersgracht

Westerdok

Admiraal de Ruyterkade

Central Station

Prinsengracht

Keizersgracht

Herengracht

Singel

Westerstraat

Leliegracht

Nieuwezijds Voorburgwal

Nieuwendijk

Damrak

Weepers Tower

Oosterdok

Gelders Kade

De Zon

Anne Frank House

Westerkerk

Rozengracht

Nieuwe Kerk

Royal Palace

Raadhuisstraat

Dam

Oude Kerk

Oudezijds Voorburgwal

Achterburgwal

Waag

Nieuwmarkt

Damstraat

Antoniebreestr

Prinsengracht

Keizersgracht

Herengracht

Singel

Kalverstraat

Rokin

Oudezijds

Kloveniersburgwal

Oudeschans

Begijnhof

Spui

House of Rembrandt

Jodenbreestr

Waterlooplein

Singelkerk

Munt

Singel

Muntplein

Floating flower market

Statue of Rembrandt

Rembrandtsplein

Amstel

Leidsegracht

Herengracht

Keizersgracht

Leidsestraat

Spiegelstraat

Kerkstraat

Regulersgracht

Utrechtse Straat

Amstel

Municipal Theater

Leidseplein

Prinsengracht

Vondelpark

P. C. Hooftstr

Vijzelgracht

Frederiksplein

N

Jan Luijkenstraat

Rijksmuseum

Weteringschans

Van Gogh Museum

Museumplein

Stedelijk Museum

Stadhouderskade

207

Amsterdam's busy Central Station is located on a large artificial island in the harbor which also serves as the terminus for the cities' and regions' trams, buses, ferries, and most recently the subway. In watery Amsterdam, the subway was built above ground in sections, then sunk to the required depth by washing away the soil under it. An excellent introduction to Amsterdam is to take a trip on one of the numerous Rondvaart boats which tour the canals and the harbor. Several of the companies have their points of departure near the Central Station. Others are located on the Rokin and the Amstel.

From the Central Station it is only a few blocks to the Dam, the heart of the city. On the Dam we see the royal palace built in 1648. It is supported by 13,659 wooden piles driven into the city's swampy soil. Since all other buildings are likewise supported, Amsterdam is sometimes called "an upside-down forest." In 1535, the Dam square was the scene of fighting between some revolutionary "Munsterite" Anabaptists and the local government, in which the *burgemeester,* several citizens, and some of the misguided revolutionaries were killed. It should be noted that Jan van Geelen and his revolutionaries did not have the support of the peaceful Anabaptists in Amsterdam. But the government nevertheless exploited the incident to prove the dangers of Anabaptism.

Opposite the palace stands the National Monument of the Liberation which commemorates the five years of German occupation and Holland's liberation by Canadian and British forces in 1945.

From the Dam we take the Kalverstraat, a busy shopping street open to pedestrians only. Soon we'll see on the right-hand side the entrance to the city orphanage (Weeshuis), dating back to 1578. The orphanage, beautifully restored for the city's 700th birthday in 1975, is open to the public. Today it houses a coffee shop and exhibits from Amsterdam's historical collection. Inside the coffee shop we find the amusing statues of David and Goliath, audiovisual aids from another era in Bible study.

As noted earlier Amsterdam has many museums and the Dutch people are among the most enthusiastic museum-goers in the world (44 museum visits per person, per year!). When we continue through the orphanage and turn left, we find that Amsterdam even takes the museum to the people: a short street has been covered over with a glass roof and enclosed at both ends to house a beautiful selection of Renaissance paintings from the national collection.

Shortly after passing through this "gallery" we turn right to enter the Begijnhof. Throughout western Holland and Flanders, are quiet courtyards of clustered dwellings, almshouses, usually grouped around a garden or a green. These houses *(hof* or *hofjes)* were made available, sometimes rent-free, to widows, single women, Beguines, and others. The Begijnhof is Amsterdam's most beautiful example. It dates back to the earliest days of the city's existence and served as a home to women devoted to charity. It is a

The Dam with the Royal Palace and Liberation monument

Canals, bridges, and excursion boats

sanctuary of peace and quiet right in the busiest part of the city. It includes the oldest house in Amsterdam, dating back to the 1300s, and the English Reformed church where the Pilgrim fathers worshiped before departing for America.

We exit Begijnhof via the entrance leading to *het Spui*. Turning to the right we cross two streets and a canal, the Singel. We turn left along the Singel and take a moment to look down the Beulingsloot, one of Amsterdam's narrower canals. Then we continue to the rounded doors of the building on Singel 452. This building, which from the outside looks much like any other of the stately homes along Amsterdam's tree-lined canals, houses the Singel Mennonite Church, the offices of the Dutch Mennonite Conference (ADS), and other agencies of the Dutch brother-sisterhood. The church itself, which dates back to 1608, is a hidden church and not visible from the street.

The church was called "Bij 't Lam" after the brewery, The Lamb, which once stood here. The church was renovated in 1839 and again in 1952. The organ, the second-earliest organ in a Dutch Mennonite meetinghouse, dates back to 1777. In the 17th century the Singel church experienced a conflict between Galenus Abramsz de Haan and a more conservative group. The conservatives eventually moved out to establish a second Mennonite meetinghouse on the Singel called "De Zon" (the Sun). It is located at Singel 118. It now serves as an auction hall. A third group also established a church on the Singel called De Toren (the Tower), no longer in existence. The disagreement became known as *"de Lammerenkrijg"* (War of the Lambs). But reconciliation did take place and in 1801 the various factions joined to form the United Mennonite Church. A gable stone in the Singelkerk shows the sun, the lamb, and the tower, with the Latin phrase "Bound in love and peace."

From the Singel church it is but a few steps to Amsterdam's floating flower market, located on permanently moored barges along the next section of the Singel between the Koningsplein and the Munt. The Munt tower with its beautiful carillon was built in 1620. It is a popular meeting place: "See you at the Munt at 5:00." The broad Munt Square, located on top of a wide bridge across the Singel, is one of Amsterdam's busiest thoroughfares. From the Munt it is not far to the Rembrandt *plein*, where we find a bronze statue of the great master surrounded by much traffic and little cafes that become noisier as the night goes on. From the Munt we can return to the Dam via the Kalverstraat.

From the Dam we turn west, go around the palace, and follow the Raadhuisstraat to the Westerkerk, a beautiful 17th-century church. The Westerkerk steeple, 85 meters (279 ft.) high, is the tallest in the city. Rembrandt lies buried in the church, but the exact place of his grave is not known.

Close to the church at Prinsengracht 263, stands the Anne Frank

The Singelkerk dates back to 1608

Baptismal service in the Singelkerk

house, the hiding place of a young Jewish girl and her family during the years of German occupation, whose world-famous diary has acquainted thousands with the tragic events of 1940 to 1945.

On the same canal, Prinsengracht 159 to 171, is the Zon's Hofje, formerly a Mennonite-owned *hofje* for the aged. It was also the site of a Mennonite meetinghouse called Kleine Zon (Little Sun), later named De Arke Noah. In this quiet courtyard, which now provides student housing, we can see a gable stone with a poem and a clock dated 1765, the year the hofje was founded.

Not far from here, in the Egelantierstraat 36 to 50, we find Anslo's Hofje. It was founded in 1626 by the Amsterdam Mennonite merchant Clasz Anslo, the son of the eloquent Mennonite preacher Cornelisz Anslo (1592-1646) who was used as a model several times by Rembrandt.

We return to the Dam for other destinations.

From the Dam we follow the Kalverstraat to the Heiligeweg, where we turn right. Then we follow the Leidsestraat to the end. This street crosses each one of the city's canals and provides the visitor with charming views in either direction from the bridges. At the end of the street we reach the Leidseplein. Two more blocks and across the Stadhouderskade (canal) lies the entrance to the Vondelpark, once the private park of a Mennonite merchant family named van Eeghen, but now a city park. In the park we find a statue of the great Dutch poet Joost van den Vondel, who was a Mennonite most of his life, but later became a Catholic.

Not far from the park and Vondel's statue, we come to a cluster of Amsterdam's world-renown cultural institutions: the Rijksmuseum, with its fabulous collection of Rembrandts and other classics; the van Gogh Museum; the Municipal Museum; and the Concertgebouw, the setting for great performances which are heard on good music stations around the world.

Taking the Dam Square as a point of departure once again, we can go past the National Monument of the Liberation, through the narrow Damstraat, the Oude- and the Nieuwe-Hoogstraat to the Jodenbreestraat is the house where Rembrandt lived during his most successful years, 1639 to 1658. It now houses a museum of his etchings and drawings and is well worth a visit.

Between the Rembrandt house and the central station we pass the Waag, which still looks like the medieval city gate it once was, but has since served as weighing house *(waag),* guild hall, fire station, and now a museum. Another tower of the same vintage stands on the Prins Hendrikkade, across from the Central Station. It is known as the Schreierstoren (Weepers Tower). This tower was the point of departure for the great sea voyages in the sailing ships days. A gable stone recalls the sorrow of the women and children left behind and of husbands who never returned.

A bronze plaque on the Schreierstoren commemorates the departure

The house where Rembrandt lived, 1639-58

from here in 1609 of Henry Hudson, who was commissioned by Amsterdam to make a voyage of discovery, during which he sailed up the bay and a river later named after him. Shortly thereafter the Dutch established New Amsterdam on the island of Manhattan. Four decades later New Amsterdam was captured by the British who renamed it New York.

The Mennonite Church of Amsterdam, though technically one congregation, is divided into five districts, each with its own meeting place. They are the Singelkerk, described earlier, the meetinghouses at Karperweg 5 in Amsterdam West, and Meerpad 9 in Amsterdam North. Services are also held in two schools, the Professor Zeemanschool in the East, and the Burgemeester Haspelschool in Amsterdam-Amstelveen. Services are also held at the Menno Simons Huis, a retirement center in Buitenveldert. The total membership is around 1,800.

When you ask for a Mennonite church in Holland, you will probably get a blank stare. The word used here is *Doopsgezind* (Anabaptist). The little Doopsgezinde Kerk on the Meerpad 9 is of historic significance and is listed as a national landmark, as are a number of other Mennonite meetinghouses throughout the country.

A Word (or Two) of Caution

Two cautions are in order before you start on any of these Amsterdam walks. For the past decade Amsterdam has been plagued with an international and youthful band of pickpockets who operate on streetcars, on the crowded Kalverstraat, in museums and in department stores. It is not a major problem, but it helps to be alert at all times. Amsterdam also has an extensive red-light district which is found throughout the oldest and most historic parts of the town. They are found extensively, though not exclusively, in the area east of the Central Station and the Dam Square.

A VISIT TO WATERLAND

The area just north of Amsterdam is called Waterland and rightly so—it is about half water. The area gave its name to a branch of the Dutch Mennonites, the Waterlanders, who often served as agents of reconciliation between the various types of Anabaptists. It is said that Hendrikje Stoffels, who moved in to keep house for Rembrandt after the death of Saskia, was a Mennonite from Ransdorp in Waterland.

In the middle of this area lies the town of Broek in Waterland, an authentic Dutch town, where it is still the custom to take off your shoes when you enter somebody's home. Even Napoleon did so when he visited Broek's mayor in 1811. The town has a cheese farm and the shop of a shoemaker of wooden shoes. Both places are open to the public.

Seven kilometers (4½ miles) farther north we come to Monickendam, one of the most attractive towns along the former Zuiderzee, an unspoiled example of a merchant town from Holland's Golden Age. Monickendam's beautiful houses and green canals are grouped around a charming 15th-

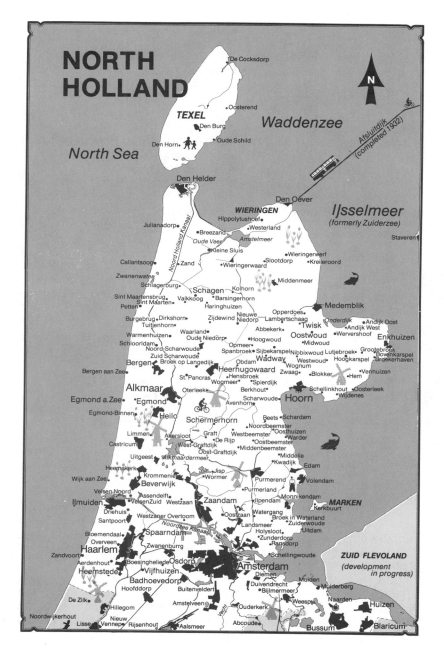

NORTH HOLLAND

TEXEL

North Sea

Waddenzee

WIERINGEN

IJsselmeer
(formerly Zuiderzee)

Afsluitdijk (completed 1932)

De Cocksdorp

Oosterend

Den Burg

Den Horn

Oude Schild

Den Helder

Den Oever

Hippolytushoef

Westerland

Julianadorp

Breezand

Amstelmeer

Oude Veer

Kleine Sluis

Wieringerwerf

Staveren

Callantsoog

Zand

Wieringerwaard

Slootdorp

Kreileroord

Zwanenwater

Schlagerburg

Schagen

Kolhorn

Middenmeer

Sint Maartensbrug

Valkoog

Barsingerhorn

Petten

Sint Maarten

Haringhuizen

Opperdoes

Medemblik

Burgebrug

Dirkshorn

Nieuwe Niedorp

Zijdewind

Lambertschaag

Onderdijk

Andijk Oost

Tuitjenhorn

Abbekerk

Twisk

Andijk West

Warmenhuizen

Waarland

Oude Niedorp

Hoogwoud

Oostwoud

Wervershoof

Enkhuizen

Schoorldam

Noord-Scharwoude

Opmeer

Midwoud

Zuid Scharwoude

Spanbroek

Sijbekarspel

Nibbixwoud

Lutjebroek

Grootebroek

Bergen

Broek op Langedijk

Obdam

Wàdway

Westwoud

Hoogkarspel

Bovenkarspel

Broekerhaven

Bergen aan Zee

St. Pancras

Heerhugowaard

Hensbroek

Zwaag

Blokker

Hem

Venhuizen

Wogmeer

Spierdijk

Alkmaar

Oterleek

Berkhout

Schellinkhout

Oosterleek

Egmond a. Zee

Egmond

Avenhorn

Scharwoude

Hoorn

Wijdenes

Egmond-Binnen

Heilo

Schermerhorn

Beets

Schardam

Limmen

Graft

Noordbeemster

Akersloot

Westbeemster

Oosthuizen

Castricum

De Rijp

Oostbeemster

Warder

West-Graftdijk

Middenbeemster

Uitgeest

Oost-Graftdijk

Middelie

Heemskerk

Alkmaardermeer

Kwadijk

Edam

Jisp

Wijk aan Zee

Krommenie

Wormer

Purmerend

Volendam

Beverwijk

Purmerland

Velsen-Noord

Assendelft

MARKEN

IJmuiden

VelsenZuid

Westzaan

Zaandam

Ilpendam

Monnikendam

Kerkbuurt

Driehuis

Westzaner Overtoom

Oostzaan

Watergang

Santpoort

Noordzee Kanaal

Landsmeer

Broek in Waterland

Zuiderwoude

Bloemendaal

Spaarndam

Holysloot

Uitdam

Overveen

Zwanenburg

Zunderdorp

Ransdorp

Zandvoort

ZUID FLEVOLAND
(development in progress)

Haarlem

Boesinghelieqe Osdorp

Schellingwoude

Aerdenhout

Vijfhuizen

Heemstede

Amsterdam

De Zilk

Hoofddorp

Badhoevedorp

Diemen

Muiden

Muiderberg

Hillegom

Buitenveldert

Duivendrecht

Bijlmermeer

Weesp

Naarden

Huizen

Noordwijkerhout

Nieuw Vennep

Amstelveen

Ouderkerk

Vecht

Lisse

Rijsenhout

Aalsmeer

Abcoude

Bussum

Blaricum

Noord Holland Kanaal

215

century brick tower, which has an 18-bell carillon, cast in 1596. On the south side of the tower, we see a small stage on which mechanical horses and riders make their rounds on the hour and on the half-hour while an angel blows a trumpet. Across from the tower stands the town hall built in 1746. Around the corner stands the old weigh-house *(waag)* built in 1600, now a pancake restaurant.

Not far from Monickendam, we come to Volendam and Marken, two places where colorful, traditional costumes are still worn by the fisherfolk and shopkeepers. More than likely, however, you'll find more tourists than natives there. Two more towns nearby round out the itinerary—Edam, known for its round Edammer cheese, and Purmerend, known for its weekly sheep and cattle markets. Of the towns mentioned above, Monickendam, Edam, and Purmerend each have a Mennonite congregation which holds biweekly church services in historic meetinghouses.

THE ZAAN RIVER

The region on both sides of the Zaan River, not more than ten kilometers (six miles) from the heart of Amsterdam, consists of a number of small towns—Zaandam, Koog aan de Zaan, Zaandijk, Westzaan, and so on—which were combined in 1974 under the new name Zaanstad, but the old names persist.

Because the Zaanlanders perfected the windmill during the 1500s as a source of power to drive all manner of machinery, the Zaan region is regarded as one of the world's oldest industrial areas. Food and spices, lumber and wood products, oil, grease, and paint are produced in large quantities for home use and for export. Cookies and biscuits in tins, packaged noodles and cereals, and prefabricated kitchens were practically invented here. Linoleum was first made in Krommenie as a by-product of the vegetable oil industry. (Do you recognize the words *lin*seed and *oil* in the name?).

People from all over Europe came to the Zaan to learn a trade. One of these visitors was Czar Peter the Great of Russia. Even today the wind may treat you to a whiff of fresh mustard, the sweet smell of chocolate, or the pungent aroma of newly sawn lumber.

The Zaanlanders developed a unique style of architecture. A typical Zaan River house is of wood construction painted dark green with white trim and ornamentation. They lend the appearance of elegance against Holland's tumultuous skies coupled with their reflections in choppy waters of the wide river.

Secret Anabaptist meetings were held in all these river towns as early as 1543, resulting in the formation of numerous Frisian, Flemish, and Waterlander congregations. During the 17th century 20 percent of the population was Mennonite. In 1687 the various traditions resolved to drop the old names to form the United Mennonite Church. Several meetinghouses were combined and the new Zaandam Church was built. In 1810 the Zaan area congregations joined those of Amsterdam and Haarlem to push for the formation of the ADS, the Dutch Mennonite General Conference.

Interesting Mennonite meetinghouses can be seen at Westzaan (Zuideinde 231) Zaandam (Westzijde 80) and Koog/Zaandijk (Lagedijk 34). All are large wooden structures with loose chairs arranged in a semicircle. The wooden floor is usually covered with fine white sand. Because they started out as "hidden churches," you may pass them before you realize it.

On the east side of the Zaan River, across from Zaandijk, lies de Zaanse Schans, a beautiful resident quarter preserved by a nonprofit foundation. The area was named Zaanse Schans for an entrenchment built in 1574 to hold back the Spanish troops in the Eighty Years' War. As we walk through de Zaanse Schans, we get the feel of what all of the Zaan region looked like until late in the 19th-century. The dikes were probably built during the 1300s.

Alongside the dike runs a main canal connected to numerous smaller ditches at right angles to it. This dike and the canal path lead to beautiful groupings of green and white Zaan River houses, as well as a half-dozen windmills ranging from small drainage mills to larger industrial sawmills and oil and paint mills.

Of the more than two hundred mills once found along the Zaan, only twelve remain and seven of these can be seen at de Zaanse Schans. The De Zoeker oil mill was built in 1608 by the Mennonite minister, inventor, and engineer, Pieter Pietersz. It is the only windmill in the world which still presses oil in the traditional way. It is open to visitors when in operation. From the mills along the dike a path leads through the marshy land to the Kwakels, once a shipyard building but now the workshop of a shoemaker of wooden shoes. He will gladly demonstrate his trade to us, and wooden shoes are for sale. We may end our visit at De Kraai (The Crow), once the storehouse of a flour mill, but now a restaurant specializing in pancakes.

ALKMAAR, HISTORY AND CHEESE

From de Zaanse Schans it isn't far to Alkmaar. The Dutch have a saying, "From Alkmaar begins the victory," which reminds us that in 1573 the city of Alkmaar withstood a siege by 16,000 Spanish soldiers for seven weeks, after which the Spanish gave up and retreated. Alkmaar was a center of Anabaptist activity as early as 1530. Between 1551 and 1578 the Anabaptist missioner Leenaert Bouwens baptized no less than 123 persons in Alkmaar. During the siege of the city by the Spanish, Mennonites aided the magistrate in holding the town but were exempt from actually bearing arms.

One of Alkmaar's outstanding Mennonite leaders was Hans de Ries (1553 to 1638), a minister in the Waterlander congregation. Throughout his

Zaan river homes in green and white

Alkmaar on Friday morning: the cheese market

life de Ries worked at the reconciliation and unification of the various Mennonite traditions. He saw it as his mission to "heal the breach." He kept a record of the martyrs, which became the basis for Tieleman Jansz van Braght's later *Martyrs Mirror,* and wrote and compiled a Mennonite hymnal first published in 1582. All in all, de Ries was a man who served the Lord faithfully and without regard for personal dangers. At the age of 84 he journeyed by boat to Zaandam to deliver a sermon. A few weeks later he became ill and died.

The Alkmaar Mennonite Church on the Koningsweg 12 is a good example of a neo-classic church building. Napoleon's soldiers occupied the church from 1795 to 1797, at which time many important books and papers were lost. The pulpit came from the now-extinct congregation at Barsingerhorn.

On Friday morning the city of Alkmaar comes alive with the colorful spectacle of the cheese market. Early in the morning the thousands of Gouda and Edammer cheeses are piled up on the square and precisely at 10:00 the sale begins. The members of four different guilds (or *Compagnies)* of carriers, recognizable by their white suits and their red, blue, green, or yellow hats, begin to carry the cheeses to the scales on *berries* of corresponding colors. Between each two guildsmen, walking at a trot, they move around 160 kilos (350 pounds) of cheese to the scales and into the buyers' trucks. The cheese market is visited by thousands of tourists and parking in town is well nigh impossible. It is better to use public transportation and then walk.

Not far from Alkmaar there are several nice clusters of from three to five windmills. They are near Ouddorp, between Oterleek and Rustenburg, and near Schermerhorn.

If you plan to return to Amsterdam, it pays to detour via De Rijp. Now a sleepy little town, it was once the center of the Dutch whaling and herring industry. It was the home of the famous waterworks engineer, Jan Adriaansz Leeghwater (1575-1650). Leeghwater, who was a Mennonite, also designed De Rijp's charming little Renaissance town hall.

On Rechtestraat 40, we find the house of Bettje Wolff (1738 to 1804) and Aagje Deken (1741 to 1804), who jointly wrote and published a number of important 18th-century poems and novels, in spite of their fundamental differences in temperament and outlook. Bettje Wolff, the wife of a Reformed pastor, was light-hearted, Aagje Deken, single and a member of the Mennonite church, was serious. Both were opposed to the low moral standards of the time and looked forward to the realized ideals of a better age when people would be governed by rational Christian morality. Aagje Deken contributed at least 74 hymns to a hymnal published by the Haarlem Mennonites, but Bettje Wolff wrote the major and the best parts of the novels on which they collaborated. The two women died seven days apart and were buried in the same grave.

THE CITIES OF WEST FRIESLAND

We now turn our attention to that part of the province of North Holland called West Friesland, located along the shores of the former Zuiderzee, opposite the province of Friesland. The area includes three old and beautiful Hanseatic cities—Hoorn, Enkhuizen, and Medemblik—and between them are miles of lush green polderland dotted with red-roofed towns. It is also a major vegetable growing region.

Hoorn is rich in well-maintained houses and civic monuments and is perhaps the best example of a late Gothic/early Renaissance trading center. After Hoorn, Enkhuizen is another good example of a dormant trading center on the shores of the former Zuider Zee. The fortifications dating back to 1600s have been preserved, including the imposing Dromedaris Gate, which is even older (1540).

Since 1983, Enkhuizen has a new open-air museum, the Zuider Zee Museum. Already considered one of Europe's finest open-air museums, it required 40 years to plan and to build. The Zuider Zee Museum combines three elements: an urban character, a totally authentic environment, and original activities. The whole set of neighborhoods and industries and the activities around the harbor present visitors with a good picture of life along the Zuider Zee between 1880 and 1930, before the building of the Afsluitdijk. The museum parking lot is located out of town. We follow the signs ZZM. The museum itself is reached by ferry boat, a 20-minute ride past a beautiful panorama of old Enkhuizen. We should allow at least a half day for the Zuider Zee Museum.

The oldest of the three West Frisian towns is Medemblik. It dates back to Count Floris V, who built the town around his Radboud Castle in 1288. The original castle can still be seen on the south side of the harbor. From the dike next to Radboud Castle there is a nice view of the Ijsselmeer. During the Golden Age, Medemblik made its fortune with spices from the Orient.

The cities of Hoorn and Medemblik and towns in between are served by a regularly scheduled steam railroad which winds its way along the canals and through fields of cabbage. Equally historic steamships provide excursions between the cities' harbors. In West Friesland, getting there is half the fun.

IN THE LAND OF MENNO SIMONS

Friesland is one of Holland's two northernmost provinces and there is no other place quite like it in the world. Because Friesland was long isolated from the rest of the country—to the southwest by the former Zuiderzee, to the east by extensive marshlands—it developed a culture and a language of its own. Its history goes back thousands of years, and only in recent decades has Friesland shown noticeable signs of change.

Friesland has no big cities. The two largest towns are the provincial

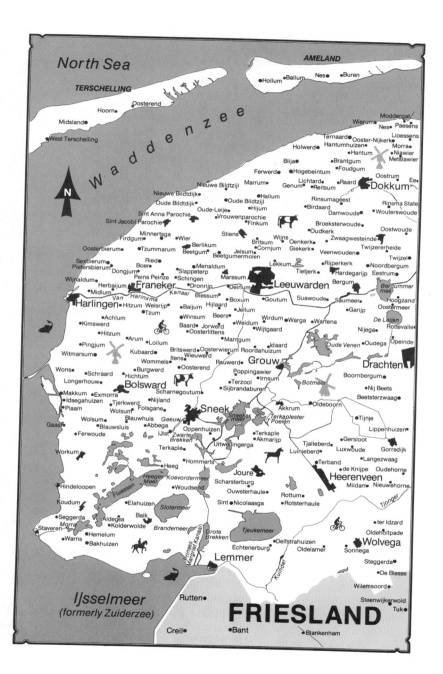

North Sea

TERSCHELLING

AMELAND

Waddenzee

IJsselmeer
(formerly Zuiderzee)

FRIESLAND

221

capital, Leeuwarden, and Sneek. The greater part of the province is used for extensive dairy farming, and the meadows are full of registered black-and-white Frisian-Holstein cows.

The Leeuwarden cattle market, held on Fridays, is the largest market of its kind in the world and sales of 10,000 cattle per day are not uncommon. There are more than one hundred dairy plants in Friesland, three quarters of which are farmer co-ops. In the north, near Berlikum, there are vegetable gardens and wide expanses of potato fields (for seed potato export). One potato is called Saskia, for Rembrandt's wife, who was born in this area.

The language spoken here is Frisian, which is quite different from the Dutch and perhaps more related to Scottish or Old English. Road signs are usually in two languages, Leeuwarden-Ljouwerd, Franeker-Frjenster, Sneek-Snits. The Bible is translated in Fries.

Friesland is reached via the 22-mile-long Afsluitdijk which connects the province to western Holland. A white observation tower and monument, seven kilometers (4½ miles) from the North Holland coast, marks the place where the dike was completed in 1932. There are some informative exhibits and a good view at this always cool and windy place.

Friesland is to the Dutch/North German Mennonite story what Zurich and Zollikon are to Swiss-South German Anabaptism. Anabaptist influences were found here as early as 1530 and nowhere was Mennonitism as deeply rooted in the general population as here. The first fellowships emerged in Leeuwarden probably through the preaching of Melchior Hofmann. In 1531 Sicke Freerks, a tailor, was beheaded for his belief.

It was Sicke's martyrdom that caused Menno Simons, the village priest at Witmarsum, to become interested in the question of infant versus adult baptism. In the spring of 1535 a group of Münsterite Anabaptists captured the monastery, Oldeklooster, near Bolsward. They were defeated and later killed by provincial forces one week later. In the fracas a brother of Menno, Pieter Simons, lost his life. Menno then wrote his booklet *Against the Blasphemy of Jan van Leyden,* and consequently withdrew from the Catholic church to join the peaceful (Obbenite) Anabaptists.

In 1537 Menno Simons was chosen to be an elder among the Anabaptists, a position he filled so capably that his followers were soon called Mennists. The number of Anabaptist congregations continued to grow, even after Menno Simons was forced to flee to Groningen, and then to Germany, when the Frisian governor offered a huge reward for his capture dead or alive. The church in Friesland also grew because of the influx of refugees from Flanders and elsewhere. This resulted in the formation of many types of Mennonite congregations, with many towns having two or more Mennonite churches in close proximity. By the 17th century most of these congregations united. In 1666 the Mennonites comprised approximately 22 percent of the population of Friesland.

Even after the outright persecution officially ended, the Mennonites of Friesland were barely tolerated by the Calvinist magistrates. In the 1670s the Mennonites were forced to make a "voluntary" contribution of more than one million guilders to the Frisian navy. On another occasion the Frisian government closed all Mennonite churches after all but one of the 150 Mennonite ministers refused to sign a formula of faith prescribed by the Calvinist authorities. Not until 1795 did the Mennonites enjoy the civil rights of their Reformed neighbors.

Today the four dozen Mennonite congregations of Friesland are organized in *Rings* (circles) which pool their facilities, ministers, and resources. The congregation at Bovenknijpe became the first congregation to have a full-time seminary-trained woman minister when Anne Mankes-Zernike accepted the pastorate in 1911.

The two most important places in Frisian Mennonite history are Witmarsum and Pingjum. Witmarsum was the birthplace of Menno Simons. According to tradition he was born in a white farmhouse that still stands just outside of town. The building was recently acquired by the Dutch Mennonites, who plan to turn it into a center where small and specialized seminars can be held.

Witmarsum is where Menno served as a Catholic priest from 1531 to the time of his withdrawal from the church on January 30, 1536. Whether or not Menno personally formed a congregation at Witmarsum remains an open question, but we do know of a congregation at Witmarsum after his departure. Until 1877 services were held in a very simple meeting place, formerly a barn. Today the Menno Simons monument stands on its site amidst the meadows.

The monument is inscribed on one side, "In memory of Menno Simons, born at Witmarsum in 1496" and "1536, Menno's departure from the Catholic Church." On the second side it reads, "According to tradition, Menno spoke to the first of his followers here." The third side reads, "For three centuries the Anabaptists of Witmarsum and surrounding areas met on this site." And finally, the fourth side carries Menno Simon's favorite Bible verse, 1 Corinthians 3:11, "Other foundation can no one lay than that which has been laid which is Jesus Christ."

The congregation moved to a new meetinghouse in town on December 16, 1877. That meetinghouse was in turn replaced by the current one, built in the early 1960s by an international group of Voluntary Service workers.

The new meetinghouse has the typical barrel-vaulted ceiling of the earlier meetinghouses, a style which was later carried to Danzig, to South Russia, and finally to the plains of Kansas and Manitoba. On a beam we read the admonition: "Hear the Word of God, believe the Word of God, live according to the Word of God." A large oil painting of Menno, twin to a painting in Hamburg-Altona, hangs on the side wall.

Pingjum: the hidden church (exterior)

Pingjum: the hidden church (interior)

224

It is only two kilometers (just over a mile) from Witmarsum to Pingjum. Menno is thought to have spent his youth at Pingjum, the home of his father's relatives, and after his ordination in 1524, he served the village as a Catholic priest. Pingjum has two points of interest for the Mennonite traveler—the old church (now Reformed) where Menno served as a priest and the charming little "hidden church" of the Mennonite congregation. From the outside, this building looks like the private homes around it, but beyond the living room and pantry, one finds a secret meeting place. In 1827 the Pingjum congregation united with Witmarsum and today the hidden church is rarely used for services.

South of Witmarsum and Pingjum lies the town of Makkum, a picturesque fishing village on the coast of the Ijsselmeer. Around 1600 three Mennonite congregations were active in Makkum, all of which were of earlier origin. The three congregations merged but decreased in size, as did the whole town of Makkum, when its importance as a seaport faded. The current meetinghouse is on Bleekstraat, and the congregation has about 35 members. This congregation is linked with the Ring Workum, Bolsward, and Hindelopen.

Makkum is famous for its Makkum pottery, equal in quality and artistic value with the better-known Delft. Since 1660 the Makkum pottery enterprise has been in the hands of a Mennonite family named Tichelaar. Many members of the family have served as deacons of the local church and as directors of both the Frisian and the Dutch Mennonite General Conference (ADS). The pottery works welcomes visitors Monday through Friday.

Eleven kilometers (seven miles) to the south of Makkum we come to the long and narrow dike town of Workum, a prosperous harbor town from the 18th century which is now two kilometers from the sea, due to a change in the coastline. Workum has a great number of interesting old houses along the one main street. The street has two Frisian names: Noard and Sud (north and south). The Mennonite meetinghouse, (Noard 100), is a hidden church that dates back to 1694. The neighboring town of Hindelopen (Hylpen in Frisian) is known for its colorful peasant art. Hindelopen chairs and tables in red and green, lavishly covered with bird and flower motifs, are purchased by eager buyers from throughout the country.

Typical for Friesland are the "head-neck-and-body" farms. They are so named because the house (head), the connecting hall (neck), and the body (a huge barn) are all under the same thatched roof.

Throughout the summer endless rows of white sails are visible, apparently floating over the green meadows but in reality skimming across the many lakes and canals. The big sailing events are the Sneek Week (pronounced snake-wake), which begins on the Friday preceding the first Saturday in August, and the *Skutsjesilen,* which is held for 15 days in June and July. Skutsjesilen hosts the sailing of the now-historic lake and canal freighters with their huge brown or black sails. Several Frisian cities and some private collectors still own a few of these ships and each year they are sailed together in various parts of the province. For the times and location of this year's Skutsjesilen, contact the VVV. (See page 27 for instructions.)

Throughout Friesland and into the neighboring province of Overijssel, we can see *klokkestoelen,* huge wooden A-frames supporting one or more church bells under a small roof. They are free-standing, frequently in a corner of the country cemetery. Throughout the centuries the bells have been rung for funerals, to warn the people of storms and floods, to signal an approaching enemy, and to celebrate a birth in the royal family.

The province of Friesland has a unique link with the United States. In 1782 the Staten Generaal (congress) of the Netherlands, meeting at Leeuwarden, voted to recognize the new American republic. Holland was the first nation to do so. The document is on display in the provincial archives at Leeuwarden.

We could go on and on describing the delights of Friesland: its neat little towns spaced evenly along the horizon between endless meadows under immense skies, Frisian-Holsteins contentedly grazing, sails and windmills moving quietly, terns and gulls winging in the wind. We may take any road away from the main highway and create our own adventure!

A TOWN WITHOUT STREETS

Giethoorn is a town of 2,500 inhabitants in the Dutch province of Overijssel. Although one access road dead-ends not far from the center of town, Giethoorn itself has no streets—only miles of tree-lined canals, countless foot bridges, and a winding path. The traditional way to get around in Giethoorn is by *punter,* a long flat-bottomed boat which is pushed ahead with a long pole. Giethoorn is surrounded by *kraggen* (floating meadows). Kraggen consist of layers of decaying water plants, thick enough to support a grazing cow, but floating nevertheless. After a hard storm you can sometimes see a farmer poling his meadow back home. When Giethoorn was first settled, in the late 1500s, more than half the people were Mennonites. This watery and almost inaccessible place made a perfect refuge for the persecuted sect. Once there were two Mennonite churches, Giethoorn North and Giethoorn South. Later the two combined at Giethoorn South. The present meetinghouse was dedicated on Christmas Day, 1871. Just outside of town there are two Mennonite campgrounds *Kraggehuis* (House on the Kragge), and *Samen Een* (Together we are one).

The Dutch Mennonites, following the lead of the British Quakers, established church camping and retreat centers earlier than the church elsewhere. In addition to the two camps at Giethoorn, the Dutch Mennonites have retreat centers in the woods at Elspeet, in the dunes at Schoorl, *Fredeshiem* (House of Peace) in the wooded sand hills near Steenwijk, and *het van Eeghenhuis* in a polder near Aardenburg, Zeeland.

A Frisian "Klokkestoel"

Everything moves by boat in Giethoorn

In addition, there is camping for youth on the island of Texel, and there is another camp next to the retreat at Aardenburg. All but Schoorl are year-round retreat centers and can be found in a telephone book under *Doops-gezinde Broederschapshuizen.* You might find one of the Broederschaps-huizen an ideal spot from which to undertake your excursions, as well as a good place to meet Dutch Mennonites.

ROTTERDAM, THE WORLD'S LARGEST SEAPORT

It is said that in Rotterdam shirts are sold with the sleeves already rolled up, underscoring the city's reputation as a hard-working community. It is almost impossible to imagine that Rotterdam was almost completely wiped off the map during World War II. The destruction of Old Rotterdam began on May 14, 1940, when German Stuka dive bombers peppered the city with incendiary bombs. Four years later Nazi demolition squads finished the job with dynamite.

But Rotterdam's civic leaders, in hiding from the Nazis, laid detailed plans for a new city to rise from the ashes as soon as the war would be over. Today Rotterdam is the second largest city in Holland and since 1956, the world's busiest harbor. And the Rotterdamers still have their sleeves rolled up.

Rotterdam is indeed overwhelming. Terms like "the world's largest", and "the world's most modern" must be used to describe so many of the city's naval enterprises that one begins to take it for granted. Some notable facts: Nearly 32,000 ocean-going ships call on the city each year to transfer their cargoes into the holds of 230,000 river ships. The harbor serves from 200 to 300 ocean-going ships daily. The average turnaround time for a ship (loading and unloading, refueling) is between six and seven hours. The world's largest container terminal holds 300,000 containers. It takes the huge traveling cranes less than a minute to move a container from the hold of a ship to the ready lines of trucks and railroad flatcars.

The Spido Boat Company, with its landing stage at the Willemsplein, offers 75-minute excursions through the heart of the harbor complex and other more extensive excursions lasting from five to nine hours.

Tucked away among Rotterdam's 37-kilometer (23 miles) stretch of docks and wharfs lies Delfshaven, where the Pilgrims boarded the *Speed-well,* which carried them to England and from there on to Massachusetts. That tiny harbor is still there, as is the church where the Pilgrims prayed before boarding the ship. Some of Delfshaven's oldest houses around the church are being restored, some as art studios, others as private homes.

For those interested in maritime history, a visit to the museum ship *de Buffel,* a steamship built in 1868, is well worth the time. Rotterdam also has a large number of contemporary sculptures, monuments, and fountains. A most impressive monument is Ossip Zadkine's "May 1940," which symbol-izes the city with its heart removed. It illustrates well the horrors of war.

Delfshaven, where the Pilgrims boarded the "Speedwell"

DEN HAAG AND SCHEVENINGEN

Holland is unique in that it has a capital, Amsterdam, as well as a seat of government or residence which is *Den Haag* (the Hague). The name is a variation of the city's official name *('s Gravenhage),* which has proven to be pronounceable only by the Dutch themselves. Translated, 's Gravenhage means the Woods of the Counts. During the 1200s the area now occupied by the city was the hunting domain of the counts of Holland.

In 1280 Count Floris V began the construction of the Ridderzaal, the hall of knights, adjacent to his chateau. The opening session of the Dutch parliament, the Staten-Generaal, still takes place in the magnificent Ridderzaal. On that solemn occasion the queen arrives at the Zaal to deliver her State of the Nation message after a ride from her palace on the Lange Voorhout in a golden coach drawn by six white horses.

When the Ridderzaal is not in use for government functions or for the reception of foreign dignitaries, the hall is open to the public daily except Sundays, between the hours of 10:00 a.m. and 16:00 (4:00 p.m.) The entry fee also covers a visit to the First and Second Chambers, providing the government is not in session. The First Chamber houses 75 senators appointed to six-year terms by the eleven provinces; the Second Chamber houses 150 deputies elected to four-year terms by the voting public.

Most of the interesting sights to see in Den Haag are within walking distance from the Ridderzaal. These include the Inner and Outer Courts surrounding the Zaal; the Doelen, which during the 1600s was the armory of a company of archers; and the Hofvijver, a beautiful pond which is illuminated at night. On het Plein we find the monument of Willem de Zwijger, the first prince of Orange. The monument is surrounded by the buildings of the ministries of the interior, defense, justice, and foreign relations.

The Maurits Huis, once the home of Prince Jan Maurits van Nassau, houses a small (approximately four hundred pieces) but very prestigious art collection, including numerous works by Rembrandt, Rubens, and Vermeer. Nearby the *Gevangenpoort* (Prison Gate), open daily April through September 10:00 a.m. to 17:00 (5:00 p.m.), contains a large collection of medieval torture instruments and execution devices. A visit to the Gevangenpoort may not be the most pleasant experience, but it helps us understand what Blaurock, Hut, Sattler, and others went through for their faith in facilities similar to this elsewhere in Europe.

During the second half of the 19th century, a group of artists living in and around Den Haag revived the art of painting directly from nature, especially landscapes. Their impressionistic style, similar to that of the Barbizon school of France, became known as the Haagse School.

Leading figures in the Haagse School were Josef Israel, J. W. Weissenbruch, Theofile de Bock, G. H. Breitner, Hendrik Willem Mesdag, and his wife, Sientje Mesdag van Houten, Anton Mauve, and Jacob Maris. Of these the Mesdags and Mauve were Mennonites.

Den Haag has two places of interest to students of this school of impressionism. One is the National Museum H. W. Mesdag at Laan van Meerdervoort 7. There we find the works of the Mesdags and others of the Haagse school, as well as representative samples from the Barbizon school (Corot, Millet, Courbet, and others), open daily 10:00 a.m. to 17:00 (5:00 p.m.) and on Sundays, 13:00 tp 17:00 (1:00–7:00 p.m.).

Also of interest to students is the *Panorama Mesdag* on Zeestraat 653. The *Panorama* is a gigantic circular painting, 120 meters in circumference and 14 meters high (394 by 46 ft.), which represents the fishing village of Scheveningen in 1881. Visitors view the painting from the top of a dune of real sand which blends in with the painted dunes 14 meters (or 46 ft.) away.

Panamora Mesdag is world famous, not only for its perfect optical illusion, but also as a unique monument to the vitality of the Haagse School. The painting was completed within two years. Willem Mesdag painted the sky, the sea, the beach, and the fishing boats. His wife, Sientje, painted the village of Scheveningen, de Bock painted the dunes, Breitner did the horse riders, and Blommers painted the costumed woman and her child.

In spite of a difference in their styles, unity prevails. The perspective is marvelous. The skies radiate a soft light which beyond Scheveningen illuminates the towers of Den Haag in the distance. In the absence of a true port Scheveningen's flat-bottom fishing boats, *(bommen,)* are seen being drawn ashore by draft horses.

A Scheveningen trawler coming home

Much of the actual town of Scheveningen was demolished by the Germans during World War II. The Kurhaus, a resort hotel built in 1885, has been restored to its former victorian glory and a new harbor has been constructed. Around the harbor it is still possible to see the older women of Scheveningen dressed in their traditional black and white costumes. On Sundays the skirts are deep pastel colors, and the Sunday bonnets are of fine lace.

Between Den Haag and Scheveningen is the miniature village of Madurodam, with everything scaled down to 1/25 actual size. This is Holland in a nutshell. Walking through Madurodam, you have the feeling of being a Gulliver among the Lilliputians. Trams move through the busy streets and ocean liners glide into port. The windmills are busy pumping water and a band plays music on the square. At the airport, planes taxi out to takeoff positions. Madurodam is open daily between the first of April and the first weekend of October, from 9:30 a.m. to 21:30 (9:30 p.m.). After dark the lights go on in the houses and in the streets of Madurodam. For children of all ages. A visit to this miniature village is indeed an adventure.

ARNHEM AND OOSTERBEEK

In the eastern part of Holland we find Arnhem. Along with the surrounding towns, especially Oosterbeek, Arnhem suffered terrible destruction during the ill-fated battles of "Operation Market Garden," which began on September 17, 1944. In Oosterbeek the British Military Cemetery contains more than 1,700 white stones marking the graves of 1,667 English draftees and 79 Polish volunteers.

Just to the north of Arnhem we come to the Netherlands Open-Air Museum. Founded in 1912, it is one of the oldest museums of its kind in the world. Situated on 44 ha. (75 acres) of wooded lands, we find farms, homes, windmills, and shops from all over Holland. Every type of regional architecture is represented, from the ancient Loshoes (in which a farmer and his animals shared the same living space) to Volendammer fishermen's cottages, a school from Drenthe, a paper mill from Gelderland, a West Frisian farm, a barn full of wagons and sleighs, sheep sheds, laundries and tollhouses. Inside these buildings costumed craftsmen demonstrate beekeeping, paper making, bread baking, corn milling, and other crafts.

The queen's personal collection of historic Dutch costumes is housed in a separate building. Two old inns provide refreshment. By following a suggested red route, a green route, or a blue route, we may visit a selected part of the museum in time spans of from one to four hours.

BELGIUM

Belgie/La Belgique

B

Belgium is one of the smaller and most densely populated countries, as well as the most highly industrialized nation in Europe. Belgium covers an area roughly the size of Maryland, but with three times as many inhabitants. In comparison with the United States as a whole, Belgium's population density is fourteen times greater. The country is so small that only one of its nine provinces, Brabant, is not bordered by another country or waterfront.

For centuries the histories of Belgium and Holland, the Low Countries, were inseparable, and after the defeat of Napoleon in 1815, the Congress of Vienna once again reestablished the United Provinces. But by this time the traditions, the interests, the language, and the religion differed greatly. In the fall of 1830 the southern provinces seceded, adopted a constitution, and elected Prince Leopold von Saxe-Coburg as their first king. The country is named after the Belgae, a tribe which lived in the area when Julius Caesar conquered it 2,000 years ago.

Belgium was attacked and occupied by the Germans during both world wars and suffered great loss of life and property twice in one half-century. During the First World War, much of the endless trench warfare took place on Belgian soil ("in Flanders fields the poppies grow") and in 1944 the Allies and the Germans wasted each other and the unfortunate countryside in the Battle of the Bulge. There are literally hundreds of military cemeteries and monuments in Belgium, with those of World War I concentrated around Ypres, and those of World War II around Bastogne.

However, Belgium was one of the first countries to recover after World War II, having had the advantage of being liberated in 1944, a full year earlier than most of northern Europe. In 1948 Belgium formed a customs union with Holland and Luxembourg (Benelux) which in turn inspired the EEC (European Common Market) three years later.

Much of Belgium is lowland similar to the Dutch landscape, stretching from the dunes along the North Sea to the foothills of the Ardennes, southeast of Brussels. The Ardennes rise to an elevation of 693 meters (2, 274 ft.) not far from the German border. Through this land a number of important rivers flow northward forming an excellent system of waterways complemented by an extensive canal system which connects practically all urban centers to the sea. Antwerpen, on the Schelde River, is Belgium's largest, and the world's third largest, port.

Rural and urban life are closely linked in Belgium and in the western provinces it is often hard to determine where the metropolitan area, the suburbs, and the rural areas begin and end. Belgium has 34 cities with a population of over 25,000 inhabitants. The largest city is Brussels, with more than a million people. All of these towns are connected by a nation-wide system of buses, trams, and railroads. In the western half of the country, everybody lives within a few minutes' walking distance from efficient mass transit—never more than five kilometers (three miles) from the nearest railroad station.

One of the world's great manufacturing countries, Belgium is sometimes called the workshop of Europe. Most of Belgium's heavy industry is found in the south. About a quarter of a million workers are employed in the steel mills and metal fabricating industries. Along with basic steel, Belgium exports many finished products, including nails, wire, barbed wire, rails, and railroad wheels, tools, and various types of machinery. Other well-known Belgian products include fine linens and lace, glass and crystal.

More than any other country, Belgium is a land of castles and most of them are still intact, much as they were in the Middle Ages. There are moated castles, castles on mountaintops, castles standing on islands in the lakes, and castles surrounded by lush green parks. Why so many castles? Since it is located at the crossroads of Europe, Belgium has always attracted visitors and some of these came carrying shields and crossbows. The same castles that were built to show these invaders that they were not welcome now welcome an invasion of curious tourists. One of the largest is the Castle of Bouillion on the Semois River, built by Geoffrey de Bouillion, a leader in the First Crusade.

Those who are interested in the arts will be pleasantly surprised by the treasures they will find in Belgium. There is never enough time to enjoy half of it. Eight centuries of intensive activity in the arts have filled Belgium's towns, castles, museums, and palaces with priceless works. It is, above all, in painting that the artistic genius of the country expressed itself.

Flemish art had two golden eras—the 15th and the 17th centuries. In the 15th century the great Flemish masters, the brothers Hubert and Jan van Eyck, invented oil painting. Also worthy of note are Rogier van der Weyden, Hans Memling, Gérard David, and others. The 16th century brought Quinten Metsys and the Breughels; Pieter Breughel the Elder and

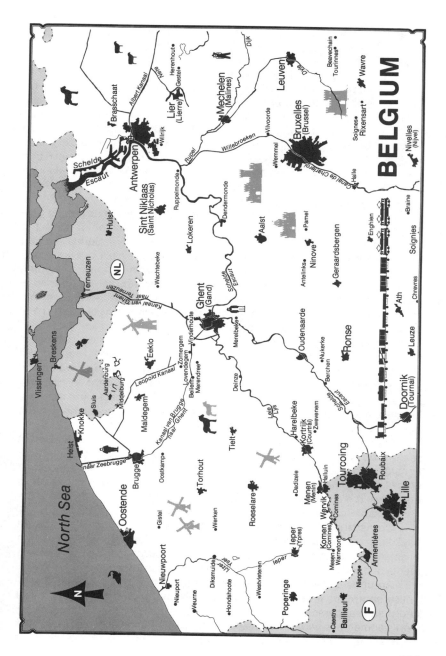

BELGIUM

North Sea

Belgian cities and towns:
Brasschaat, Lier (Lierre), Herenhout, Gestel, Mechelen (Malines), Leuven, Bewerchain, Tourinnes, Wavre, Vilvoorde, Bruxelles (Brussel), Soignes, Rixensart, Nivelles (Nijvel), Braine, Halle, Wemmel, Willebroeken, Rupel, Wilrijk, Antwerpen, Ruppelmonde, Dendermonde, Aalst, Pamel, Enghien, Soignies, Ath, Chevres, Leuze, Doornik (Tournai), Ronse, Oudenaarde, Nukerke, Berchen, Merelbeke, Ghent (Gand), Vinderhoute, Zomergem, Lowendegem, Merendree, Bellem, Deinze, Eeklo, Maldegem, Aardenburg, Middelburg, Kanaal van Brugge naar Ghent, Oostkamp, Brugge, naar Zeebrugge, Helst, Knokke, Sluis, Breskens, Vlissingen, Oostende, Gistel, Torhout, Werken, Tielt, Roeselare, Dadizele, Menen (Menin), Wervik, Halluin, Tourcoing, Roubaix, Lille, Komen (Comines), Mesen, Warneton, Comines, Armentières, Nieppe, Bailleul, Caestre, Hondshoote, Westvleteren, Poperinge, Ieper (Ypres), Diksmuide, Nieuwpoort, Nieuport, Veurne, Sint Niklaas (Saint Nicholas), Lokeren, Wachtebeke, Hulst, Terneuzen, naar Terneuzen, Kanaal van Ghent, Ninove, Antelinks, Geraardsbergen, Harelbeke, Kortrijk (Courtrai), Zwevenem, Leie Lys, Schelde Escaut, Albert Kanaal, Nete, Dijk, Dijle, Leopold Kanaal, Canal de Charleroi, Kanaal naar Ghent

NL

F

N

235

Pieter Breughel the Younger. The 17th century ushered in the age of Flemish baroque with Peter Paul Rubens as the undisputed master and Anthony van Dyck and Jacob Jordaens as his best-known pupils.

In the 19th century another artistic revival occurred which is still continuing. James Ensor and Rick Wouters are the leading figures of this revival. Another well-known contemporary Belgian painter is Paul Delvaux, whose melancholy figures inhabit moonlit Belgian townscapes. Belgium has had a number of great writers and poets, but because of the limited range of the Flemish language, they are hardly known beyond Belgium's borders. It is unfortunate that Guido Gezelle's lovely poems defy translation in other languages. Charles Coster wrote *Til Eulenspiegel,* and Maurice Maeterlinck was a poet-philosopher and dramatist of significance. Maeterlinck was awarded the Nobel Prize for Literature in 1911.

While French cooking has the reputation, many connoisseurs give Belgian cuisine an edge over the French. I agree, but the point is hard to argue. So why not judge for yourself. The *New York Times* Sunday edition sometimes features Belgian recipes. One suggestion: even if you are not by nature a desert eater, save some room for it in Belgium. All foods, including deserts, are prepared from fresh and natural ingredients without preservatives and artificial additives. In Ghent or Brugge, we might try some waffles or *poffertjes* for lunch. In Dinant the bakeries specialize in cookies, and one can buy a superbly detailed gingerbread man more than two feet tall.

The Ardennes have enough caverns and grottoes to keep geologists and those interested in spelunking, occupied for weeks. There is the Merveilleuse Grotto at Dinant, and a cavern at Remonchamps, which has the world's longest underground navigable river. The cave at Han-sur-Lesse, with its underground lake, is considered the loveliest and most extensive cave in Europe. It also has the tallest underground chamber in the world, 128 meters (420 ft.) high.

For those interested in folklore and festivals, Belgium offers an almost year-round spectacle. Ancient customs, processions, and commemorations of religious, historic, or legendary events bring gaiety to many towns and villages. Binche has one of the oldest festivals in Europe and features the Gilles, the costumed dancers first brought out in 1549 to celebrate the conquest of Peru. The dress was inspired by the Incas.

On Ascension Day, the Shrine of the Holy Blood, which was brought back from the Second Crusade by Count Thierry d'Alsace in 1150, is carried in solemn procession through the streets of Brugge, followed by reenactments of principal stories from the Old and New Testaments.

An unusual feature of most festivals and processions are the Giants. These enormous lavishly and colorfully dressed figures represent biblical and medieval personalities. The figures are shaped around wicker frameworks sometimes two or three stories high. The most elaborate pageant of them all, the *Ommegang* (walk about), is held on the Grand Place of

"The Presentation in the Temple" by Hans Memling (1430?-1495)

Brussels on the first Thursday in July, but tickets for a place to stand are sold out months in advance. Our chances are much better along the 35-kilometer (22-mile) parade route of the March of St. Roland at Gerpinnes on the Monday following Whitsunday. On other occasions cities decorate entire squares with a rich tapestry of cut flowers, called *Fleuralia*.

ANABAPTISM IN FLANDERS

The precise moment that Anabaptism came to Flanders is not known. But it is believed that there were congregations in Brugge and Ghent as early as 1530. The persecution of Anabaptists in Flanders was extremely severe. Because the vice-regent governing the Low Countries lived in Brussels, he was able to crack down hardest on the Anabaptists nearest to him. In cooperation with the Spanish rulers, the Catholic Church hired inquisitors, like the zealous monk Cornelis Adriaansz, who kept negative sentiments toward the Anabaptists alive. Later when the Calvinists rose to power, the Anabaptists were still considered heretics and still not permitted to worship freely. So in Flanders the Anabaptists got it from all sides. The *Martyrs Mirror* and other sources list 400 martyrs in this small area. But more recent scholarship estimates the actual number to be closer to 1,000. Many of the Anabaptists in Flanders fled the persecution and moved to the northern Netherlands, to England, and to the Lower Rhine (see "Germany").

In Flanders the relentless persecution succeeded. The last secret congregations in Flanders probably shared the same fate as the one in Ghent, which was dissolved in 1634.

The Flemish Anabaptists differed from their brethren in the north in that they had no elders. Elders traveling down from Holland ministered to them infrequently. In the absence of elders, the total brotherhood took on more of the responsibility, including that of baptism. Eventually this became one of the points of contention between the Flemish refugees in Holland and the Frisians. Many of the Flemish Anabaptists were weavers or otherwise engaged in the textile industry. This caused additional problems between the Flemish and the Frisians because the Flemish wore more elaborate and costly clothing than the plainer Frisians. Credit must be given to Hans de Ries, of Flemish origin, and the Waterlander Mennonites of North Holland for attempting to bring about mutual understanding and reconciliation between these culturally diverse groups.

Since the 1950s there is again an organized Mennonite presence in Belgium, after more than 300 years. Largely the result of MCC work following World War II and mission work thereafter, there are now around 100 persons in Belgium who affiliate with various French, Spanish, and Slavic language Mennonite fellowships.

A Bilingual Nation

Belgium has two official languages. Flemish, a language related to the Dutch, is spoken by the Flemish people who live in the north. French is the official language of the Walloons, who live in the south. The linguistic frontier established by law in 1963 draws a line east-west just to the south of Brussels. In addition, some German is spoken around Eupen and St. Vith in the eastern provinces. Along most highways the signs are in both languages. For instance, Luik is Liège, Doornik is Tournai, Kortrijk is Courtrai.

The Climate

Because the warm gulf stream comes past the coast of Flanders, the climate in most of Belgium is moderate. Summers are pleasant but not too hot. The winters tend to be mild. As in Holland, a prevailing wind comes from the west and it may rain during part or all of 200 days per year. To the southeast, in the Ardennes Mountains, the influence of the continental climate is felt in colder winters and warmer summers.

The Best Times to See Belgium

Because Belgium enjoys a mild climate, tours of towns and country can be made throughout the year. But between April and the beginning of November the country is most picturesque. In the springtime the acacias planted along the streets and canals add a lively green to the stucco and the brick. The orchards of Flanders will be in bloom and wild iris provide color in abundance along the canals. Summer is a good time to explore the dunes and the white beaches along the North Sea. Fall and winter are both good seasons to explore the immense forests of the Ardennes Mountains.

Holidays and Store Hours

In addition to the major holidays—New Years Day, Christmas, and Easter—Belgium celebrates Labor Day (May 1), Independence Day (July 21), Maria Ascension Day (in midsummer), All Saints' Day (November 1), and Armistice Day (November 11). Stores, banks, and post offices are closed on these days. The second day of Christmas is not a holiday in Belgium and neither is Good Friday.

Belgium has no laws regulating store hours. Many stores are open in the evening or on Sunday. The grocery chains and department stores are open from 9:00 a.m. to 18:00 (6:00 p.m.) and until 21:00 (9:00 p.m.) on Friday.

Special Rules of the Road

All traffic coming from the right, also the slower vehicle, has the right-of-way unless indicated otherwise. Public transportation—trams, buses, taxis—always has the absolute right-of-way over all other traffic.

If a parked car or van or any baggage on top of the vehicle obscures a traffic sign for the driver coming from behind, it is illegally parked.

Sleeping in cars along the roadside is forbidden.

Using cables for towing is illegal. Towing rods are required.

Children under 12 are not allowed in the front seats of cars.

Evening scene near Brugge

The Monetary System

Belgium's monetary unit is the Belgian Franc (BF). The Franc is subdivided into 100 centimes. Coins come in the values of 25 centimes, 1, 5, and 10 BF, all in white metal. Recently a gold-colored 20 BF coin in copper/nickel/aluminum was introduced. Of these 60 million new coins one half have been minted with the Flemish inscription *Belgie,* the other half with the French *Belgique.* Paper money comes in the values of 50, 100, 500 and 1000 BF notes and higher.

STROLLING THROUGH THE HEART OF BRUSSELS

Although known collectively as Brussels, the city is actually organized as a conurbation of 19 separate communes, the central and largest of which is Brussels. The city has just over a million people, of which nearly one fourth are foreign residents. During the last four centuries Brussels has taken the lead over the other towns of Belgium and in 1830 it quite naturally became the capital of the new kingdom of Belgium. Today many of the authorities of the European Economic Community have established their headquarters in Brussels, as has NATO.

It seems that Brussels is always restructuring its future and diggings and detours seem to go on forever, a process started by the ambitious burgemeester Anspach more than 100 years ago. Some of the "temporary" overpasses over the construction sites are now 30 years old, and I have yet to see the area around the Gare du Nord without barriers and bulldozers. One can only hope that the Brussels of tomorrow, once rid of its unsightly construction sites and detours, will emerge a truly modern capital while preserving the wealth of its great heritage.

The heart of Brussels is the Grand Place, the historic trade center of the old city. This sumptuous square in the Italo-Flemish Baroque style bears testimony to the power of the guilds which rebuilt it after the bombardment ordered by the French king Louis XIV in 1695. It is today, one of the most beautiful squares in the world.

The *Hotel de Ville* (town hall), begun in 1402 and finished in 1480, is a unique example of 15th-century civic architecture. Its tower, designed by Jan van Ruysbroeck, supports a lacy spire topped by a five meter (16-ft.) weather vane in the form of the archangel Michael, patron saint of the city. It still houses the offices of the city council. Across from it, the *Maison du Roi* (the King's House) over the years served as bread market, the seat of various tribunals, as customs house, and as a place to receive foreign dignitaries. Under Spanish rule it was used as a prison. Today it houses a museum.

The square and the two civic structures are surrounded by no less than 39 guildhouses and private mansions, the one more lavish than the other. They are (starting at the corner of the Rue au Beurre/Boterstraat and going counter-clockwise) (1 and 2) *the King of Spain,* guildhouse of the bakers; (3) *the Wheelbarrow,* guildhouse of the tallow merchants; (4) *the*

Brussels: the Grand Place by night

Sack, corporation house of the joiners and coopers from 1444 onwards; (5) the Wolf, the house of the archers, completed in 1691, the only building to escape the shelling by Marshall de Villeroy; (6) the Horn, house of the boatmen; and (7) the Fox, guildhouse of the haberdashers.

To the left of the town hall, the lineup continues with (8) the Star, the smallest and one of the oldest of the buildings on the Grand Place, but not a guildhouse; (9) the Swan, which became a guildhouse only in 1720 when it was acquired by the butchers; (10) the Golden Tree, better known as the brewers' house; (11) the Rose, once occupied by the guild of St. Sebastian; (12) Mont Tabor, later called The Three Colors; and (13) the Fame, a small corner house.

On the east side of the square we find numbers 14 through 19, the house of the Dukes of Brabant and six buildings grouped under one single ornamental pedament. They are (14) the Hermitage, house of the wine sellers and vegetable merchants; (15) the Fortune, house of the tanners; (16) the Windmill, house of the millers' guild; (17) the Pewter Pot, house of the cabinetmakers; (18) the Hill, house of the stonecutters, slaters, masons, and sculptors guild, and (19) the Purse.

On the north side of the square we find (20) the Deer, also known as the Flying Deer, purchased in 1696 by the tailors; (21 and 22) Joseph and Anna, also occupied by the brewers' guild; (23) the Angel; (24 and 25) the House of the Tailors; (26 and 27) the Pigeon, which in 1510 became the guildhouse of the painters; and (28), which served as the magistrates' chambers. Past the Maison du Roi is (34) the Helmet, where the fruit merchants used to display their wares in front of the house; (35) the Peacock, which always has been a private home; (36) the Little Fox, previously known as the Samaritan; (37) the Oak, house of the hosiery weavers; (38) Santa Barbara; and (39) the Donkey.

If at all possible, we should visit the Grand Place at least twice: once late in the evening around 23:00 (11:00 p.m.) when it finally gets dark enough to bring out the beauty of the buildings with artful illumination, and once again in the morning when the flower vendors have set out their blooming plants and cut flowers for the benefit of buying housewives and visiting photographers.

The square was the scene of many historic events. In 1568, Counts Egmont and van Hoorne were executed here by the Spanish because they dared ask for basic freedoms. Anabaptists were also burned at the stake here. The last Anabaptist martyr in Brussels was Anneken van den Hove, buried alive a mile out of town on July 19, 1597, after two years and seven months of imprisonment. The execution was carried out by Jesuit priests who danced on her body as she lay dying.

Other interesting sights are found in the Sablon District. The Grand Sablon Square, majestically flanked by old houses of the master crafts, is always lively. On weekends an array of red and green stalls (the official

Flower vendor on the Grand Place

colors of Brussels) houses an antique and book market under the protective wing of the Notre Dame du Sablon. This church, a fine example of 15th-century Gothic architecture, owes its splendor to the city's crossbowmen who built it.

Nearby the enchanting parklet of the Petit Sablon is ringed by a wrought iron fence topped by 48 delicate statues depicting medieval crafts and trades. In the park are the statues of Egmont and van Hoorne, heroes of the Low Countries' resistance to Spanish tyranny, as well as statues of the great 16th-century humanists. Behind the park stands Egmont Palace. In 1972, Great Britain and Ireland signed their entry into the European Economic Community in this building.

The Park of Brussels, once the private hunting ground of the dukes of Brabant, was redesigned as a formal French garden during the 18th century. On the one side of the park stands the Royal Palace, on the other side the Palace of the Nation, which houses the chamber and the senate.

The Place de la Monnaie is dominated by the Theatre Royal de la Monnaie, one of Europe's major opera houses. Here, in 1830, the revolution broke out during a performance of Aubert's opera *La Muette di Portici,* which resulted in Belgium's secession from the Netherlands. Today it is best known as the home of contemporary ballet.

One of Brussels' outstanding churches is the Cathedral of Saints Michel and Gudule. With its remarkable stained-glass windows, it is considered a textbook of Gothic styles. Also notable are the Church of Saint Magdalene, the Church of Saint Niklaas, and the Notre Dame de la Chapelle, in which Pieter Breughel the Elder lies buried. At night the streets immediately to the north of the Grand Place come alive with sidewalk cafes, artisans selling their wares, and performing street musicians.

At 32 Rue de ten Bosch is the Brussels' Children's Museum. Open on Wednesday and Saturday afternoons, this living museum was especially created for three-and-four-year-olds. Inside in addition to admiring the objects, children can actually touch them and operate them. The exhibits, which are always changing, have included the making of bread, a model of the human body, a printshop, musical instruments, a demonstration of use of carpenter's tools, and more.

Eighteen kilometers (eleven miles) southeast of Brussels we find Waterloo, site of the battle which ended Napoleon's reign on June 18, 1815. The battle left 49,000 dead and thousands wounded. The site is marked by an artificial mound, 45 meters (148 ft.) high, which supports a bronze lion weighing 28 tons. Contrary to the popular legend, the monument was not cast from the cannons left behind.

FLANDERS UNDER SPANISH RULE

The Flanders plain stretches across northwestern Belgium from the French border to the southern Netherlands. East Flanders (capital Ghent) is more crisscrossed with canals and rivers than West Flanders (capital Brugge). At one time Flanders also included the French department Nord from Dunkirk to Lille, then called Duinkerken and Rijssel. The language spoken here is Flemish.

It is strange that this part of Belgium is now largely Catholic, for during the Middle Ages it was a center for all sorts of pre-Reformation renewal movements. In the 16th century there were at first Anabaptist congregations in nearly every town and village, followed later by still more numerous Reformed congregations. Both were met with unparalleled persecution. The Spanish Duke of Alva and his Blood Council claimed the lives of hundreds of martyrs. There is no corner in Europe where the soil was so thoroughly soaked with the blood of martyrs and where the execution stakes were so frequently erected as in Flanders. The *Martyrs Mirror* lists about 400 Anabaptist martyrs in Flanders, but recent research in the ar-

Quiet reflections at Lissewege, Flanders

chives has already brought this number to more than 800. The first martyrs were Willem Mulaer, beheaded in Ghent on July 15, 1535, and Arendt de Jaeger and Jan van Ghentbrugge, beheaded four days later.

The continued executions caused a mass migration to the north. Thousands upon thousands of Flemish Protestants moved to Amsterdam, to Friesland, to Emden, and even to Danzig. By 1634 Anabaptism ceased to exist in Belgium. That the Anabaptists in Flanders were numerous can be ascertained from the number of Flemish congregations among the Mennonite churches in Germany and from the originally Flemish names which still exist among the Mennonites. Some of these names are Craen (Krahn), Falck, de Wael (Wall), van der Smissen, Couwenhoven (Kauenhoven), Claesz (Klaassen, etc.), Rose (Roosen), Willems, and Wijnands (Wiens).

Since the Second World War, three small Mennonite congregations have emerged in Belgium, two in Brussels and one in nearby Rixensart.

245

GHENT AND HET GRAVENSTEEN

Ghent is the richest of all Belgian cities in architectural treasures. But unlike Brussels, Ghent has had the gift of being able to incorporate them into its continuing life. In the city's center we are surrounded by the cathedral of St. Bavo, the Cloth Hall, the Belfort, and the Church of St. Niklaas. These are but a stone's throw from the incomparable Graslei, so we have no sense of being in an old city. The modern world and all its hustle and bustle is all around us. Truly, this area is home to the most remarkable collections of architectural treasures anywhere.

Inside the St. Bavo's is the priceless *Adoration of the Lamb,* by Hubert and Jan van Eyck, an early oil painting by the brothers who invented the technique. It has been in the church since 1432. The nearby town hall has two distinct styles. We can readily see where the Gothic builders stopped and where the Renaissance architects resumed the work 60 years later. Along the Graslei, mentioned earlier, stands an interrupted row of ancient mansions, quietly reflected in the water of the Leie River. These stately homes were built between the 12th and the 16th centuries.

For students of Anabaptist Mennonite history, the chief attraction in Ghent is het Gravensteen, the castle of the counts of Flanders. With the exception of Antwerp, no other Flemish city has a longer list of martyrs as Ghent and the grim castle played a large role in their suffering. All in all, 146 Anabaptist Mennonite martyrs were imprisoned and executed here (105 were burned at the stake just outside the castle's main gate).

The castle was built in 1180 by Philip d'Alsace on the remains of a much older fortification whose walls now form the bottom of the dungeons. More than likely, Philip had seen similar castles built by the crusaders in the Middle East, which explains the likeness of het Gravensteen to the fortress ruins in Lebanon and northern Israel. A tour of the moated castle takes about 1½ hours. Inside we find dungeons, torture rooms, the castellan's residence, supply stores, and the large hall of knights, in which the Order of the Golden Fleece held its meetings. There is an extensive collection of torture instruments and branding irons.

The dungeons of het Gravensteen were in use until well into the 18th century. Accused persons stayed here from six weeks to thirteen months for preventive imprisonment, that is to say, before their trial. The unsanitary conditions and, the intense winter cold of the dungeons, all but killed the unfortunate prisoners. Once the trial was held, punishment was swift and little time was wasted in erecting the pyres for burning. The exhibits which show man's inhumanity to man are sobering, especially when one realizes that the use of torture is on the increase again in many parts of the world. Currently the countries violating human rights and/or using torture number 117, with the United States and the United Kingdom conveniently looking the other way when it involves their allies.

Other points of interest in Ghent include the Little Begijnhof and the

Ghent: het Gravensteen

Ghent: merchants houses along the Graslei

Old Begijnhof, both established in 1234 to provide homes for Beguines (a women's lay order), and the *Dulle Griet* (hoarse Margaret), a massive 15th-century cannon known better for its dull roar than for its effectiveness in lobbing cannon balls.

BRUGGE: THE CITY AS A LIVING MUSEUM

Sometime during the fifth century forces of nature created Het Zwin, an inlet from the North Sea. Four centuries later the Vikings penetrated Het Zwin as far as it was navigable and built there a wooden dock or *Bryggja,* as they called it. Unsure of the motives of these Scandinavian visitors, Count Bauduin of Flanders built a castle nearby to observe the Norsemen.

In less than one century Bryggja, or Brugge, as the Flemish called it, became the greatest trading center between the Mediterranean and the Baltic seas. By 1340 Brugge had a population of 35,000 people, unheard of at that time. The new port was enlarged so that 1,700 sailing ships could be tied up there at one time. Out of their holds came lumber from Sweden, furs from Novgorod, metals from Poland, fruits from Spain and Egypt, and wine from France.

To ensure continued active trading, Brugge sponsored international trade fairs, the first one in 958. Soon seventeen trading nations stored their goods in Brugge's warehouses and twenty governments established embassies and consulates in the city. Then the forces of nature, which had created Het Zwin in the first place, turned against Brugge. During the 15th century, the harbor silted up and Brugge found itself 14 kilometers (8½ miles) from the sea. When the sea, and with it the merchants, departed from Brugge for Antwerp and elsewhere, they left behind a magnificent city which became a sleeping princess. It wasn't until 1907 that a canal was dug and a new harbor built, so that once again Brugge plays a minor role in Belgian commerce.

The Anabaptist movement was very prominent in medieval Brugge. One hunter of the Anabaptist heretics complained that there were no less than 700 Anabaptists in the city. We know of 47 martyrs here, of whom two died in prison, two were buried alive, and 43 were burned at the stake. Other Anabaptists from Brugge were captured and executed elsewhere and by 1630 the last survivors had moved north into the Netherlands.

For tourists, Brugge has much to offer. Four of the original city gates remain, as do three of the original 27 windmills on the ramparts. More than 2,000 medieval buildings are still inhabited by Brugge citizens who live and work there.

The heart of Brugge is the market square established by Count Bauduin III in 958. Dominating this busy square is the 83 meter-high (260 ft.) Belfort, by far the most imposing tower in all Belgium. The tower has a beautiful carillon of 47 bells, weighing a total of 27 tons, which sends its music tinkling over the red rooftops every quarter hour. During the summer

Brugge, where time stood still

Brugge: two-horsepower cab service

months, extensive carillon concerts can be heard every Monday and Wednesday evening. A climb up the 366 steps of the Belfort will reward the ambitious person with tired feet, a faster heartbeat, and a splendid panoramic view.

Away from the market square, on the Minnewater, an old bridge leads into Brugge's Begijnhof. Established in 1225 by Jeanne van Constantinopol, the countess of Flanders, it used to house women whose husbands had gone off to the Crusades. Today it is a convent for Benedectine nuns. When the bell of the Begijnhof chapel tolls, the sisters in their outsized starched white caps hurry along the brick streets to the sanctuary. The nuns are themselves walking museum pieces, reminders of Brugge's former glory.

The Memling Museum, the Groen Museum, and a number of other museums together own the largest collection of works by Flemish masters anywhere in the world. Other museums display the works of gold- and silversmiths, the pottery and the lace, the tapestries and the sculptures of Brugge's golden era. Near the Minnewater one can still see ladies sitting in their doorways making lace by hand.

The age-old craft of lacemaking

Estimates put the number of remaining lacemakers in Belgium between three and four hundred women, most of them between the ages of 60 and 80. However, Myriam de Saedeleer, whose family has been bobbing lace for 135 years, refuses to call lacemaking "a dying art," and points to the growing number of young women who are taking up the craft as a hobby.

The city's information service, located in the base of the Belfort, can supply you with a map and useful advice on what to see in Brugge. In my book, no visit to Belgium is complete without a visit to Ghent and Brugge.

ANTWERP (ANTWERPEN)

The city of Antwerp received its name from a third-century legend about a battle between the Roman soldier, Silvius Brabo, and a giant—or at least a person of large proportions—who terrorized the shippers and the fishermen on the Schelde River. He managed to chop off the giant's hand and throw it in the Schelde. (H) ant = hand and werpen = to throw. By the 1300s Antwerp had developed into a commercial center specializing in fish, salt, grains, and products from England. By the 15th century Antwerp joined the Hanseatic League.

Not too long after Johannes Gutenberg invented the art of printing from moveable type, Antwerp became a center of printing and publishing with no less than sixteen printing establishments, of which Christopher Plantin's was the best known. Historians see a definite link between the rapid spread of Protestantism (and Anabaptism) in and around Antwerp and the city's many printing presses. But the spread of the new ideas also resulted in early persecution. Already on July 1, 1523, Hendrik Vos and Johan van Essen were burned as martyrs.

Around 1560 there were about 2,000 Mennonites in Antwerp, meeting in groups of from 35 to 70 persons in private homes. In 1569 a great number of them lost their lives when a service in the home of Jan Boote was surprised by informers. In 1573, 35 people worshiping in the home of Jan de Chardis met the same fate. Since Mennonite congregations had their own midwives, the authorities were not informed about the children that were born and the children could remain unbaptized. Announcers would visit the members and tell them when and where the next secret meeting would be held. With the coming of the duke of Alva, the persecution increased. This period became known as the time of the Spanish Fury. On August 16, 1585, more than 35,000 people fled the city and environs of Antwerp, among them the last of the once numerous Mennonites.

After the decline of Ghent and Brugge during the 16th century, Antwerp became Belgium's second largest city. More recently it has become known as the third largest port in the world. The Flandria Company offers tours of the Schelde and the harbor complex ranging from 50 minutes to three hours from its docks, next to the Steen Castle.

In the heart of the old city we find the irregular-shaped *Groote Markt* (Grand Place) surrounded by guildhouses and mansions. On one side of it stands Antwerp's city hall, built in 1564, in the Italo-Flemish Renaissance style. On the square itself we see the Silvius Brabo fountain, which depicts the Roman soldier tossing the defeated giant's hand in the river. Not far away stands the Cathedral of our Lady, remarkable not only for its beauty but also for its size. The entire church covers more than one hectare (2½ acres) and the interior, 117 by 65 meters (384 × 213 ft.), is one of the largest enclosed spaces in Europe. The cathedral's ceiling is supported by 125 pillars.

The Plantin Moretus museum, the 33-room home and printshop of the printer Christopher Plantin, is located on the Friday Market. Built during the 16th century, the shops were enlarged to the present size by Plantin's descendants, the Moretuses, during the 17th and 18th centuries. In the printshop demonstrations are given on the original 17th-century hand presses. The library exhibit contains a 1455 Gutenberg Bible and Plantin's *Biblia Regia,* which is printed in Hebrew, Syriac, Greek, Latin, and Aramaic.

The het Steen Castle was built along the Schelde in 843. In the 13th century the castle was enlarged to accommodate the prison and these facilities were again enlarged in 1520, just in time for the Spanish to incarcerate, torture, and execute a great number of Protestant and Anabaptist heretics. The death of 72 of these martyrs is remembered in the so-called *Antwerpen Lied,* published in 1560. The poem begins with these lines: "Here, O God, our heavenly Father, are tales of woe in these times." Today het Steen houses a maritime museum.

For lovers of contemporary sculpture there is no place like Antwerp's Middelheim Park. For decades the city has been buying more than 200 sculptures by the great masters, from Rodin to Maillol to Giacometti and Moore, and has placed them in the 20-hectare (50 acres) park. New acquisitions are added to the park regularly. A pavilion, open to the public during the afternoons, houses a collection of smaller and more fragile works in wood, copper, and terra cotta. And every other year Middelheim Park hosts an international sculpture festival, the *Biennale.*

MORE TO SEE IN BELGIUM

Because many of the places of tourist interest and nearly all the places of Mennonite historical interest are located in Flanders, we have so far provided the reader with itineraries from western Belgium. A significant place to visit is the Domains of Bokrijk (near Hasselt), one of Belgium's outstanding tourist attractions. Owned and operated by the government, the 1,300-hectare (3,200 acres) park combines the features of a national forest with those of historic recreation like Williamsburg. It includes an open-air museum, the national arboretum, a deer park, and a forest preserve with fourteen small lakes and fens. In the open-air museum an authentic

Antwerpen: het Steen

Flemish village, a Kempen village, and a Brabant village have been reconstructed in the most minute detail.

South of Brussels at Ronquières, it is possible to observe a unique method of transportation: an inclined plane for canal barges located on the Bruxelles-Charleroi Canal. Two steel basins filled with up to four meters (thirteen ft.) of water can carry from two to four ships up or down a 1,432-meter-long (4698 ft.) inclined plane to overcome an altitude of 64 meters (210 ft.). Visitors have an excellent view of the operations from the 150 meter (492 ft.) high steel observation tower.

The Walloon province of Namur is especially known for its lovely stretch of the Meuse (Maas) River as it flows north from France toward the provincial capital, also called Namur. A favorite destination is Dinant, a charming town with a long and turbulent history. Today excursion boats come up the river daily from Namur and the streets are full of tourists. A cable tram takes you from river level to the citadel, from where you have a magnificent view over Dinant's busy streets and the river.

In the winding valley of the Semois lies Bouillion, where we can see the best preserved and most spectacular medieval fortress castle in Belgium. It once belonged to Geoffrey de Bouillion, a prominent figure in the First Crusade (1096-1099). Before leaving for Jerusalem, Geoffrey sold his fortress to the prince-bishop of Liège.

The Hautes Fagnes region (highland moors), between the towns of Eupen and Malmédy, is all but snowbound in the winter. But in the spring it wakes up to a riot of color in the form of its sub-Alpine flora. The area is visited by professional and amateur botanists from all over the world. Organized hikes are available.

Spa, the town from which all other spas derived their name, is the famous place of mineral springs and baths, popular with the royalty and the high society of the 18th and 19th centuries. Spa continues to attract visitors from all over the world in search of a cure from its mineral waters or simply to enjoy the town's lovely environment.

In Flanders, in addition to the towns already mentioned, we might enjoy the cities of Kortrijk (Courtrai), Ieper (Ypres), and Doornik (Tournai). In the Kempen area of North Belgium, Tongeren (the oldest town in Belgium) and Sint Truiden are worth a visit.

Jan Gleysteen /84

Luxembourg/Letzeburg

The Grand Duchy of Luxembourg is one of the smallest industrial nations of the world with a total of 2,586 square kilometers (just under 1,000 square miles) and a population of about 350,000. Luxembourg has a long and convoluted history during which it has been either occupied or ruled by the Romans, the Germans, the French, the Dutch, the Austrians, and the Spanish. Despite these changing allegiances, the Luxembourgers have been able to maintain an identity and a national motto: "Mir wolle bleiwe wat mir sin" ("We plan to remain who we are") has stood the test of time.

A major change came in 1830 when Belgium, along with Luxembourg, a part of the Netherlands, revolted and seceded. The European powers attempting to solve the differences among the Low Countries, suggested that the [Old Dutch] province of Luxembourg be divided in two, with the western (French-speaking) part becoming a province of the new Belgium, and the remaining part, by virtue of its ties to the house of Orange-Nassau, forming a personal union with the Netherlands. The resulting new Belgian province, also called Luxembourg, is actually larger than the duchy of Luxembourg itself.

The union with the Netherlands came to an end when Wilhelmina ascended the Dutch throne and the Luxembourg constitution did not permit a female ruler. Luxembourg then passed on to another branch of the house of Nassau and became a grand duchy under Grand Duke Adolphus. In later years the reign did pass on to Adolphus' female descendents, with Marie Adelaide and Charlotte as the successive rulers.

The Nazis smashed through all three Low Countries on May 10, 1940, and in August 1942, Adolf Hitler proclaimed Luxembourg a province of Germany. The Luxembourgers responded with a general protest strike. The Germans retaliated with mass deportations, carting off 10 percent of the country's population, including all the young men.

The Allies arrived to liberate the country in September 1944, and Luxembourg City became General Omar Bradley's headquarters from which he directed the ill-fated Battle of the Bulge. The northern part of the grand duchy, along with much of Belgium, suffered greatly under this offensive.

After the war Luxembourg linked its economic future with that of Belgium and the Netherlands in a customs union (*Benelux*), which in turn formed the core of the EEC (the European Economic Community).

Despite its small size, Luxembourg ranks among the world's leading steel producers, and the steel mills along the Alzette account for 30 percent of the duchy's gross national product. For this small country to survive, export is a must. Incidently, nearly all of the nation's electricity is generated from the heat captured at the steel mills.

Counting meadows and pastures as well as fields, about half of the hilly land is cultivated. The farms are small and the soil is generally poor. Phosphate fertilizers, a by-product of the steel mills, are widely used. Yet the yields per acre are considerably below the levels achieved in Holland and Belgium. Along the Mosel there are some excellent vineyards and there is some logging.

Within the country, both the Luxembourg Franc and the Belgian Franc, which are of equal value, circulate as legal tender. But because Luxembourg does not have a national bank and currency is issued through the savings and loan institution, Luxembourg Francs are hard to dispose of outside of the country.

Luxembourg plays an important part in radio broadcasting. Radio Luxembourg, with the most modern facilities in the world, easily covers all of Europe, including the Soviet Union.

During the 1960s a new harbor was opened on the Mosel River near Wasserbillig. A canal connected it with the system of Rhine waterways, which opened up a new avenue for the export of Luxembourg products. A creative liaison with another small country, Iceland, and the national airline *Flugleidir* (Icelandair) makes Luxembourg's airport at Findel a much more popular destination than the size of the country might suggest.

LUXEMBOURG'S AMISH-MENNONITES

Mennonites have come to Luxembourg only in recent times. It was not until the 1840s that three Amish-Mennonite families from the Alsace and from Germany came here at the same time that their cousins were migrating to western Ontario, Illinois, and Iowa. Initially, they rented, then later purchased, farms in the hills north of Luxembourg City. A few others joined them, or married into the families, over the next 30 years. The Mennonites in Luxembourg today are still largely the descendants of three families named Oesch, Nafziger, and Schertz.

For more than a century, worship services were held on their farms

The Rosswinkelhof meetinghouse

uphill from Diekirch. In 1948 the congregation purchased a small wooden army barrack in Diekirch and converted it into a meetinghouse. Only six years later a new stone meetinghouse was built on the Rosswinkelhof near Scheidgen/Consdorf and dedicated on September 26, 1954. Also during the 1950s two missionary families, serving under the eastern and the conservative Amish mission boards, began working in the southern part of the country at Esch-sur-Alzette and at Dudelange. Their mission extended into the steel-making regions of northern France at Metz and Thionville. The baptized membership of the two Mennonite congregations in Luxembourg totals just short of a hundred persons.

In the Grand Duchy of Luxembourg three languages are used: "*Letzeburgsch*," a patois spoken in the Mosel Valley; German, used for general conversation; and French, the official and cultural language. In parliamentary sessions, French, Letzeburgsch, and German are used interchangeably without translation.

Luxembourg has a greater number of nice sunny days and less rainy days than its neighboring countries. This is caused by the Ardennes Mountains which constitute a barrier against the rain-carrying westerly winds from the Belgian coast and the cold winds from the north. The Mosel Valley, which forms the border between Luxembourg and Germany, has the most agreeable climate.

Holidays and Store Hours

In addition to the major holidays of the Christian year, Luxembourg recognizes Carnivals Monday, Day of Labor (May 1), the National Holiday (June 23), Maria Ascension Day (midsummer), Schobermesse (end of August), and All Saints' Day (November 1). Stores and banks are closed on these days. Most stores in Luxembourg are open Tuesday through Saturday from 8:00 a.m. to noon and from 14:00 to 18:00 (2:00-6:00 p.m.), closing an hour earlier on Saturday. Post offices and banks are always closed on Saturday.

Special Rules of the Road

Public transportation has the priority over all other traffic. Sleeping in cars along the highway is illegal.

The Monetary System

The Luxembourg Frank or Franc is on a par with the Belgian Franc, has the same divisions, and comes in identical sizes with its Belgian counterparts, both in metal and paper. Within the country the BF and the LF are used interchangeably. But because Luxembourg, unlike other nations, does not have a national bank, Luxembourg Franks are not easily disposed of outside the country.

A DRIVE THRU THE DUCHY

For centuries the city of Luxembourg was one of the most formidable fortresses in the world. Dismantled between 1867 and 1883, many relics of its ancient past have been preserved, including the Citadel of the Saint Esprit and the remains of the Bock, a fortification dating back to the tenth century. Not far from the Bock, one may explore a section of the more than 23 kilometers (14 miles) of underground tunnels which once connected the various parts of the former Luxembourg fortress.

The city, located along both sides of the deep winding ravine of the Alzette, has no less than 80 bridges and viaducts. They range in style from the graceful curves of Roman arches to bold and modern steel spans. A good view over the entire city can be had from the Plateau du Kirchberg. During the tourist season, the bridges and many of the historic buildings are magnificently illuminated.

Diekirch is a small town on the Sûre River, at the foot of the steep Herrenberg, on which several of the old Mennonite farmsteads are located. In town it is possible to see some interesting Roman mosaics discovered at construction sites in 1926 and in 1950. Two kilometers to the south, on the road to Larochette, we find a Celtic dolmen, known as the Devil's Altar.

Diekirch is the starting point for more than 60 kilometers (40 miles) of marked hiking trails, including one which leads through the spectacularly beautiful Sure Valley to Esch-sur-Sûre and Hochfels. Esch-sur-Sûre is a typical Ardennes market town, clustered around the ancient ruins of a castle and completely surrounded by a loop of the Sûre. It is probably the most photographed spot in the entire grand duchy.

Two of Luxembourg city's eighty bridges and viaducts

"The House I Live in, by the Bridge"—Sketch by Victor Hugo, 1871

Another spot of beauty in Luxembourg is the town of Vianden. The town dates back to the ninth century and its Gothic church of 1248 is the oldest religious structure in the country. The ruins of the Castle of the Oranje-Nassaus, built in 1417 and destroyed in 1820, dominate the scene. There is a good view of Vianden from the bridge across the Our. The castle is floodlighted every evening during the summer months.

The great French author Victor Hugo (1802—1885), who wrote *The Hunchback of Notre Dame* and *Les Miserables* was an early champion of human rights, a proponent of free public education and quite progressive on a number of other issues. When Louis Napoleon declared himself the dictator of France in 1851, under the title Napoleon III, Victor Hugo, in protest, went into self-imposed exile for almost twenty years. He spent the summer of 1871 in Vianden. The house in which he lived is now the Victor Hugo Museum. Facing the house is a bust of Hugo by Auguste Rodin.

The area between Diekirch, Consdorf, Scheidgen, and Echternach is known as Luxembourg's Little Switzerland, an area of wooded glens and ravines and exotic red sandstone rock formations. Little Switzerland, along with the valley of the Sûre, the Mullerthal, and the Our Valley, forms part of the great Germano-Luxembourgois Natural Park, its hundreds of miles of hiking trails clearly marked by holly berry symbols. The German part of this park is located in the adjoining Eifel Mountains. The Mullertal contains four picturesque villages. Echternach is known for its unusual dancing procession on Whitsunday, in which thousands of devout pilgrims participate under the eyes of an equal number of interested spectators.

For a different vacation, one might try to see Luxembourg from a duck's perspective. With its many scenic rivers, Luxembourg is an ideal country for canoeing. Both the Luxembourg Railways and the local buses will transport folding boats or lightweight kayaks (maximum: 40 kilos) for the price of one bicycle ticket when accompanied by the owner. Good navigational maps of Luxembourg's rivers have been published by the Luxembourg Kayak Club, and canoes can be rented from the same organization.

FRANCE

France

Apart from European Russia, France is the largest country in Europe. Except for the borders it shares with Belgium and Luxembourg, France has more or less natural boundaries on all sides. To the west France is bordered by the Atlantic Ocean, the English Channel, and the North Sea. To the south there are the Pyrenees along the Spanish border and the Mediterranean Sea. Southeastern France is separated from Italy by the Alps and from Switzerland by the Jura. Finally, the upper Rhine River forms the border between France and Germany.

France has only four great rivers: the Seine, the Loire, the Garonne, and the Rhone, of which the Loire is the longest. Each of France's four major ports — Le Havre, Nantes, Bordeaux, and Marseille — is located at the mouth of these streams. Northern and northeastern France have extensive canal systems — often linking river to river — on which some 10,000 barges move thirty million tons of commodities annually.

The Pyrennes, unlike most of Europe's other mountain ranges, were not as greatly affected by the working of the Ice Ages and therefore lack the large lakes and broad valleys characteristic of the Alps. Consequently, the Pyrennes' high, difficult, and infrequent passes have restricted the flow of commerce and culture between France and Spain for centuries.

France has long had the largest population in continental Europe, but since World War II West Germany and Italy have exceeded France by significant numbers. France's reputation as a great cultural center has always attracted expatriate writers, artists, and composers (Hemingway, Picasso, Stravinsky, and Honegger, for example). On the other hand, few Frenchmen ever leave their homeland permanently.

Natural resources play an important part in France's economy and a variety of good soils contributes considerably to this fact. More than 90 percent of the French land area is considered fertile. However, compared to the other European nations, French agriculture absorbs an inordinate proportion of the labor force and productivity per worker is low.

Except for some large cooperative farms located mostly in the north, the average French farmer farms the same fifty acres that have been in his family for generations and, in spite of electricity and mechanized transportation, the French farmer lives much like his grandparents did. It is these masses of small farmers who uphold the conservative traditions of France and are often at odds with the country's best interests, putting France at a disadvantage in competing with its European trading partners.

Only the farms in the north produce more wheat than France can use, and there wheat is rotated with potatoes and sugar beets. France also produces some 300 different kinds of cheese, the best known of which include Roquefort, Camembert, and Brie. Iron ore, found in the Lorraine, is France's most important mineral and helps to make that region a major steel producer. The Alsace once had major deposits of potash, but these reserves are now declining. Bauxite was first discovered near Le Baux in southeastern France in 1821, which accounts for the mineral's name. Larger reserves of bauxite, used in making alumina, have since been found in Jamaica and in Surinam.

One not immediately noticeable but striking difference between France and the rest of Europe is the extent to which French business and industry is directly controlled by the government. Not only are the postal, telecommunications, rail, and air services wholly nationalized, but the government also holds a monopoly on the production of electricity, coal, gas, oil, alcohol, tobacco, and matches. The North American traveler may find it handy to know that you can therefore always buy postage stamps after hours in the government-owned tobacco shops.

Government ownership also extends to the manufacturing of cars, trucks, buses, locomotives, planes, fertilizer, and the movie industry. Since they are involved in making movies, the government has passed a law that French theaters must show French movies twenty weeks out of the year. And when we buy a Renault, a Peugeot, a Citroen, or a Simca, we are dealing with the French government.

Consequently, the French do indeed have more bureaucrats than anyone else. The government employs more than one fifth of the nation's work force and has the responsibility for one third of the nation's investments. The stories we may have heard about needing just one more stamp and signature from a minor official in the back room of the *deuxième bureau* before beginning a project are probably true. It is also true that many Frenchmen have found ways to work around the system.

The French are avid readers with more than a quarter of the population reading at least two good books per month. Fine bookstores can be found even in the smallest of towns. Well-known French writers and poets include Honoré de Balzac, George Bernanos, Antoine de St. Exupéry, Jean-

Vegetable farms near Amiens

France's natural borders provide magnificent beaches

Paul Sartre, Albert Camus, Simone de Beauvoir, Paul Verlaine, and Guillaume Appolinaris. One contemporary French novelist, André Malraux, was appointed minister of cultural affairs. He promptly set out to revitalize the French National Theater. Malraux also gets the credit for the ambitious cleanup and restoration of Paris.

French music continues to distinguish itself by innovation and experimentation. The works of Claude Debussy, Maurice Ravel, Arthur Honegger (born Swiss), and Igor Stravinsky (born in Russia) have become part of the world's musical repertoire.

A number of industrial firsts can be attributed to the French. Peugeot build the world's first diesel car. Citroen developed the front-wheel drive and the four-wheel drive. The European electric railways, developing independently, ran on many different currents and voltages. The French Alsthom Locomotive Works developed a silicone rectifier unit making it possible for locomotives to cross borders and to continue running on another voltage whether AC or DC. Recently the French have added to their own fabulous system of trains the TGV — trains of *Tres Grande Vitesse* (very high speed).

In 1961 the French began the world's first tidal power plant and completed it by 1966. It harnesses the tides of the English Channel at the mouth of the Rance River, which may differ as much as fifteen meters (44 ft.) between ebb and flow. The world's longest automobile tunnel, 12 kilometers (7.25 miles) in length, connects France with Italy through the base of the Mont Blanc.

Two areas of France of great interest to Mennonite visitors are the Alsace and the Lorraine. The entire Alsace and part of the Lorraine have at times been German, then French again, then German, and currently French. In the treaty of Versailles, signed in 1919, France again recovered the Alsace and the Lorraine from Germany.

Unfortunately, the Mennonites living on both sides of the Franco-German border around Wissembourg, France, and Landau, Germany were always among the first to see their farms destroyed in the renewed hostilities of 1870-1871, 1914-1918, and 1940-1945. In those same areas we still find visible reminders of the Maginot Line, France's costly tribute to the foolishness of war.

The Maginot Line is an almost continuous fortified line of defense facing Germany along the entire eastern border of France. It begins at Sedan, just below the Belgian border town of Bouillion, and ends at Huningue not far from Basel, Switzerland. This line of defense was the brainchild of the French minister of defense, Andre Maginot, 1877-1932. Only the bunkers and observation posts were exposed. These were constructed of thick reinforced concrete, dressed by a special nickel-chrome-clad steel.

Here and there sunken roads lead to overhead doors weighing seven tons, entrances to six- or seven-story underground complexes of workshops, power plants, hangars, living quarters, dorms, war rooms, communication centers, hospitals, and immense reservoirs of diesel oil, all connected by underground roads and narrow-gauge railways. The air pressure within the Maginot Line was kept above normal to keep out gas.

Each of seven main facilities along the more than 500 kilometer-long (310 miles) line were capable of housing 12,000 men with enough food and supplies to hold out three months. In reality they were never occupied by more than 30,000 men. In June 1940 the Germans simply invaded France through Belgium and easily captured the Maginot Line from the rear.

It is reported that mushrooms are now raised in part of it and one of the line's subterranean fortresses, Simserhof (near Bitche), is open to the public several times a year for a 2½-hour tour on foot and by train covering half of the fortress's ten-kilometer (six miles) underground route.

THE FRENCH AMISH-MENNONITES

The city of Strasbourg in the Alsace became an important center for the early Anabaptist movement. Many Anabaptists came to Starsbourg from Augsburg when persecution increased there. At that time Strasbourg was referred to as "the City of Hope" because it had a history of being tolerant on external matters. Since many other religious groups found freedom and refuge in Strasbourg, it became a city of great diversity.

In 1526 many prominent Anabaptist leaders spent some time in Strasbourg. These included Balthasar Hubmaier, Wilhelm Reublin, Michael Sattler, Melchior Hofmann, Hans Denck, and Pilgram Marpeck. In Strasburg each man had his own little group of followers, each identified by the leader's name and each stressing some idea peculiar to that leader. In spite of the tolerance and great leaders, a strong, stable, and lasting Anabaptist congregation never developed in Strasbourg. Nevertheless, Strasbourg was an important meeting place for Anabaptists. At least six conferences of Anabaptist ministers were held there between 1554 and 1607. Thus Strasbourg has had a lasting influence on European Mennonitism.

Pilgram Marpeck — an engineer, mining judge, and forester — fled from Austria to Strasbourg around 1528 and soon became the leader of the fellowship there. Marpeck was an educated man and wrote several books, including *An Account* and *An Admonition*. He was also working on a New Testament concordance. Marpeck's writings were used by both Anabaptists and Hutterites as authoritative works. Marpeck also held the only public debate with the Strasbourg city clergy. While living in Strasbourg he designed a complex waterway for the city that was built to transport lumber from the Black Forest to the Rhine harbors. When Strasbourg finally got tough with the Anabaptists, they did so by persecuting the leaders. Pilgram Marpeck was forced to leave Strasbourg in 1531. The leadership of the Strasbourg congregation was taken over by Leopold Scharnslager, one of the most capable remaining leaders.

Following the Thirty Years' War, Mennonites fleeing Switzerland set-
tled near Colmar and in the valley of Sainte Marie-aux-Mines (Markirch).
Among a large group that settled in Markirch in 1696 was Jakob Ammann,
leader of the Ammann-Leut or Amish. Ammann was very influential among
the French Mennonites and many of the congregations in France have
Amish histories. Most of the Amish in western Pennsylvania, Ohio, and
Iowa can trace their origins back to the 19th-century migrations from
France. During the past 150 years, more Swiss Mennonites migrated into
France. Newcomers took over the leadership of congregations and soon
the conservative modes of the Amish disappeared.

During the 18th century, Mennonites from the Alsace migrated to the
Palatinate across the Vosges Mountains into the Lorraine and down to
Montbeliard and Belfort. Although the groups were then widely scattered,
they managed to keep the faith and in this century there has been a renewal
among the French Mennonites. Until recently there were two French Mennonite conferences: the Association, which was primarily German-speaking, and the Groupe, which was primarily French-speaking. In 1980 the two
conferences united. The new conference is called Association des Eglises
Mennonites de France, with about 2,000 baptized members in 25 congregations. This count includes one church in Belgium and the Holleestrasse
congregation of Basel, Switzerland.

On Parle Francais

The official language in France is French. In the Alsace most of the older people
also speak Elsassisch, a German dialect. The traveler will soon discover that the
French are not nearly as multilingual as their neighbors.

The Climate

The climate throughout much of France is influenced by the Atlantic Ocean.
The summers are therefore cool and the winters mild. This moderating influence
diminishes the farther one travels eastward toward the Rhine or southeast toward
the Alps and the Mediterranean. In the Alsace-Lorraine the winters are longer and
colder and it can get quite hot in the summer. The southern Vosges Mountains are
among the rainiest areas of France.

The Maritime Alps have a Mediterranean climate: warm, dry summers, and
gentle, rainy winters. The *Mistral* is a strong wind which blows south through the
Rhone Valley, then continues east and west along the Mediterranean Coast. The
Maritime Alps shield the French and Italian Rivieras from this wind for most of the
year.

The Best Times to See France

You have heard the words from the familiar song: "*I love Paris in the Springtime
... I love Paris in the fall.*" I agree. But Paris is really a city for all seasons. We may sit
down at an outdoor cafe on a summer evening and watch the people go by or walk
the streets decorated for Christmas in December.

For the rest of France it might be best to study the climatic character of the specific regions we may wish to visit. The Natioanl Tourist Office can advise you.

The Alsace-Lorraine, discussed in greater detail elsewhere in this chapter, has a truly continental climate — long hard winters, quite warm summers. Abundant precipitation comes in the form of thundershowers in the summer and heavy snows in the winter. The springtime is quite pleasant, dressed in the light greens of new leaves, of hedges and vineyards seen against the still snow-capped Ballons of the blue-purple Vosges Mountains.

Holidays and Store Hours

In addition to New Year's Day, Easter, and Christmas, France celebrates the following national holidays: Labor Day (May 1), the National Holiday (July 14), All Saints' Day (November 1), and Armistice Day (November 11). The second day of Christmas is not considered a holiday in France. The banks close at noon on the day before any holiday. Many museums in France are closed on Tuesdays. Stores are generally open between 8:00 or 9:00 a.m. and about 19:00 (7:00 p.m.), closed on Monday, with a two-hour break around noon. The post offices are closed on Saturdays, but stamps can always be bought at stores of the government tobacco monopoly, the so-called Bureaux de Tabac.

Special Rules of the Road

The one rule which vexes foreign visitors the most — often with disastrous results — is that in France, within towns and villages, all traffic coming in from side streets on the right has the right-of-way and faster traffic already on the street has no priority over the slower traffic coming in.

The sign "No Passing" remains in effect until repealed by another sign: *Fin d'Interdiction de Dépasser* (end of prohibition to pass). That second sign may be miles away, so don't forget the first sign in the meantime. Sleeping in cars along the highways, as well as in rest areas or on parking lots, is forbidden in France. Children under twelve must travel in the rear seat.

The Monetary System

The French monetary unit is the French Franc (FFr), which is subdivided into 100 centimes. It comes in brass coins of 5, 10, and 20 centimes, white metal coins of ½, 1 and 2 Francs, and in the copper / nickel / aluminum 10 Franc coin. Notes of 50, 100, 1000 or more come full of pinholes because of the French habit of keeping 10 notes of the same kind together with a straight pin. Do not be surprised to receive pinned bundles of paper money from the banks, or as change in the stores.

A Word of Caution

Throughout France, in cities and towns large and small, we may have to push our way past persistent crowds of North Africans peddling an amazing array of native carvings, hand-crafted belts, hats, clothing, as well as products from the entire industrial world. Unless we have sufficient time to get involved, we should not even begin. On the other hand, if they have something we really want, we will find that the price is right.

In Paris, especially around the former Halles and the new Pompidou Centre, as well as in most tourist sections of the other cities of France, we must be on the alert for pickpockets. Boys and girls, no more than ten or twelve years old, will surround, distract, and fast-talk the victim, even grab our hands in successful attention-diverting ways. Then, all at once they're gone again. And so is our billfold.

ON BOTH SIDES OF THE VOSGES

For tourists in the Anabaptist Mennonite tradition, the region on both sides of the Vosges Mountains, the Alsace and the Lorraine, are the most important part of France and we will therefore begin our itineraries with that area.

The chain of mountains called the Vosges (Vogesen in German) runs parallel with its counterpart the Black Forest in Germany and with the Rhine for a distance of 170 kilometers (100 miles) and, as with the Black Forest described in the chapter on Germany, the slopes of the Vosges are likewise dis-symetric. To the east the hills drop off sharply above the Alsatian Plains. Toward the west they descend gently, sometimes almost unnoticeably, toward the plains of the Paris Basin. Between the Vosges and the Rhine lies a rich and fertile plain of glacial origin, seldom more than 30 kilometers (20 miles) wide.

The Vosges consists of crystalline rock, predominantly granite, near the peaks and the far more dominant red sandstone, which for centuries has provided the Alsatian people with an excellent building material for

Alsatian women in their Sunday best

268

homes, castles, and cathedrals. Here and there erosion has shaped the red sandstone into playful formations, so do not be surprised to find around the next curve of the road a mushroom, a camel, or a castle not build by human hands.

With the exception of a small area near the Grand Ballon d'Alsace, which lies above the timberline, the Vosges are densely forested. Ever since the Middle Ages, with the exploitation of the forest products governed by the abbeys and monasteries, the forests have been well managed. The Anabaptist leader, Pilgram Marpeck, was a manager of these resources here for some time following his sudden departure from Tirol in 1528.

For ages the cut lumber was lowered — rather dangerously — from the slopes on sledways, by *Schlitteurs,* who carried the empty sleds back up the mountain for the next downhill delivery. At Muhlbach, a museum devoted to the Schlitteurs, is open to the public during the months of July and August.

Near the crest on either side of the Vosges, there are innumerable small lakes and ponds. The Lac de Gerardner with a surface of 115 ha. (285 acres) is the largest of these, and the Lac Blanc is the deepest at 72 meters (236 feet). These tranquil lakes are popular for canoing and fishing. Some municipalities permit licensed fishing on their lake during the even years, some during the odd years, and some not at all. Above all, these lakes serve as natural reservoirs and guard the villagers below from sudden runoff after rainstorms.

The most important city in the Alsace is Strasbourg and the chief city of the Lorraine is Nancy.

STRASBOURG, CAPITAL OF EUROPE

During the days of Julius Caesar, the little settlement of hunters and fishermen called *Argentoratum* developed rapidly into a prosperous city located on the Rhine and at the junction of several major trade routes. Hence its new name: *Strateburgum* (city of roads). In times of peace Strasbourg's location had tremendous advantages. In times of war the armies always funneled through the city, leaving the Strasbourgers to rebuild and to repopulate their pillaged and burnt-out town again and again.

Not until the 1200s did Strasbourg seem to gain on these circumstances. In 1262 the city declared itself free from the rule of the archbishop, who had been the city's highest authorities for ages. Henceforth Strasbourg's population increased and the city experienced a growing prosperity.

During the second half of the 14th century, a large bridge was constructed across the Rhine. From that time forward a steady stream of northern and central Europe's products — lumber, wine, textiles, and produce — passed through Strasbourg's customs gates and the city itself became a veritable warehouse for Europe's needs. Within a century Strasbourg became an independent city-republic governed by a city council appointed by the powerful guilds.

In 1434 Johannes Gutenberg, of Mainz, arrived in Strasbourg. He formed a partnership with three Alsatians to develop certain secret procedures of which he was the inventor. There was talk about lead and presses. Things didn't work out too well for Gutenberg in Strasbourg and around 1448 Gutenberg and one of his associates, Johann Fust, returned to Mainz to perfect their invention, the art of printing from movable type.

Both Strasbourg's central location and the city's independence from the bishop attracted thousands of Protestant believers and seekers from north and south. In Strasbourg's tolerant and hospitable environment, all found a chance to share their thoughts, to add to and to profit from Strasbourg's rich and pulsating cultural and religious life. By way of exception in medieval Europe, Strasbourg even welcomed and tolerated the Anabaptists for several decades.

By the end of the 1600s a time of decline set in for Strasbourg hastened by the endless wars in Central Europe. The Thirty Years' War, the city's annexation by the kingdom of France in 1697, the turbulence of the French Revolution, Napoleon's ill-fated adventures, and the Second Empire of Napoleon III, all spelled disaster for the city.

In 1870, during the Franco-Prussian War the city suffered a 50-day bombardment in which 600 soldiers and 1,500 civilians were killed. This bombardment also reduced Strasbourg's great historic properties and monuments to one fourth of their former numbers. Between 1870 and 1918 Strasbourg was the capital of a German state called Elsass-Lothringen (Alsace-Lorraine). During the Second World War Strasbourg again suffered heavily, especially when in August and September of 1944 the Allies bombed the city by mistake.

Since World War II Strasbourg has done an admirable job of restoring the remaining historical properties, including the cathedral, a task which continues to this day. And it seems that Strasbourg is at last recovering the role it played in European history during the city's golden years. In 1949 Strasbourg was named the seat of the Council of Europe and since 1979 Strasbourg has become the seat of the nine-nation European Parliament.

Dominating the skyline of Strasbourg stands the city's single-spired red sandstone cathedral. Built over the remains of a Roman temple dedicated to Hercules, the cathedral was started in 1015 in the Romanesque style. By 1176 the building process was resumed in the Gothic style, new for the Alsace. In 1284 Erwin von Steinbach designed the present facade in the purest Gothic style. In 1365 the work came to a halt again at the level of the so-called Platform and before either spire was started. Eventually only the north tower was completed.

The Reformers came to Strasbourg shortly thereafter, in 1523. For years the old and the new traditions existed peacefully side by side in the

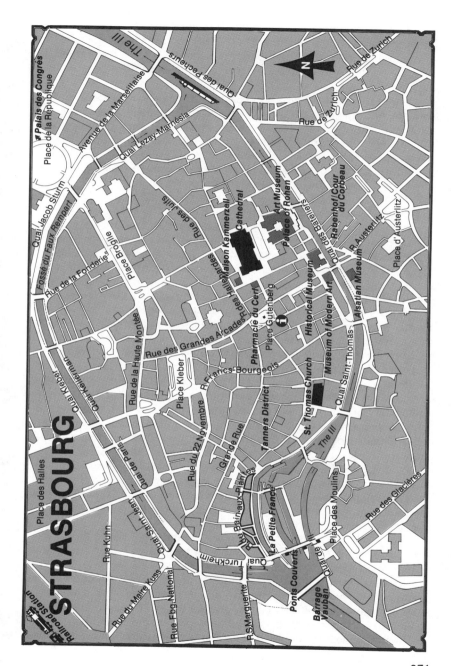

STRASBOURG

Railroad Station
Place des Halles
Place de la République
Palais des Congrès
Avenue de la Marseillaise
The Ill
Quai des Pecheurs
Rue de Zurich
Rue de Zurich
Quai Lezay-Marnésia
Quai Jacob Sturm
Fossé du Faux Rempart
Rue de la Fonderie
Place Broglie
Rue des Juits
Maison Kammerzell
Arcades des Halles
Cathedral
Art Museum
Palace of Rohan
Rabenhof / Cour du Corbeau
R. Austerlitz
Place d'Austerlitz
Rue de la Haute Montée
Pharmacie du Cerf
Place Gutenberg
Historical Museum
Museum of Modern Art
Quai des Bateliers
Alsatian Museum
Quai Kellerman
Quai Kléber
Place Kléber
Rue des Grandes Arcades
R. Francs-Bourgeois
St. Thomas Church
Quai Saint-Thomas
Place des Halles
Quai de Paris
Rue du 22 Novembre
Grande Rue
Tanners District
The Ill
Rue Kuhn
Quai Saint-Jean
Rue du Maire Kuss
Rue Bâteaux-Plantes
La Petite France
Quai Turckheim
Place des Moulins
Rue des Glacières
Rue Fbg-National
R.S.Marguerite
Ponts Couverts
Quai de
Barrage Vauban

271

old cathedral, with Martin Bucer (1491-1551) representing the Protestant viewpoint and Geiler von Kayserberg, his capable Catholic counterpart. In 1681, during the reign of Louis XIV, the cathedral became once more fully Catholic.

The best place from which to see the cathedral is from the short Rue Mercière. An inspiring sight is the Great Portal, completely covered with the statues of Old and New Testament personalities, saints, prophets, and apostles, and the Rosette Window, together measuring 42 by 66 meters (138 by 217 ft.), loaded with busy details.

Having started out as a Romanesque cathedral, the interior appears rather dark. The stained-glass windows consist of more than 500,000 leaded parts in 4,600 panes and date back to the 12th through the 14th centuries. However, they have been repaired repeatedly after each war.

A popular attraction inside the cathedral is the three-story-high astronomical clock. The present clock replaces an earlier clock from the 1400s. Work on this clock started in 1457 and continued through 1574. The final team of builders included the mathematician Conrad Dasypodius, the clockmaking brothers Isaac and Josias Habrecht, the architect Hans-Thomas Uhlberger, and the painter Tobias Stimmer, all of them Swiss.

The mechanism is extremely complicated, for it must perform numerous astronomical and timekeeping tasks simultaneously, as well as drive a number of automated figures. Currently the clock is about one-half hour behind time, but it is rewarding to go inside before noon for a good spot from which to watch the noontime spectacle sometime later.

Every fifteen minutes Christ conquers death, represented by a skeleton. The skelteon succeeds in ringing the bell only once every hour, while most of the time one of the four male figures beat him to it. The four figures represent the four ages of man. At noon the twelve apostles pass before Christ, each kneeling in turn to accept his blessing. At Peter's passing, a rooster flaps its wings and crows three times. Finally Christ turns to bless the spectators. Chariots representing the days of the week, and other movements representing the phases of the moon and a variety of other things, may take weeks, months, or years to make their rounds. The clock can be wound to run for eight days and its astronomical movements are calculated to run far into the future.

Not far from the astronomical clock stands the Pillar of the Angels, also known as the Pillar of the Last Judgment, a masterpiece in stone by an unknown 13th-century Gothic sculptor.

Against the wall on the opposite side of the interior we come to the Garden of Gethsemane. This massive and detailed "eyewitness report" in stone was created in 1498 by Veit Wagner for the St. Thomas Cemetery, but in 1667 it was fortunately transferred to its present inside location. A five-franc coin pushed in a timer will provide good illumination on this Bible story in stone.

Strasbourg's single-spired cathedral

Also worth studying is the beautiful pulpit built especially for the Catholic pastor Geiler von Kayserberg. Among the lovely biblical and church-historical sculptures which decorate this pulpit, we see a sleeping dog. According to tradition, this dog, in real life, belonged to the famous preacher himself and usually slept through his master's lengthy sermons.

During daylight hours it is possible to climb the unfinished south tower. It takes 328 stair steps to reach the Platform, 66 meters (217 ft.) above the steep roofs of old Strasbourg. Legend has it that young Goethe, who was a student at Strasbourg's University in 1770-71, and who was afraid of high places, regularly trekked up to this lofty platform to exercise his will-power.

The Cathedral Square and a number of the adjacent streets are for pedestrians only. On the corner of the square and the Rue Mercière stands the *Pharmacie du Cerf* (or *Hirschen Apotheke*), established in 1268, the oldest pharmacy in France. To the left of the cathedral stands the Maison Kammerzell. Its red sandstone first floor dates back to 1427. The four elaborate half-timbered upper stories received their present look in 1589. Restored in 1954, Maison Kammerzell is one of the most striking examples of medieval Alsatian architecture.

If we would like to dine in a medieval environment, Maison Kammerzell is a good restaurant specializing in Alsatian cuisine. One of the murals in this restaurant recalls an interesting anecdote from Strasbourg's history. In 1576 the city of Zurich shipped a huge kettle of soup to Strasbourg. The soup was still warm after the 18-hour trip down the Limmat, the Aare, and the Rhine. The Zurichers wanted to prove that in case of need, they could come quickly to the aid of Strasbourg. The remains of the original soup kettle are in the Strasbourg Museum.

Across the street from the Kammerzell, the Dauphin also offers Alsatian gastronomic specialties in historic surroundings. Just off the square the Rue de Maroquin features arts and crafts shops and numerous sidewalk cafes.

Between the cathedral and the Ill River stands the Palace of Rohan, once the residence of the Strasbourg bishops. It was built between 1731 and 1742 in rococo style. One of the residents of the palace, Cardinal Louis de Rohan, made a name for himself by his immoral behavior and for running up huge unpaid bills at jewelers and goldsmiths in several countries.

Today the palace houses three museums: a Fine Arts Museum, an Archaeological Museum, and a Decorative Arts Museum. The latter contains the best collection of ceramics in Europe.

Directly behind the Palace Rohan are the docks of the Strasbourg Excursion Boat Company. The 1½ hour boat trip on the Ill and on the canals of Strasbourg is well worth the money. The same company offers two- and three-hour excursions through the Rhine harbors from their docks at Bassin d'Austerlitz.

Strasbourg: in the Tanners District

Strasbourg: the Ponts Couverts

The museum row along the Ill continues with the Historical Museum of the City of Strasbourg located in the former butcher halls of 1587; the Museum of Modern Art, located in the old Customs House of 1358; the Museum of the Alsace, located in three 16th-century patrician homes.

Finally, there is the Rabenhof (Cour du Corbeau), an old stagecoach stop first opened in 1528 and operated continuously as an inn until 1854. Behind its unassuming facade we discover a delightful inner court surrounded by two or three tiers of balconies. Tradition has it that the wood was originally stained with ox blood from the butcher's hall already mentioned. Past guests at the inn have included Emperor Frederick the Great, the philosopher Voltaire, and King Jan Kasimir of Poland.

Still following the Ill we soon reach one of the most picturesque parts of old Strasbourg, the area called La Petite France. We get our first good view of the area from the Pont Saint Martin, right beside the old mills and tanneries which line the river here. For ages hides were dried in the open breezeways and balconies, most of which were enclosed one by one and made into rooms as the tanning business died out in Strasbourg. If we are aware of this, we can still recognize the former two- and three-story breeze-ways on the riverside of most of the large houses in the Tanners District. At the far end of La Petite France we find the Ponts Couverts (covered bridges) and the fortification of Vauban. The covered bridges now exist in name only. During an early period in Strasbourg's history where the various branches of the Ill entered the city strong defensible bridges once supplemented the city walls. Eventually these bridges were covered with tile roofs, which remained until 1784. Now only the name Ponts Couverts remains, along with three mighty medieval towers.

In the Tower of the Executioner we can still see the various cells in which prisoners awaited their final hours. The Tower of the French was used as a soldiers' barracks, and the Tower of Chains was reserved for those unfortunate condemned to galley slavery.

On top of the Barrage Vauban there is a panoramic terrace with a good view of Old Strasbourg with the Covered Bridges in the foreground, La Petite France off to the left, and the great cathedral in the center.

Returning now to the cathedral via the charming little streets of the Tanners District, the Grand Rue, and the Rue Gutenberg, we arrive at Gutenberg Square. On the square we find a statue of Gutenberg standing beside his press, displaying a proof of a Bible page with the words "And there was light." On the base, four panels illustrate the blessings Gutenberg's invention have brought to all mankind.

Ultramodern additions to Strasbourg's rich architectural heritage are the Palace of Human Rights, completed in 1964, and the Europa Palace, completed in 1976. The latter can be compared to a giant translucent oyster shell of laminated beams and glass. In it the ten-member European Parliament meets in public sessions.

For modern French cities, to have a Palais des Congrès is a must. In Strasbourg, however, which hosts a music festival every June what was built was a *Palais de la Musique et des Congrès*, (concert and convention center), featuring a 2,000-seat auditorium designed primarily as a concert hall.

COLMAR: URBAN RENEWAL AT ITS VERY BEST

Another Alsatian city of importance and considerable charm is Colmar, located halfway between Strasbourg and Basel, Switzerland, and across the Rhine from Frieburg in Germany. First mentioned during the eighth century, Colmar became a favorite stopping place on the travels of that tireless emperor and extender of civilization, Charlemagne, and later for his son Louis the Debonair. Colmar was a town of craftsmen, small merchants, and wine growers. It received its city rights around 1220 and later played a leading role in the Decapole, an association of ten Alsatian towns formed in 1354.

The implantation during the 19th century of textile and metallurgical industries in the town did not affect the charm and richness of Colmar's old quarters which have withstood the vicissitudes of time and circumstances very well.

The acclaimed restoration of the Tanners District, begun in 1968, constitutes the first stage in a general scheme for the protection and preservation of all of Colmar's historic buildings. The project, undertaken by the city with considerable financial aid from the French government, shows outstanding results. Behind the authentic medieval half-timbered gables, we discover modern and comfortable apartments and functional office space. Understandably, the entire quarter of cobblestoned streets is classified as a pedestrian zone. So we park our car and go for a stroll. There are many sights we will not want to miss.

The Museum Unterlinden was constructed as a cloister during the 13th century, housing first an Augustinian and later a Dominican order. The place was secularized during the French Revolution and after serving as an army barracks for half a century, it became a museum in 1879. The Museum Unterlinden is especially famous for one single piece, the Issenheimer Altar, painted in the early 1500s by Mathis Gothardt-Mithardt, better known as Matthias Grünewald. More than 350,000 visitors a year flock to Colmar just to see that one piece which so vividly portrays the agony of Christ on the cross and the suffering of his mother, Mary.

One art historian explains it thus: "By blending mysticism and realism, interpretation and dramatization, and by the use of surrealistic lighting, Grünewald created a work so unique that it has no known counterpart in any era in any country." The Museum Unterlinden also houses two famous pieces by Martin Schöngauer, painted around 1470. The second floor of the museum is devoted to Alsatian folk art and history.

In the streets of Colmar

Leaving the lovely Unterlinden Square, we follow the Rue des Clefs to the Place Jeanne d'Arc. Along the way we pass the city's 18th-century town hall. Turning to the right at the end of the Rue des Clefs behind the St. Matthew's Church, we find ourselves in the heart of Colmar's restored section. Here the Old Hospital, the 1609 House of the Arcades, the Custom's House of 1480, the Pfister House of 1537, the 13th-century St. Martin's Church, the Schöngauer House, and the Maison des Têtes of 1608, all crowd together within a few square blocks.

From the *Place de l'Ancienne Douane* (the Square of the Old Customs House), it takes only a few more minutes through the beautiful Quartier des Tanneurs to reach La Petite Venise, Colmar's little Venice, located along the Lauch.

The best view of La Petite Venise is from the Bridge of Saint Pierre. Here we see the old houses and the weeping willows reflected in the quiet stream, with St. Martin's in the distance. The entire scene is illuminated at night.

On the Rue des Marchands, near St. Martin's Church, we find the home and studio of the sculptor Frederic August Bartholdi, 1834-1904, the artist who created both the Lion of Belfort and the Statue of Liberty, France's birthday present to the United States in 1876. The Bartholdi house is open to the public and a statue of Bartholdi himself is located on Poincaré Avenue.

MULHOUSE, TOWN OF TEXTILES

Located on the Ill and the Rhine-to-Rhône Canal, Mulhouse is an industrial city which owes its prosperity to a long-established textile industry and since the turn of the century to potash mining. More recently international chemical concerns have established plants in Mulhouse, manufacturing such products as plastics and lubricants.

Mulhouse has several interesting museums. Among them are a museum dedicated to the history of imprinting of textile and wallpapers from the 1700s to our times; the French National Railway Museum, with a marvelous collection of locomotives, coaches, and boxcars dating back to 1844; and the Firefighting Museum next door. The National Automobile Museum specializes in, but does not limit itself to, Bugattis. It was near Mulhouse that Ettore Bugatti forged his exacting standards into the superb automobiles that bore his name, and the museum at Mulhouse has 208 of them, including the Bugatti Royale.

FRANCE'S NORTHEAST CORNER

North of Strasbourg we find the cities of Hagenau and Wissembourg. Hagenau is situated on the Moder and at the southern edge of the Forest of Hagenau. The town has two old churches, the 12th-century St. George's and the 14th-century St. Nicholas, and a few remnants of its old city walls.

Wissembourg

In the 15th-century town hall and hostelry we find the Museum of Alsatian Culture with exhibits of pottery, utensils, costumes, tools, and the like.

Wissembourg with just under 7,000 inhabitants, one of the smaller of the Alsatian cities, is located directly on the Franco-German border. Founded before 700 as the Benedictine Abbey, the charming town on the Lauter has retained much of its historic and colorful past.

In the 1720s the deposed king of Poland, Stanislas, settled in Wissembourg with his daughter Marie and a small group of loyalists. The king was very depressed, not so much because of his lost domains and fortunes, but above all for the now uncertain future of his beloved daughter.

But in 1725 the Duc d'Autin arrived from Paris with incredible news: Louis XV, King of France, desired the daughter of ex-King Stanislas, and Marie would become queen of France. Stanislas contacted a money lender in Frankfurt, Germany, for a sum sufficient to purchase back part of the family jewels left behind in Poland and some additional money for coaches, horses, and groomsmen.

The marriage took place in Strasbourg. As part of the festivities, King Louis of France installed his father-in-law, Stanislas, as the (last) duke of Lorraine. The house in Wissembourg where King Stanislas lived is now known as the Old Hospital.

Other places of note are the 13th-century Gothic church of St. Peter and Paul, the so-called Salt House of 1450, and the bridge across the Lauter in the Bruch District. The old city walls and ramparts can be explored and afford excellent views of the red-tiled roofs within.

Four kilometers (about 2½ miles) west of town lies the village of Weiler and the Mennonite children's home, Mont des Oiseaux (Vogelsberg). Southeast of Wissembourg we find the historic Mennonite settlement of Geisberg / Schaffbusch.

THE ALSATIAN ROUTES TOURISTIQUES

Throughout the Alsace the smaller towns and little villages are no less charming. In fact there are some real jewels. To make it easier for visitors to see the best of the best in a systematic way, the government has established a number of Routes Touristiques. Of these the Route du Vin d'Alsace, the Route des Villages Pittoresques, the Route des Crêtes, and two separate Routes des Châteaux are the most important.

Let's start with the Route du Vin, the Alsatian Wine Road. The 120-kilometer-long (75 miles) Alsatian Wine Road winds around the sub-Vosgien foothills between Thann, west of Mulhouse, and Marlenheim, west of Strasbourg. The road is dotted with ancient villages, castles, and castle ruins, all surrounded by meticulously kept vineyards which have been in cultivation since the third century.

An old Alsatian saying goes like this: "The tower in Strasbourg is the highest. The tower in Freiburg is the most impressive. But the tower of Thann is the most beautiful." The Church of Saint Thibaud is indeed a magnificent example of Alsatian Gothic, with more than 500 sculptures decorating the portal alone.

From Thann the Wine Road moves in and out of villages, most of which have less than 1,000 inhabitants but are complete with city gates, lovely fountains, and ancient houses in red sandstone and timber. It may be trite to say that these are places "where time stood still," but not until we learn that Turkheim, for instance, still has a nightwatchman who goes around with a lantern, do we realize that we are indeed in a different world.

Though it is hard to make a choice, perhaps the three most important villages on the Wine Road are Kaysersberg, Riquewihr, and Ribauville. In visiting these three it is advisable—in fact, at Riquewihr it is required—to leave your car outside the town and explore its treasures on foot. Kaysersberg (the Emperor's Mountain) dates back to Roman days, when it was located on the Roman road linking Gaul with the Rhine Valley.

Kaysersberg is the birthplace of Albert Schweitzer (1875-1965), the famous organist, pastor, humanist, and physician, who won the 1952 Nobel Peace prize. Today the Schweitzer birthplace at 124 Rue du General de Gaulle houses a museum devoted to Schweitzer's life of Christian service to mankind. Next door stands the Lutheran Church, where Schweitzer's father served as pastor.

Other points of interest in Kaysersberg include the fortified bridge, the town hall, numerous old mansions, and a lovely Renaissance town fountain.

We can spent as much time as we like in Riquewihr (pedestrians only) savoring the atmosphere of its ancient streets and courts. The main street of Riquewihr, also called Rue du General de Gaulle, runs slightly uphill toward the Dolder, a beautiful city gate dating back to 1291. Just off the main street is the little square of the Three Churches. Riquewihr's historic château houses the Alsatian postal museum, which traces the progress of communications from the Gallo-Roman days to our times.

In neighboring Ribeauville, a 13th-century belfort, known as the Butcher's Tower, separates the higher village from the middle village. The clock on this tower dates back to 1536. Between the tower and either end of the village, we come past many picturesque old houses and a beautiful Renaissance fountain. Four kilometers west of Ribeauville we find the three castles of St. Ulrich, of the Girsberg, and of Ribeaupierre, each of which rewards the visitor with a nice panoramic view of the valleys below.

Local costumes in black, red, and white, are still worn on special occasions and with a little bit of luck you may also observe storks nesting on chimneys and rooftops. Ribeauville, for instance, has two stork nests near the corners of the lower town, but they are not always occupied.

The town of Hunawihr is making a scientific effort to reestablish the stork, an endangered species (down to twelve in 1975), on the red roofs of the Alsatian villages. The migratory storks spend their winters along the Nile in Egypt, but due to excessive hunting in Africa, not all of them make it back to the Alsace in the spring.

Dominating the vineyards and the plains of the Rhine for miles around is the massive castle of Haut Koenigsbourg, perched on a 757-meter (2,484 ft.) summit of the Vosges not far from Saint Hyppolite. Once the property of Swiss nobles, the interior of the château was burned out by Swedish troops in 1633. During the years that Elsass-Lothringen was a German state, Kaiser Wilhelm ordered the castle's careful restoration, except that a new square keep has replaced the original round tower of the 15th century. A steep two-kilometer-long (just over a mile) access road now leads to Haut Koenigsbourg's moat and drawbridge.

The Route du Vin continues through the villages of Dambach, Andlau, Obernai, and Molsheim, all worth exploring, to Marlenheim, where the road ends.

Beyond Strasbourg and Haguenau in the northeastern corner of France runs the Road of the Picturesque Villages. These small peasant villages, about eighteen in all, have actually competed among themselves for quite some time for the title of the most beautiful. Most of the ancient villages' half-timbered farm homes are meticulously maintained and painted, and surrounded by a profusion of flowers and plantings. Antique

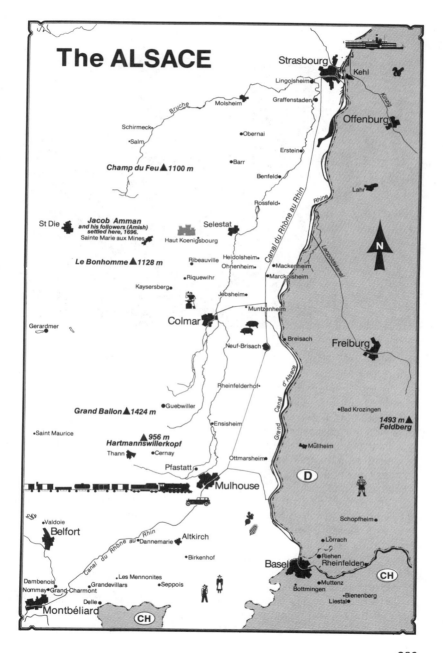

The ALSACE

Strasbourg
Kehl
Lingolsheim
Molsheim
Graffenstaden
Offenburg
Schirmeck
Obernai
•Salm
Erstein
Champ du Feu ▲ 1100 m
•Barr
Benfeld•
Lahr
Rossfeld
St Die
Jacob Amman
and his followers (Amish)
settled here, 1696.
Sainte Marie aux Mines
Selestat
Rhine
Haut Koenigsbourg
Le Bonhomme ▲ 1128 m
Ribeauville
Heidolsheim
•Ohnenheim
Mackenheim•
•Riquewihr
•Marckolsheim
Kaysersberg•
Jebsheim
Gerardmer
Colmar
Muntzenheim
•Breisach
Freiburg
Neuf-Brisach
Rheinfelderhof•
Grand Ballon ▲ 1424 m
•Guebwiller
Bad Krozingen•
•Ensisheim
1493 m ▲
Feldberg
•Saint Maurice
▲ 956 m
Hartmannswillerkopf
Thann
•Cernay
Müllheim•
Ottmarsheim•
Pfastatt
D
Mulhouse
Schopfheim•
•Valdoie
Belfort
•Lörrach
Altkirch
Canal du Rhône au Rhin
•Dannemarie
•Birkenhof
•Riehen
Basel
Rheinfelden
CH
Dambenois
•Les Mennonites
•Seppois
Muttenz•
Nommay• Grand-Charmont
Grandevillars
Bottmingen
•Bienenberg
Delle•
Liestal•
Montbéliard
CH

Chateau Haut Koenigsbourg

farm carts, wheelbarrows, and milk cans, artistically placed, complete the picture.

In my opinion the villages of Ober- and Unter-Seebach, recently combined under a single municipality, and Hunsbach are among the nicest. But please don't quote me locally. I don't want to get into an argument with the folks from Pechelbronn.

In the southern Alsace, between Ottmarsheim, Marckolsheim, and Diepolsheim, a number of towns located along the Route of the Flowering Villages (secondary road D468) also compete with each other in decorative artistry and floral profusion.

The Route des Crêtes, a skyline drive on the top of Vosges, was originally laid out between the two World Wars as a military highway. Designed to have a clear command over the valleys on either side, the Route des Crêtes runs on or just below the crest of the mountain. The road looks down on luscious forests. Between June and October each year, a number of farm-inns along this skyline drive stand ready to serve the tourists with simple home-cooked meals.

The road provides nice views over sixteen of the mountain lakes and includes the highest point of the Vosges Mountains, the 1,424-meter (4,672 ft.) Grand Ballon. From its top we can see the immediate Vosges, the

An Alsatian farm

German Black Forest, and in extremely clear weather, the Swiss Jura and the peaks of the Alps. Not far away is the Hartmannswillerkopf, a mountain slope that was contested by the French and the Germans throughout 1915 at a cost of 30,000 lives and many more wounded. There are numerous monuments to proclaim the glory and the victory but Hartmannswillerkopf demonstrates once again that "war is hell."

The two castle roads are the Route des Châteaux-forts between Wissembourg and Obersteinbach, which runs past fourteen castles and the shorter Route des Châteaux, which takes in three castles west of Colmar. Since these tourist roads were developed, local interests have pushed for additional routes, such as the Circuit of the Rhine Plains, the Cabbage Route (yes, you are in sauerkraut country), and a Cheese Route. But not all these roads are worth your time. More interesting is the Green Road, developed jointly by France and Germany to foster good neighborly relations. This road starts in Donaueschingen beyond the Black Forest and ends at Domrémy in the heart of France.

Let us now turn our attention to the other side of the Vosges to the Lorraine. Although often mentioned as the second half of the hyphenated term "Alsace-Lorraine," the latter region has always had a spirit and a feel quite different from its Germanic counterpart.

THE LORRAINE AND ITS GLAMOROUS CAPITAL

The capital of Lorraine is Nancy. Although fifth-century coins with the inscription "Nancy" have been found, the city does not again appear in written history until 1073. In 1588 Charles III, Duc de Lorraine, rebuilt the city with straight streets and open squares.

Once upon a time the dukes of the Lorraine were powerful and prestigious rulers given to tremendous pageantry. In 1608, for instance, the funeral service for the above-mentioned Charles III lasted two months and four days, involving thousands of people in a carefully orchestrated ceremony.

But in 1737 one of his successors, Duc Francois III, left the throne at Nancy unoccupied as he accepted the opportunity to become the Duc of Toscane. It was then that King Louis XV of France installed his father-in-law, the deposed king of Poland, Stanislas Leczynski, as the new Duc de Lorraine. Stanislas was to be the last duke of the Lorraine, but he was also the most beloved for his magnanimity and goodwill.

For three fruitful decades, Stanislas enjoyed his role as governor of the Lorraine to the fullest. He spent much of his time and most of the income that came with his position on embellishing the capital of Nancy and on improving the life of its citizens. Stanislas was a man of peace who dearly loved his daughter Marie, the queen of France, a man who strove for goodwill among people and nations, and a man of broadminded philosophies, and tolerant in religious matters.

Above all, King Stanislas loved to build. He spent much time poring over architectural plans, visiting work sites, and talking with the craftsmen. Almost daily he consulted with the architect Emanuel Héré and with Jean Lamour, that genial artist in wrought iron who fashioned Nancy's elaborate gates. Thanks to the tireless Stanislas, Nancy became one of the outstanding monuments of 18th-century French art and architecture. At the death of Stanislas in 1766, the Lorraine became a permanent part of France.

A tour of Nancy simply has to start with the Place Stanislas, one of the finest architectural accomplishments of the 18th century. Originally called the Place Royale, the square, measuring 124 by 106 meters (407 by 348 ft.), once featured the statue of Louis XV. It was pulled down during the French Revolution, at which time the square was renamed Place Stanislas. A statue of Stanislas was placed on the empty pedestal in 1831.

The corners of the square and the entries of two main streets, the Rue Stanislas and the Rue Catherine, are enriched by the playful wrought-iron grillwork and portals of Jean Lamour, finished in part with gold-leaf application. On one side of the square this grillwork extends around two classical fountains of great beauty.

The largest of the buildings on the Place Stanislas is the Hotel de Ville, or city hall, completed between 1752 and 1755. Inside we find a magnificent staircase of which the wrought-iron banister—27 yards long in one single

Nancy: artistry in iron by Jean Lamour

piece—represents the ultimate expression of Lamour's artistry in iron. The town hall, open to visitors every day except Monday morning and all of Tuesday, also contains the Square Salon and the Small Salon, also known as the Salon of the Empress. As we peer down from the windows of the salons over the square, we can well imagine the legitimate pride of the Polish king on the day of the square's dedication ceremonies as he observed the spectacle from these very same windows.

In the immediate neighborhood of the Place Stanislas lies the much older Place de la Carrière, which was transformed by the architect Héré to harmonize with the Place Stanislas. The square is surrounded by beautiful 18th-century buildings, by the government palace, once the residence of the governors of the Lorraine, and the Ducal Palace, now the Museum of Lorraine History. Alongside these squares the 23 hectare (57 acres) Pépinière Park offers the visitors a large rosarium, a formal English garden, and a small zoo. About two blocks away the much smaller Botanical Gardens of Nancy specialize in Alpine and carnivorous plants.

Of Nancy's many churches we mention the cathedral, built between the 10th century and 1742, the Church of St. Sebastien (1720-1731), and the octagonal Church of the Cordeliers or Ducal Chapel. Inspired by the burial chapel of the Medicis in Florence, this chapel contains the tombs of numerous dukes and duchesses of the Lorraine and several cardinals of the church.

ROUND ABOUT NANCY

About sixteen kilometers (10 miles) southeast of Nancy at Jarville, we find the Museum of the History of Iron. This vast building, which in itself gives witness to the importance of iron as an architectural component, houses exhibits of the history of iron making and metal working from the prehistoric days to the present. The museum is open to the public every afternoon except on Tuesdays.

Thirty kilometers from Nancy on the road to Strasbourg lies Lunéville, known for its wide streets and spacious parks and its porcelain factories. The town is sometimes called Le Petit Versailles. It was in Lunéville that Stanislas died on February 23, 1766. For lovers of two-wheeled transportation, Lunéville has a small but significant museum devoted to the history of bicycles and tricycles built prior to 1939.

Located along both banks of the Mosel River, Epinal lies at the junction of a half-dozen major highways. During the 17th century, Epinal rose to fame for its printmaking. The Museum of the Vosges and Print Making, with exhibits ranging from old woodcuts to modern lithographs, is well worth a visit for the graphic artist. Since 1969 practically all of the fine wire used in Michelin steel-belted radial tires is drawn at a factory in the northern section of Epinal.

SOUTH OF THE VOSGES

Between the Alsace and the Lorraine and the Swiss Jura lies the territory of Belfort and the land of Montbéliard, both of which were independent regions of long-standing.

Belfort is located in a thirty-kilometer-long (18 miles) trough between the Vosges and the Jura, connecting the great valleys of Rhine and Rhone. Understandably, these narrows became a natural passageway for foreign invaders from the prehistoric Celts to Hitler's armies. Belfort, therefore, developed essentially into a military settlement and was the birthplace of more than twenty leading French generals in this century alone.

Around 1780 Swiss Mennonites appeared in the territory of Belfort to settle on the farms around the fortress. They regularly met for worship at a farm named La Maye. In 1812 one of the members of the La Maye congregation, Jacques Klopfenstein began the publication of an agricultural almanac entitled *L'Anabaptiste ou le Cultivateur par Experience* (The Anabaptist, or experienced, farmer), taking advantage of the Mennonite reputation as master farmers. The almanac remained in print for more than sixty years, but toward the end was no longer under Mennonite editorship.

Apart from the remains of Belfort's fortifications, known as the Citadel, the main attraction in town is the Lion of Belfort, carved out of red Vosgien sandstone by Frederic August Bartholdi, who also created the Statue of Liberty. Sculpturing the giant Lion, 22 meters long and 11 meters (72 by 36 ft.) high, took five years (1875-1880).

In 1950 the French Mennonites purchased, with financial assistance from MCC, the Château La Cote, the long-abandoned estate of one of Belfort's generals, M. Charpentier, located in the suburb Valdoie. Restored by a group of Mennonite young people from many nations, the estate was renamed Villa des Sapins. The heavy shell casings, bombs, and grenades General Charpentier had used to decorate his villa's large room were hauled off to the scrap dealer for a nice sum of francs, which greatly reduced the actual cost of restoration.

For the first eight years, the Villa des Sapins housed about 35 war orphans and some twenty retired persons at one time. In more recent years the estate has mainly served as a conference and retreat center. It is located at 68 Rue de Turenne, Belfort-Valdoie.

The land of Montbéliard was formed prior to 1793 out of five ancient hereditary principalities. In German-language Mennonite documents, Montbéliard is often referred to as Mumpelgart.

The first Mennonites came to Montbéliard around 1700 as refugees from the adjoining bishopric of Basel. In 1712 hundreds more joined them after Louis XIV issued his harsh orders to expel all Amish and Mennonites from the Alsace. The refugees settled almost exclusively on the estate of Duc Leopold-Eberhard, who desperately needed people to repopulate and to restore his war-ravaged estate. The duke was especially pleased when these foreigners proved to be hardworking and capable farmers. The Mennonites were instrumental in developing a breed of red and white cattle still known as the "Montbéliarde." This same kind of cattle can be seen on the Mennonite hofs in Bavaria. Because the Mennonites were still resented by their French Catholic neighbors, the dukes would never put any agreement with the Mennonites in writing.

Around 1750 the Mennonites in the land of Montbéliard began to keep church records. They are the oldest church records in the history of the Swiss Anabaptists. Family names frequently found among them were Kauffmann, Rich(e), Mosimann, Stoll, Gerber, Schmucker, Wähltly (Welty), Meyer, Witmer, Kohler, and Baumgartner. In 1832 they built a meetinghouse along the canal which was replaced by the current meetinghouse in use since 1930. The French Mennonite periodical, *Christ Seul,* published with some interruptions since 1902, is edited and published in nearby Grand-Charmont.

Two of the major industries in the area employing tens of thousands of workers are the Peugeot assembly plant at Socheaux-Montbéliard and the Alsthom Locomotive Works, near Belfort. On the fourth of May 1924 a Montbéliardais named Etienne Oehmichen, who enjoyed experimenting with the laws of aerodynamics, flew the world's first helicopter.

THE BOUNTY THAT IS PARIS

Early morning mists over the Seine, flowering chestnut trees on the squares, patient fishermen, slow-moving barges, the awe-inspiring sight of the Notre Dame, the shedding of the sycamores along the quais, artists at their easels, the secondhand bookstalls along the Left Bank, charming parklets—all that and so much more is Paris, City of Light and City of the Four Seasons.

The Carnavalet Museum already houses more than 400,000 books written about the city. What can we do within a few paragraphs?

The 2,000-year-old village of Paris, established by the River Tribe the Parisii, has now grown into a city of more than ten million (counting the suburbs). And thanks to the efforts initiated during the 1950s by the French novelist (then Minister of Culture) André Malraux, Paris is now even more magnificent than ever before.

Getting around in Paris is surprisingly simple. On July 19, 1900, the Parisian subway named *Métropolitain* began to serve the public with a line along the Right Bank of the Seine, between the Porte de Maillot and the Porte de Vincennes. The Art Nouveau design of the standard Metro entrance, affectionately dubbed the "wet noodle" style, dates from that period.

Today no spot in Paris is more than 500 meters (1,600 ft.) from a Métro entrance. The traditional Métro alone transports more than four million persons daily. In addition, Paris has an extensive bus system with 196 routes, as well as a new Express Métro (RER) between downtown and the farthest suburbs. Through an active sales organization, Paris sells its Métro know-how and rolling stock to cities around the world from Haifa to Mexico City.

Even so, Paris has over a million private cars and only about 1,200 kilometers (750 miles) of streets suitable for through traffic. It is easy to see how one or two fender benders during the rush hour can bring the whole

Morning sun along the Seine

works to a chaotic standstill. Consequently, Paris police are strict but fair and any driving or parking violation will cost you. And even though we are "just tourist," "didn't know where we were going," or "couldn't read the sign," such excuses do not hold water with Parisian gendarmes intent on keeping things moving as smoothly as possible.

During the Second Empire (1848-1870) a gigantic urban renewal plan was initiated by Baron Haussmann. The plan included the creation of the Grands Boulevards, the administrative division of the city into twenty arrondisements, the transformation of the fortress Louvre into a museum second to none, and the giant undertaking of the Paris sewers. Beneath each Paris street lies a giant duct which carries both industrial and drinking water, sewage, telephone and telegraph lines, electric cables, compressed air and pneumatic air tubes where needed, and steam heat for public buildings. Tours of the Paris sewers (Egouts) are conducted on Monday and

Wednesday afternoons, except during heavy rains or when the Seine floods. The visitors' entrance to the sewers is found opposite No. 93 Quay d'Orsay (Métro: Alma).

And, believe it or not, though far inland, Paris is also France's fourth largest port with 800 hectare (2,000 acres) of basins and 500 kilometers (320 miles) of docks and waterside facilities.

To get the most out of our visit to Paris, the 178-page *Michelin Green Guide: Paris,* available in several languages, is indispensable. In addition the publications *7 jours a Paris/7 days in Paris* and the *Pariscop,* available in railroad stations and hotel lobbies, may be of some help. Excellent city maps are available from the Paris Tourist Office and from the public transit system, RATP. The Maison d'Information Culturelle, 1 Rue Pierre Lescot (Métro: Chatelet) can advise on current concerts, operas, stage plays, art shows, dinner theater, flower shows, and the like. It is open daily except Sundays from 10:00 a.m. to 20:00 (8:00 p.m.).

No river seems to love the city the way the Seine loves Paris. The two seem inseparable. For fifteen kilometers (nine miles) the Seine wends its way through the different *faubourgs* and *quartiers.* To get the feel of Paris, we should take a trip on one of the boats on the Seine which enables us to see a majority of the city's famous landmarks from an unusual angle, while at the same time saving our feet for more walking later. Paris offers two types of boat excursions.

The most popular are the large restaurant ships known as Bateaux-Mouches, which depart three times daily except Monday at 11:00, at 14:30 and 16:00 (2:30 and 4:00 p.m.) for a combination excursion/luncheon, or / dinner. In addition there are the Vedettes du Pont Neuf and the Bateaux Parisiens-Tour Eiffel, which leave approximately every half hour from their docks at the Vert Gallant Square and the Jena Bridge respectively. During the week the last of these boats leaves at 17:00 (5:00 p.m.). On weekends the boats continue to run until 21:00. The glass-top boats are similar to the well-known Rondvaart boats of Amsterdam and most of Paris's boats are of Dutch manufacture.

If we would rather look down on Paris and the Parisians, there are about a half-dozen good spots from which to do so. The most obvious place, of course, is from the second or third levels of the famous Eiffel Tower (see description on page 296). From the top level, closed in winter, we can look down all over Paris, a distance of about 60 kilometers (37 miles) in all directions.

From the top of the south tower of Notre Dame (see description on page 294), we have a close-up look at the Gothic cathedral's flying buttresses and gargoyles, as well as a good overview of the heart of Paris, the Ile de la Cité, the Ile St. Louis, and the Seine. The Place du Parvis, in front of Notre Dame, is the point from which all road distances to and from Paris are measured.

Paris' most famous landmark: the Eiffel Tower

Another extensive view over Paris and the artists' village of Montmartre is from the Church of the Sacré Coeur. If we do not want to tackle the stairstep streets up to the Basilica, a funicular railway will take us there from the Marché St. Pierre.

From the top of the Arc de Triomphe, you will have a nice view of the twelve avenues, including the world-famous Champs-Elysees, which converge at this point in a star pattern, with the Bois de Boulogne in the background.

The 56th and the 59th floors of the Tour Montparnasse are also ideal for a complete view of Paris. And from the top floor of the Beaubourg, also known as the Pompidou Center for Art and Culture, there is a lovely vista of traditional Paris with the more modern buildings visible in the distance.

In the heart of Paris the Seine flows around two boat-shaped islands, the Ile de la Cité and the slightly smaller Ile St. Louis. These islands have been inhabited for more than 2,200 years, first by the tribe of the Parisii. Around the fourth century the city adopted the name of its founding tribe and the riverboat of the Parisii can still be seen on the city's official coat of arms. During the Middle Ages, the growing population spread from the islands to both banks of the Seine. As we circle the islands and cross any of the fourteen beautiful bridges to the opposite banks, we enjoy the most lovely sights Paris has to offer.

Of these two the Ile St. Louis remains the classical and more provincial one. More than likely Conrad Grebel strolled around its quais while he was a young student in Paris (1518-1519). However, all the present facades were built between 1627 and 1664.

The larger Ile de la Cité, once covered by a multitude of chapels, convents, monasteries, and school, has undergone drastic transformations over the centuries, especially during the reigns of Louis-Philippe and of Napoleon III, when the entire center of the island was evacuated to make room for large administrative buildings. New since those days are the massive Hôtel de Dieu, a police prefecture, and the Courts of Law. The Place du Parvis in front of Notre Dame was quadrupled in size allowing for an unobstructed view of the great cathedral.

Notre Dame was built and completed between 1163 and 1345, according to the original and unmodified plans of the architects Jean de Chelles and Pierre de Montreuil. In the annals of cathedral building this was a relatively short construction period.

Notre Dame was the scene of many great, as well as ignoble, moments in French history, including the official opening of the First States-General by Philippe de Fair in 1302, the coronation of Henry VI of England in 1430, and the coronation of Mary Stuart as queen of France following her marriage to Francois II in 1559. In 1572 Henri de Navarre, a Huguenot, stood outside the door while his bride Marguerite de Valois, a Catholic, stood at the altar alone for their wedding ceremony.

The Notre Dame of Paris

Following the French Revolution the cathedral was desecrated and turned into a hall dedicated to the Cult of Reason, though most of the space was simply used for warehousing commodities. In 1804 the church was restored and redecorated for the occasion of Napoleon's coronation as emperor by Pope Pius VII. But, as the history books tell us, Napoleon took the crowns out of the hands of the pope to crown first himself and then his wife, Josephine.

With the emergence of Romanticism and the popular feelings aroused by Victor Hugo's novel *The Hunchback of Notre Dame,* France's republican government ordered the cathedral restored, a task that took from 1841 to 1864. In recent history the state funerals of General de Gaulle and of President Pompidou were conducted in the cathedral.

During the restorations of 1841 to 1864 the architect Viollet-le-Duc completely rebuilt Notre Dame's 90-meter (295 ft.) central spire, using more than 500 tons of oak timber and 250 tons of lead in the restoration process. He also included himself among the myriad copper sculptures of apostles and evangelists.

Before we leave this area, we may enjoy browsing on the quais on the Left Bank, which are still lined with bookstalls, where secondhand books, prints, photos, and antique postcards can be bought. But the bargains are not what they used to be when I was a young student bicycling through France. Many of the bridges across the Seine are works of art in themselves and have been the frequent subjects of paintings by the French impressionists. The Pont des Arts, completed in 1803, was the world's first iron bridge.

The Champs de Mars is one vast level garden spanning both sides of the Seine, enclosed on the north by the Palais de Chaillot and on the south by the Ecole Militaire. The area was established as a combination military parade and fair grounds in 1780. Three years later the world's first hydrogen-filled balloon lifted from the Champs de Mars.

In 1798 the tenth anniversary of the republic was celebrated with a mammoth Industrial Exhibition, with the novel idea that exhibitors had to pay to exhibit. This was followed by the World's Fairs of 1867, 1878, 1889, 1900, and 1937. The Eiffel Tower remains as a souvenir of the 1889 World's Fair. Alexandre Gustave Eiffel, born in Dijon, was a brilliant engineer of international renown. During his life he produced such works as the Douro Bridge in Porto, Portugal, and the framework for Bartholdi's Statue of Liberty. For the astronomical observatory of Nice he designed the moveable dome that has become standard for observatories the world over.

The idea of a tower for the 1889 World's Fair came as a natural for Eiffel, skilled as he was at constructing iron structures of enormous size. The Eiffel Tower was put together in two years by an army of 300 iron workers using more than 2½ million hot rivets. When it was finished it was the tallest structure in the world. Eiffel laughed and said, "Well, there you have it. A 300-meter flagpole for France!"

Scores of traditional French artists and writers were outraged, however, and more than 300 of them signed a petition to have the thing pulled down. Since then the furor has calmed down and today the Eiffel Tower is ... well, it's just part of the Paris skyline visited by more than three million tourists annually. In 1953 a twenty-meter high transmission tower for radio and television was added to it, bringing the tower to a new total height of 320.75 meters or 1,051 feet.

From a technical point ov view the Eiffel Tower is a masterpiece. While the tower's weight in iron is more than 7,000 tons, it is so well distributed that the dead weight pressure on the four corner blocks is not more than that of a person sitting on a chair. Even in strong winds it does not sway more than twelve centimeters (four inches). But on hot summer days when the iron expands, the tower can grow as much as fifteen centimeters (five inches).

You may climb the 1,652 steps to the observation platform for five francs or you can take the elevator for fifteen francs (1982 fees). In 1983 the tower's original hydraulic elevators were replaced by modern ones, glass boxes that offer a dizzying view over town as you go up. And two new restaurants have been added, both on the first level: *La Belle France* is a brasserie-type place with a 1920's Paris decor; the other one, *Le Parisien,* is for those a bit more in a hurry and features a limited menu. Below the tower we find a sculptured portrait of Eiffel himself.

The collection of buildings called the Louvre has a long and turbulent history. Originally constructed as a fortress by Philippe-Auguste around 1200, it ceased to serve its military purposes two centuries later when the city walls of Paris were moved further out. It wasn't until 1546 that Francois I commissioned Pierre Lescot to transform the Louvre into a royal residence. Francois died a year later but the work was begun and the transformation and enlargement of the Louvre continued with many starts, stops, and setbacks for three centuries.

In the third year of the French Revolution, a mob of Parisians attacked the Louvre and the adjoining Tuilleries, killing 600 guardsmen and thoroughly looting the place. The leaders of this revolt installed themselves in the Opera House and in the royal apartments. Years later Napoleon evicted these squatters and began the Louvre's long overdue restoration, a task not completed until 1860 under the reign of Napoleon III. The Louvre, the largest palace in the world, was finished as last.

During the May riots of 1871 the western parts of the palace were set on fire by the insurrectionists, but the main buildings escaped major damage. The burned-out parts were pulled down and the Third Republic commissioned the rebuilding of the Marsan and the Fiore pavilions as end pieces of the Louvre complex. The resulting two arms of the Louvre now enclose a formal garden.

Today the Louvre houses the world's largest art museum. The so-called Grande Galerie extends 442 meters (1,450 ft.), the longest museum hall in the world. The entire museum is divided into five basic departments: paintings and drawings, Egyptian antiquities, Oriental antiquities, Greek and Roman antiquities, and sculptures and artifacts. For a floor plan and information on where to find certain departments of interest, we inquire at the main desk in the Salle de Manege,

The museum is so overwhelmingly large and the number of exhibits so enormous that we could spend weeks here studying the more than 400, 000 paintings and objects on display. The story goes that during the 1950s, in the days when Americans were the only ones who had the money to travel, one couple was "doing" Europe in two weeks. Breathlessly they rushed up to a Louvre guard and whispered, "Quick, quick, tell us. Which way to the Mona Lisa? We are double-parked!"

A charming and very different part of Paris is Montmartre, also known locally as the Butte. The name Montmartre dates back to Roman times

Montmartre, a favorite with painters and poets

when it was known as the Mount of Mercury. In later Christian days the hill was crowned with abbeys and convents. Montmartre is located over vast gypsum quarries, all closed around 1800, when subsidence threatened to undermine the entire hill.

During the 19th century it became the well-known abode of artists and writers who immortalized the village within the city with flowery songs (Aristide Bruant) or in drawings or lithographs (Toulouse Lautrec). In the evening they all met at the Moulin Rouge to applaud the singers and the entertainers.

Walking through the winding streets of Montmartre we will probably be reminded of the paintings of Utrillo or the drawings of Dubuffet. Two of Montmartre's famous windmills, once numbering more than thirty, are now in the process of restoration. The Place du Tertre, long the meeting place of famous artists and writers, is of interest and nearby the diminutive Place du Calvaire offers the visitor one more exceptional panorama over Paris.

After the disastrous Franco-Prussian War of 1870 to 1871, some Catholic survivors of the ordeal made a vow to build a basilica dedicated to the Sacred Heart on the hills of Montmartre. The idea caught on and soon the French government placed itself firmly behind the project.

A Romano-Byzantine-style building was started in 1876 and completed in 1910, at a cost of forty million old francs. The result is impressive, even if its aesthetic merits remain a point of disagreement. In the Sacré Coeur tower hangs the Savoyarde, cast in 1895, one of the world's largest bells (weighing nineteen tons).

For people who like to visit cemeteries, I recommend the Cemetery of Père Lachaise. In 1626 the Jesuits bought this site, then outside of Paris, as a place on which to build a house of retreat. This hilly terrain became the favorite place of meditation for Father La Chaise. In 1763 the city expelled the Jesuits and turned the hillside into a cemetery, now the largest in Paris. In the Cimetiere Pere Lachaise are the graves of Frederic Chopin, Victor Hugo, Camille Corot, Oscar Wilde, Honore de Balzac, Amadeo Modigliani, Sarah Bernhardt, Baron Haussmann, Paul Eluard, and many other notable persons.

The Cimetiere Père Lachaise was the scene of the last battle of the 1871 riots when 147 survivors were lined up against the cemetery wall and shot. This spot has ever since been known as the wall of the Federalists. Other cemeteries of interest are those of Montmartre and of Montparnasse, each holding the graves of numerous famous artists, writers, and composers.

There are many more things to see in Paris—great museums, churches, parks, and monuments, but we will end our admittedly short description with the Champs-Elysées. The world's most famous avenue created by Maria de Medici, under the name Cours de la Reine in 1616, received its present name (translated the "Elysian Fields"), in 1667 when the shade trees were planted. In 1724 it was extended to the site of the present Arc de Triomphe, which dominates the scene in this part of Paris. In 1814 occupation troups from many nationalities camped on the avenue, leaving behind a monumental mess that took two years to clean up.

Today the Champs-Elysées is the second-widest avenue in Paris, measuring 71 meters (233 feet) between the fashionable buildings. Only Foch Avenue, 120 meters (394 ft.) is wider. Lining the Champs-Elysées are the headquarters and showrooms of luxury car companies, the houses of high fashion and the big-name perfumeries, major world banks and airline companies, and a dozen cinemas. At times of great national celebration or sorrow the Champs-Elysées become the spontaneous rallying point for the French.

THE SPLENDOR OF VERSAILLES

Just outside of Paris, and easily accessible by various means of public transportation, lies Versailles, a town and a palace. Versailles, of course, is the palace of all palaces, enlarged and embellished under the Sun King, Louis XIV, during the most glorious days of the French monarchy.

The palace complex is so extensive that its Bureau of Visits offers a choice of twelve suggested visits, one of which is by car. It is open daily except Mondays. Let me emphasize that the Palace of Versailles, the gardens, and the Trianon cannot possibly be seen during one single vacation. If possible a good first general impression needs to be followed by future returns to see specific buildings or gardens.

The creation of Versailles in its present form began under the architect Jules Mansart in 1678 and continued under his personal direction for thirty years. Working with him were the interior decorator Le Brun and the landscape architect Le Nôtre. Together they kept 36,000 men and 6,000 horses busy. Their work included the diversion of a river, the reclamation of 16,000 hectare (37,000 acres) of swampland, the installation of 1,400 working fountains, and the continuous job of raising and then planting 150,000 annuals in the flower beds. With the coming of each winter season, more than 3,000 subtropical trees needed to be moved inside the Orangeries.

When the palace came into use, even while construction continued for many decades, the court staff numbered more than 20,000 from ceremonial guards to secretaries, from ladies-in-waiting to servants. In addition more than 1,000 princes and nobles, with their own 4,000 attendants, lived in the palace. Living a life of incredible splendor and luxury, the inhabitants lost touch with the real world beyond their opulent setting.

Somewhere on the immense grounds there was even a charming village of twelve thatch-roofed cottages where Queen Marie Antoinette and her lady friends could go and play at "being simple peasants," dressed in rustic costumes, herding their sheep, churning butter, and eating food brought along in baskets. The real peasants and citizens eventually responded to this unreal situation with the French Revolution and Marie Antoinette was tied to a real peasant cart and hauled off to lose her head under the guillotine.

THE CHATEAUX OF THE LOIRE

A popular destination with many vacationers is the beautiful Loire Valley and its châteaux. Sometimes called the Garden of France, the Loire landscape is known for the subtle light illuminating lazily winding stretches of river in the midst of a peaceful and idyllic landscape. All along the Loire, there are a great number of the finest Renaissance châteaux immaginable and a number of older medieval castles. Several of these buildings formed a backdrop to significant events which had momentous effect on French, English, and European history.

It was the weakness of the French Carolingian kings that allowed for the rise in power of these ambitious lords of the Loire. Soon one baron after another raised his own army, struck his own coins, and for all practical purposes, the king's authority was hardly recognized in this valley. Soon every strategic place on the river, from Orleans to Angers, was occupied by the stronghold of an independent warlord.

Chenonceau, one of the chateaux of the Loire

The chateau of Chambord

During the 12th century these rivals fought one another. The principal antagonists among many were the Capets and the Plantagenets. In 1154 one of the Plantagenets became Henry II of England. As a result, the English then controlled an empire which stretched from the north of England to the Spanish border. In 1216, half a century later, one of the Capets, Philippe-Auguste, recaptured all of the French provinces from King John of England and the Loire Valley was French again. But the Hundred Years' War (1337-1445) brought back the English.

It was then that Joan of Arc (Jeanne d'Arc) appeared on the scene. Following a divine vision, the simple unlettered French girl from Domremy in the Lorraine, with an escort of six men, traveled all the way to Chinon on the Loire without encountering a single one of the murderous armed bands that terrorized the countryside. This was seen as further evidence of her divine calling.

Joan of Arc was barely eighteen when she arrived at the court of the as yet uncrowned king of France, Charles VII. Charles was a good man, but he had little support and no money. The Hundred Years' War had left France divided, and the British had won every battle so far. But when he heard of this young peasant girl who had a divine revelation, Charles experienced a glimmer of hope.

But just to be sure of Joan and her divine vision, Charles decided to put her to a test. When she arrived, the Great Hall of the castle of Chinon was lit by 50 torches, and 300 lords in their finest apparel milled about in the room. Charles left one of them occupy the throne and he himself slipped in among the foot soldiers. When Joan came in, she gave the man on the throne barely a glance and walked right up to Charles, whom she had never seen before. Then she said to him, "Gentle Dauphin [crown prince], my name is Joan the Maiden and the King of Heaven has revealed to me that you will be anointed and crowned king in the great city of Reims." She continued, "I'll tell you in the name of our Lord Jesus Christ, that you are the heir to the throne of France."

Charles was now assured of his heroine's divine mission, but his advisers were full of doubt. Joan was taken to court and cross-examined for three weeks by a bench of theologians who were to decide whether she was insane or inspired. In the end she was recognized as a true messenger of God.

Captured by the Burgundians at Compiègne one year later, Joan was sold by them to the English for the fabulous sum of 16,000 pounds. To the English, Joan represented the soul of French resistance to their supremacy. She was burned at the stake at Rouen on May 30, 1431. Joan's mother and King Charles VII submitted her case to the pope, who ordered a new trial. She was declared innocent in 1456, beatified in 1909, and declared a saint in 1920. The day of her execution, May 30, is commemorated throughout France.

Joan's "recognizing" of Crown Prince Charles made the Château de Chinon forever famous, but the other châteaux are no less magnificent and their stories just as intriguing. The great names of the châteaux along the Loire include Chenonceau, Chambord, Blois, Amboise, Azay-le-Rideau, Beaugency, Usse, and Saumur. At the site of at least ten of these châteaux the history of the particular château and their illustrious occupants is presented in late-night *Son et Lumiere* (Sound and Light) performances lasting from twenty minutes to two hours. Sometimes recorded English translations are available upon request and sometimes the program ends with spectacular fireworks.

The most beautiful of all the castles on the Loire is Chenonceau. It was successively owned and occupied by six women, among them Diane de Poitiers, a woman of legendary beauty. In a power struggle with Catherina de Medici, Diane de Poitiers was forced to trade Chenonceau for the lesser, but nevertheless magnificent, castle of Chaumont.

IN THE FOOTSTEPS OF THE EMPEROR

One of my favorite excursions through France is on Route Napoleon, which runs from the French Riviera through the Maritime Alps to the high Alps of Savoy and ends at Grenoble. Essentially Route Napoleon is identical to the current Route Nationale 85, except that close to Grenoble Napoleon's actual travels took him via the Routes Departementales No. 4 and 5.

The Route Napoleon takes us through an incredible variety of spectacular landscapes from quaint Mediterranean villages surrounded by 2,000-year-old terraced olive groves to the windy heights of the Savoyard Alps. The road can easily be covered in two days at any time of year. The SNCF/Europabus 256, Nice-Grenoble completes the route in one day with short stops at several historic sites. Holders of a Eurailpass will get a 50 percent reduction on this line.

All along the Route Napoleon there are historical markers and monuments topped by the emblem of a soaring eagle, reminiscent of Napoleon's words, "This eagle will fly from tower to tower until it rests on the tower of Notre Dame."

Following his escape from the isle of Elba, Napoleon disembarked at Golfe-Juan on the first of March in 1815. From there Napoleon and his little band of followers moved to nearby Cannes, where he arrived late, only to leave early the next morning. Wanting to avoid the easier road to Paris through the Rhône Valley because he expected it to be hostile, Napoleon had no other choice but to take the road to Grasse and from there to cross the Alps. Beyond Grasse, when the road was no longer fit for wagons, the small band followed the rough path and trails mostly used by peasants and their donkeys.

By the third day they had reached Castellane and by noon Barrême.

The next morning, March 4, they ate breakfast at Digne. That night the group lodged at the Château Matijai, while Napoleon waited with some impatience for the news from Sisteron, where a mighty citadel controlled the narrow passage of the Durance River.

Then came the incredible news—Sisteron was left unoccupied! Napoleon pressed on, stopping there for breakfast on March 5 and leaving the place with growing confidence and the admiration of the locals. Coming to better roads, Napoleon made it to Gap, where he was enthusiastically welcomed. On the sixth, he ordered a short night's rest for his people at Corps.

In the meantime troops under Marshall Michel Ney were sent to Paris to arrest him. The encounter took place on the March 7, somewhere between Corps and Laffrey. But when the soldiers saw their old leader, they joyfully joined him. Together they entered Grenoble, as the citizens shouted, "Vive l'Empereur," and thus began the second reign of Napoleon, known in history as the Hundred Days.

In recognition of their loyal support, Napoleon appropriated to the Department of the Haut-Alpes a sum sufficient to construct hostelries on six of its mountain passes most exposed to the severe winter weather. They are found on the highway passes of Izoard, Manse, Vars, and Noyers, and on the mule-trail passes of la Croix and Agnel leading into Italy's Piemonte. Of these hostelries, the last two are now in ruins, while the one in Noyers has been replaced by a hotel. A monument marks the "Meadow of the Encounter," where Napoleon met the soldiers sent from Paris.

ITALY

Italia

The Republica Italiana occupies most of the boot-shaped peninsula in the Mediterranean Sea, except for the 23 square kilometers (9 square miles) of the Republic of San Marino and eight acres of Vatican State. Italy also includes two large islands, Sardinia and Sicily, and a number of smaller ones. Elba, once the home of Napoleon in exile, and Capri are perhaps the better-known of these islands. The country was given its name 800 years before Christ by Greek settlers who called the southern part "Itala," which means "land of oxen" or "grazing land."

For century upon century the history of Italy was synonymous with the history of Western civilization. The Roman Empire shaped the government, the trading practices, the architecture, and the arts, all around the Mediterranean Sea and as far north as Holland's Rhine River delta, and in the southern half of what is today England.

After the fall of the Roman Empire in AD 476, Italy was subjected to wave upon wave of foreign invasions and all political unity was lost for the next 1400 years. To use the words of Klemens von Metternich in 1814, Italy had become "a geographical illusion," fragmented as it was into a multitude of petty principalities and kingdoms forever at war with one another and constantly subjected to foreign domination.

The tradition of Roman leadership, however, survived through the church, which managed to preserve and extend Western civilization, even during the barbaric eras. At the same time, the power and prosperity of the great cities, which began during the 11th century, proved to be a stronger force than the political chaos around them. In these city-states—Venice, Florence, Genoa, Pisa, Livorno, Ravenna, Turin, to mention just a few—a whole new approach to arts and ideas was born. The Renaissance, as it was called, marks the beginning of modern times, not only for Italy but for all of us to this day.

Indeed, the cultural tradition of Italy is one of the richest in the world. Whether in painting, sculpture, music and poetry, or science, Italian creative genius has led the way and has stimulated cultural development far beyond Italy's borders. It is impossible, for instance, to think of Holland's Golden Age without first giving credit to the Italians. Among the city-states, Venice achieved greatness in the arts later than the other cities, but retained it longer. The Renaissance masters of the island city included Titian, Giorgione, Tintoretto, and Veronese. Venetian art experienced a revival during the 18th century with the landscape artist Canaletto and the frescoist Tiepolo as the leading figures.

The Italian people are quite conscious and justifiably proud of this great heritage. Their tradition is not confined to museums and archives, but it is part of their daily life. On his way to work in the morning, the Italian may drive past buildings designed by Giotto and Brunnelleschi, past sculptures of Michelangelo and Donatello, or fountains designed by Bernini or Ghiberti. On the stereo in his Fiat he listens and hums along with the world's best-loved melodies, written by his countryman in his language. When he goes to worship, the church he attends may be adorned with original paintings by Ghirlandaio and Botticelli.

Whenever the Austrians or the Spanish occupied parts of Italy, the Italians had little say-so in their own political destiny and played no active role in European politics. But when the French conquered parts of Italy, republican administrations were set up. The French introduced representative forms of government as well as laws that were the same for all parts of the country. Therefore during times of French rule, Italian poets, intellectuals, and idealists began to see the possibility of a united and free Italy. Years later, in 1860, Giuseppi Garibaldi, aided by a small personal army of enthusiasts (the Red Shirts), set out to subdue the separate principalities and kingdoms, a task partially completed by 1861. Victor Emmanuel, king of Sardinia, was chosen king of Italy. In 1866 Venetia joined Italy and in 1871 the Papal States were reduced to Vatican City, at which time Rome also became the new nation's capital.

The new kingdom had many problems. Chief among them was to weld together a heterogeneous people who, through a millennium and a half of fragmentation, presented anything but uniform views and aspirations. The long wars to unite the country had left them with monumental debts. Italy had few material resources and it lagged far behind the rest of the world in entering the age of industry. The economic and social differences between the north and the south were [and still are] enormous. The pope, Pius IX, angry about losing the Papal States, locked himself up in his palace and did not permit Catholics to participate in the politics of the new kingdom. In Italy that meant that the government was without support.

Relations between the Vatican and Italy remained unfriendly under five successive popes, for another 50 years, until the signing of the Lateran

Treaty on February 11, 1929. At that time a drastically reduced Vatican was recognized as a sovereign state. The pope, in turn, recognized the kingdom of Italy but retained decisive authority in the fields of education and marriage for all Italians.

During the first half century, the new nation faced a number of setbacks. Belated efforts to enter the colonial era were costly and ultimately unsuccessful. Italy's halfhearted participation in both world wars was equally disastrous. In World War I it took the Italians two years of bloody fighting to gain ten miles of territory, only to have to surrender it again before the war was over. When the war ended, Italy was given about 9,000 square miles of Austrian territory, but this was far less than the British had promised them in a secret agreement, or than the Italians thought they deserved. The annexed territories include the site of Georg Blaurock's last journeys, his capture and execution, as well as sites related to the beginning of the Hutterite movement. On June 13, 1946, the monarchy itself ended after 85 years, to give way to the present-day Italian republic.

Education in Italy is free and compulsory for all children between six and fourteen years of age. Within a century, Italy has made tremendous progress in the task of reducing the 73 percent illiteracy of 1871 to less than 5 percent today. However, in the rural south, due to poverty and lack of facilities, the quality and amount of education remain unsatisfactory and the dropout rate is high. Near the "sole" of Italy's "boot," many children stop attending school at the age of ten or eleven.

At the same time, Italy has 29 universities, eighteen of which are more than 400 years old. The University of Bologna, one of the oldest in the Western world, dates back to the mid-1000's. In addition there are hundreds of schools and institutions of art, music, architecture, and engineering.

Italy has two Central National Libraries similar to the United States' Library of Congress: one in Rome and one in Florence. Both libraries receive all new books that are published in Italian. The one in Rome is the center for non-Italian publications.

The contrast between the developed and industrial North and the underdeveloped agricultural South remain. To this day, no important industries are located south of Naples and the wages in the South are roughly half of those in the North. This results in an internal annual migration of 300,000 southern Italians who hope to find work to the overcrowded northern cities. Other Italians try to find their fortune in the other EEC nations and chances are that our waiters in Belgium and the road workers in Germany are indeed Italians.

If Americans are said to have a love affair with the automobile, then the Italians seem to have a double dose of it, and they are inspired tinkerers. The principal automobile factory in Italy is Fiat of Turino, which manufactures a complete line of cars, trucks, buses, rail cars, marine engines, and

In Italy's industrial north: mass housing for southern job seekers

farm equipment. In addition there are Lancia, Alfa Romeo, Masserati and Ferrari, Lamborghini, and Tomaso, all of which create exotic and expensive machines; and Autobianchi and Innocenti, which produce medium-prized cars for the domestic market. Other fine products of Italy's technology include sewing machines, fine precision-built bicycles and bicycle parts, and Olivetti typewriters and business machines.

The Italians are also masters in the art of stonework, masonry, and cement construction. The Motorway to the Sun (the Autostradas A-1, A-2, and A-3) which links Milan with the "toe" of Calabria, is a masterpiece of construction carried out through difficult terrain, particularly where it crosses the Appenines.

The architect Pier Luigi Nervi, master of reinforced concrete, designed the permanent buildings of the Turino Trade Fair, the Pirelli Building in Milan, and co-designed the UNESCO Headquarters in Paris. As a professor at the University of Rome, Nervi taught that a designer can develop effective solutions three ways: by understanding the harmony of the laws of physics which regulate the balance of forces and the resistance of materials, by honestly interpreting the factors of each assignment, and by rejecting the limitations of previous solutions.

ON THE TRAILS OF BLAUROCK AND HUTTER

The entry on Italy in *The Mennonite Encyclopedia,* Volume III (published in 1957), concludes that there was no Anabaptist movement in Italy and little or no contact between persons previously thought to have had Anabaptist ideas and their contemporaries to the north. It is a surprising and erroneous but understandable conclusion. First of all, many of the articles describing persons, places, and events in *The Mennonite Encyclopedia* were originally written for and translated from the earlier *Mennonitisches Lexicon.* Many of the contributing editors, Neff, Loserth, Friedmann, and others, were native Germans and Austrians who [then correctly] treated the northern Italian story under Austrian Anabaptism and who may not have recognized the transfer of Austria's southern regions to Italy as permanent. Furthermore, recent scholarship has found new traces of Anabaptism in Italy and in Yugoslavia and connoisseurs of ceramics have linked the appearance of certain new glazes and certain specific designs in 16th and 17th-century Habaner (Hutterite) pottery to the arrival in the Moravian colonies of Italian believers, mainly from Venice, where certain ceramic designs "disappeared" in the early 1560s, only to resurface a few years later among the Hutterites. Certainly when one recognizes today's borders, both the final journeys of Georg Blaurock and the beginnings of Hutterite Anabaptism are found within the boundaries of present-day Italy.

Since the 1950s there is again a Mennonite presence in Italy, the Chiesa Evangelica Mennonita. The church, located on the island of Sicily, relates to the Virginia Conference of the Mennonite Church and has 66 baptized members in two congregations.

A Melodious Language

The official language of Italy is Italian. Many varieties of Italian are spoken, but the Tuscan dialect, spoken around Florence, forms the basis of modern Italian. In the northern region, bordering Austria and Switzerland, German is spoken as well and most towns have dual names (for instance, Brixen/Bressanone, Schlanders/Silandro, Toblach/Dobbiaco).

The Climate

Southern and middle Italy are affected by the Sirocco, a moisture-laden warm wind. In the northwest we experience the cold Mistral, a wind which originates in France's Rhône Valley. In the south, the spring and the fall are the rainy seasons.

In the Dolomiti, bordering the Swiss and Austrian Alps, daytime temperatures can be rather high in the summer, but the air is dry and not oppressive. The winters in northern Italy are severe. The spring and the fall are delightful. In the north the rains come mainly during the summer.

On the plains along Italy's longest river, the Po, the summers can be hot and dry, but in the springtime and in the fall, it rains so constantly that major floods are the rule, rather than the exception. Already around 300 BC the Etruscans built elaborate embankments to contain the Po. But the river's own continuous deposits of silt make that a never-ending process.

The Best Times to See Italy

Most people will visit Italy during the spring and the summer, but the best possible time to tour Italy depends, of course, on the region you wish to see. The summer is a good time to visit the Alps and the Dolomites, but most knowledgeable travelers favor the springtime or the fall for trips to Venice, to Florence, and to the Po Valley. Winter and springtime are mild on the Italian Riviera, where the weather is nearly always pleasant.

Holidays, Holy Days, and Store Hours

In addition to the normal holidays of the church year, Italy recognizes as legal holidays Three Kings Day (January 8), the Festival of Saint Joseph (in March), Liberation Day (April 25), Labor Day (May 1), Sacraments Day (the second Tuesday after Pentecost), the Day of the Republic (June 2), St. Peter and St. Paul's Day (early in the summer), Maria Ascension Day (late summer), All Saints' Day (November 1), Armistice Day (November 11), and Maria Emmaculate Conception Day (in December). The second day of Pentecost is not a holiday in Italy. In addition there are many local holidays related to patron saints of certain towns and villages.

In general, stores are open between 8:00 to noon and again from 15:00 to 19:30 (3:00 - 7:30 p.m.). The farther south we travel, the later these noon hour siestas start and the longer they last. Prescription drugs are available only from a registered pharmacist. Banks are open from 8:30 to 13:30 (1:30 p.m.), Monday through Friday. In Italy, as in the rest of Europe, one can nearly always exchange money at all major railroad stations and at the airport.

Special Rules of the Road

Public transportation, trams, buses, and taxis, have the right-of-way. In mountainous areas, uphill traffic has the right-of-way over descending traffic. If your car or van is parked in such a way that traffic signs are obscured to other drivers, you are parked illegally. Sleeping in cars along the highway is permitted, providing the car is legally and safely parked.

The Monetary System

Italy's money is called the Lira (plural: Lire). Theoretically the Lira is still divided into 100 centesimi, but since the Lira itself is only worth about 1/14th of a penny, further division is hardly necessary. The Lira comes in coins of 2, 5 and 10 Lire (aluminum), 100 L (white metal) and in bills of 500, 1000, 5000, 10,000 and higher. A cup of coffee may cost you 1000 Lire, a room for two with breakfast at a moderately priced hotel: 70,650 Lire per night.

A Travelers' Warning

A word of caution about traveling in Italy. The stories you may have heard about crimes against tourists in Italy are probably true. Should anything happen to you while traveling there, you will find the bystanders extremely sympathetic, the police seemingly unconcerned. They are not. It is just that they have heard your story, or one like it, too many times before.

Police authorities in Italy have published a small brochure with helpful suggestions and you will probably find a copy of it on your hotel bed. Here are a few of their hints.

Since much of the purse and camera snatching in Italy is motorized—done from small cars and motor scooters—it is advisable to walk two feet away from the curb, to carry cameras, shoulder bags, with the straps bandolier-fashion across the chest, with the object itself away from the curb.

Do not carry all your cash, credit cards, and travelers' checks in one place. In the big cities do not take more money out on the street than what you may actually need.

The city of Naples in particular is plagued by impostors, handsome young men in sharp uniforms who offer their services to incoming tourists at the railroad station and at the ferry terminals. Claiming to represent the municipal tourist office and equipped with official-looking credentials, they welcome the visitors and seem ready to help the stranger with just about anything from checking your baggage to helping to cash your travelers checks. Chances are that you will not see these friendly guides, your baggage, or your money again.

When traveling on trains and ferries, do not accept candy or drinks from friendly strangers. They may be laced with drugs. Once you are feeling drowsy, your belongings may disappear with your new friends.

If possible, travel at least in pairs or in small groups and keep an eye on each other's situation in the crowd. Copy the important pages of your passport and leave the original passport with the hotel clerk for safekeeping.

Having said all this, enjoy the incomparable sights of Italy and the genuine friendliness of the Italian people as a whole. From my own experience I have found that Italians, eager to help, may walk along with you for five blocks to get you back on the right course and/or to practice their English. In some cases complete strangers have even taken the day off to show me around. Only a few of them would do so with ulterior motives, but such persons do exist.

THE DOLOMITES

We will begin our itinerary of Italy with a trip through the Dolomites— in particular through the valleys of the Eisack (Isarco), the Etsch (Adige), and their tributaries. Throughout this section we will use the historic Tirolian names as they appear in the *Martyrs Mirror,* the Hutterite *Chronicles,* and *The Mennonite Encyclopedia,* followed by the current Italian name in parentheses. Without such a system, cross-referencing our historic publications and this tour guide would be impossible since the new names are often quite different, i.e., Sterzing = Vipiteno.

The Dolomites are a rugged and spectacular massif in multicolored limestone which takes on ever new shades through the movement of light and shadow as the day progresses. The range was named Dolomites after the French geologist Gratet de Dolomieu, who studied the formation during the 1700s. The nature of the material and the effects of erosion have created a distinct landscape of steep, rugged rocks that take the form of giant towers and domes, standing on gentle slopes covered with Alpine pasture and clusters of conifers. The southern exposure and the steepness of the upper slopes account for the complete absence of glaciers in these Alps. In the spring, the Dolomites are the place par excellence to photograph Alpine flora. Miles and miles of white and mauve crocuses, accentuated by blue enzians and delicate Turkish bells, are not uncommon.

Running from north to south through this valley is the ancient Brenner Road. This Roman road was first improved during the Middle Ages by Venetian traders transporting their wares to Germany, and then again in 1895, and once more between the two world wars. Today a new limited access road, developed during the 1970s, winds through the narrow valley on stilts, leaving the historic road and its market villages in its shadow.

Just to the north of Brixen (Bressanone), the Rienz (Rienza), and the Puster (Pusteria) join the Eisack (Isarco). From the west, high up on the Reschen Pass (Passo di Resia), no more than ten kilometers (six miles) from Austria's Upper Inn Valley, the Etsch (Adige) comes to join the Eisack (Isarco) at Bozen (Bolzano). Each of these river valleys and their tributary ravines played an important role in the story of Georg Blaurock's last years and the beginning of Hutterite Anabaptism.

ANABAPTIST ACTIVITIES IN THE DOLOMITES

Following his bloody treatment and subsequent expulsion from Zurich in January 1527—on the same day that Felix Manz lost his life as a martyr—Georg Blaurock became increasingly active in South Tirol until his own life was snuffed out there two years later. The Anabaptist fellowships, which had been formed along the Etsch (Adige) and the Eisack (Isarco) had just lost their leader Michael Kurschner by death at the stake after a long imprisonment. When Georg Blaurock heard that the brethren called for someone to bring the Word of God to them, he spared himself no trouble or effort to go at once to the orphaned congregations. Accompanied by Hans Langenegger, a weaver from Ritten (Renon), just north of Bozen, Blaurock traveled through the Vintsgau (Val Venosta), strengthening existing fellowships and establishing new congregations at Glurns (Glorenza), in Schlanders (Silandro), in Meran (Merano), in Bozen (Bolzano), as well as on the heights of Ritten (Renon).

Blaurock's field of mission was indeed extensive. In the Eisack Valley (Valle d'Isarco) his chief centers of activity were the cities of Klausen (Chiusa), Gufidaun (Gudon), and Wels (Valles), as well as in the mines of the Pfunderberg (Mont Fundres). As a rule the congregations met secretly at night, on or near a bridge separating two principalities, to escape if necessary to the "safe" side, beyond the jurisdiction of a local sheriff. But since Blaurock's ministry was quite successful, it became harder and harder to conceal the great numbers of believers. To escape the ever-present government spies, Blaurock frequently changed his meeting sites and never hesitated to make strenuous journeys to meet with his people. At

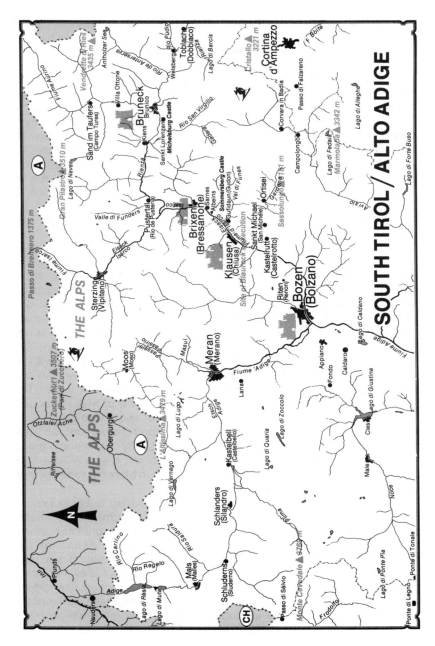

SOUTH TIROL / ALTO ADIGE

313

times he ministered in the Pustertal (Valle di Pusteria) and in the villages along the Rienz (Rienza). He had the largest number of followers in Klausen (Chiusa), the town to which he always returned after each journey.

All this made the imperial authorities in Innsbruck more and more determined to capture Blaurock in particular and to smash the Anabaptist movement in its entirety. The emperor even threatened to depose the local rulers unless they immediately "put an end to the mischief." On August 14, 1529, Blaurock and Langenegger were caught and thrown into the dungeon of the castle Sommersberg at Gufidaun. Ten days later, on August 24, the two brethren were severely tortured in the hope of extorting valuable information from them regarding the Anabaptist movement. On September 6, 1529, Georg and Hans were burnt at the stake in Klausen (Chiusa). While he was being prepared for his execution, Blaurock took the occasion to preach his farewell sermon to the assembled populace.

A new and different, but equally dedicated leader, would soon take Blaurock's place. Jakob Hutter (as his name implies, a hat maker) was from Moos (Moso) near Sankt Lorenzen (San Lorenzo) in the Puster Valley (Val de Pusteria). Hutter's first congregation was at Welsberg (Monguelfo). While meeting in the house of a relative, he once baptized ten new members into the congregation. The government got word of this "synagogue" in the spring of 1529, and ordered the sheriff of Toblach (Dobbiaco) to surprise the meeting and to catch the heretics. Some were caught but others escaped, among them Jakob Hutter himself. Hutter's sister Agnes was not so lucky. She was captured and executed.

The government continued to pursue the Anabaptists with a vengeance. Already in 1529, the government reported that more than 700 persons had been executed or expelled, while others had fled, leaving behind property as well as their children. During this time of trial, Hutter and his co-laborer Jorg Zaunring led one group after another to Moravia. In time these exiles in Moravia formed a well-organized brotherhood, ably led by Hutter himself. As the *Great Chronicle* records, "By the help and grace of God, he put the true church in pretty good order. Hence we are now called Hutterites." New people continued to arrive in Moravia, sometimes at the rate of 120 to 130 persons per week.

In the summer of 1535, Hutter and his wife returned to South Tirol to start a new work of evangelizing in this most dangerous environment. Within a year they, and two aged local women, were captured at Klausen (Chiusa) and taken to the bishop's fortress of Brandzell (Bronzolo). On December 9, 1535, when the weather was extremely cold, Hutter was marched off to Innsbruck to be cross-examined two days later. For more than two months, Hutter was interrogated under every degree of torture and barbarous whippings. He was finally burned at the stake on February 25, 1536. Hutter's wife was executed two years later, after having been transferred to Sommersberg Castle at Gufidaun (Gudon), spending her final

In the Dolomites: the Sassolungo range

Klausen (Chiusa), site of Blaurock's execution

days in the same dungeon which had earlier housed Georg Blaurock.

In 1557 Hans Kräl, a very active preacher in the Pustertal, was captured and thrown in the dungeon at Taufers (Tubre or Tures). Surrounded by bats, rats, and vermin, the clothing rotted from his body and he nearly perished. During this time in the hole, he spent no less than thirty-seven weeks in the blocks. But he survived to become one of the outstanding leaders of the Hutterite movement in Moravia, where he served as a bishop (1578-1583).

The Dolomites combine fabulous scenery with a concentrated history of intense Anabaptist activities for over a decade during the 1500s. Coming from the Brenner Pass, we soon reach Sterzing (Vipiteno), a picturesque little town with an old city gate dating back to 1468. From Sterzing (Vipiteno) the road continues to Brixen (Bressanone), where the Rienz joins the Eisack. The bishop of Brixen and the emperor at Innsbruck were often at odds with each other on any number of issues, but on the matter of Anabaptism they were agreed. Hence there were many victims in Brixen. The palace of the prince-bishops is still in existence and can be entered via a bridge over a moat.

Just above Brixen one can turn off to Bruneck (Brunico) and to Toblach (Dobbiaco). The area includes Welsberg (Monguelfo), the site of

Gufidaun (Gudon), and the Sommersberg castle

Hutter's first congregation, and the ruins of the Michelsberg Castle near Sankt Lorenzen (San Lorenzo)—for long a notorious prison for Anabaptist captives. In the very beginning, this valley yielded great numbers of persons to the Hutterite colonies in Moravia. Below Brixen (Bressanone) we come to Gufidaun (Gudon) and Klausen (Chiusa).

The areas around Gufidaun were frequently used by Blaurock and his followers for their secret meetings and it was in the castle dungeon at Gufidaun that Blaurock spent his last days on earth. Sommersberg Castle at Gufidaun is still intact but it is privately owned and not open to visitors. Klausen (Chiusa) is the site of both Blaurock's and Langenegger's execution and of Hutter's imprisonment. Klausen has retained its historic Tirolean character. Its stuccoed houses are painted with frescoes and embellished with wrought-iron signs along the narrow main street. In the days of Blaurock, both the castle of Brandzel and the Sabiona Monastery overlooking the town belonged to the bishop of Brixen.

From Klausen it is but 30 kilometers (19 miles) until we reach Bozen (Bolzano), today the capital of the Alto Adige. Bolzano is a bilingual city and the point where two cultures meet. While the old city center has a distinct Germanic character, the observant visitor will note that in Bolzano the deliberate and serious style of northern life and the easygoing and more exuberant lifestyles of the south complement each other in harmony.

A good place to observe this meeting of the cultures is in the Laubengasse (Via dei Portici) and on the Obstmarkt (Piazza delle Erbe), where a lively fruit and vegetable market is held in front of the 15th- and 16th-century houses and arcades.

For a splendid view of the town and the surrounding valleys, as well as of the Dolomites to the north, we take the cable tramway to Soprabolzano, 1,221 meters (4,006 ft.) above sea level. From the summit at Soprabolzano, it is not far to the "Crowned Girls," a curious limestone formation. From Soprabolzano, a cog railway continues to Ritten (Renon), home of Blaurock's closest companion, Hans Langenegger.

Traveling northwest from Bolzano we arrive at Meran (Merano) which was, until the 15th century, the capital of South Tirol. In 1528 the city, by permission of the emperor himself, offered a pardon to all Anabaptists who would voluntarily report to the authorities, recant, and ask for mercy. But few of them responded. In 1529 Georg Blaurock preached in Meran on his way to the congregations along the Eisack (Isarco). But his visits did not lead to the establishment of a congregation within the city. The immediate vicinity of Merano is known for its table grapes, of which it produces 3,000 tons annually. If we have the time, we will stroll on the Winter- and the Summer Promenades along the Passeier (Passirio) River, a tribute of the Etsch (Adige), or on the Tappeiner Prominade through the mountains about town. Also it should be noted that in the Etsch (Adige) Valley, Schlanders (Silandro) was long an Anabaptist center.

VENICE ON THE ADRIATIC

The Dolomites are a good point of departure for a side trip to Venice. We will travel Route 47 from Trento to a point five kilometers south of Bassano, where Route 245 branches off to the island city. But whichever road we take, all roads end at the Piazzale Roma, where we must leave our car on an artificial island. During the summer months, allow at least one hour to get the car parked.

Venice can be visited only by boat or on foot. The city consists of 117 islands separated by 150 canals and joined by more than 400 bridges. The narrow *calle* (alleys), found on each island square, have no sidewalks. Vendors pushing their wares through the calle on wheelbarrows yell out, *"Le gambe, le gambe,"* which is short for "Watch your legs." You'll do well to heed their warning.

Meandering through the entire city like a giant "S" in reverse in the Canal Grande, nearly three kilometers (two miles) long, lined with more than 200 marble palaces, the former houses of the rich and the famous of the Renaissance era. The best way to see Venice is to hop on board the *Vaporettos* (little steamers) or the faster *Motoscafi* (motor boats).

The traditional way to see Venice is, of course, by gondola. That is a delightful experience. But be sure to agree on the price before you set your foot on one. The gondoliers, wearing black pantaloons, sailors' shirts, and straw hats, stand at the rear of their craft, moving it with the motions of a single oar.

Venice's Piazza San Marco is one of the most famous squares in the whole world. It is surrounded on three sides by beautiful cafes and shops and opens up toward the St. Mark's Cathedral, once the state church of the Venetian Republic. St. Mark's, begun in AD 828 and mostly finished between 1063 and 1073, is a busy mixture of Byzantine and Western styles. Its rich decorations, in marble, gold, and mosaic, earned the basilica the name Chiesa d'Oro (the Golden Church). The central doorway is surmounted by the famous four bronze horses from the Greco-Roman period, brought to the city as war booty from Constantinople in 1204 by the Doge Dandolo.

Also on the square we find the 99-meter (324 ft.) high free-standing Campanile, or bell tower. In its simplicity the Campanile stands in stark contrast to the riot of detail and colors of the basilica. The original Campanile, dating back to the 10th century, collapsed in 1902. Rebuilt according to the old plans, the new Campanile has an elevator which takes us to a platform from where we can take excellent panoramic photos of the city.

Nestled between St. Mark's and the open waterfront is the Doge's Palace, which served both as the seat of the government and residence of the Doges. Over the narrow canal behind it we find the Bridge of Sighs, which led from the courtrooms to the prison and which owes its name to the sighs of the prisoners on the way to their executions.

Venice: the Rialto Bridge

The Rialto Bridge is probably the most famous of all the bridges in Venice. Built from 1588 to 1592, the bridge was designed to let a fully equipped galley pass under it, and it has, therefore, a distinct hump. The middle of the bridge is lined with shops, and from the galleries on either side there are marvelous views of the Canal Grande. Fish and produce markets line the west bank.

A quick count of all churches and chapels in Venice soon adds up to more than 60. The most significant of these, from an artistic point of view, are the Santa Maria della Salute (17th century), the San Giorgio Maggiore (1566-1610), the Santa Maria Gloriosa (a Gothic church and the largest in Venice), the San Zaccaria (a Renaissance church with a 13th-century campanile), and Santos Giovanni e Paolo (1234-1430). The Beggars' Canal, which runs past this church, has been the subject of countless paintings and drawings by Canaletto and other great artists.

Three Venetian Protestants—Giulio Ghirlandi, Francesco della Saga, and Antonio Rizetto—fled Italy in 1541 to join the Hutterites at Pausram in Moravia. Returning to Venice in later years as Hutterite missionaries, all three were captured and executed by drowning in the Adriatic Sea—Ghirlandi in 1562, della Saga and Rizetto in 1563. But as della Saga pointed out to his executioner, "In the end the sea will give up its dead on the day of judgment."

The inside passage of the Bridge of Sighs was known to other Anabaptists as well. In 1540 a group of 90 Anabaptist men and boys were captured when their congregations were betrayed. They were marched from Falkenstein Castle, north of Vienna in Austria, to be sold as galley slaves to the mighty Admiral Andrea Doria, then the doge of Venice. Somewhere along the road all managed to escape, but twenty of them were recaptured and later ended their lives on the doge's galleys.

The punishment of galley slavery was one of the severest penalties in use among the Mediterranean sea-faring nations, and as such it was also used to combat heresy. France was the first nation to do so by condemning Huguenots to lifelong galley service.

The last Anabaptists to be taken to the galleys were five men from Berne in 1714. Two of them died at sea, but in 1716 Dutch Mennonites were able to buy the three survivors for a ransom. When the Bernese government again sent four Anabaptists to the galleys in 1717, it was the Dutch government that bought their freedom.

About 120 kilometers (75 miles) east of Venice we find Trieste, the largest port on the Adriatic. At times a free and independent state, but more often a disputed territory, Trieste was placed under United Nations control at the end of World War II. In 1954 the citizens in a plebiscite voted to become part of Italy.

Trieste is the maritime outlet for landlocked Austria and the starting point of the massive Trans-Alpine Pipeline which pumps crude oil from the Mediterranean to the refineries at Ingolstadt in Germany. The line has the capacity to move 50 million tons of crude per year.

FLORENCE, THE RENAISSANCE CITY

There are three good reasons to visit Florence: the beauty of the city itself, the city's outstanding collection of art, and its cuisine. For over three centuries, Florence was the capital of the Renaissance, the lively center of arts and sciences in Europe. Along the shores of the Arno, those artists lived and labored who led Europe out of the Middle Ages into modern times. And wherever you may wander in Florence, you are always following in the footsteps of Dante, Giotto, Michelangelo, Brunellesschi, Donatello, Galileo, and da Vinci.

Before starting to explore the city in detail, it is helpful to observe the panoramic view of Florence's red sea of tile roofs, its towers and villas surrounded by tall cypresses and gnarled olives, and the hills beyond the Arno. To enjoy this view, the best places to go are the Piazzale Michelangelo (just above the downtown area), the terrace of the Fort Belvedere, and the Bellosguardo Hill (all on the south side of the Arno), and the Hills of Fiesole to the northeast. We will agree that the natural setting of Florence is second to none.

The heart of the city is the Piazza del Duomo. On the piazza is the Cathedral (Duomo) of Santa Maria dei Fiore, built and paid for by the Florentine Republic and the clothmakers' guild. It is one of the largest cathedrals in the Christian world. It was begun in 1296 and dedicated a century and a half later in 1436. The huge and magnificent dome by Brunelleschi took fourteen years to

Florence: Brunelleschi's Duomo and Giotto's tower

build. The church's tall and slim campanile is sometimes called Giotto's tower because the great painter drew the plans for it. Unfortunately, Giotto died two years after the construction had started. Rounding out the cathedral complex is the baptistry. The three bronze doors of the baptistry by Lorenzo Ghiberti are world-famous. The east door, created between 1425 and 1452, facing the Duomo, is so beautiful that Michelangelo declared it worthy of being "the gate into Paradise."

About five blocks away near the Arno River, we come to the Piazza della Signoria, a square down by the Palazzo Vecchio, which together with the Loggia della Signoria and the Piazzale degli Uffizi, makes up an ensemble which is unique in the world. The square was, and still is, the political stage of Florence, while the many statues around it make it virtually an open-air museum. Near the Neptune Fountain of 1576, a bronze plaque marks the spot where Savonarola was burned at the stake in 1491. In front of the Palazza Vecchio, we find a copy of Michelangelo's David and Donatello's Judith and Holofernes.

The Uffizi Gallery is one of the finest museums in the world. It contains a marvelous collection of tapestries, sculptures, prints, and paintings, in which the great Italian masters from Botticelli to Michelangelo are represented by the best of their works.

The 14th-century Ponte Vecchio across the Arno is unique in appearance. On either side of the bridge we find jewelers' shops and leather goods stores, while above these shops a corridor connects the Uffizi Palace with the Pitti Palace, in itself a worthy complement to the Uffizi. Once the

Florence: the Ponte Vecchio

322

palace of Maria de Medici, the Pitti houses a wonderful collection of Titians and Raphaels, as well as works of other artists.

On the Piazza Santa Croce, one of the oldest squares in town, we find the 13th-century church and cloisters of Santa Croce. Inside the Santa Croce there are the tomb of Michelangelo, a funerary monument to Dante (who is, however, buried at Ravenna), and the tomb of Galileo.

It would take many more pages to describe the many other palaces and churches, events, and celebrations of Florence. The *Michelin Green Guide for Italy* recommends a minimum of four days just to see the main sights of Florence.

At least while we are in the neighborhood, it would be good to devote an afternoon to Fiesole, eight kilometers (five miles) to the north. Fiesole, an ancient Etruscan settlement, is sometimes called the Mother of Florence. A well-preserved Roman amphitheater dating back to 80 BC is still being used for plays today. Fiesole's quiet and rustic setting inspired writers from Boccaccio, who drafted his *Decameron* here, to Charles Dickens and Anatole France.

MORE THAN A LEANING TOWER

Even older than Florence is Pisa, which was first Greek, then Etruscan and Roman, then for a long time a great independent maritime republic, and finally part of de Medicis' duchy of Toscane. No wonder that Pisa developed its own architectural style by blending the classical and the Oriental. While splendid buildings recall the glorious past of the Pisan Republic, in our time the city leads a somewhat dormant existence.

In Pisa most tourists will immediately head for that remarkable grouping of buildings consisting of the cathedral, the baptistery, the leaning tower, and the cemetery, which together form one of the most solemn and enchanting corners in all of Italy. And, as was the case with Florence, we can hardly begin to list the great works of art which adorn the exterior and the interior of each of these structures, from the late 12th-century bronze doors by Bonano to the mosaics and paintings by Cimabue.

Few monuments in the world are as well known as Pisa's leaning tower. The famous bell tower is already more than eight centuries old. The tower's inclination at present is 4.54 meters (almost 15 ft.) and it continues to tilt at the rate of a millimeter per year, adding to the worries of art historians and technicians who someday hope to stabilize the famous landmark permanently.

The astronomer and physicist Galileo utilized the cathedral of his native Pisa to study the movement of the pendulum and the leaning tower to work out the laws of acceleration of falling objects according to their specific weight. It was in Pisa that he quarreled with the church fathers about his findings and was forced to renounce his theories before the Inquisition. It should please Galileo to know that in 1982 the church finally admitted that their scientist had been unjustly treated and that his theories of the movement of sun and earth were indeed correct—just as Galileo had whispered after the Inquisition, "Nevertheless, it does turn."

Other sights in Pisa include the National Museum of Art located in the 15th-century San Matteo Cloister and the Quais of the Arno lined with serene palaces and the Gothic church of San Paolo on the Arno.

THE ITALIAN RIVIERA

The continuation of the French Riviera is a paradise for nature lovers. From Ventimiglia and San Remo, just this side of the French border, all the way to La Spezia, the Riviera is known for its perpetual mild climate. The mountains to the north shield the towns and villages from the cold winds while the entire coast turns its face to a full day of warm sunshine. The slopes are covered with flowers and fruit.

The rich harvest from these sunny slopes are utilized by the candied fruit factories, the perfumeries, and the olive oil presses. The best way to see the region is from the ancient, narrow, and winding Via Aurelia, hacked out by the Romans. Sometimes below it, beside it, or above it, the railway darts in and out of hundreds of tunnels. By far the most picturesque part of the entire Riviera is around Portofino.

The town of Portofino itself is a perfectly sheltered natural port, nestled in a rocky promontory surrounded by a nest of pastel-colored houses. It is a favorite with artists. From Portofino it is possible to take two hikes, one short and the other one long. Just before sunset is the ideal time to take the shorter walk to the lighthouse which starts out with a series of steps as far as the little church of San Giorgio. After the sun has set on the Gulf of Rapallo, the lights of La Spezia become visible in the distance, while the lighthouse begins to sweep its beams across the Mediterranean.

While the round-trip to the lighthouse takes only half an hour, plus the time spent enjoying the spectacle, it will take 4½ hours round-trip to reach the pretty fishing village of San Fruttuoso. The beautiful scenery along the trail and the fairy tale setting of the village itself make it worth the effort.

Located at the center of the Italian Riviera lies Genoa, a large and busy port city. Genoa is a city of contrasts where imposing palaces share the scene with narrow alleys housing the poorest of the poor. Genoa's great sons of the past include the sailor-explorer Christopher Columbus and the Admiral Andrea Doria. So rich was Genoa at one time that in 1533 Andrea Doria lavishly entertained the emperor and his court for twelve days and every time the gold-plated silverware was dirty, it was thrown in the harbor to be replaced by clean cutlery.

Of interest to the visitor are a number of the palaces, the city's oldest lighthouse (Lanterna) built in 1544, and the house of Columbus. A good view over Genoa can be had from Monte Righi, which can be reached by cable tram from the Largo della Zecca.

Rome: the Ponte Sant'Angelo across the Tiber

ROME, THE ETERNAL CITY

In this modest book we will make no attempt to relate the history of Rome throughout the centuries, nor to describe its features in detail. Rome's monuments and artistic properties run into the ten thousands and are scattered over an immense geographic area. Fortunately, good books about Rome abound, including a 200-plus-page *Michelin Green Guide*. Serious students of art and architecture, archaeology and church history, come to the Eternal City for a whole year, only to leave many of its sights to be explored the next time.

The city has had its ups and downs. In the imperial times it may have had nearly two million inhabitants. By the time of the Middle Ages, it had shrunk to less than 60,000. Today there are nearly three million Romans.

Most guides to Rome advise the first-time visitors to head for the Piazza Venezia and to climb Michelangelo's monumental staircase to the capital for a select view of the ancient Forum—its marbles, its columns and arches, with the Palatino in the background. To one side of the Forum stands the Mamertine Prison where, according to legend, both Paul and Peter were imprisoned.

Nearby stands the Coliseum, an amphitheater of colossal dimensions and a masterpiece of the architecture of antiquity. On the Coliseum's topmost gallery, 57 meters (187 ft.) above the ground, brackets used to support a circle of poles making it possible to stretch a linen cloth (vellum) over the

50,000 spectators in case of too much sun or rain. Between the Coliseum and the Forum stands the Triumphal Arch of Constantine, commemorating the emperor's victory over Maxentius in AD 315.

On the other side of the Tiber, we find Papal Rome, with the city and gardens of the Vatican and St. Peter's Cathedral at its center. Because of the harmony of its proportions, which take into account the effects of distance and perspective, the gigantic dimensions of St. Peter's are not at first apparent. But the size of St. Peter's can be compared to other great churches of the world by means of markers placed in the floor inside. Upon entering St. Peter's, the first chapel on the right contains Michelangelo's famous Pieta. St. Peter's dome, designed by Michelangelo and completed by himself as far as the lantern, may be climbed during the winter months, October through March, except when papal audiences and religious ceremonies are in progress.

We conclude this brief write-up with a mention of the Castel Sant'Angelo, the fortress built in AD 135 as a mausoleum for Emperor Hadrian. The castle's summit offers the visitor a marvelous view of old Rome, while the castle itself is linked to the old town by the graceful Ponte Sant' Angelo, an ancient bridge decorated with baroque angels by Bernini.

MILANO, HOME OF DA VINCI AND VERDI

Milan (Milano) is Italy's second city in population and first in economic importance. For tourists Milan has two main centers of attraction: the Dom Square (Piazza del Duomo) and the Simplon Park (Parco Sempione). From the Piazza del Duomo we can enter the glass-enclosed Galleria, the 200-year-old forerunner of today's shopping malls. In the spacious Galleria the Milanese shop for gifts or sit down to read their papers over a cup of espresso at a sidewalk cafe.

Outside on the square stands the *duomo* (cathedral) in all its dazzling glory. It is the largest Gothic structure in Italy, begun in 1386 and continued in the same style over many centuries. The last of the spires were not finished until 1809. There are 135 of them and the highest of these, bearing a gilded statue of the Madonna, reaches a height of 108 meters (354 ft.).

The spires, the nooks and crannies, and the doorways of this vast cathedral are covered with no less than 2,245 statues, while almost 2,000 more share the interior of the church with 58 mighty pillars and a mass of Lombardian works of art. A visit to the duomo should be topped by a walk on the roof (access via stairs or elevator) for a closer look at some of the sculptures and for a magnificent view of Milan.

The Parco Sempione is a pleasant park dominated by the square and massive castle of the dukes of Milan, the Sforzas. Begun in 1450 over the ruins of an earlier castle, the Castello Sforzesco has been remodeled over the centuries.

Milan is also the city of opera and of Giuseppe Verdi. In 1832 Verdi was

Milan's dazzling Duomo

refused admission to the Milan Conservatory because he lacked formal training and besides that he was too old. Verdi simply went on to become the composer par excellence whose operatic masterpieces are still performed more frequently than those of any other composer. His best-known compositions include *Rigoletto, La Traviata* and *Aida*. Most of Verdi's works premiered at La Scala, Milan's leading opera house. Verdi had frequent conflicts with the Austrian occupation forces who felt, not incorrectly, that Verdi's stirring melodies fostered Italian nationalism.

Twice during his lifetime, Milan was also home to that greatest genius of the Renaissance, if not of all times, Leonardo da Vinci. In the early 1480s da Vinci entered the service of Lodovico Sforza, the duke of Milan. During this time da Vinci painted *The Last Supper,* a mural in the dining hall of the monastery of Santa Maria della Grazie. Although many people considered this one of the greatest paintings of all times, it has been restored so often that it can hardly be considered, any more, a da Vinci original. It is currently again undergoing restoration after damages incurred during the summer of 1980. (See the Nov. 1983 issue of *National Geographic* for an "in progress" report.)

When the French marched into Milan in 1499, Leonardo fled to

Florence where he painted *La Gioconda,* better known as the *Mona Lisa.* In 1506 he returned to Milan to concentrate on engineering, hydraulics, anatomy, and aeronautics. Copies of Leonardo's drawings, letters, notes, and models can be seen in the Leonardo da Vinci Museum of Science and Technology on the Via San Vittore, open daily except on Mondays and holidays.

AUTOMOBILE CITY

Turin (Torino), with a population of over one million, is the capital of Italian engineering. It was in Turin that the Italian automobile industry, represented by Fiat and Lancia, was born. Today Turin produces more than 85 percent of all Italian motor vehicles.

Automotive engineers from around the world come to advance their knowledge at Turin's Politechnico. Tire companies like Michelin and Pirelli have major works here and the world's best-known custom coach builders, including Pinin Farina, all add to the prosperity of Turin. South of town on the road to Savona, a large modern automobile museum also houses a library of more than 8,000 volumes on automotive history.

For students of church history, Turin makes an excellent point of departure for a trip to the remote villages of the Waldenses, beyond Pinerolo to the southwest. The trip to Prali, Torre Pellice, and Bobbio Pellice, goes into rugged terrain. Some of the roads (?) trails (?) leading to the sites and monuments of Waldensian history may not be recognized as such by the everyday tourist, and considerable driving skill is required to get there. The Waldensian Conference Center, Agape, located in this area does not look like it has changed much since Mennonite Voluntary Service workers helped with its construction during the early 1950s.

WHO GOES THERE?

In most countries all vehicles are required to carry an oval nationality plate or sticker, in addition to the license plate. When driving in Europe you will soon discover that you are surrounded by a highly international community on the move. Until recently that was even more so, but the skirmishes in Lebanon, Iran, Iraq, and the takeover of Afghanistan have pretty well eliminated the trucks with exotic lettering that used to transport goods between Great Britain and Kuwait, Germany and Iran. Here are some of the plates you are most likely to encounter:

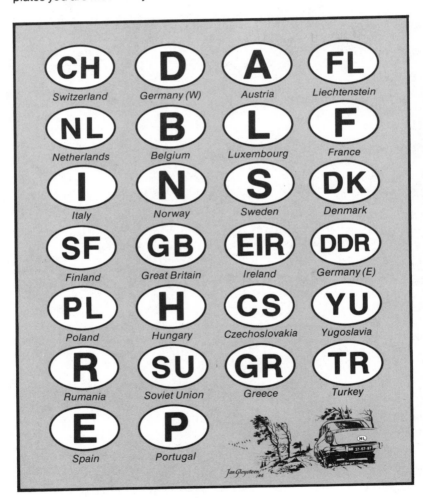

CH Switzerland	**D** Germany (W)	**A** Austria	**FL** Liechtenstein
NL Netherlands	**B** Belgium	**L** Luxembourg	**F** France
I Italy	**N** Norway	**S** Sweden	**DK** Denmark
SF Finland	**GB** Great Britain	**EIR** Ireland	**DDR** Germany (E)
PL Poland	**H** Hungary	**CS** Czechoslovakia	**YU** Yugoslavia
R Rumania	**SU** Soviet Union	**GR** Greece	**TR** Turkey
E Spain	**P** Portugal		

Jan Gleysteen '86

IN APPRECIATION

A guidebook of this kind is by nature not the work of one person but rather one person's selection from the collective memory of many people, past and present. For me the process began long ago when, as a child, and later as a young man, I followed in the footsteps of my father as he shared with me the rich heritage of the places we visited. To his teachings and shared materials I have since added my own collection of clipped articles and marked-up books and the personal experience of many journeys. The eleventh Mennonite World Conference in Strasbourg, France, provides the occasion to share some of these treasures with a wider audience.

Only those who have labored with manuscripts of this kind can appreciate the impossibility of listing all those persons and organizations who have contributed, editorially or otherwise, to the end product. Within our family, credit must be given to our daughter Linda Gleysteen Yoder, who, working from my notes, wrote the Anabaptist-Mennonite history summaries for each of the chapters. Our son Richard David drew the twelve national and regional maps, while I take responsibility for the five city maps in this *Tourguide*. The typographical detail and the meticulous cutting of second-color overlays for all these maps was completed under my direction by Maria Friesen, Birgitt Rohde, Cathy Depta, and Paula Johnson. My wife, Barbara, worked out the metric-to-American equivalents throughout the book, as well as fueled the author with good meals and plenty of hot coffee.

To Pat Bailey goes the credit for keyboarding and correcting all this "stuff" through several stages of computer printouts, and to Glenn Millslagle and Carl Shawley for turning the corrected information into clean and sharp typography. I especially wish to thank Leonard Gross and Rachel Shenk at the Archives of the Mennonite Church in Goshen, Indiana, for a critical reading of an early printout and for their many helpful suggestions and additions. I am grateful for the sharp minds and the sharp pencils of Paul M. Schrock and Dolores Rizza, book editor and copyeditor at MPH, who styled the manuscript prior to final typesetting, and to Naomi Moon for conscientious proofreading.

In addition, I wish to thank Robert Blosser and Don Echard in the camera and stripping department, and those people in the pressroom and the bindery who saw the product to completion. The help I have received from all has been more than practical and material—I have experienced a community of Christian love. To these my friends and family, I now return the fruits of our endeavor.

—Jan Gleysteen

Personal notes, additions, record of passport numbers, important addresses and phone numbers, dates of concerts, exhibits, and special events . . .

Jan Gleysteen grew up in Amsterdam, Holland, where he took his training in illustration and design at the Municipal School for Applied Arts and the Royal Academy. In the early 1950s he spent much time crisscrossing Europe by bike, sketching and painting along the way. He came to the States in the fall of 1953 to study (at Goshen College) and to work (at Mennonite Publishing House). He has now served MPH for more than three decades, initially as an artist, more recently as writer, editor, and lecturer, primarily in the field of Anabaptist-Mennonite historiography.

For years Gleysteen enjoyed creating travel itineraries for church workers going overseas and for missionaries coming home. In 1969 John L. Ruth and Jan Gleysteen embarked on the first of a series of research trips to document European Mennonite history. This first excursion resulted in the *Martyrs Mirror Oratorio,* the film *The Quiet in the Land,* and the novel *Conrad Grebel, Son of Zurich,* all by John Ruth, and the beginning of Gleysteen's widely used slide lectures. Jan's black-and-white photos from this and later expeditions have since been used to illustrate countless publications here and abroad.

In 1970 Jan first took a group of friends on a three-week bus tour of Europe to visit the places he knew so well. This was the beginning of Tour-Magination, a tour company which specializes in travel with an emphasis on Anabaptist-Mennonite life and thought. Throughout the Mennonite denomination Gleysteen is perhaps best known for his heritage lectures, and for his part in seminars on church architecture.

Jan Gleysteen and his wife, Barbara, are members of the Mennonite Church of Scottdale, Pa. The Gleysteens have two grown children, Linda Jo and Richard David, and a son-in-law, Michael. Jan serves on the Worship and the Arts Committee of the Mennonite Church and sits in on the meetings of the Mennonite Historical Committee. He also serves on the advisory board of *Mennonite Weekly Review,* and is a columnist for *Festival Quarterly.* At MPH he is editor/designer of church bulletins. In all these endeavors Jan has found it difficult to tell the difference between work and creative enjoyment.